Codename
VALKYRIE

Codename VALKYRIE

General Friedrich Olbricht and the Plot Against Hitler

HELENA SCHRADER

Haynes Publishing

A catalogue record for this book is available from the British Library

ISBN 978 1 84425 533 7

Library of Congress catalog card No. 2008933799

Published by Haynes Publishing,
Sparkford, Yeovil, Somerset BA22 7JJ, UK
Tel: 01963 442030 Fax: 01963 440001
Int. tel: +44 1963 442030 Int. fax: +44 1963 440001
E-mail: sales@haynes.co.uk
Website: www.haynes.co.uk

Haynes North America Inc., 861 Lawrence Drive, Newbury Park, California 91320, USA

Designed and typeset by James Robertson
Printed and bound in Britain by J.H. Haynes & Co. Ltd., Sparkford

CONTENTS

Acknowledgements and Introduction   7
German Military Ranks   11
Glossary   12

1   The Last Attempt: 20 July 1944   15
2   The Age of Innocence   24
3   The War to End All Wars   30
4   Between Revolution and Reaction   41
5   The Fragile Republic   59
6   National Socialist Peace   75
7   The Formation of an Anti-Hitler Conspiracy   106
8   Hitler's General?   119
9   Organising Hitler's War   145
10   Resistance to Hitler   171
11   The Reasons Why   200
12   The Consummate Conspirator   211
13   The Conspiracy Fails   236

Conclusion   258
Notes   263
Bibliography   268
Index   284

ACKNOWLEDGEMENTS AND INTRODUCTION

O n a spring day in 1942 *Hauptmann* Axel Freiherr von dem Bussche-Streithorst, then the adjutant of the Reserve Regiment 23, based in Potsdam near Berlin, received a call informing him that the chief of the General Army Office, General Friedrich Olbricht, was on his way. As Axel explained to me in one of the many personal talks we had over our decade-long friendship, the chief of the General Army Office was as far removed from a mere regimental adjutant as 'the dear God is from earth'. Bussche, however, had been warned by a fellow opponent of Hitler, Fritz-Dietlof Graf von der Schulenburg, that this General Olbricht was 'one of them' — i.e. part of the conspiracy against Hitler. Bussche therefore knew, without being told, that if this *General der Infanterie* was going to visit a lowly regimental adjutant, then it had nothing to do with official duties.

More than forty years later, Bussche could still vividly remember the ensuing encounter. With open enthusiasm and delight, Bussche related spontaneously how on a warm and sunny spring day in Potsdam the three-star general approached the (as Bussche described himself) wary first lieutenant with warmth and charm. Olbricht was, as Bussche remembered it, a bit on the stocky side, and he could speak with a slight Saxon accent — when he wanted to break the ice. He spoke cheerfully about a variety of completely unimportant official topics (which in Bussche's eyes clearly did not warrant such a high-ranking inspection) and then 'suggested' to Bussche that they take a walk together. While crossing the open exercise fields where no one else could possibly hear them, Olbricht began to lecture Bussche about a certain General Staff plan with the codename 'Valkyrie'.

'Valkyrie' was, as Bussche described it, a 'well-organised plan of the Home Army that was to be used in the event that the millions of forced labourers in Germany rose up in revolt'.[1] But Bussche had already been warned by Schulenburg that the plan was also intended to serve as a blueprint for a coup d'état against Hitler. Bussche therefore understood perfectly when Olbricht, in his relaxed Saxon inflection, 'explained' to him: 'Now, Valkyrie: that is for when the forced labourers strike and we have to restore order, you understand?' And Bussche assured the General, '*Jawohl, Herr General.*' And then Olbricht continued, smiling, 'And if it gets really bad, then we'll have to take control of the radio stations and the ministries in Berlin, you understand what I mean?' '*Jawohl, Herr General.*' And so on and so forth.

Axel von dem Bussche would later volunteer to blow himself up while holding on to Hitler. For several days in late November 1943 he waited in Hitler's headquarters, the *Wolfschanze*, for the opportunity to gain access to Hitler and so carry out the assassination. The pretext for his presentation to Hitler was the modelling of a new uniform. But the model uniform was destroyed in an air raid before it reached the *Wolfschanze*. Bussche returned to his unit at the front and was severely wounded. After the amputation of a leg, he was never fit enough to make a second assassination attempt.

Friedrich Olbricht, on the other hand, continued to work on perfecting Plan Valkyrie. The officers of his staff routinely updated the official aspects of it while co-conspirators worked on the secret components such as the announcement of Hitler's death, the orders to close the concentration camps and to arrest SS and Gestapo leaders. Twice, on 15 July and again on 20 July 1944, General Olbricht issued the Valkyrie orders. He did so although he was not authorised to do so and hence risked not only military disciplinary action, but also arrest for treason if the true purposes of Valkyrie were revealed. Both times he took these supreme risks because his chief of staff, *Oberst* Claus Graf Stauffenberg, had promised he would − regardless of what happened − set off a bomb during Hitler's daily briefing. But twice Stauffenberg failed. On 15 July he did not even set off the bomb, and on 20 July, he managed to set off the bomb but not to kill Hitler. On 15 July, Olbricht was able to 'disguise' his illegal actions as a training drill − but not without arousing the intense suspicion of the commander of the SS, Heinrich Himmler. On 20 July, there was no going back and the coup attempt was made. It failed because Hitler was still alive and so able to give counter-orders. It cost thousands of opponents of Hitler their lives, and the first to die was Friedrich Olbricht.

Olbricht − a man whose opposition to Hitler went back to 1923, who actively sought to remove him from power from 1938 onwards, and who originated and issued Valkyrie — is the real hero of the so-called 'German generals' plot' against Hitler. Sadly, he has been largely eclipsed and even maligned in the existing literature. This book is an attempt to set the record straight.

The research done for my dissertation in history at the University of Hamburg, culminating in a PhD *cum laude* in 1991, is the basis for this book. At the time the research was being conducted, Germany was still divided into two hostile states, and access to the archives and citizens of East Germany was difficult and uncertain. Furthermore, a great many key sources had been lost or destroyed either in the Second World War or thereafter. Witnesses were dying or losing the clarity of memory essential for writing a reliable biography. Indeed, the sources for the work were so meagre that many in the German academic community strongly advised against even attempting a biography of General Olbricht. As one of them put it: 'If it were possible to write a biography of Friedrich Olbricht, then a good German historian would already have done so.'

I went ahead with my research anyway, on the simple premise that even if the source material were scanty, it would only get worse as more and more witnesses died. More significantly, since Olbricht's role in the German Resistance had been absolutely crucial, even a weak biography was better than none. As so often happens, persistence was rewarded. In contrast to the historians, those who had actually known Olbricht were enthusiastic about my efforts. Axel von dem Bussche greeted the news that I was working on a biography of Olbricht with a resounding: 'Finally!' and immediately launched into the above description of his walk with Olbricht in Potsdam.

Even more surprising was an incident at a government reception. The superintendent of RIAS (Radio in the American Sector), Ludwig Freiherr von Hammerstein, was chatting with someone about my work on Olbricht when he was interrupted by the superintendent of the *Deutsche Oper*, Prof. Götz Friedrich. Friedrich, who had been involved in a different conversation with a different set of guests, had overheard the name 'Friedrich Olbricht' and at once broke in to ask Hammerstein more. He too expressed his delight that Olbricht was 'at last' getting some recognition and explained that his father had served on Olbricht's staff. He asked Hammerstein to give me his telephone number and ask me to call him. I did so with some trepidation — he was a very busy man, after all. But his secretary had been warned and assured me he would call me back 'as soon as the rehearsal was over'. He not only did, he invited me to his home for tea, provided me with his father's memoirs, and wrote the introduction to my German biography of Olbricht, all out of devotion to a man his father had talked about repeatedly when he was growing up.

Before I had finished, I had uncovered no fewer than 41 witnesses who had personally known Friedrich Olbricht and could contribute critical insights into his personality and role both in terms of military career and Resistance activities. I gained unprecedented access to the archives in East Germany and received help from East German historians and researchers. I was able to dig up additional, previously unused material in both the National Archives in Washington and the *Bundesarchiv* in Freiberg. In the end, a picture of Friedrich Olbricht emerged that fundamentally altered the prevalent and popular view of the German Resistance and particularly the 20 July Plot.

While I am indebted to all those who contributed their memories of Olbricht to my research, I would like to express my particular thanks to the family of Friedrich Olbricht, especially his widow Eva and his son-in-law Dr Friedrich Georgi. Both helped me in every way possible, welcoming me into their home and sharing with me their feelings as well as their few remaining mementos. I am also deeply indebted to Ludwig Freiherr von Hammerstein for acting as the consummate mentor and facilitator in helping me establish contact with many key survivors of the Resistance or their relatives. Nor would any acknowledgements be complete without mentioning that Axel Freiherr von dem Bussche provided me with some of the most dramatic, significant, and surprising information about Olbricht's role in the anti-Hitler conspiracy, while Prof. Götz Friedrich shared his affectionate and admiring memories of the man. All these fascinating witnesses of history are no longer with us.

Let me end, however, by thanking Jonathan Falconer and Haynes Publishing for giving me the opportunity to tell Olbricht's story in English for an English-speaking audience. It is an important story for anyone interested in the Second World War or in resistance against totalitarian regimes anywhere in the world, at any time in history.

Helena Schrader
Oslo, May 2008

GERMAN MILITARY RANKS

German Army	British Army	US Army	SS	SA
Generalfeldmarschall	Field Marshal	–	Reichsführer SS	Stabschef
Generaloberst	–	General (4*)	Oberstgruppenführer	–
General der (Waffengattung)	General	Lieutenant General (3*)	Obergruppenführer	Obergruppenführer
Generalleutnant	Lieutenant General	Major General (2*)	Gruppenführer	Gruppenführer
Generalmajor	Major General	Brigadier General (1*)	Brigadeführer	Brigadeführer
Oberst	Colonel	Colonel	Standartenführer	Standartenführer
Oberstleutnant	Lieutenant Colonel	Lieutenant Colonel	Obersturmbahnführer	Obersturmbahnführer
Major	Major	Major	Sturmbahnführer	Sturmbahnführer
Hauptmann/Rittmeister	Captain	Captain	Hauptsturmführer	Hauptsturmführer
Oberleutnant	1st Lieutenant	1st Lieutenant	Obersturmführer	Obersturmführer
Leutnant	2nd Lieutenant	2nd Lieutenant	Untersturmführer	Untersturmführer
Feldwebel	Sergeant	Sergeant	Oberscharführer	Truppführer
Gefreiter	Lance Corporal	Corporal	Rottenführer	Rottenführer

GLOSSARY

Abbreviation	German Term	Definition
	Abitur	Equivalent of a High School
AK	Armeekorps	Corps Command
	Bendlerstrasse	The street on which the German General Staff HQ building was situated. The term 'Bendlerstrasse' became synonymous with the Army General Staff during the interwar period, and during the war itself it referred to the HQ of the Home Army
d.G.	der Generalstab	German General Staff Officer (member of the trained elite corps)
	Einsatzgruppen/ Einsatzkommandos	SS Special Forces deployed behind the front lines to exterminate Jews and Gypsies
	Ersatz	Replacement (e.g: ersatz coffee)
	Freiherr	Baron
	Freikorps	Military units formed to fight the German revolutionaries in 1918–20, after the disintegration of the Army following defeat in the First World War
FüHQ	Führer Hauptquartier	Hitler's Headquarters
	Gauleiter	Regional Party Official
Gestapo	Geheime Staatspolizei	Secret State Police
	Graf	Count
	Gräfin	Countess
Ia, Ib, Ic		Ia First General Staff Officer (Operations); Ib Second General Staff Officer (Logistics); Ic Third General Staff Officer (Intelligence)
ID	Infanterie Division	Infantry Division
i.G.	im Generalstab	Officer serving in a staff position, perhaps temporarily assigned to the General Staff
IR	Infanterie-Regiment	Infantry Regiment

KPD	Kommunistische Partei Deutschlands	German Communist Party
NS	Nationalsozialistisch (e/er)	Nazi (adjective)
NSDAP	Nationalsozialistische Deutsche Arbeiterpartei	Nazi Party (subjective)
OB	Oberbefehlshaber	Commanding Officer/CO
OKH	Oberkommando des Heeres	Army High Command
OKW	Oberkommando der Wehrmacht	Armed Forces High Command
Ord.O	Ordonnanzoffizier	Aide-de-Camp – ADC
	Polizeipräsident	Chief of Police
PzD	Panzerdivision	Armoured Division
	Putsch	Coup d'état
	Reich	The German Empire, common term for Germany at the time
	Reichstag	German Parliament/the building in which it met
	Reichswehr	100,000-man army allowed by the Treaty of Versailles; politically neutral and highly trained
	Reichswehrminister/um	Minister/Ministry of Defence
SA	Sturmabteilung	SA – 'Brown Shirts'
SPD	Sozialistische Partei Deutschland	Social (Democratic) Party, the Majority Socialists
SS	Schützstaffel	SS
	Truppenamt	Disguised General Staff during the Weimar Republic
USDP	Unabhänigige Sozialistische Partei Deutsch	Independent Socialist Party
	Waffen-SS	SS units engaged in military operations rather than racial policies and police work
WK	Wehrkreis	Military District
	Wehrmacht	Armed Forces, the expanded military forces of Germany after the Treaty of Versailles was abrogated by Hitler

Chapter 1

THE LAST ATTEMPT: 20 JULY 1944

The morning of 20 July 1944 broke hot and humid over the capital of the Thousand-Year Reich. Although still a throbbing population centre and the hub of National Socialist Germany, Berlin was already badly battered. In the eleven months since the RAF had opened its bomber offensive against the German capital, more than 10,000 bomber sorties had been flown against Berlin, delivering 30,000 tons of explosive. Since March 1944 the USAAF had joined in this aerial 'Battle of Berlin', hitting the city by day as well as by night. Bomb damage – from completely smashed and gutted buildings to shattered windows and fallen plaster – had become commonplace for Berliners. Daily life now included frequent disruption to water and electricity supplies, public transport that did not run on time, and the forced billeting of the homeless in those dwellings still habitable.

But the city was definitely still functioning. On this hot, sunny Thursday morning people went to work as they did every day: the workers to the factories, the shopkeepers to their stores, and the secretaries and bureaucrats to their offices. They rode the ageing buses, the trams, and the extensive underground. They were orderly and ordinary, but there were few who were indifferent to the latest news.

The Red Army was in the process of smashing its way through Army Group Centre on the Eastern Front. On 3 July, the 100,000-strong 4th Army had been encircled at Minsk and by 11 July it had been eliminated in what amounted to a mini-Stalingrad. By 17 July, the Russian Army had crossed the old Curzon Line, thereby passing into territory that belonged to Germany's traditional 'sphere of influence'; which had been turned over to Germany by the Molotov-Ribbentrop Pact of 1939. The advancing Soviet juggernaut not only appeared unstoppable, it seemed to be virtually feeding on the divisions, corps, and armies that the *Wehrmacht* threw against it.

On the other side of the Continent, German forces were faring no better. After four years of peace and German supremacy in the West, German defensive positions had been breached by a massive seaborne invasion in Normandy on 6 June. One month later, almost a million Allied troops had been landed in the West. Meanwhile, the armies of the Western Allies also continued to advance up the Italian peninsula.

By 20 July 1944, even ordinary Germans knew that the German Army was overstretched and fighting desperately. It was increasingly clear to even the most trusting and loyal supporters of the Nazi regime that only a miracle of some kind could turn the situation around. A great deal of faith, genuine or merely expedient, was being placed in the 'wonder weapons' that were allegedly about to be unleashed upon Germany's enemies.

The supreme leader of the Thousand-Year Empire and commander-in-chief of the armed forces facing this dire military situation was not in his capital. He was at his specially built headquarters, consisting of a complex of underground bunkers hidden deep inside the Polish forest, the so-called 'Wolf's Lair', or *Wolfschanze*. He had a busy day ahead of him, filled with the usual briefings and highlighted by a meeting with his fellow (but now deposed) dictator, Benito Mussolini, scheduled for 14:30. To accommodate the arrival of the Italian visitor, the usual daily briefing was moved forward by half an hour, to 12:30.

Perhaps because of the heat of the day, or for some other unrecorded reason, the briefing was scheduled to take place in a wooden hut above ground rather than in an underground bunker. The various members of Hitler's entourage and the senior military commanders due to report at the briefing gathered in the hut. Although there were several senior officers of the Army, Navy and Air Force (altogether 23 men), neither Hitler's deputy, Hermann Goering, nor the commander of the SS, *Reichsführer* Heinrich Himmler, were present at the briefing.

The newly appointed chief of staff of the Home Army, however, was scheduled to give a presentation. The Home Army was responsible for conscripting, clothing, equipping, training, and organising the replacements vitally needed to sustain the fighting units of the German Army, which was haemorrhaging entire divisions. The dictator wanted to be sure that more cannon fodder was on the way for his depleted armies.

Because the chief of staff of the Home Army had assumed his position less than three weeks earlier, he had to be introduced to his commander-in-chief and dictator by the commander of the *Oberkommando der Wehrmacht* (OKW), the Joint Armed Forces Command, *Feldmarschall* von Keitel. This was somewhat awkward inasmuch as the chief of staff of the Home Army, *Oberst* Claus Graf von Stauffenberg, had lost his right hand and two fingers of his left hand, as well as his left eye, in Africa. The Colonel, having been introduced, left the hut to make a phone call with his superior in Berlin, leaving his heavy briefcase under the table.

Only minutes later, a huge explosion racked the briefing hut. Debris was blown into the air. People started screaming and calling for medical help. Smoke rose up in a slow, lethargic cloud above the hut. Except for those in the immediate vicinity, however, the explosion did not arouse excessive alarm. Wild boars and other game often detonated one of the many landmines placed around the perimeter of the *Wolfschanze*.

Security procedures included locking down the entire complex after any suspicious event, but the soldiers manning the innermost checkpoint let *Oberst* Graf von Stauffenberg pass without difficulty because he was in possession of a valid ID. At the second checkpoint the guards were more punctilious, however, and refused to let him pass. They were not intimidated by his insistence that he had orders to fly back to Berlin immediately. Stauffenberg demanded to speak to the commandant of the *Wolfschanze*, but since the commandant was already on his way to the scene of the explosion, he spoke to the adjutant instead. The adjutant vouched for Stauffenberg, who was then allowed to pass out of the secured area.

Shortly afterwards Stauffenberg — having now escaped the explosion by minutes and bluffed his way out of the tightly guarded security zone surrounding the dictator — climbed aboard a waiting transport plane. He was barely in the air before the pilot received word that all flights from the airfield were grounded.

But it was too late to stop Stauffenberg. The one-eyed, one-armed count had apparently succeeded where more than 40 other would-be assassins had failed. Not since the Beer Hall bomb in November 1939 had an explosive device intended to eliminate Hitler actually detonated in his vicinity. Various other attempts had failed silently. Stauffenberg — handsome, rich, and successful — had long since earned the nickname

'Darling of the Gods'. Apparently they still smiled on him, despite the mutilation of his good looks at the hands of American fighter aircraft in the African desert.

As he flew back towards Berlin, Stauffenberg was confident that his action had set a coup d'état in motion. The coup had been planned for years and tested as recently as five days earlier. It was, furthermore, a scheme that had been disguised as a legitimate contingency plan for the suppression of a revolt by the millions of forced labourers working inside the Third Reich or to counter enemy commandos parachuted into the German capital. The plan authorised, indeed required, the German Army to cordon off the government sector, take over radio stations, and seize control of the nerve centres of the capital. Furthermore, it called upon the German Army to take over all the subordinate military districts, including those in occupied territories.

Not surprisingly, given the immense powers the plan contained, the only person authorised to set Valkyrie into motion was Adolf Hitler himself or, in the event that he was incapacitated, the commander-in-chief of the Home Army, *Generaloberst* Fromm. As Stauffenberg flew back towards Berlin on the afternoon of 20 July 1944, he presumed Hitler was dead, and so he felt confident that his immediate superior, *Generaloberst* Fromm, would now set the plan in motion, thereby enabling the conspirators to carry out their coup.

The conspirators were a loose coalition of anti-Nazi elements. They had come together in an active conspiracy to depose Hitler out of a shared determination to put an end to the criminal regime he led. On the military side they included some of the most senior officers in the German Army: first and foremost, the former chief of the General Staff, *Generaloberst* Ludwig Beck. Beck had been so appalled by Hitler's proposed invasion of the Sudetenland in late 1938 that he had urged his fellow generals to resign collectively in protest. His colleagues had not then been prepared to sacrifice their careers for the sake of principle, however, and so *Generaloberst* Beck had resigned alone and in silence. With this act of moral rectitude Beck removed himself from a position of direct influence on German policy, but he became a beacon of decency and a centre of opposition to those still on active service in the German Army who opposed the regime on moral grounds. Other senior military officers who shared Beck's views of the Nazi regime and its policies — for example, the military governor in France, General von Stülpnagel, the head of German Counter-Intelligence, Admiral Canaris, and the chief of the General Army Office, *General der Infanterie* Friedrich Olbricht — coalesced around Beck. Over time they established contact with civilian opposition circles: men such as the former Mayor of Leipzig, Carl Friedrich Goerdeler, and the circle of intellectuals collected in the so-called *Kreisauer Kreis* which met to draft a post-Nazi constitution.

The majority of the military and civilian opponents of the Nazi regime had gradually come to the conclusion that Hitler had to be eliminated, by violence if necessary. Initial plans for his arrest and trial were dropped in favour of an assassination, and both the coup plans and the schemes for an interim government until democratic elections could take place were constantly revised and adjusted to take account of changing events. While the plans for a post-Hitler government were more the preserve of the civilian conspirators, the plans for the coup d'état were the responsibility of the military conspirators. As he flew back to Berlin on the afternoon of 20 July 1944, *Oberst* Stauffenberg believed that the coup was already in progress.

On arrival at Rangsdorf two hours later, however, Stauffenberg learned that the coup had not been set in motion at all. The Valkyrie orders had not been issued. The German Army was not on alert, let alone moving to seize control of government buildings, radio stations, and communications networks throughout the Third Reich. Two critical hours, in which the German Army should have been stealing a march on Hitler's loyal minions of the SS and SA, had been lost. Stauffenberg, incredulous, put a call through to the headquarters of the Home Army, the *Bendlerstrasse*, and demanded to speak to General Friedrich Olbricht.

General Olbricht was the man he called for several reasons. First, it was Olbricht who had recruited Stauffenberg to the anti-Hitler conspiracy roughly a year earlier. He had recruited Stauffenberg to be his own chief of staff so that he would have a talented and energetic chief willing to devote his energies to Valkyrie and the coup plans, because Olbricht's own senior position did not afford him sufficient time to do so himself any more. Thus, up to three weeks earlier, Olbricht had been Stauffenberg's military superior. While that function had passed to General Fromm when Stauffenberg changed military jobs, Olbricht remained Stauffenberg's superior in Resistance matters. This was because Olbricht had been a leading conspirator for five times as long as Stauffenberg, and was marked down to be minister of war in a post-Hitler government. It was psychologically significant that Olbricht was also three ranks superior to Stauffenberg and almost 20 years older. Their relationship, by all first-hand accounts, was very good and congenial – but with Olbricht clearly in the position of senior officer.

Accounts vary, but Stauffenberg was clearly upset that Valkyrie had not been set in motion. Olbricht, however, countered that the reports to reach Berlin had been ambiguous at best and negative at worst. The only information to reach Berlin was that an assassination *attempt* had been made, but that Hitler was still alive. Stauffenberg countered vehemently that this was not true: that Hitler was dead and that the coup should be set in motion immediately. Never mind that Stauffenberg did not and could not know this. Never mind that this was not true. On the basis of Stauffenberg's statement, the entire coup apparatus was indeed now, three hours after the explosion at the *Wolfschanze*, set in motion.

This meant not only that the official Valkyrie orders were issued, and that German Army units started to take control of designated installations, it also meant that the conspirators – those designated to take over key positions in an interim government – started to assemble. These men, such as the dismissed *Generalfeldmarschall* von Witzleben or General Hoepner, were men who had chosen disobedience to Hitler for the sake of their troops and paid for it with dismissal and disgrace. They came to replace opportunistic officers such as *Generaloberst* Fromm and so ensure that the Army would remain loyal to the conspirators even after the subordinate military commanders and troops realised what was happening.

On Stauffenberg's insistence that the coup go ahead, civilians and junior officers of known anti-Nazi sentiments were also summoned to the *Bendlerstrasse*. Their function was to support the very thin layer of actual conspirators in carrying out the coup. Yet the appearance of these individuals, who had no business in the headquarters of the Home Army, both betrayed the fact that Valkyrie was *not* a normal military plan and revealed the political sentiments of the participants. By activating these elements, both the disgraced military men and the civilians, the coup had in effect come out of the closet, and everyone involved had put their head in the noose in the event of failure.

Although on his arrival in the *Bendlerstrasse*, Stauffenberg continued to insist with ever-increasing drama that Hitler was dead, the facts were against him. No amount of bragging that he had himself set the bomb or that he had 'seen Hitler carried out', or even that 'no one could have survived the blast', could change this single fact. While Stauffenberg and Olbricht continued to send out the Valkyrie orders and tried to push ahead with the coup, the word was already escaping from the *Wolfschanze* that Hitler was very much alive.

What this meant was that subordinate military commanders were soon receiving two sets of contradictory orders. Orders from the Home Army stated that 'the *Führer*' Adolf Hitler was dead and declared a state of emergency. The orders furthermore placed the SS and police under Army orders; ordered the arrest of party leaders and the occupation of the concentration camps and Gestapo offices by military units; and named the dismissed *Generalfeldmarschall* von Witzleben commander-in-chief of the armed forces. Altogether, the Valkyrie orders contained a series of measures that were designed to enable the Army to wrest control of the nation away from the Nazis. But from the *Wolfschanze* came orders to arrest Stauffenberg and ignore orders signed by Witzleben.

Faced with contradictory orders, many commanders called in to the *Bendlerstrasse* to try to find out what was going on, trusting the word of their military superiors more than what came out of Hitler's lair in Poland. But when Propaganda Minister Josef Goebbels, the only senior Nazi official then in Berlin, realised that Army units were surrounding the government district, he also recognised he was in acute danger. He called the commander of the '*Gross Deutschland*' Guard Battalion in charge of those troops to his office and patched through a call to Hitler personally. The sound of Hitler's familiar voice proved that the Valkyrie orders were false, and that Hitler lived. Hitler furthermore ordered the Guard Battalion commander to ruthlessly put down what was now clearly exposed as a coup.

Within just a few hours the coup collapsed, because those who had not been part of it ceased to obey orders that they now knew were illegal. Those conspirators who could slip away in the darkness did so, hoping to escape detection and arrest. The leaders — Olbricht, Stauffenberg, and

Beck — did not have that choice. They continued to try to salvage their coup until officers of their own staff turned against them.

Just after midnight on the night of 20/21 July 1944, General Olbricht was shot in the courtyard of the *Bendlerstrasse*, followed shortly afterwards by *Oberst* Stauffenberg, while in the room above them *Generaloberst* Beck was allowed to shoot himself. A bloody retribution against all known opponents of the regime followed.

The misrepresentation of what had happened in Berlin on 20 July 1944 started immediately. That same night, Hitler announced in his speech to the nation that 'a tiny clique of ambitious, unscrupulous, and criminally stupid officers' had plotted to kill him. The only conspirator he named was Stauffenberg. Rarely had Hitler been so successful in shaping opinion, even to this day.

The Western Allies picked up Hitler's theme at once: only a tiny clique of officers had been involved. A 'tiny' clique meant that not enough people had been involved to change the call for unconditional surrender or to upset the policy of collective guilt. Furthermore, the civilian component in the conspiracy was completely ignored. The West insisted on seeing the 20 July Plot as a 'generals' plot'. And because the attempt came so late, it was assumed, without further investigation, that the conspirators had supported the war, and Hitler, earlier. Hitler's epithet of 'ambitious' was accepted at face value.

Because the attempt failed, it was equally easy to accept Hitler's characterisation of the conspirators as incompetent. In retrospect, they had done everything wrong. The bomb had failed to kill the victim. The orders had gone out too late. The conspirators didn't have control of the communications network, and so counter-orders soon came from the *Wolfschanze*. They failed to seize control of the radio station in Berlin, and so Goebbels could broadcast. The conspirators didn't even have control of their own troops, who soon turned against them. Was any more evidence needed that these men were 'criminally stupid'?

And just as Hitler named only one person, the predominant image presented in the literature even today is of a single heroic figure — Stauffenberg — struggling alone to achieve the goal of eliminating Hitler. Just like Hitler, many modern portrayals of 20 July reduce the entire German Resistance to a single individual: Stauffenberg. And since

Stauffenberg is the hero of the modern myth about the German Resistance, it is not possible that he failed or that he made mistakes. Rather the blame for his failure must be pushed off on to the other, less charismatic, less glamorous, less handsome co-conspirators — especially General Olbricht, the man who 'wasted' three critical hours after the assassination attempt.

But the world rarely corresponds to Hitler's — or Hollywood's — vision of it. And if one is prepared to suspend one's prejudices and follow the journey of an individual man through the forge of history, one can come closer to the truth. What follows is Friedrich Olbricht's story.

Chapter 2

THE AGE OF INNOCENCE

A Childhood in the Kingdom of Saxony, 1888–1913

It has been said that there was no better period in which to live than the closing years of the nineteenth century. It was a period characterised by optimism, an unshaken faith in 'progress', and a Pax Europa maintained by a balance of power. It was an age in which people widely believed that mankind was the master of nature and that science could be harnessed for the good of humanity without negative side effects. No one then could conceive the horror of the coming century – not the slaughter of a generation in the trenches of the First World War, nor the industrialised genocide of the Nazis, nor the decades of totalitarian terror and oppression of the Soviet Union. It was into this happy world that Friedrich Olbricht was born in Leisnig, a small town in Saxony, on 4 October 1888.

At the time of his birth, Saxony had already been absorbed into the newly unified Germany, but Saxony was still a quasi-independent kingdom within the so-called German Empire (*Deutsches Reich*), and it retained its own identity. Furthermore, Saxony had a long, proud history, one in which artistic and academic rather than military achievements took pride of place. Indeed, the Saxons tended to look down on their austere, 'uncultured', and militaristic northern neighbour, Prussia.

Yet for all its cultural traditions and fondness for the arts, Saxony by the late nineteenth century was primarily defined by its high level of industrial development. Saxony was one of Germany's industrial heartlands, with a prosperous and self-confident middle class. Here titles and bloodlines counted less than success, and there was both room and respect for the 'self-made man'.

Furthermore, nineteenth-century industry was very labour intensive, and large-scale industrialisation generated a large urban working class. This section of society, cut off from traditional social structures and largely alienated from the authority of the Church, was susceptible to new ideas and ideologies, and in the latter half of the nineteenth century there were plenty of these in circulation. This was, after all, the age in which socialism was flourishing in many varieties – not just the Marxist strain – and Lenin had not yet put his stamp to it. Although not all socialists were revolutionary, the working class in Saxony was known for its radicalism: so much so that Saxony was often referred to as 'the Red Kingdom' because the left wing of the Social Democratic Party had a firm grip on unions and the organised working class.

Thus Friedrich Olbricht was born into a 'happy' but also a highly volatile environment. He was the son of a young teacher who himself came from a family of educators. Friedrich's grandfather was a school principal. His great-uncle was tutor to the Saxon princes. His father, Emil, had a PhD in physics, after which he went on to have a highly successful career as a teacher. It is notable that despite his excellent qualifications (he later earned the title of Professor in addition to his doctorate), Emil Olbricht devoted his career to educating not the elite, but rather the increasingly important and independent lower classes. With the exception of two years spent at a gymnasium, Emil Olbricht devoted his entire career bringing education to those students not destined for higher education. In his final post, however, he proudly oversaw the expansion of the elementary *Realschule* into an *Oberrealschule*, or middle school, offering longer and more comprehensive education to the underprivileged.

That Emil Olbricht was committed to his charges is demonstrated by the fact that he did not confine his activities on their behalf to the schoolroom. Emil Olbricht was instrumental in introducing free school breakfasts to counter the fact that many of his pupils came to school too hungry to concentrate. He was also the founder of a society for adult education. He was praised for being hard-working, organised, and fair, but the characteristic that shone through most in people's memories of him was his 'warmth'. This must indeed have been exceptional, because even those of his students who later became leftist revolutionaries remembered him with affection – a fact for which his son Friedrich would have good reason to be thankful.

Friedrich Olbricht himself was the only child of this exemplary educator, and as such he undoubtedly enjoyed more than his fair share of his parent's attention. After a somewhat shaky start (he was at the bottom of his class at the end of primary school), he apparently found his stride and followed in the footsteps of his forefathers by demonstrating strong academic ability. In retrospect, it is significant that Olbricht did not go to a cadet academy, as did the future chief of staff of the *Wehrmacht*, Alfred Jodl. He did not, therefore, start school with the admonition that he was there 'to learn how to die well'. Rather, he − and the majority of the men who would later be his co-conspirators in the fight against Hitler − enjoyed what was known as a 'humanistic' or enlightened education. Schools that were categorised as such placed a strong emphasis on history, literature, art, and languages. This education was furthermore characterised by striving to instil in students an open mind, tolerance for conflicting opinions, and respect for differences, combined with reliability, circumspection, and self-restraint. All these were traits that Olbricht was later to demonstrate to a high degree.

Olbricht graduated near the top of his gymnasium class in 1907. A career in any field of his choosing lay open to him. Certainly, given Olbricht's background and academic success, a university education seemed a logical next step. But already at the age of 18 Olbricht had decided he wanted to be a professional soldier. Indeed, despite being a product of landlocked Saxony, Olbricht first wanted to pursue a career at sea. It appears he was attracted by the idea of travel, or he may have felt that the expanding Navy offered more opportunities, or perhaps he thought the work of a naval officer was more intellectually challenging. Whatever his reasoning, the German Navy was beyond his reach because Olbricht was short-sighted and so could not pass the physical requirements. He settled, therefore, for his second choice: the Army. On 1 March 1907 he joined the Royal Saxon Infantry Regiment 106 as a cadet. At that time Stauffenberg had not even been born.

Although Olbricht's career choice represented a conscious break with his family heritage, his decision is less surprising than it may seem. In 1907, when Olbricht chose a military career, the military was 'the pride of the nation'. The officer corps enjoyed the highest prestige possible throughout the German Empire − indeed, no profession was respected more. Furthermore, this was the period when the Army in Saxony was trying hard to counter Socialist influences by breaking with authoritarian traditions and seeking to 'win the hearts and minds' of soldiers for the nation.

Indeed, the age of *Kadavergehorsam*, corpse-like obedience, was long since over, even in Prussia. In its place was a conscious policy to respect the 'human dignity' of each individual soldier. By 1907, the doctrines of *Feldmarschall* von Moltke the Elder had long been integrated into the military ethos, and these included the concept that every soldier should be a *thinking* soldier. German military doctrine of this period, in contrast to popular conceptions of it, stressed individual initiative and even tolerated disobedience if it served stated objectives. In short, the German, and especially the Saxon, Army was consciously modernising.

Lastly, because universal male conscription ensured that every German youth passed through the ranks of the Army, the military was conscious, and proud, of its role as an educator. The military leadership saw universal male conscription as a means to indoctrinate the nation's youth with fundamental military virtues and patriotic values. The Army provided more mundane training as well, on health, hygiene, and technology.

It is conceivable that Olbricht was attracted to the challenge of countering Socialist influences, or that it was the educational role of the Army that appealed to the young man. Certainly he did not have to fear being cut off from all intellectual stimulation. On the contrary, the tradition of academic training for officers in Saxony went back hundreds of years. The Elector of Saxony, Johann Georg III, had made the first attempt at creating an officers' training school as early as 1687, and in his institution only one-quarter of the courses addressed military subjects. The rest of the training was devoted to language, dance, fencing, and riding.

More importantly, even in Olbricht's time the Saxon Army was famous (or infamous, depending on perspective) for an elsewhere inconceivable freedom from bureaucracy. Saxon officers prided themselves on not taking the letter of the law too seriously. The Saxon Army also had a reputation for superior food and excellent support services; only the actual combat skills of the Saxon Army were considered less than outstanding. Olbricht would go on to a career in which he ended up as the most senior officer in the entire German Army with responsibility for exactly these non-combat functions.

Last of all, it was widely believed that officers of non-aristocratic background had a better chance of advancement in the Saxon Army than in any other in Germany. Some bourgeois officers left their native regions in order to take service in Saxon regiments because they felt they had better chances there than at home. Only one-seventh of the officers in Olbricht's regiment were aristocrats. The tone was clearly set by the majority of bourgeois officers coming from families like Olbricht's own: the urban, educated elite, rather than the rural gentry as was still largely the case in Prussia.

Olbricht's career progressed rapidly from the start. After 17 months he was promoted to lieutenant, in just three years he was battalion adjutant, and in five he was regimental adjutant − the latter a highly respected and coveted position for a junior officer, which foreshadowed a career in the General Staff. However, not all was going well for Friedrich Olbricht.

In July 1912, when Olbricht was not yet 22, his father was killed in a fatal accident while mountain climbing. Olbricht himself went to bring his father's remains home and learned that his father had not been killed in the fall, but had bled to death slowly before help could arrive. For a 21-year-old with a very close relationship to his father, this was a severe blow. The impact seems to have resulted in, as psychiatrists have often noted, an early maturity. Olbricht's youth ended with his father's death. As an only child, he assumed responsibility for his widowed mother, and his entire career suggests that he rapidly learned to form his own opinions and go his own way, as is often the case for youth who cannot rely on the advice of their elders.

One indication of this early maturity is the following incident. Fritz Nölting, one of Olbricht's regimental comrades, had become addicted to gambling. Certainly, gambling was very much part of the officer lifestyle in the early twentieth century, but German officer pay was notoriously poor. One was supposed to serve with the colours for the honour of it − or have a rich family capable of supplementing one's income. At all events, gambling debts were 'debts of honour'. An officer unable to pay his gambling debts was expected, at the very least, to resign his commission. A bullet through the head was more likely.

Fritz Nölting was a passionate soldier − and gambler. By his own account, he found himself in a rapid downward spiral, and was not far from facing the muzzle of his revolver when his younger and junior comrade, Friedrich Olbricht, intervened. Olbricht recognised that Nölting took his word of honour as seriously as any debt of honour. He set about wringing from the more senior officer a promise never to touch a playing card again. Over time — but in time — he wore Nölting down to the point where he gave his word never to gamble again. Nölting was convinced that Olbricht saved his career and life. While this is only a tiny incident, it does demonstrate that Olbricht not only felt responsible for his fellows, he was also willing to work tirelessly towards a goal that brought him no particular gain.

But the days when gaming in the officers' casino dominated the lives of German officers were rapidly drawing to a close. By 1913 this peaceful, optimistic, smug Europe was rushing headlong into the first great catastrophe of the young twentieth century. In the last, golden summer of an age innocent of modern genocide and totalitarian dictatorship, Friedrich Olbricht met a young woman who captivated his heart.

She was the 19-year-old Eva Koeppel. The daughter of a large landowner in Pomerania, Eva found the Saxon Olbricht notably different from the young men she had previously met. She related years later that she was attracted to the 26-year-old Saxon Army lieutenant because she found him witty and by no means as one-sided as the officers from her native Pomerania. Fritz Olbricht did not talk only of horses, hunting, and gambling. He was well read and open-minded. She later learned to value his reliability and his goodness, but in that first summer of their acquaintance there was no real opportunity to get to know one another well. Before the relationship could truly blossom, the First World War shattered the façade of orderly human progress.

Chapter 3

THE WAR TO END ALL WARS

An Officer in the First World War, 1914–18

With the Fighting Troops

The outbreak of the war prevented the planned posting of Friedrich Olbricht to General Staff College. Instead of reporting to the War College in Berlin to begin training for the German General Staff, Olbricht, still acting as regimental adjutant, went to war.

Only months earlier, the leadership of the Saxon Army had raised objections to the mobilisation plans because of the scheduled simultaneous deployment to the front of the two Leipzig regiments, including Olbricht's own 106th. The Saxon military leadership feared that any outbreak of war would ignite widespread riots and strikes on the part of the notoriously radical Leipzig working class. The Socialist International, a federation of the labour unions and workers' political parties which represented nearly a million workers, was a vehemently pacifist organisation. During the war scare of 1913, it had agitated furiously against an outbreak of hostilities. That the Socialist International might call on its members to join a general strike to stop mobilisation and that the Leipzig workers would follow such an appeal appeared a genuine threat – at least to the generals in Saxony.

But the German mobilisation plans were rigid and allowed no last-minute adjustments for local threats. These plans called for the Saxon Army to deploy more or less as a cohesive unit, the Leipzig regiments forming the 48th Brigade of the XIXth Saxon Corps, one of three Army corps that made up the Saxon Army.

Fortunately from the generals' point of view, the Socialist International disintegrated almost instantly at the declaration of war. The various national organisations within the federation proved more Nationalist than Socialist. By the thousands, workers – no less than their bourgeois brothers – rushed to join the colours. In August 1914, everyone thought that war was a glorious thing and would be over by Christmas.

The XIXth Corps was assigned the task of crossing immediately into Luxembourg and securing an important railway line. The 48th Brigade was assigned the vanguard and came into contact with the enemy on 21 August 1914. On 23 August, the brigade led the assault across the River Maas and suffered significant losses when it was pinned down by French artillery and attacked from behind by civilian 'partisans' including, according to the regimental history, women and girls. Only the coming of darkness saved it from worse casualties. Just three weeks into the war, Olbricht had endured his first bloody battle. He had also distinguished himself to such a degree that he was recommended for a citation.

There followed two weeks of intermittent but hard fighting in which the Saxon Army, including the corps to which Olbricht was attached, was both on the offensive and the defensive. This fighting eventually climaxed in the First Battle of the Marne, which lasted from 6 to 12 September 1914.

At the start of this battle, the German Army was just 30 miles from Paris and the French government had fled to Bordeaux. In a desperate gamble, the French forces under General Michel-Joseph Maunoury attacked the German flank under General von Kluck. Although desperately needed French reinforcements only reached the front using a shuttle service of 600 Paris taxis transporting five soldiers at a time in two daily trips each, the French halted the German advance and forced the German Army to dig in. The chance for a quick German victory was over, and the trench warfare that was to dominate the war for the next three and a half years began.

The battle was not yet over, however, when Friedrich Olbricht became the first officer in his regiment to earn the Iron Cross (2nd class). Just weeks later, he was promoted to *Oberleutnant* and awarded the highest Saxon military order, the Royal Saxon Military St Heinrich Order. He was the sixth person of a total of just 66 to receive this honour during the First World War. The citation read:

As Regimental Adjutant of Infantry Regiment 106, Oberleutnant Olbricht provided outstanding support to his regimental and corps commanders. To an exceptional degree, he proved himself a bold and fearless transmitter of orders during the advance in the autumn of 1914 and during the First Battle of the Marne. By accompanying the rapidly advancing infantry to the foremost positions, he was able to give excellent first-hand accounts on the progress of the fighting and on the enemy positions to the regimental commanders during this battle. Especially on 8 and 9 September, he distinguished himself with intrepid rides through intense fire to reach brigade and Army headquarters when the telephone connections were disrupted. He thereby ensured that headquarters was rapidly informed about the situation of his regiment.[1]

The First Battle of the Marne was the swansong of the Saxon Army. Almost immediately afterwards, on 3 October 1914, the Saxon commanding general was replaced by a Prussian. After that, one after another, the Saxon divisions were detached from the Saxon corps and Army and thrown into the war wherever the German High Command felt they were needed. Never again would a Saxon Army fight as such.

Olbricht's regiment found itself attached to the newly created 58th Infantry Division, and in this unit it participated in the Battle of the Loretto Heights. Although this is not one of the most famous battles of the First World War, it was nevertheless typical in that it lasted for days and in the end achieved nothing but great loss of life on both sides. Olbricht's regiment was one of the most severely decimated. Within three days the regiment lost 49 officers – almost the entire complement – and 1,355 men. It was so badly mauled, in fact, that it was withdrawn from the division altogether until it could be refreshed and reconstituted. By the end of this battle in early May 1915, less than a year since the start of the war, Olbricht had lost almost all of his peacetime comrades.

When the regiment was again deemed combat ready, it was, probably to the relief of the few remaining veterans of the devastating fighting in the West, sent to the Eastern Front as part of the 58th Division. Here a war of movement was still in progress, and Olbricht's regiment took part in an offensive lasting from late July until September 1915. But this offensive wore itself out, and the forward progress ground to a halt at the end of September. Less than a month later, on 20 October 1915, the 58th Division was sent back to the Western Front.

Although only a short interlude in the entire span of the war, these few months fighting in the East gave Olbricht exposure not only to the Russian Army but, more importantly, to Russian geography. Olbricht saw at first hand the vastness of the land, the harshness of the climate, and the underdeveloped state of the infrastructure. The extreme difficulties the German armies experienced in maintaining their lines of communication made a deep impression on him – one that he did not 'conveniently' forget a quarter of a century later.

That he was a thinking observer of what he encountered is evidenced by the fact that he was tasked with providing a briefing about the war on the Eastern Front to all officers of the Army to which the regiment was next attached. This suggests that Olbricht was perceived by his superiors as the kind of officer who could put together a worthwhile briefing even for superior officers. Independent of this, he was awarded the Iron Cross (1st Class) on 10 December 1915 for his role in the fighting on the Eastern Front.

On 13 March 1916, Olbricht's division was thrown into the ongoing Battle of Verdun. For 12 days, Infantry Regiment 106 held its own. Then, exhausted and depleted, it was withdrawn. A description of these 12 days at Verdun is one of the very few documents written by Olbricht that has survived. It was produced on 26 March 1916 – the day that the regiment was finally pulled out of the front line. The simple and direct style and the criticism of superior commands are both noteworthy. For example, Olbricht wrote: 'A systematic artillery barrage was not possible, since no artillery spotters came forward. The heavy artillery preferred to comfortably carry out carpet barrages – which often ended in our trenches. ... A German shell in German trenches demoralises more than hunger, thirst, and cold.'[2]

Interestingly, Olbricht placed the words 'hero's death' in quotation marks in his report of Verdun, which was written in 1916 – long before war weariness had become widespread. Equally notable is his willingness to confess his own reluctance and fears. He excuses his remarks with the words that 'unfortunately' he was there himself. Olbricht refused in the midst of this slaughter to speak of 'heroes' for *Volk und Vaterland* – the German equivalent of King and Country. Rather, he focused on the human suffering in an inhuman fight. He was not above relating even the banal side of the operations, such as reporting that 'Two treacherous direct hits turned our humble WC into a wasteland.'[3] He wrote, too: 'The delivery of food, munitions, and materiel was, as a result of the described conditions, always a dance with death. Warm meals were completely impossible, since it would have been nearly impossible to bring food in pots down the long access trenches, and it would in any case have arrived cold and filthy to the extent that it arrived at all.'[4]

Highly significant is that Olbricht, although himself decorated for daring rides through heavy enemy fire, demonstrated an unusual degree of respect for the support troops − the 'tail' rather than the 'teeth' of the Army. Instead of focusing exclusively on the fighting troops, as is more common in such reports, he emphasised the daily courage and sacrifice of the engineers and signals soldiers, the men driving the supply wagons, and the cooks.

Lastly, he is blunt in stating that the 'battle was completely ignominious for the regiment', adding: 'We, who were there, don't want any praise. We simply wish to say … that the days at Verdun were some of the hardest this regiment has ever experienced.'[5]

Olbricht was promoted to *Hauptmann* on 18 April 1916 and transferred to the post of brigade adjutant. In this position, he accompanied the 58th Infantry Division to the Somme Front. The division took up its position on 31 October 1916, although the division was considered in need of rest. Just 12 days later a British counter-offensive opened before the division could be relieved. The British rolled over neighbouring divisions on 14 November, taking more than 5,000 prisoners. After another four days, the 58th Division was also forced to give ground. While this was another German 'defeat', the British had nevertheless failed to achieve the needed breakthrough. The offensive stalled and the war resumed its static character.

By the end of 1916, Friedrich Olbricht, now 28 years old, had fought against all three of Germany's main enemies: France, Russia, and Britain. He had participated in both offensive and defensive operations and engaged in both mobile and trench warfare. At the Somme, he had furthermore witnessed one of the very first tank attacks in history. While perhaps the most amazing aspect of his biography up to this point was simply the fact of his survival, he had clearly not done so by shirking his duty as his three decorations prove. On the contrary, he had proved beyond a doubt that he was an exceptionally courageous officer, capable of performing even under immense pressure and the most intense fire in military history. He had also convinced his superiors that he was a thinking officer, capable and deserving of training for higher command. In the German Army of this time that meant only one thing: acceptance into the General Staff.

With the General Staff

The German General Staff was a unique institution which differed in essential features from the staffs of other nations of the period. It had its roots in the Wars of Liberation against Napoleon and was founded by the 'revolutionary' Prussian officers around Gerhard Scharnhorst and August Wilhelm Graf von Gneisenau. These great innovators broke with the tradition of Prussia's 'Soldier King' Friedrich Wilhelm II and his son Friedrich II 'the Great'. Those Prussian monarchs had built up an Army and a military reputation based on rigid, even draconian, discipline in the other ranks, coupled with 'hereditary' courage and a spirit of sacrifice on the part of an aristocratic, but largely uneducated, officer corps. The Great Reformers introduced a Napoleonic spirit into the Prussian Army by emphasising advancement by merit (rather than birth), and added to this the critical component of professionalism.

In addition to these general reforms, they established the General Staff. The goal was to provide 'competent advisers' to military commanders because, as they unabashedly acknowledged, the commanders were often incompetent (i.e. hereditary monarchs and their close relatives). Acceptance into the General Staff, unlike acceptance into a regiment or appointment to High Command, was only possible after passing an objective entrance examination *and* passing successfully out of rigorous training. Membership in the General Staff was, therefore, not governed by family tradition or title. Furthermore, it was a distinct branch of service, equivalent — but superior — to the infantry, cavalry, and artillery. A General Staff officer, once he was selected through competitive examination and had successfully completed intensive specialised training, wore a distinctive uniform with the insignia of the General Staff. Only with the rank of general did a General Staff officer lose this distinction and become indistinguishable from other officers.

In the century between the defeat of Napoleon in 1815 and the start of the First World War, the Prussian General Staff proved its worth. In a quick series of short but decisive wars, Prussia established its military supremacy on the Continent of Europe and created a new, unified German state. The Austrian officers, who laughed and lost interest in the Prussian 'war games' because there was no mechanism for betting, soon learned what had been at stake when the German Empire was formed at Austria's expense. The French likewise learned that genius need not be embodied in a great leader à la Napoleon, but could also be found in an institution that systematically rewarded competence and initiative.

Nothing demonstrates this better than the career of *Generalfeldmarschall* von Moltke, the chief of the German General Staff during the Franco-Prussian War. Moltke came from an obscure and impoverished family. He was so poor, in fact, that he could only pay for his uniforms by publishing short stories and essays and doing translations from English. He served first in the Danish Army, but later managed to transfer to the Prussian Army. Here his intellectual capabilities were quickly recognised and he was rapidly accepted for training at General Staff College. Having successfully completed this training, he spent the rest of his career as a staff officer, never commanding a unit larger than a platoon, until he commanded an Army Group (i.e. multiple armies). But when he did take command, at the express wish of the King, Prussian military forces reshaped the political map of a continent in a series of short, successful wars.

Following these successes, it is hardly surprising that Moltke's doctrines became those that dominated the German Army for nearly half a century. And these are very revealing. Moltke believed in careful staff planning in advance of any manoeuvre or military campaign – but warned that 'No plan survives contact with the enemy.' He believed that 'from the youngest soldier to the highest general' every soldier should understand that it was 'better to do the wrong thing than to do nothing at all'. Yet he insisted that when mistakes were made, they had to be acknowledged, analysed, and learned from.

By the end of the nineteenth century, no army in Europe was more admired than the German. No profession was more admired in Germany than that of military officers. And within the officer corps, nothing was more prestigious than the General Staff. Indeed, by the First World War, so great was the prestige and power of the General Staff, that military success or failure was attributed more to the chief of staff than to the commander. Poor performance cost the chief of staff – not the commander – his job.

But the great planners of the German General Staff had expected the First World War to be over in weeks, just as Prussia's last three wars had been. So the General Staff College was closed at the start of the war. There was no graduating class of 1915 or 1916, and by 1917 – with no end to the war in sight – attrition made the German Army desperate for staff officers. The solution was a sharp break with General Staff tradition: prospective candidates for the General Staff were selected predominantly from the ranks of regimental and brigade adjutants, who were presumed to have had insight into planning, organisational, and leadership responsibilities, and they were given only hasty ad hoc training. They were then transferred to the General Staff without further ado.

Olbricht was one of the officers who underwent this highly abbreviated training. At the end of January 1917 he was sent on a one-month training course and then reassigned, *as a General Staff officer*, to the XIXth Corps. In this new position, Olbricht was witness to a catastrophic defeat at what was known in German sources as the '*Wytschaete-Bogen*'.

In this obscure battle, the Germans suffered severe casualties – many to gas and phosphorous attacks – and were pushed back decisively by British forces that paid a comparatively low price for their successes. Postwar analysis of the battle blamed two factors. Some commentators attributed the failure to reluctance of the divisional, corps, and army commanders to withdraw – although this was explicitly left to their discretion by their superiors at Army Group level – because of insufficiently prepared positions to their rear. Other sources blamed British air superiority. The significance of the battle for Olbricht was twofold. He learned respect for the importance of air power, and he drew the right conclusion about the advantage of prepared rearward positions.

This local disaster was followed, in Olbricht's career, by the far more appalling waste of life in the fighting in Flanders. Again, both sides in this conflict suffered almost unendurable misery in a battle characterised by massive artillery attacks combined with gas and phosphorous assaults against units that had no warm food, dry clothing, or shelter.

After this battle, Olbricht was given another four-week course in General Staff work at Sedan, before being sent to the staff of the 3rd Army on 2 August 1918. His position there was a highly responsible one, essentially as the deputy of the first General Staff officer, i.e. the officer with tactical responsibility. But Olbricht was not happy there. He did not like or respect the Army's commanding general, General von Einem. According to Olbricht's widow, then his fiancée, Olbricht was upset because Einem 'plundered' so much, and Olbricht argued with him about it, despite being nothing but a lowly staff officer with the rank of *Hauptmann*.

He did not have long to worry about such things, however, since a major British offensive hit the 3rd Army on 26 September 1918. After an 11-hour artillery barrage, the British attacked with strong armoured and infantry units supported by powerful air squadrons. Three days later, the 3rd Army was forced to give ground, but there was no breakthrough. The Army chief of staff attributed this to 'flexible defence', which allowed the troops to move back to prepared positions, regroup, and rest before attacking again.

It is notable that this kind of 'elastic defence' on a much larger scale proved remarkably successful when exercised in the Second World War by competent generals such as Field Marshals von Kluge and von Manstein. Hitler, in contrast, clung to the tactics of static defence that had caused so much misery, and proved obsolete, in the course of the First World War. There can be no doubt that this is one of the reasons why Olbricht later despised the 'greatest military genius of all time', as Hitler liked to characterise himself.

But the 'elastic' defence of the 3rd Army could not save Germany from defeat. A breakthrough in the neighbouring 5th Army at the beginning of November 1918 forced the 3rd Army to withdraw. Meanwhile, the German Army was starting to disintegrate. The first references to disorder and disobedience on the part of the troops are registered in the war diary of the 3rd Army on 8 November 1918. On 11 November the Armistice was signed, and the German High Command ordered the formation of Soldiers' Councils (known elsewhere as 'Soviets').

Although the 3rd Army, still largely Saxon in composition, reported no serious 'incidents' with the Soldiers' Council, it had to admit that their reception at home was not a hero's welcome. The German Army returned in defeat to a nation that was seething with discontent and embittered towards a leadership that had demanded unprecedented sacrifices of them for worse than nothing.

Although Friedrich Olbricht's role in the withdrawal of the German Army was that of a tiny cog in a massive machine, his presence was apparently 'indispensable'. He had planned to marry Eva Koeppel in Berlin on 9 November 1918, but he was not given leave. Not until

28 December 1918, after all the units of Saxony's armed forces had been repatriated to Saxony, was Olbricht granted leave.

His courtship of Eva Koeppel had taken place almost exclusively by mail. Only once since they had first met in the summer of 1913 had the young couple had the chance to meet personally. In March 1917, Eva travelled to Wiesbaden, where her brother was recuperating from a wound, and Olbricht was able to obtain leave to spend time with her there. They spent 'several weeks' together, albeit well chaperoned as was then the custom.

Nevertheless, it would be wrong to suppose that Eva and Friedrich did not know each other well. Not only had the relationship survived over five years of separation – itself an indication of the strength of the relationship – but written communication, as many modern Internet correspondents can testify, often allows people to gain deeper insight into one another than 'dating'. Letters, unlike dances, teas, or other social contact in the early twentieth century, were private, and they enabled the writer to open up in a way often difficult face to face. Over a five-year period, in which both partners had experienced the loss of beloved friends and watched a world slowly crumble under the weight of the war, Eva and Friedrich had shared their thoughts and feelings. Through the exchange of letters revealing emotions and values, they had drawn closer. Unfortunately, none of the letters these young lovers exchanged during their courtship have survived. They were lost when the SS took over Olbricht's home just hours after he was shot. But the success of Olbricht's marriage suggests that the letters did indeed provide the foundation for a sound relationship.

As one of the few survivors of a generation largely slaughtered in the trenches, Friedrich Olbricht certainly had other options than Eva Koeppel, but the future was to prove the wisdom of his choice. Throughout Friedrich Olbricht's married life, and most especially in the difficult years of opposition and resistance, Eva not only stood by him, but supported him in his activities. She was a courageous and independent woman who, far from needing protection or sheltering, took an active interest in his career and never held back with her opinions. Indeed, she quite honestly admitted in later life that she would have enjoyed being a General Staff officer herself! In a different age and society, she would certainly have studied and had a career of her own. To the end of her days she read avidly, kept up with current events, and had firm views on political and social developments.

It is especially notable that while most Resistance leaders sent their wives 'to safety' in the countryside and carefully shielded them from any knowledge of their illegal activities, Eva Olbricht was fully involved in her husband's Resistance activities. It is highly doubtful, for example, that Nina Gräfin Stauffenberg knew anything whatever about what her husband was up to before Hitler announced his name over the radio on the night of 20 July 1944. The wives of other Resistance figures were given only vague hints or were aware of their husband's *sentiments*, but not their concrete activities and plans. A few wives, however, were full partners who assisted the Resistance. Gräfin Yorck and Gräfin Moltke of the Kreisauer Circle, for example, attended meetings of this Resistance circle and took notes. Erika von Tresckow actually helped in typing up the secret supplementary orders for Valkyrie. Eva Olbricht was present at several key meetings between Resistance leaders. She hosted dinners at the Olbricht villa for military and civilian leaders in which opposition views could be exchanged and plans discussed. The dinners were particularly important for bringing retired and disgraced generals such as Beck, Hoepner, and Witzleben together with active officers, and for bringing civilians such as Adam von Trott zu Solz together with members of Counter-Intelligence such as Admiral Canaris and Hans Oster. Most importantly, she witnessed the fateful conversation between her husband and Stauffenberg on 15 July 1944.

Her strength of character aroused the disapproval of men who thought women should be passive and mute. She was sometimes referred to derogatorily by subordinates of Friedrich Olbricht as the '*Frau Generälin*', implying undue influence on her husband. Her daughter and son-in-law, however, firmly reject the idea that Eva was the dominant partner in the marriage. According to those closest to them, Olbricht tolerated his wife's independent and outspoken ways because he respected her – but he also knew exactly where to draw the line and could very sharply rebuke attempts at interference that were inappropriate. But that was all in the future.

On 28 December 1918, Friedrich and Eva married in a small ceremony at her home in Rozdnazeno, Pomerania. On the same day, a Polish government was formed. The newly-weds just managed to catch the very last train for the West before the border was closed behind them.

Chapter 4

BETWEEN REVOLUTION AND REACTION

The Political Crisis, 1918–21

Revolution in Germany, 1918–19

The German Revolution, like most unsuccessful revolts, is largely forgotten. It was short-lived and appeared to have been quickly put down, but the legacy of the Revolution was more significant than is generally assumed by foreign observers. Certainly the character of the Weimar Republic would have been different, and arguably Hitler's rise to power impossible, if Germany had not still been recovering from the trauma of a revolution that almost succeeded.

In looking back upon the German Revolution, it is essential to remember that the Bolshevik Revolution had succeeded in Russia almost exactly a year earlier and that the Bolsheviks had even less support in the population at large than their German equivalents, the Independent Socialists. Furthermore, from a Marxist point of view, Germany had achieved the necessary preconditions for successful revolution, while Russia had not. Germany, in contrast to Russia, had a large, well-organised, and – thanks to people like Olbricht's father – comparatively well-educated working class. This working class was represented by the internationally respected Social Democratic Party (*Sozialdemokratische Partei Deutschlands*, or SPD).

Although in the early days of its existence under Bismarck the SPD had been outlawed, by the outbreak of the First World War the SPD had grown, completely legally and simply by winning elections, into the largest and most powerful party in the (admittedly weak) German parliament, the *Reichstag*. While the SPD still preached that the Revolution was 'inevitable', what it actually did was to participate in the German constitutional system. Rather than seeking to overthrow the bourgeois system and establish a 'dictatorship of the proletariat' by violent means, it sought to change that system into a socialist society by peaceful and democratic means. Furthermore, while socialist ideology held that class interests were more important than national interests, the identification of the SPD with Germany was so great that when the First World War broke out, the party loyally voted for the necessary budgets.

As is typical in leftist parties, however, a small minority within the SPD was not prepared to accept majority rule for long. This faction split off in 1917 and established the Independent Socialist Party. Their initial popularity was based on a single policy: opposition to the war. By 1917 the war was causing ever greater and more acute misery, particularly to the urban poor. As a result, more and more workers turned against the loyal 'majority' Socialists, who continued to support the war cabinet (nominally under the Kaiser but effectively controlled by the German Army High Command), and gave their support to the vehemently pacifist Independent Socialists. But the leadership of the Independent Socialists was more than pacifist; they were also genuinely revolutionary. After the example of the successful revolution in Russia, the Independent Socialists became impatient with seeking change within the existing system. They believed the time was ripe at last for a German Socialist revolution. And so the stage was set for a bizarre revolution in which the left fought more among themselves than against the right.

On 29 September 1918, the German High Command announced to a completely unsuspecting and trusting German government that Germany had lost the war. The news shocked and devastated the political ruling class, including the majority Socialists, because they had been kept in the dark about the real military situation and believed their own slogans about how close they were to victory. The Independent Socialists, consistent opponents of the war, were the only political party that was neither stunned by the news nor at a loss about what to do next. While the other parties had programmes only for 'after the victory', the Independent Socialists had been expecting and longing for defeat because they saw it as the prelude to revolution.

While the Kaiser, the government, the civil service, the bourgeois parties, and the SPD were still reeling from learning that the war was lost, the German Army leadership was already insisting on the next logical step: an end to hostilities on the best possible terms. Yet while the German Army Command demanded peace and the still-dazed German government was feverishly trying to obtain an armistice, the German Navy ordered the High Seas Fleet to sail out to what could only be a futile, even if successful, last battle.

That was one senseless sacrifice too many, and the sailors mutinied. Notably, their mutiny was entirely in line with the policy of the Kaiser's government and the German General Staff, which wanted an 'acceptable' armistice sooner rather than later – something that would have slipped out of their grasp if the German Navy had attacked at such a time. In addition, the sailors themselves greeted the elected parliamentary representatives sent to negotiate with them as heroes, not enemies. Germany's sailors and – as we shall soon see – soldiers were essentially war-weary, but not revolutionary.

But having once revolted against their officers, they had no choice but to force changes on their society, or face being shot as mutineers. So the German Revolution began not really as an attempt to bring down a government, but rather as a way of averting a counter-revolution by the reactionary naval leadership and a means of securing the peace that the government was already seeking.

Once ignited, however, the spirit of revolt was hard to control. The example of Russia was close at hand, and in contrast to the soldiers and sailors, there were elements of the German working class that were radical and revolutionary. Even while the German Army was still fighting desperately – but with discipline – against the advancing Western Allies, the garrisons of the German home front joined forces with the revolutionary workers to take power from the institutions of the old regime: first and foremost from the military officers and headquarters, the police, and the civil administration. They set up 'Workers' and Soldiers' Councils' in place of the existing organs of government. This is where the legend of the 'stab in the back' originated.

With a revolution now brewing at their backs, the German military leadership and government were forced to accept virtually any terms the Western Allies put before them – and they did. But the military and political leadership also recognised that the Kaiser had to go if they were to have any chance of putting down the rebellion. The leadership of the Social Democratic Party additionally recognised that they were going to have to *take control* of the incipient revolution. Otherwise, they knew it might develop its own momentum and go in directions that the orderly and hard-working democratic majority abhorred: the way of the Russian Revolution.

On 7 November 1918, massive demonstrations in Munich demanding the end of the monarchy and the war drove the King of Bavaria to flight. In the night, the revolutionary forces took control of the garrison and the arms in the city. The next morning the leader of this revolt, Kurt Eisner, demanded that the government turn over their offices to him, and they did. Thus on 8 November, Munich was in the hands of the revolutionaries.

On 9 November, a massive strike and demonstration by workers with the same demands, now directed at the Kaiser and the central government, were held in Berlin. The German chancellor, Prince Max of Baden, knowing that the Army had already accepted that the Kaiser must go, proclaimed the Kaiser's abdication (in fact, before he had been persuaded by his military advisers to do so) and then he himself resigned. With the crowds still screaming for a republic, the leaders of the SPD and the Independent Socialists, Friedrich Ebert and Karl Liebknecht, independently but more or less simultaneously, proclaimed the establishment of a republic. Significantly, the SPD proclaimed a 'German' republic, while the Independent Socialists declared a 'Socialist' republic.

In fact, Germany had no government whatsoever. Prince Max of Baden had turned the 'government' over to the head of the majority Socialists, Friedrich Ebert, but the latter took over a 'government' that constitutionally could not exist without the Kaiser. Meanwhile, the spontaneous seizure of city halls and the disarming of officers continued across the country. The only force that seemed capable of restoring order and establishing the authority of the now Social Democratic and self-proclaimed republican government was the returning field army.

But this army was exhausted and came from the same elements that were now setting up Workers' and Soldiers' Councils around the country. The army disintegrated almost as soon as it crossed the border into Germany. What remained were hundreds of Workers' and Soldiers' Councils which had placed themselves in power. Control of Germany would clearly go to whatever party or group could take control of those councils and re-establish central authority.

The only contestants in the struggle for power over the Workers' and Soldiers' Councils were the majority Socialists and the Independent Socialists. The bourgeois parties had no hope of controlling them, and disdained them even while buckling under their decrees. The Independent Socialists hoped to repeat the success of the Bolsheviks in Russia and steer Germany straight into Socialism. The majority Socialists, on the other hand, wanted to set up a parliamentary democracy in which they could expect, as the largest political party, to form a government and implement their far more moderate programme of reform. The Independent Socialists planned a 'dictatorship of the proletariat' that recognised only the rights of the 'progressive elements' in society: the working class. The majority Socialists, in contrast, wanted the power of the majority party within a democratic system without disenfranchising the majority of the population, which was not Socialist at all.

The bourgeoisie, lamed and demoralised as they were by the double blows of a lost war and the abdication of the Kaiser, were intelligent enough to recognise that the majority Socialists were preferable to the Independent Socialists. Likewise, the military leadership recognised that they had to support the SPD government, or Germany would go the way of Russia.

This coalition of forces – the majority Socialists, the bourgeoisie including the civil service and industrial leaders, and the Army leadership – effectively managed to put out the flames of radicalism and take control of the German Revolution. The ultimate result was a very progressive republic: the so-called Weimar Republic. But it did not always look so certain that the forces of reason and gradual change would win, and the situation was particularly precarious in Leipzig, the home of Olbricht's regiment.

The Revolution in Saxony

Even before the war or the split of the Social Democrats into two parties, the *Leipziger Volkszeitung* was known as the voice of the radical leftist elements inside the SPD. In the course of the war, the discontent and radicalism of the Leipzig workers grew disproportionately to the discontent of the nation at large. Indeed, Socialist historians claim that the first Workers' and Soldiers' Council on German soil was established in Leipzig in April 1917, more than a year before the mutiny of the High Seas Fleet. The occasion was a massive strike in which spokesmen were elected to send a catalogue of political demands to the government in Berlin.

By the time the German November Revolution came more than 18 months later, the politically active working class of Leipzig had already split unevenly between the two Socialist parties; there were 35,000 registered members of the Independent Socialists, compared to a mere 250 loyal members of the majority Socialists. On 8 November 1918, the same day as the successful leftist revolution in Bavaria and a day before striking workers and demonstrators in Berlin forced the German chancellor to resign and the Kaiser to abdicate, the garrison troops in Leipzig arrested their officers, seized control of the weapons depots, and elected 'Soldiers' Councils'.

However, the balance of power was reversed in Dresden, the capital of Saxony. There the majority Socialists held power. Thus, when the King of Saxony abdicated in Dresden on 13 November, the relationship between the two Socialist parties in Saxony as a whole was more or less balanced. The Saxon Assembly of Workers' and Soldiers' Councils elected a six-man government in which each of the two Socialist parties named three ministers. The Independents claimed the ministries of Interior, Finance, and Defence. The very next day, 14 November, this Saxon government was already protesting against the SPD government in Berlin, demanding a more revolutionary programme.

Just over a month later, on 23 December 1918, the Saxon government refused point-blank to recognise the orders of the central government in Berlin, which was led by the majority Socialist Chancellor Ebert. By 8 January 1919, the Saxon Assembly of Workers' and Soldiers' Councils went further and demanded the resignation of Ebert and his majority Socialist government.

Meanwhile, however, the Independent Socialists had lost support among their own clientele. In an election to the Workers' and Soldiers' Councils held in Chemnitz in late December, the lion's share of the votes went decisively to the majority Socialists, leaving Leipzig alone staunchly 'Independent'. Forced by the changing balance of power into a minority position in the Saxon government, the Independent Socialists chose to withdraw altogether rather than be part of a government that was no longer revolutionary enough in their eyes. The Independent Socialist leadership withdrew to Leipzig.

All this had happened before Friedrich Olbricht and his bride arrived in Leipzig on the morning of 29 December 1918. Up to the point of his arrival, Olbricht had been with the field army – and in the 9 November election of Soldiers' Councils, the soldiers of that army had either elected officers or majority Socialists. The result was that the Leipzig Regiments 106 and 107 returned to the very stronghold of German revolutionary

Socialism still marching in their best peacetime parade tradition, only to be met with indifference from the population and outright hostility from the revolutionary elements that now controlled the city. No sooner had the two regiments reached Leipzig than they melted away. Men did not wait for an official 'demobilisation'; they had fought too long and hard for nothing and now wanted only to go home – and they did. All that remained in the barracks were the dregs: men without families, men without job prospects, men who had come to love the killing.

It was to these pathetic remnants of an army that Olbricht returned 'to duty' at the start of 1919. To be fair, Olbricht was much better prepared for the situation than many of his comrades and later co-conspirators. On the one hand, Olbricht's family had ties to the Saxon royal family, and the King of Saxony had advocated peace more than a year before the Kaiser was forced to accept defeat; on the other, from his father's former pupils, Olbricht knew just how war-weary the nation was. He may not have fully realised, however, just how *explosive* the situation had become in the meantime.

While Olbricht officially returned to Leipzig as a General Staff officer assigned to the XIXth Corps with responsibility for demobilisation, in fact, as noted above, the troops had demobilised themselves. Furthermore, the XIXth Corps had turned over control of its HQ and all military installations – including weapons depots – to the Workers' and Soldiers' Council. Worst of all, the commanding officer of the XIXth Corps had officially submitted to the Council: i.e. accepted that the XIXth Corps took its orders from the Council, not from the German military district command (which was working together with the Ebert government) in Berlin. In short, Olbricht was officially a subordinate of the Workers' and Soldiers' Council of Leipzig. And while the XIXth Corps commanded virtually no troops at all, the Council had disarmed the police and replaced them with a revolutionary militia. By the time Olbricht arrived in Leipzig, this militia was almost 1,500 strong and well armed.

The situation was soon further complicated by the founding of the German Communist Party, the KPD, another competing leftist party with an even more radical programme than that of the Independent Socialists. This party sprang from the radical left wing of the Independent Socialists, which had previously called itself the Spartacus League. Breaking with the pacifists in the Independent Socialist Party, the KPD advocated the use of force to establish the 'dictatorship of the proletariat' and followed the Leninist ideal of an elite party (the 'vanguard of the proletariat') rather than a mass party. This extremely small fragment of the German working-class movement started a revolt against the Ebert government at the end of December 1918.

If he wanted to avoid the fate of the Russian majority Socialists, Ebert had no choice but to ask for help from the bourgeoisie and even reactionary elements of the population. They were alone in commanding the loyalty of the only troops still capable of putting down the rebellion and restoring order. Ebert needed order if he was going to establish a functioning government, hold a constitutional assembly, and legitimise his own rule.

Fortunately for Ebert and the majority of Germany's population, which abhorred the idea of a Bolshevik-style regime, there were German officers who had, in the vacuum created by the collapse of the old Imperial Army, forged new voluntary military units out of the remnants of the old. These so-called *Freikorps* (Free Corps because they were not part of any larger, functioning organisation, but simply mercenary units organised by charismatic leaders) were the only disciplined armed forces left at the disposal of the Ebert government.

When one of these *Freikorps* needed to pass through Leipzig on their way to put down the Spartacus rebellion in Berlin, the workers and the workers' militia of Leipzig attacked the troop train. The clash resulted in casualties on both sides. In February 1919, the Leipzig Workers' and Soldiers' Council called for a general strike. The goals were more power to the Councils, the creation of a national workers' militia, and the disbanding of all the *Freikorps*. Clearly a confrontation was coming between a provocatively rebellious Leipzig controlled by the Workers' and Soldiers' Council and the anti-revolutionary government of Friedrich Ebert.

Furthermore, although the Independent Socialists had controlled Leipzig ever since the collapse of the old regime, large portions of the population opposed their policies. Leipzig had a large radical working class, but it did not house only workers. The majority Socialists were weak in Leipzig, but there were still many monarchists, other conservatives, and even liberal elements in Leipzig's population. They had initially been helpless against the Independent Socialist Party because it was well organised and belligerent, but they existed. As the threat from the radical workers grew, so did the defensive instincts of the 'reactionary' majority. Particularly among the students, a strong bourgeois element existed that, as it recovered from the shock of the lost war and the Revolution, started to resist the rule of the minority. And not only had the soldiers returned from the war; their officers had, too. There were still officers in Leipzig in early 1919 who were determined to 'exterminate' the Revolution and its leaders. These forces clearly sided with the central government under Ebert and opposed the local radical government.

Olbricht's personal role in these troubled times is as unclear as the situation itself. It is recorded that he was 'elected' to 'commissions' and 'committees'. By whom? It is said that he 'arbitrated'. Between whom? He allegedly enjoyed the 'trust' of the Workers' and Soldiers' Council as well as that of his own military commanders. Yet while Olbricht's actual activities and role remain shrouded in a blanket of vagueness, the qualities that made him successful at mediation are much clearer. Olbricht had been brought up to respect men regardless of their origins. To the end of his life, Olbricht could not stand arrogance or patronising behaviour. He was a good listener, and furthermore possessed the ability to defuse tension with dry wit. But not even gallows humour could help as the situation continued to deteriorate.

By March 1919 the general strike called by the Independent Socialists had collapsed, and the KPD too was in retreat. The leadership of the KPD, after the murder of Karl Liebknecht and Rosa Luxemburg, conceded Berlin to the forces of 'counter-revolution' and fled to Leipzig. Meanwhile, in Dresden, a KPD demonstration got out of hand and ended in the murder of one of the majority Socialist Saxon ministers. The government of Saxony responded to the murder of one of their own by asking Berlin for help in the 're-establishment of law and order' in Saxony. The central government, for the first time fully in control of the capital, responded by ordering *Freikorps* Maerker to do exactly that.

No one in Leipzig was in any doubt that this *Freikorps* under the command of General Maerker would attack. By now the revolutionary militia numbered 2,500 men, and some 20,000 firearms had been taken from the military depots and distributed to 'loyal workers'. Impressive as that sounded, the *Freikorps* Maerker was 20,000 strong and it was a disciplined and experienced unit. The Leipzig Workers' and Soldiers'

Council therefore decided that military resistance would be hopeless and decided to resist with a general strike instead. The problem with such strikes, though, was that they also hurt the workers, who lost pay and, being poor to start with, could least sustain long periods without income. So the Council decided it would be best not to start the strike until the *Freikorps* Maerker was about to enter Leipzig.

Maerker, however, had no intention of rushing into Leipzig. He preferred to prepare his campaign carefully, and that meant painstaking reconnaissance. He wanted to know in advance where the key installations were, where the enemy was likely to be concentrated, and what the transport and communications networks of the city looked like.

No one was better suited to provide the commander of the *Freikorps* with first-rate information about Leipzig than Friedrich Olbricht. Not only did he know Leipzig intimately, his former regimental barracks was now serving as the HQ of the revolutionary militia. Furthermore, by now he had been in revolutionary Leipzig for more than three months. He knew the leaders of the Workers' and Soldiers' Council – in some cases personally. Many had been students of his father, and he benefited from the high regard in which these men still held the elder Olbricht. And so Olbricht became Maerker's undercover intelligence operative inside Leipzig.

Decades later, Olbricht's widow remembered how he had worn his General Staff trousers (i.e. those with the distinctive red seam-stripe that identified a General Staff officer) under his civilian clothing. This was so that he could move around Leipzig without difficulty but, on reaching Maerker's HQ, could command the respect due to a General Staff officer.

The quality of the information provided to Maerker is demonstrated by the effectiveness of his operation and the fact that it was carried out with hardly any bloodshed. Maerker moved his units into the surrounding area and into Leipzig itself in small units by rail. None of the individual units knew where they were going or the plans of the others, but they arrived in and around the city simultaneously. Before the Workers' and Soldiers' Council could call a general strike, the city was in Maerker's hands.

It is to Maerker's credit that his troops retained their discipline despite their success. There was no rounding up of opponents, no mass executions, and the corpses of the leaders of Leipzig's radical workers did not turn up in the River Elster at dawn. Maerker's reputation as a reliable and competent commander was confirmed. He went on to provide protection for the constitutional assembly at Weimar.

Olbricht's role in the episode was that of a good General Staff officer, nameless and in the background. Yet it was highly significant. Olbricht had placed himself decidedly on the side of the republican government, which had ordered the *Freikorps* Maerker to restore order in Saxony. By assisting Maerker so effectively, he had helped prevent bloodshed, and he had also been instrumental in putting an end to the rule of a radical and increasingly dictatorial minority. The Workers' and Soldiers' Council of Leipzig no longer represented the majority of even the working class. It certainly did not represent the interests of the middle and upper classes. And it had been fighting for a lost cause ever since the Independent Socialists had lost parity in the Saxon government. Olbricht helped restore order in the stronghold of the revolutionary Socialists, and in so doing he helped suppress the German Revolution and gave the majority Socialist government in Berlin a chance to build a new democratic Germany.

Nation Building, 1919–21
The suppression of the Spartacus League and KPD in Berlin and the Independent Socialists in Saxony enabled the restoration of order and so set the stage for a new beginning in Germany, politically, socially, and militarily. Already, in mid-January 1919, a Constitutional Assembly had been elected on the basis of universal suffrage for all citizens – men *and women* – over the age of 20. This Assembly reflected well the political sentiments of the time, and the three pro-republican parties in the Assembly – the majority Socialists (SPD), the Centre Party, and the Democrats – together commanded more than three-quarters of the vote. The SPD polled no less than 38 per cent of the entire popular vote, making it the largest party in the Assembly. Popular support for the Independent Socialists, in contrast, shrank (now that the war was over) to only 8 per cent of the vote. The Communists boycotted the election altogether because they did not believe in elections or constitutions; they espoused instead the 'dictatorship of the proletariat' as exercised by the 'vanguard of the proletariat' (i.e. the KPD) and the primacy of revolution over evolution.

The Constitutional Assembly that met in Weimar from 6 February to 31 July 1919 produced one of the most liberal constitutions then known to man. It provided for a parliament with proportional representation, a directly elected president, and an independent judiciary. Although the president had certain emergency powers, the actual balance of power lay firmly with the parliament. Furthermore, there was a very robust bill of rights guaranteeing individual and minority freedoms. At the time this constitution was approved by an overwhelming majority in the Constitutional Assembly, it was almost universally considered a model of progressive democracy by scholars around the world.

History was to reveal the weaknesses of this 'model' constitution, but a far heavier burden for the young republic was the continuation of war by other means on the part of the Western Allies. First, the Allies maintained their choking blockade of Germany throughout the period of revolution and nation building, causing indescribable misery for the entire civilian population despite the cessation of hostilities. Then, adding insult to injury, the Allies presented Germany with an ultimatum: they could either sign the so-called peace treaty hammered out among the victorious powers at a congress in Versailles – or they could resume the war.

It is important to remember that the diplomatic conference held at Versailles in the aftermath of the First World War was, much like the Potsdam Conference after the Second, a conference of the victors. It did not qualify as a peace conference any more than the Potsdam Conference did 26 years later, because Germany was not present at the negotiating table. The Treaty of Versailles did not represent a negotiated peace between the parties to the war. It was a document that articulated the demands of the victorious powers. Germany was told it had to accept these terms unaltered or resume the war.

There was, however, by now no way whatsoever that Germany could resume the war. The German Army and Navy had been defeated by September 1918, but at that time they still very much existed as highly effective and deadly forces, which the Allies dreaded. By July 1919, they did not properly exist at all. Thus Germany had no choice but to sign the 'Treaty', albeit under protest, and the first German republic was forced, literally at gunpoint, to swallow the poison that would kill it.

The Treaty of Versailles contained clauses placing the blame for the now universally hated war solely on the Germans and requiring that they surrender to the Allies for trial a long list of war criminals, including the

Kaiser, the Crown Prince, and *Feldmarschall* von Hindenburg. It took away territories that had been controlled and settled by Germans for centuries. It demanded that all German territories west of the Rhine be demilitarised. It imposed restrictions on economic activity and required the payment of vast sums of reparations. The economic provisions of the Treaty of Versailles were so draconian, in fact, that the English economist John Maynard Keynes condemned them heartily in a small but prescient book published in 1919 and titled *The Economic Consequences of the Peace*. Keynes rightly predicted that the economic burden heaped on Germany would prove unsustainable and that the search for relief would drive Germany to political extremes. He did not know Hitler by name, but he clearly saw the conditions and forces that would soon help bring him to power.

Meanwhile, nothing united the otherwise bitterly divided Germans so completely as their hatred of Versailles. Germans of all political persuasions were equally determined to evade it. Nothing contributed so surely and powerfully to Hitler's later popularity as his systematic and effective defiance of Versailles. Nothing tainted the Social Democrats more damagingly than the fact that a Social Democratic government had been forced to sign the Treaty – no matter that they did so under protest, or that the majority at the Constitutional Assembly had agreed that it was necessary, or that the military leadership likewise admitted there was no choice.

But that lay in the future. For Major Friedrich Olbricht in the summer of 1919, the immediate reality was that the Treaty of Versailles restricted the German armed forces to just 100,000 men, including an officer corps of just 4,000 officers. This Army was to be just one-sixth the size of France's, one-third the size of Poland's, and indeed smaller even than the Army of the newly created Czechoslovakia. It was denied heavy artillery and armour, but burdened with expensive but obsolete cavalry. It was denied air support as well, because the Treaty of Versailles forbade Germany from having any kind of air force. It was also forbidden from retaining or establishing any kind of General Staff: a left-handed tribute to the effectiveness of this uniquely German institution.

The two key personalities behind the creation of the new Army, christened *Reichswehr* (Imperial Defence Force) despite the complete morbidity of the *Reich*, were Generals Wilhelm Groener, the last quartermaster general of the old Imperial Army, and Hans von Seeckt, the effective chief of the General

Staff of the new Army. It had been Groener who, as quartermaster general, had told the Kaiser that he had to resign, and Groener who assured Ebert of the support of the returning field army for the Social Democratic government. Groener, too, had taken responsibility for admitting to Ebert that Germany had no means to resist the Allies in 1919 and so had to accept the hated Treaty of Versailles. But having taken this responsibility, Groener resigned. In his place Hans von Seeckt, until then an obscure if successful General Staff officer, was appointed to head the Army and left with the task of trying to salvage something of Germany's military heritage and traditions without openly violating the provisions of Versailles.

From the start, Seeckt recognised that he had to start from scratch and create something new. He urged his colleagues to 'Stop trying to resuscitate a corpse. … It is impossible to revitalise the old Army. It is dead.'[1] At the same time, he recognised that not every aspect of German military tradition was worthless. Thus on the one hand he was ruthless in analysing the causes of Germany's military defeat, but he was just as rigorous in defending those aspects of Germany's military traditions that deserved preservation. For example, Seeckt was the man who ensured that there was secret development and training of both armoured and air-force units. He also ensured that a disproportionately high percentage of General Staff officers were retained in the tiny officer corps of the *Reichswehr* and that a disguised General Staff continued to exist and operate under the innocuous title of *Truppenamt* (Troop Office). Most importantly, he tried to instil in the entire *Reichswehr* the best traditions of the old General Staff: advancement by merit, open and critical discussion of options, and decisiveness in action – even if it meant taking risks or disobeying orders for the sake of achieving an objective.

The Western Allies required that *Reichswehr* recruits sign on for 12-year tours, in an effort to prevent Germany from creating a vast 'reserve' army by turning over the troops in the 100,000-man Army rapidly. Seeckt exploited this provision to create an elite corps that would be capable of training up a mass Army when the time came. To this end, Seeckt wanted a thinking Army: an Army in which every soldier had the qualifications required of a non-commissioned officer, every NCO had the qualities and potential to hold a commission, and every junior officer had the makings of a future general.

But to get there, Seeckt first had to demobilise the old Army and select with great care the men he wanted to retain. At the time the Germans accepted the terms of the Versailles 'Treaty', the once millions-strong Imperial Army had been reduced to somewhere between 325,000 and 400,000 men, including 15,000 officers. To meet the provisions of Versailles, more than two out of every three officers would have to be sent home. Obviously, not all those officers and men wanted to serve in the *Reichswehr*. There were many, even professional officers, who came back from the First World War embittered and disillusioned. No doubt many others lost interest in a career that offered such slim prospects of advancement or prestige. Still others were outraged and insulted by the thought of serving a republic, most especially one headed by a Social Democratic government. Nevertheless, there were many others who had no other training, no other prospects, and desperately clung to the familiar in an uncertain age. It is a fact that the *Reichswehr* had the luxury of selecting only those candidates considered the absolute best. It is equally certain that many men became embittered by the fact that they were *not* selected and later flocked to the SA and SS, where they then spent much of their time and energy trying to destroy the *Reichswehr* that had scorned them.

According to his widow, Olbricht never for a moment considered another career. He almost certainly had other career opportunities, given the fact that he was still young (31) and came from an academic rather than a military family. That he chose to remain in the new Army is, therefore, an indication that Friedrich Olbricht was comfortable with the prospect of serving a republic. The fact that he was selected for the *Reichswehr* is, on the other hand, a very clear indication of how highly he was regarded by the senior officers now in control of the new Army. In fact, he was so highly thought of that he was selected for the secret General Staff and assigned to the staff of one of the 12 divisions that the *Reichswehr* was allowed to establish: the 4th.

Olbricht was still managing the demobilisation of Saxon troops in Leipzig (or more accurately, administratively cleaning up the spontaneous demobilisation of the year before), when the so-called 'Kapp Putsch' occurred in March 1921. This putsch was in reality an attempt by the most senior officer in the German Army, General Walther von Lüttwitz, to prevent the government from complying with some of the more onerous provisions of the Versailles 'Treaty'. In particular, Lüttwitz objected to the surrender of 'war criminals' such as the German Crown Prince and *Feldmarschall* von Hindenburg to the Allies and to the disbanding of some of the still existing and effective *Freikorps*. Lüttwitz allied himself with the arch-conservative politician Dr Wolfgang Kapp, and relied on one of the *Freikorps* scheduled for dissolution to seize control of the government in Berlin.

Seeckt had word of the impending coup attempt and tried to persuade the Minister of War, Gustav Noske, to take action to prevent it. However, Noske did not take the threat seriously – until he was confronted by it. He then, at the last minute, demanded that the infant *Reichswehr*, or more accurately, the Berlin garrison of the *Reichswehr*, which was much smaller than the advancing *Freikorps*, defend the government. In a retort that became infamous, Seeckt told the Minister of War that '*Reichswehr* would not shoot at *Reichswehr*'. This retort is usually quoted out of context and the impression given that Seeckt then walked out of the meeting. In fact, Seeckt continued to argue hotly that the *Reichswehr* could not take to the streets without igniting a civil war and bloodshed on a scale worse than what had been seen two years earlier during the Revolution and the Spartacus League revolt. Furthermore, although Seeckt refused to support the use of force to put down the coup attempt, he nevertheless unambiguously supported the elected government. He had first warned it and urged it to take preventive action, and when his warnings were not heeded and the coup was in progress he sent out signals to the chiefs of staff of all *Reichswehr* divisions informing them that Lüttwitz had been suspended from his duties and that all orders originating from him or Kapp were illegal.

Meanwhile, feeling unsafe, the elected government of Germany fled Berlin. The leaders of the coup took over the government offices without a shot being fired. But their victory proved hollow. The civil servants refused to recognise them or obey their orders. The bulk of the Army, following Seeckt's orders, likewise ignored their orders and, most importantly, the workers went out on strike (whether spontaneously or at the instigation of the Social Democrats remains controversial). Kapp sat in the Chancellery surrounded by the machine guns of the 'Ehrhardt Brigade' and gave orders, but nobody followed them. In fact, the resistance to Lüttwitz included his own son-in-law, Major Kurt von Hammerstein-Equord, whom he arrested in exasperation.

Olbricht's corps in Leipzig followed Seeckt's orders, not those of Lüttwitz. But Leipzig was still a powder keg. The radical elements used the reactionary coup in Berlin as an excuse for new riots of a revolutionary character. The *Reichswehr* was called upon to restore order. In Dresden similar clashes were so violent that they resulted in 59 dead and over 200 wounded. The central government, which had fled from Berlin to Dresden, again felt compelled to move – this time in fear of a revolution from the left rather than a coup from the right. Meanwhile in Berlin, the Kapp Putsch collapsed from sheer lack of support. Passive resistance, not bloodshed, had defeated it.

The importance of the Kapp Putsch for Olbricht is not in what he personally did – he was not involved – but in the lessons he learned. First, he had seen that control of the government could be achieved without bloodshed, without *Reichswehr* shooting at *Reichswehr*. Even more important, he had seen that by using the General Staff communications network General von Seeckt had been able to take virtual control of the entire military apparatus and stop the most senior active officer in the German Army from carrying out his plans. Last but not least, it was clear that both Kapp and Lüttwitz had acted without proper planning or preparation. When the time came, Olbricht would do his best to ensure that his coup made use of these 'lessons learned'.

Olbricht's own loyalty to the Republic was never in doubt. In fact, he was viewed as so reliably 'republican' that he was appointed *Reichswehr* liaison officer to the Social Democratic *Oberpräsident* Hörsing in Magdeburg. The reason for the appointment was the fact that officers of the *Reichswehr*'s 4th Brigade garrisoned in Magdeburg had supported the Kapp Putsch, and it was felt that an unquestionably republican officer was needed to restore the provincial government's trust in the *Reichswehr*. Olbricht was chosen for the job.

It was a thankless task in which Hörsing often bypassed Olbricht in various matters and even leaked sensitive material against the *Reichswehr* to the Social Democratic press. Nevertheless, on 30 June 1921 Olbricht was recalled to the staff of the 4th Division after roughly seven weeks in Magdeburg, with the explicit agreement of *Oberpräsident* Hörsing, in consequence of the 'relaxation of tension in the situation'.[2]

From this highly politicised chapter of Olbricht's life, two reports written by him have survived. Today we know nothing about the assignment that resulted in their production, nor even for whom they were written or why. One of the reports describes developments in the newly created Czechoslovakia. It details the splintering of the Czech Socialist Party and the founding of the Czech Communist Party, describes tensions in the German-speaking north, a school strike against the Czech educational policies, and the founding of the Little Entente. All of this information could have been gleaned from public sources, and the entire account appears to be more a summary of press reporting on Czechoslovakia than a product of particular intelligence.

The other report, in contrast, reveals astonishing insight and understanding of developments inside the Independent Socialist Party. Olbricht writes, for example, that the splintering of the Independent Socialist Party was completed during a Party Congress in Halle in which 237 of 632 representatives at the Independent Socialist Party Congress voted for an alliance with the KPD. The majority rejected this course of action, but, as Olbricht observes: 'As a result of this division, the up-to-now strongest radical party has been significantly weakened and rendered incapable of carrying out major revolutionary initiatives. In particular, an internal battle has now begun for control over the Party treasury and press.'[3]

Olbricht also reports upon a secret meeting of roughly 120 armed leftist radicals in Leipzig. These were remnants of the armed workers' militia created during the rule of the Workers' and Soldiers' Council. The objective of the meeting appears to have been to discuss tactics for pursuing the goal of the creation of a 'Soviet German state' – i.e. one ruled by Workers' and Soldiers' Councils or rather, the KPD. It would be fascinating to learn who or what Olbricht's source for this information was. This meeting, guarded as it was by sentries at all the key crossroads, was most certainly *not* reported even in the radical leftist press.

It is also noteworthy that, in his reporting on the developments inside the radical workers' movement, Olbricht makes a clear distinction between political and economic actions. He refers to two strikes that he describes as being 'purely economic in character and without political content'.[4] At the same time he draws attention to the relationship between economic misery and political extremism, pointing out that the unemployed and the hungry are more easily seduced by revolutionary ideas. While many of Germany's future leaders were still mourning the monarchy or dreaming of revenge against the Western Allies, Olbricht was looking at the revolutionaries up close, and recognising the power of the revolutionary parties' appeal.

Chapter 5

THE FRAGILE REPUBLIC

In the *Reichswehr* and the
Weimar Republic

With the Troops in Saxony

The tiny Army in which Olbricht now served had a very different character from that of the Imperial and Royal Army, which he had joined as an idealistic youth in 1907. Not only was it very small, but it was also a professional rather than a conscript Army. Troops were required to sign on for no less than 12 years and officers for 25. As mentioned earlier, Seeckt sought to turn these terms of service into a virtue by converting the *Reichswehr* into a cadre of men capable of performing above their actual grade. To create such a cadre, he set entrance requirements high and trained troops rigorously and in several specialities. Never before had the German Army had such well-educated officers and men. Furthermore, to keep the Army from ageing, requirements for further training and qualifications were used to weed out 'unsuitable' material and open places for new recruits. Within a relatively short period, the quality of the little Army was so excellent that it was viewed with admiration, and envy, by Germany's former enemies.

But this high level of professionalism had a price. The price was homogeneity of a dangerous kind. The officer corps, naturally, came predominantly from the ranks of the old Imperial Army. Seeckt sought to select the most competent officers and gave preference to General Staff officers; but the pool of officers with strong democratic, let alone socialist, credentials was very tiny to begin with, so there was a clear conservative bias in the material available. Seeckt was nevertheless remarkably successful in weeding out officers with reactionary views. *Freikorps* officers had a notoriously hard time getting a billet in the new *Reichswehr*, because Seeckt viewed them as dangerously politicised and independent. Throughout the short-lived Weimar Republic, the officer corps of the *Reichswehr* was to prove far more moderate than the various paramilitary organisations that thrived in the aftermath of the First World War.

Yet nothing could change the fact that the officer corps of the *Reichswehr* was inevitably dominated by the same classes that had always dominated the Imperial Army: the aristocracy, the gentry, and to a limited degree the urban elites, to which Olbricht belonged.

Whereas the conscript Army of the *Kaiserreich* had drawn the other ranks from literally all sectors of society and so encompassed some of every political colour, the *Reichswehr*, as a volunteer Army, could only draw from those segments of the population with a desire to join. The leftist parties – particularly the pacifist Independent Socialists and the revolutionary Communists – abhorred the *Reichswehr*. They viewed it as the heir of the Imperial Army and an instrument of 'capitalist and monarchist oppression'. Their adherents viewed themselves as enemies of the *Reichswehr*, not potential members. Even the attitude of the majority Socialists towards the *Reichswehr* was at best ambivalent and at worst hostile. To be sure, the SPD recognised the dependency of the Republic on the *Reichswehr*, for although it was worthless against external enemies (being too weak and without modern weapons), it was nevertheless indispensable as a shield against revolution from the left and reaction from the right. Yet the SPD has never warmed to the military, even to this day. Thus the SPD saw the military, any military, as a 'necessary evil' that one *used* – not something of which one was proud, much less something one wanted one's son to join. So the other ranks of the *Reichswehr* came from the conservative elements of the population, and it is arguable that on the whole, the troops of the *Reichswehr* were more hostile to the Republic than were their officers.

The relationship between the *Reichswehr* leadership and the Republic remains controversial to this day and was undoubtedly contradictory and ambiguous from start to finish. On the one hand, Seeckt clearly recognised that there was no alternative to parliamentary democracy in the post-First World War era. Moreover, the *Reichswehr* defended the Republic again and again, against attacks from both the left and the right. Last but not least, even when handed 'emergency powers' by parliament during the Emergency of 1923–4, the *Reichswehr* leadership was scrupulous about returning power to parliament at the end of that emergency. And yet there can be little doubt that there was no love lost between Republic and *Reichswehr*. The *Reichswehr* consciously served not the government or the parliament, but rather an abstract 'state' or 'nation'. Indeed, many officers and men of the *Reichswehr* viewed themselves as the defenders of something greater and more enduring than the 'temporary' or 'interim' form of government then in power.

The leadership of the *Reichswehr* consequently made every effort to ensure that the *Reichswehr* would not become mired in 'party politics'. Neither soldiers nor officers were allowed to belong to political parties, they were not allowed to take part in political demonstrations or rallies, and they did not even have the right to vote. But it was precisely this conscious distancing from the 'filth of politics' that over time created an even greater alienation from the Republic.

This alienation was reinforced, at least in the early years, by the *Reichswehr*'s lack of popularity. The Right despised the *Reichswehr* because it had betrayed the Kaiser, and the Left hated it because it had suppressed the Revolution. And as noted above, even the governing parties viewed it as a necessary evil. Although Seeckt tried to improve the image of the *Reichswehr* by opening soup kitchens for the destitute in the worst years of inflation and by implementing similar measures, nothing could really help it as long as it was being asked, repeatedly, to turn its guns against its fellow citizens.

The year 1923 was particularly disastrous in this regard. In this catastrophic year, during which the French occupied the Ruhr and the Rhineland and the German currency was completely debased by an irresponsible fiscal policy, the *Reichswehr* was asked to suppress uprisings from the Left and the Right, both of which resulted in bloodshed. The year started with the French declaring the Germans in default on their reparations and, despite objections from both the British and the Americans, the French occupied the Ruhr to secure payments in kind directly. The Germans responded with passive resistance: the workers in the Ruhr went on strike. The French escalated the crisis by extending their occupation to the Rhineland and using brutal military law against the civilian population that defied them. The German government, meanwhile, was cut off from the revenues of its most productive region but burdened with paying the unemployment and social benefits of the idle workforce. Their response of simply printing worthless money led to the worst inflation in human memory. The mark became completely worthless. People's savings (and debts) were wiped out, rewarding the profligate and punishing the honest. Those dependent on fixed incomes – pensioners, widows, the unemployed, students – had effectively no income at all and had to sell their possessions or their services just to eat. People who had money over-indulged in everything consumable and those with nothing resorted to crime, prostitution, and suicide. The harvest was good that year, but the farmers refused to sell it for any monetary sum.

On 12 August 1923 the architect of these disastrous policies, the government headed by Chancellor Cuno, resigned and was replaced by a government under Gustav Stresemann. Stresemann recognised that Germany had to capitulate to the French yet again – a hugely unpopular and humiliating act, but as in 1918 Germany had no alternative. On 26 September 1923, he officially ended the policy of passive resistance.

This was not, however, the end of the crisis. On the contrary, the end of passive resistance was so unpopular that leaders on both the Left and the Right thought the time had come to bring down the Republic and replace it with a form of government more to their liking. The centre of right-wing opposition was in Bavaria, where the government defied the central government and sought to break away from Germany altogether. The forces at work here were partly monarchist (in favour of a restoration of the Wittelsbach dynasty), but also included some ultra-nationalists such as *Feldmarschall* von Ludendorff and the obscure political agitator Adolf Hitler.

The leftist opposition was, not surprisingly, centred in Saxony. Because of the high degree of industrialisation and the fact that the Saxon economy was particularly dependent on exports, the hyperinflation of 1923 had a disproportionately devastating impact in Saxony. The shortage of foodstuffs was especially severe, and economic misery rapidly turned to political radicalism. Already in the spring of 1923 an extreme leftist government had been elected. This government, led by Dr Zeigner, could only hold on to power with the support of the KPD faction in the provincial parliament. This dependence upon Communist support made the government even more radical.

Within a short period of time, the provincial government had approved a number of measures that earned it the displeasure of the central government in Berlin. Among others, the Saxon government passed laws providing for the creation of 'proletarian companies'. Not only did the provincial government form these units, it gave them quasi-police functions, and also tried to integrate them in a border-defence role.

Obviously, all issues with respect to defence were reserved to the central government. More seriously, the creation of additional armed forces could easily have been viewed as a violation of Versailles. With the French already in occupation of most of Germany's industrial heartland, and the *Reichswehr* helpless against the six times stronger and better-equipped French Army, further provocation of France was the last thing Germany needed. The central government and the *Reichswehr* leadership therefore protested vehemently against these provocative measures.

Zeigner's government responded to the angry protests of the *Reichswehrministerium* (Ministry of Defence) by going on the offensive. Zeigner accused the *Reichswehr* of maintaining illegal weapons and munitions depots. The fact that these accusations were probably true made them all the more dangerous. Zeigner threatened to reveal proof of these illegal depots to the Allies, and the Communists supported the Saxon government by demanding ever more 'parliamentary inquiries' into the misdeeds of the *Reichswehr*.

So when on 26 September 1923 the central government ended passive resistance to the French occupation, the Bavarian government immediately declared an emergency – and announced that it (the Bavarian government) had taken over control of the local *Reichswehr* units, effectively declaring the independence of Bavaria from the central government. The central government responded by placing the entire country under martial law and transferring emergency powers to the Minister of Defence. Individual district commanders became his deputies, and in Saxony this meant that the commanding general of the IVth *Wehrkreiskommando* (4th Military District), General Müller, exercised executive powers throughout Saxony. One of Müller's first measures was to prohibit the 'proletarian companies' and arrest the most prominent of their leaders. Zeigner responded by placing the 'proletarian companies' under police jurisdiction and inviting the KPD into his government. After getting the approval of the Communist Party of the Soviet Union, the KPD agreed to join the Saxon government. The condition of their support was the immediate arming of 50,000–60,000 workers and open confrontation with the *Reichswehr*.

On 10 October 1923, Stalin commented on events in Germany in an open letter published in the German Communist Party newspaper *Rote Fahne*: 'The approaching revolution in Germany is the most important world event in our time. The victory of the revolution in Germany will have greater importance for the proletariat of Europe and America than the victory of the Russian Revolution six years ago. The victory of the German proletariat will undoubtedly shift the centre of world revolution from Moscow to Berlin.'[1]

Inspired by this opinion, or perhaps on instructions direct from Moscow, Böttcher, the Communist finance minister of Saxony, gave an inflammatory speech on 13 October 1923, which both attacked the central government in Berlin and called for revolution. On 17 October General Müller reacted with an ultimatum, insisting that the Saxon government distance itself from the sentiments expressed by their finance minister. Zeigner then demanded the resignation of the Minister of Defence, *Reichswehrminister* Gessler, instead. The latter responded by placing the police in Saxony under *Reichswehr* control and reinforcing the *Reichswehr* in Saxony.

Obviously, the KPD had expected this response and was in no way distressed by it. Rather, they saw it as the necessary opening of the revolution they blatantly advocated. Their strategy was to respond with a general strike followed by armed revolt. But at this late stage in the game, the rest of Zeigler's government started to get cold feet. They could decide neither to denounce the finance minister and so bow to the authority of the central government and *Reichswehr*, nor to openly ignite civil war. They set up a committee to discuss the problem.

Meanwhile, *Reichswehr* reinforcements were moving into Saxony. They were met with uncoordinated but bitter resistance on the part of radical workers. The radicalised workers, inspired by the speeches of the KPD leadership and the example of the successful Russian Revolution, fought fanatically, but without cohesion. They were confronted by well-disciplined and well-trained troops that harboured no sympathy for the Left. The forces of the 'Revolution' were soon defeated.

The *Reichswehr* 'invasion' of Saxony in October 1923 went down in the history of the German Left, and particularly the German Democratic Republic, as a brutal and barbaric action characterised by atrocities on the part of the *Reichswehr*. The British ambassador to Berlin at the time, Viscount d'Abernon, in contrast, wrote on 25 November 1923 that there was every indication that the *Reichswehr* carried out the actions against the KPD effectively, but *without* unnecessary harshness. While isolated incidents of brutality occurred, there is no evidence to support the thesis that these were policy.

Meanwhile, at the political level, the struggle between the central and provincial governments was continuing. On 27 October 1923, the Stresemann government in Berlin demanded the resignation of Zeigner's provincial government. On 28 October, Zeigner and his government refused. On 29 October, *Reichswehr* Infantry Regiment 10 was given orders to seize control of the government buildings and remove the defiant Saxon government. Most of the ministers capitulated in the face of force. Only Finance Minister Böttcher (KPD) refused to leave peacefully and was carried out against his will. So ended the defiance of the Saxon government.

Olbricht and his young wife experienced these events at first hand. Until 1 October 1923, Olbricht was serving on the staff of the 4th Division in Dresden and so sat at the very centre of the crisis. He would have sensed the increasing escalation of tension in a very acute manner – indeed, he must almost have felt a sense of déjà vu as the *Reichswehr* prepared once again to move against rebellious workers. On 1 October, however, he became commander of the 9th Company, IIIrd Battalion, IR 10 and was, therefore, actively engaged in putting down the rebellion. Whether his company actually had to fire in anger is not recorded, but it cannot be excluded.

Certainly, Eva Olbricht remembered being very frightened during this period. Arms had been distributed to (or more accurately, retained by) thousands of radical workers, whether they were organised into the 'proletarian companies' or not. Undisciplined adherents of an ideology that glorified violence and class struggle felt justified in carrying on the 'defence of class interests' by attacking 'class enemies' such as 'monopoly capitalists' or 'militarists' at will. The Olbrichts lived in a ground-floor apartment in Dresden. With Friedrich often away, Eva was alone with her two small children, Rosemarie (born 29 November 1919) and Klaus (born 10 May 1922). Eva remembers that she sometimes felt so unsafe that she sought refuge with a Jewish furrier who lived in the apartment above her.

After the tensions of 1923, the Olbrichts undoubtedly welcomed the relative calm of the remaining years of Friedrich's tenure as company commander. Normal garrison life was restored, punctuated by the spring and autumn manoeuvres. It was here in Dresden that the Olbricht children experienced their carefree pre-school years, and Dresden would be viewed as 'home' by the Olbricht family long after they had moved away.

The happiness with which the family remembers these years may have been in part coloured by the fact that in retrospect it was not only an objectively peaceful period, but also one in which Olbricht was at peace with his situation. He loved serving with the troops, and most officers will agree that the position of company commander is one of the most rewarding. Added to this, in Olbricht's case, was the fact that he 'was one of the few officers who was happy to serve the Republic and did so with inner conviction'.[2] This fact made him an exception rather than the rule among his colleagues, and it goes a long way to explaining his behaviour in the years to come.

Even among those officers who later chose the path of resistance and rebellion against Hitler, sincere support for the Weimar Republic was rare. The majority of the older officers – Beck, Halder, and even Hammerstein and Oster – were at heart monarchists. Tresckow favoured a constitutional monarchy similar to that of Britain. Stauffenberg, in contrast, was already under the influence of the poet Stefan George, who loathed the 'bourgeois mentality' and so had little sympathy for parliamentary democracy. While it is wrong to equate George's teachings precisely with Hitler's movement, nevertheless George preached the need for a national renewal that would result in a 'New Reich'; and indeed, the phrase 'Thousand-Year Reich' originated with him. Stauffenberg's conviction that he belonged to a 'secret' elite that would fulfil Germany's destiny clearly came from his days as Stefan George's disciple, and he is said to have died with the phrase 'Long live Secret Germany' on his lips. Olbricht's sincere acceptance of the Weimar Republic and its constitution is a fundamental difference between the two men that would clearly have its consequences.

Finally, it was during these peaceful years in Dresden that Olbricht became acquainted with many of his future co-conspirators against Hitler. Here he met Hans Oster, Georg Thomas, Erwin von Witzleben, and, most importantly, Ludwig Beck. These men, together with Stülpnagel and Hoepner, were to form the core of the Military Resistance movement to Hitler right up to the invasion of the Soviet Union in the summer of 1941.

With the Truppenamt in Berlin

On 1 March 1926, *Hauptmann* Friedrich Olbricht was posted to the *Truppenamt* in Berlin. The *Truppenamt* was the innocuous name given to the organisation within the *Reichswehr* that performed the bulk, albeit not all, of the functions of the pre-war General Staff. It was, compared to the

General Staff of the Imperial Army, much less powerful and had been stripped of a number of key functions (such as personnel management), but it nevertheless carried on the tradition of the General Staff.

The *Truppenamt* was composed of 4 departments in which a total of 60 officers served. The first department, or T-1, was the Department for National Defence (*Landesverteidigung*), and was responsible for mobilisation and operational planning, thereby fulfilling the function of the old Prussian General Staff. The second department, or T-2, was the Organisational Department, with responsibility for peacetime organisational issues. The third department, or T-3, was known as the Statistical Department until 1931, and thereafter by the more informative designation of Foreign Armies Department; it was, in fact, the intelligence department. The fourth department, or T-4, was the Training Department. Olbricht was assigned to T-3.

The officers of T-3 were divided into groups with responsibility for different countries or regions. Their job was to analyse the reports of the German military attachés, to read the press from and about their respective countries of responsibility, and otherwise by whatever means possible to follow developments in 'their' countries. Any German officer who had any contact with a foreign power was likewise required to report to T-3, whether they were taking part in a horse show or studying abroad. Last but not least, the officers of T-3 were expected to travel to the countries for which they were responsible. During his service in T-3, Olbricht is known to have travelled to France, Belgium, Italy, Hungary, Austria, Switzerland, and the Soviet Union. Eva Olbricht stressed that this work, whether at home or abroad, was by no means focused exclusively on military affairs, but rather offered her husband comprehensive insights into the political and economic situation of the countries followed and visited.

Initially, Olbricht was responsible for following Austria, but his responsibilities were soon broadened to include Hungary, Switzerland, Italy, and the Balkans. By 1928 he had moved up to the position of deputy director of the department, with no single area of responsibility. As deputy director, Olbricht acted as the liaison officer to foreign attachés stationed in Berlin, which meant, among other things, that it was his job to accompany the foreign attachés when they observed German military exercises. Most significantly, he was also accountable for personnel matters and management responsibilities within the department. He combined success in his mission with good leadership skills, which made him popular with his subordinates. Hans-Joachim von Horn served under Olbricht in T-3 and remembers him as follows:

> Olbricht was very bright. He was a clever man, but as a person he was very pleasant and helpful. He knew how to help out when someone in the department was having difficulties, and he did it in a very positive way. He was very popular. He had charm and got along with everyone. He was always there when you needed him. And he had common sense and a sound sense of humour. He had a wonderful way of dealing with his subordinates. [3]

The importance of Olbricht's more than five years in T-3 was, however, primarily the exposure it provided to the external world. While many *Reichswehr* officers spent their entire career moving from one small garrison town to the next, Olbricht was dealing with foreign officers and visiting foreign countries. The result was an exceptional understanding of Germany's international situation. An added side effect was that many of the diplomats whom Olbricht met while serving in T-3 remained friends long after he had left the department, providing him with alternative perspectives later in his career. As chief of the *Allgemeine Heeresamt* from 1940 to 1944, Olbricht continued to entertain members of the Diplomatic Corps at his home.

At all events, Olbricht's job in T-3 required diplomatic skills not often found in military men. Olbricht had already demonstrated a degree of diplomatic talent during the Revolution, when he had succeeded in winning trust and decreasing tension. In T-3 he was noted more for his warmth, charm, and wit, which people found attractive. Observers of him during his years in T-3 stress that his charm often made him the unintentional centre of any social event. It was only a small step from attracting and charming to becoming the recipient of delicate and candid information.

Not that things were always easy. Relations with France were at a low ebb during Olbricht's period of service in T-3, a period in which the French were only reluctantly withdrawing from the Ruhr and so increasing their intelligence inside Germany. In April 1931 the French deputy attaché, Major Mierry, with two other French officers and the French consul, was caught red-handed taking photos of a *Reichswehr* artillery barracks in

Konigsberg – an obviously restricted area. The American military attaché summarised the situation in his report, stating:

> One could imagine what would happen if three German officers, one of whom was a senior officer of the Intelligence Department, were caught doing the same thing in France. … The general feeling seems to be that it is a good joke on the French, that it was tactless and even stupid on their part, and that they deserve all that they will get in the way of a call-down, both from the Germans and from their own government.[4]

The consequence was a letter (signed by Friedrich Olbricht) stating that the German ministry of defence wanted nothing more to do with Major Mierry. The French major was immediately recalled to Paris and replaced.

On the whole, however, Olbricht had more contact with the countries of Eastern rather than those of Western Europe. As is well known, the *Reichswehr* and the Red Army maintained an illicit relationship throughout much of the Weimar Republic. The first secret contacts between Trotsky and Seeckt took place even prior to the Treaty of Rapollo. As early as summer 1921, the first *Reichswehr* officers visited the Soviet Union, and a special subdivision of the T-3 Department had been established (T-3V) to manage the secret contacts with the Soviet Union and the programmes that resulted from them.

The principal point of interest on the German side was cooperation with the Soviet Union with respect to the development, production, and testing of those weapons forbidden to the *Reichswehr* by the Treaty of Versailles, particularly armour and aircraft. The training of *Reichswehr* personnel on these forbidden weapons systems followed as a logical second step. In 1927, however, in accordance with Stresemann's policy of 'understanding' with the Western powers in conjunction with the Treaty of Locarno, the secret training programme was largely discontinued in favour of a more conventional exchange of General Staff officers. It was in this context, as an official General Staff 'exchange officer', that Friedrich Olbricht spent six weeks travelling about the Soviet Union in 1930.

Olbricht made his trip there in the middle of a social revolution. In 1929 Trotsky had been permanently banned from the Soviet Union, and it was in the second half of that year that Stalin began his programme of expropriating the land of the independent peasants, the so-called 'kulaks', and forcing the collectivisation of Soviet agriculture. In October 1929, at the start of this campaign, only 4 per cent of all Soviet farms were collectives; by the end of March 1930, just six months later, 58 per cent were collectives. The price was horrendous.

The programme was announced like a declaration of war in which Stalin promised to 'smash the kulaks' and 'eliminate them as a class'.[5] Not only were landless and poorer peasants encouraged to seize the land and property and to loot the homes of their luckier neighbours, but military force was used as well. The Red Army surrounded any village offering resistance to collectivisation and the population was rounded up and deported, or gunned down mercilessly. In addition to the literally millions of peasants 'exterminated' outright in the 'operations', the damage to the agricultural productive capacity of the country as a result of the elimination of the most productive and progressive farms was desperate famine. Modern historians estimate that as many as 5 million Russian peasants were killed outright, 10 million were deported to Siberia, and possibly the same number again died of starvation. The numbers will never be known, but Stalin appears to have given credence to this number at Potsdam by abruptly inflating the previously reported Soviet casualties in 'the Great Patriotic War' by a figure of close to 30 million. While this figure would have included many other victims of Soviet policies, from purges to forced deportations and slave labour as well as the victims of collectivisation, it is clear that population losses of the pre-war period were abruptly reported as 'war' casualties. Stalin thereby neatly shifted the blame for his own handiwork on to the Germans. This sleight of hand was readily accepted by the West without question, and modern Russia prefers to see Stalin as a hero rather than a murderer, so the lie continues.

But Friedrich Olbricht visited the Soviet Union in the midst of this unprecedented self-inflicted massacre. Furthermore, Olbricht was not sent for training in clandestine facilities completely cut off from the rest of the Soviet Union like many other German officers who had gone there before him, nor was he sent to attend manoeuvres of the Soviet Army. On the contrary, his mission was a 'study tour' of the Soviet Union itself. This means that the objective of his trip was to study the Soviet system – economically, socially, and politically – not just the Red Army. Significantly, he was accompanied by another, more junior but Russian-speaking, officer of the T-3 Department, *Hauptmann* von Horn.

Olbricht's journey took him by train to Moscow, where he was 'received' in the Kremlin; by whom is not recorded. From Moscow, Olbricht was taken – by his constantly attentive Soviet escort officers – to Tolstoy's former estate at Yasnaja Poljana, then to Charkow in the Ukraine, and on to Rostow. From Rostow the trip continued to Tiflis, Gory, Borschum, Batum, and finally Sotschi on the Black Sea. This was the furthest reach of his visit, and from there Olbricht returned to Moscow via Krasnodar and Rostow.

The trip included not only Red Army installations, but also many industrial and agricultural 'sites'. For example, Olbricht and Horn spent two full days in 'Gigant', the showpiece state farm. Naturally, the programme included museums and entertainment as well. Both Olbricht and Horn reported that the Russians also made repeated offers of sexual procurement, which the German officers found inappropriate.

Significantly, Olbricht's visit was the first by a German General Staff officer to the Soviet Union after the forced collectivisation. It is, therefore, significant that General von Hammerstein, then the chief of the *Truppenamt*, remarked to the American attaché, Colonel Carpenter, in early 1931 that 'recent' reports (Olbricht's report would have reached him only a few months earlier) from the Soviet Union indicated a deterioration in the discipline, training, and morale of the Soviet Army. Horn, furthermore, remembered that Olbricht and he had been particularly impressed by the calibre of the formerly Tsarist officers still serving with the Red Army, but notably less impressed by the younger or revolutionary cadres. It appears that the Red Army consciously selected ex-Tsarist officers to maintain the bulk of the contacts with the *Reichswehr*, it being correctly perceived that they got along better with their German counterparts.

Whether Communist or Tsarist, however, the great majority of those officers with whom Olbricht interacted during his visit did not survive the purges of the Soviet officer corps that soon followed. Estimates of the number of officers executed in these purges run at roughly 35,000, or about 50 per cent of the total Soviet officer corps. The victims included 13 of 15 Army commanders, 57 of 58 corps commanders, and 110 of 195 divisional commanders, or 90 per cent of all generals and 80 per cent of all colonels. In short, any personal contacts Olbricht made during his trip were of no relevance for the war.

What would prove very useful for the future, however, were Olbricht's observations about the Soviet Union itself – and this was true despite the severe restrictions put upon his freedom of movement by his Soviet hosts. The Soviet escort officers were intent upon showing the image of the Soviet Union that propaganda about the 'Workers' Paradise' prescribed: technological progress, modern lifestyle, equality, and a high standard of living for all. But this was a Potemkin Village: a façade only, with no substance. Thus, while the officers travelled in luxurious first-class railway carriages, Olbricht noticed that everywhere they went, 'small boys climbed on to the roofs of the trains and then reached in through the windows to steal'[6] – a clear indication of appalling poverty just outside the 'official' picture. Likewise, both Olbricht and Horn remembered with discomfort the manner in which the Soviet officials treated their own population, including throwing people out of train compartments or hotel rooms without warning to make room for the foreign guests. Olbricht and Horn also witnessed the power – and the extremity – of Soviet propaganda. Horn remembered particularly one lecture to Soviet troops in which the lecturer, possibly unaware that Horn was fluent in Russian, told his audience that every day ten people starved to death in Hamburg.

Whether it was the presence of the Russian-speaking Horn or simply a greater ability to observe and interpret that which was *not* on the agenda of his hosts, Olbricht returned to Germany with a sober assessment of Soviet reality that contrasted sharply with the enthusiasm of many other Western observers. Stalin's ability to hoodwink the Left is legendary. While the Soviet people were enslaved, imprisoned, and executed without trial by the hundreds of thousands, Western observers wrote: 'The labour camps have won a high reputation throughout the Soviet Union as places where tens of thousands of men have been reclaimed. ... So well-known and effective is the Soviet method of remaking human beings that criminals occasionally now apply to be admitted.'[7] H.G. Wells reported of Stalin that he had never met a man 'more candid, fair and honest. ... No one is afraid of him and everybody trusts him.'[8] If some of the world's intellectuals from Wells to G.B. Shaw, Pablo Neruda, and Lady Astor were charmed into believing that Stalin's Soviet Union was paradise on earth, it is hardly surprising that a mediocre German general such as Werner von Blomberg also came away feeling that the Soviet example of 'disciplining the masses' almost made him a 'Bolshevik' – before making him an enthusiastic 'National Socialist'.

Olbricht wanted none of either, and it is not too far-fetched to argue that it was his exposure to the Soviet Union in 1930 that 'immunised' him against National Socialism in Germany. While there is evidence that Olbricht had read Lenin and was familiar with the essential works and doctrines of Communism, he remained a critic of the political system. His later opposition to the war against the Soviet Union was not ideological, but rather based on his understanding of the sheer dimensions of the country, its deplorable infrastructure, and the capacity for suffering of its vast population. Olbricht did not believe Germany could win a war of aggression against the Soviet Union, and so he opposed it; that is very different from being an admirer of the brutal, totalitarian system that then held Russia in its iron grip.

In addition to these important insights into the nation that would be Germany's most embittered enemy just over a decade later, Olbricht's five and a half years in T-3 also gave him an exceptional insight into domestic politics at a very critical period. Unlike the idyllic world of garrison duty, as an officer of T-3 Olbricht was in the midst of political developments. He was in this highly political position in Berlin when Seeckt was forced to resign, when Germany was finally admitted to the League of Nations, when the Ruhr was at last evacuated by the French, and when the Kellogg-Briand Pact was signed. In short, he filled a political job in Berlin during the peak years of Stresemann's 'policy of understanding' with the West.

These were the good years of the Weimar Republic: the years in which the economy boomed and the arts flourished. There appeared to be a hope for reconciliation with the former enemies and a chance for a better future for all. It was precisely during Olbricht's years of responsibility for the region that the Weimar Republic worked successfully to expand the 'spirit of Locarno' to the new countries carved out of the former Hapsburg Empire. In short, Olbricht experienced a period of decreasing tension and witnessed at first hand the benefits of peaceful cooperation.

It is also significant that the chiefs of the *Truppenamt* under whom Olbricht served the bulk of his time were Generals Heye and Hammerstein. Both of these men recognised the primacy of civilian control over the military, and General Kurt von Hammerstein particularly favoured reducing the 'inner alienation' between *Reichswehr* and Republic. Likewise, the Minister of War during the larger portion of Olbricht's service in T-3 was none other than the retired general Wilhelm Groener, a convinced supporter of parliamentary democracy. These, then, were the men whom Friedrich Olbricht had to look up to when he came to work in a central staff position in Berlin for the first time. Significantly, he was also surrounded more by future opponents of National Socialism than by future adherents. Here too, as in Dresden, he met many of his future co-conspirators: Hammerstein, Adam, and Speidel.

Yet in T-3 Olbricht witnessed not only the blooming of Weimar, but the beginning of the end as well. Before his time in T-3 was up, he had been through three government crises, and the NSDAP had increased its seats in the *Reichstag* from 12 to 107. Furthermore, the 'spirit of Locarno' was already waning. The dreadful year 1929 saw not only the death of Gustav Stresemann, but the start of the Great Depression. The political and social conflicts that had briefly been overshadowed by apparent prosperity and artistic creativity began to come to the surface again. The allure of the 'Workers' Paradise', praised so highly by most visitors, made the German working class impatient for improvements faster than a parliamentary democracy burdened with the huge reparations of a lost war could deliver. In May 1929 the barricades went up in the streets of Berlin again and only after days of fighting, with 19 dead and 36 wounded, could the 'riots' be put down. By 1932, the number of dead lost to 'political unrest' had climbed to 147.

Unemployment was increasing, too. It went from 1.2 million in summer 1929 to 3.2 million in the winter of the same year. By the start of 1931 it had reached 4.4 million, and one year later it climbed above 6 million. It was the pressure of this rising flood of unemployment and the apparent inability of parliamentary democracy to deliver a government capable of taking firm, and possibly unpopular, action that seduced many into looking for – if not an alternative system of government altogether – 'a strong man' capable of leading them out of the chaos. When Olbricht left Berlin at the end of 1931 to return to Dresden as battalion commander, the NSDAP had become the second largest political party in Germany. Although it would be another two years before it was in a position to take control of government, in fact, by early 1931 the National Socialist 'seizure of power' was already on the horizon.

Chapter 6

NATIONAL SOCIALIST PEACE

In the Peaceful Years of the Nazi Regime, 1933–8

The National Socialist 'Seizure of Power'

In autumn 1931, Friedrich Olbricht returned to his beloved Dresden to assume command of the 1st (Ranger) Battalion of Infantry Regiment (IR) 10. The Rangers were an elite troop, and both the troops and their NCOs were expected to fulfil extra requirements to qualify as Rangers. Contemporaries report that Olbricht was both respected by his superiors and popular with his troops. Since Olbricht had never himself been a Ranger, his assignment was an honour, and his acceptance by his subordinates a particular success. His popularity may have had to do with the fact that he 'knew how to party and how to break up the hard and often monotonous duty with cheerful interludes'.[1]

Yet much as Olbricht enjoyed his duties as battalion commander and was pleased to be back in Dresden, the worsening political crisis in Germany cast a long and deepening shadow. Less than a year after his return to Dresden, the Republic was on its deathbed. Parliamentary democracy was suspended in June 1932 in favour of rule by decree under the Emergency paragraph of the constitution; and despite this legal suspension of the constitution, the government was unable to confront effectively the deepening economic crisis. The army of unemployed continued to grow and, in desperation, the population looked for ever more radical political solutions. The parties of the two extremes – the Communists and the National Socialists – benefited most from the public mood, and they fought one another viciously not only in the *Reichstag* and at the ballot box, but in the streets and the pubs as well. During the election campaign of July 1932, no fewer than 47 people were killed and roughly 500 injured in politically motivated violence.

These elections were also a major victory for the National Socialists. Hitler's party increased its representation in parliament from 107 to 230 and so became the strongest party in the *Reichstag*, with 37.8 per cent of the popular vote. The second largest party in parliament, the Social Democrats, trailed by almost 100 seats with just 103 parliamentary mandates, or 17 per cent of the vote. At this point, in a sound democracy, the Nazis should have been asked to form a government. However, the distrust of and distaste for the National Socialists was so great that the president of the Republic, *Feldmarschall* von Hindenburg, emphatically refused to appoint Adolf Hitler chancellor. Instead, the government remained in the hands of Franz von Papen who, lacking a majority in parliament, could only govern by presidential decree under the Emergency paragraph. Meanwhile, however, the economic situation deteriorated further and political violence continued to escalate. Clashes and even politically motivated murders were most common between the so-called 'storm troopers' (*Sturmabteilung*, or SA) of the NSDAP and the Communists. Within months of this inconclusive election, the KPD, the fourth largest party in the *Reichstag* with 89 seats, initiated a vote of no confidence in the government, and *with the support of the NSDAP* forced the president to call yet again for new elections – less than six months after the previous ones.

The elections of November 1932 brought the Communists a less than 3 per cent improvement in their popularity (from 14.7 per cent to 17.1 per cent of the popular vote), but they cost the Nazis 2 million votes and 34 seats, as their percentage of the popular vote fell from 37.8 per cent to 33.5 per cent of the popular vote. Yet even so, the Nazis remained the largest faction, and the overall vote was still so fragmented that no other party was able to form a stable coalition government in the face of the opposition from both the NSDAP and the KPD.

Feldmarschall von Hindenburg, despite personal antipathy for Hitler and sincere inner reservations, felt he could no longer ignore the dictates of parliamentary democracy. He felt that he had to invite the leader of the largest party in parliament to form a government. In consequence, on 30 January 1933 he appointed Adolf Hitler chancellor of Germany.

No sooner had Hitler obtained his position than his own party started to create and nurture the myth of the 'seizure of power'. This terminology always implied a coup, if not a revolution; but this propaganda of the Nazis is extremely misleading. Certainly, Hitler rapidly exploited the legal powers invested in him, along with completely *un*constitutional means, to turn his chancellorship into a totalitarian dictatorship. Nevertheless, when analysing the options open to opponents of Hitler, it must never be forgotten that he initially came to power by completely legal means. Furthermore, at the time of his appointment, any attempt to prevent him from becoming chancellor would have entailed an open violation of the the Weimar constitution. Most especially, the *Reichswehr* could not have taken action against Hitler without itself breaking the constitution and initiating an illegal coup d'état against the legally elected president and the legally appointed government supported by the largest, albeit not majority, political party in Germany.

Certainly many factors led to the downfall of the Weimar Republic. The economic and political burdens of the lost war were undoubtedly the greatest of handicaps. A constitution that bequeathed proportional representation without limits, and hence resulted in the severe fragmentation of votes and a permanent absence of a viable majority in the legislature, was another serious weakness. Individual personalities, from the incompetent Chancellor von Papen to the intriguing *Reichswehrminister* von Schleicher, all had their role to play. Yet there was nothing inevitable about the failure of Weimar. Another constellation of personalities and events might have enabled the Republic to survive, perhaps after constitutional reforms of a constructive kind. But by January 1933, almost no one in Germany believed in the Republic any more, and the country on the whole was ready for something new.

The majority of the officers of the *Reichswehr* were no exception. As noted earlier, most of the *Reichswehr* officers served the Republic with inner reservations and without enthusiasm. While they accepted it as the legal form of government, most longed for something else. Either they were nostalgic for a return to the monarchy or they dreamed of a new national 'renaissance' or 'rebirth'. Hitler had long since recognised this, and knew too that he would ease his path to power if he won the *Reichswehr* over to his cause. In consequence, long before he was appointed chancellor, Hitler tried hard to woo the *Reichswehr*.

His success, however, was notably meagre. In only one case was it ever proved that *Reichswehr* officers violated their constitutional duty to abstain from party politics and actually supported the NSDAP. Three junior officers were brought to trial in Ulm, and their trial revealed just how little the young officers involved actually understood National Socialism. What attracted them, and many civilians, was the National Socialist promise to make Germany a military power again, to restore its dignity among nations, and to regain its lost territories and lost respect. Nothing whatever suggests that the young *Reichswehr* officers at any time supported the racial or even the aggressive policies of the NSDAP. It is most accurate to say that these misguided supporters of the NSDAP, like millions of others in Germany, saw in the Nazi Party only what they *wanted* to see.

For the vast majority of *Reichswehr* officers, those who remained true to their oath and never actively supported any political party, the NSDAP nevertheless *appeared* to offer what they secretly longed for: a national renewal. And most *Reichswehr* officers, like almost all the other elites in Germany at the time, overestimated their own power and influence. Indeed, most believed themselves to be vastly superior to the bombastic, uneducated leaders of the populist Nazi Party. The leaders of the *Reichswehr* consequently believed that they would be able to control and use the Nazis for their own goals, if ever the NSDAP should come to power.

In short, as long as the Nazis were *not* in government, the *Reichswehr* leadership remained loyal to the Republic and the vast majority of younger officers remained strictly neutral, regardless of any personal sympathies for National Socialism (as they misunderstood it). Had Hitler attempted to 'seize power' in a coup in 1932 or 1933, he would have faced the guns of the *Reichswehr* – just as he had in Bavaria in 1923. But he did *not* 'seize' power in a coup d'état, and that was what rendered the *Reichswehr* utterly helpless to stop him.

To be sure, the commander-in-chief of the German Army, General Kurt von Hammerstein, met both Chancellor Kurt von Schleicher and Adolf Hitler on 29 January 1933, the day before Hitler was asked to form a government. The purpose of this first meeting, which was attended by one or two other generals (the exact cast varies depending on the source of the account), was to discuss whether there was anything the *Reichswehr* could and should do to prevent Hindenburg from appointing Hitler chancellor.

Hammerstein recorded his version of both events in an unpublished memorandum written in 1935 – just two years after the events but, notably, while Hitler was still in power. Hammerstein's memo provides a clear and succinct explanation of the *Reichswehr*'s position on that fateful January day after Schleicher's resignation and before Hindenburg had taken the constitutional step of asking Hitler to form a government. He writes:

> On 29 January a meeting took place in my offices between myself and Schleicher, who had already resigned but was still acting chancellor. It was clear to both of us that Hitler had to be named chancellor. Any other choice would lead inevitably to a general strike, if not to civil war, and hence result in the extremely intolerable situation of the *Reichswehr* being deployed domestically against two fronts, the National Socialists and the Left. We both searched for any means whatever that would enable us to avoid this undesirable situation. The results of our deliberations were negative. ... Finally I decided, with Schleicher's consent, to seek a meeting with Hitler.[2]

Several points are critical about this account. First, Hammerstein was emphatically and passionately opposed to Hitler. This fact is evidenced not only by what he wrote but by his subsequent career. Hitler found it necessary to remove him from office within a year of becoming chancellor. Hammerstein was prepared to arrest Hitler and try him for treason in 1940. Both his sons were active participants in the coup attempt on 20 July 1944. Thus there can be no doubt that Hammerstein would indeed have liked very much to find an alternative to Hitler's appointment. But he didn't, because he (and Schleicher) was convinced that failure to appoint Hitler would lead to a general strike at best, and possibly civil war.

It should never be forgotten that at this time, Hitler's 'storm troopers' (*Sturmabteilung* or SA) numbered roughly 500,000 men. That was *five times* the strength of the *Reichswehr*. Even if one assumes that the SA consisted mostly of unemployed men with no particular military training, let alone weapons, it still possessed such a serious superiority in numbers that any confrontation between the *Reichswehr* and SA would have led inevitably to bloodshed. It is not too far-fetched to hypothesise that the *Reichswehr* might well have won every clash – inflicting casualties five or even ten times higher than those it suffered – and yet still have lost the conflict. The *Reichswehr* gunning down hundreds or thousands of civilians who were out in the streets supporting the largest political party and demanding the fulfilment of the constitution might even have drawn in foreign powers. It was, quite simply, a battle the *Reichswehr* could not have won politically. And so the *Reichswehr* had no choice but to accept Adolf Hitler as German chancellor.

In addition, that legal assumption of power by the National Socialists changed everything. Suddenly, officers who had inwardly sympathised with the NSDAP no longer needed to pretend otherwise; and even those officers who rejected the violence, radicalism, and proletarian character of the Nazis succumbed to the hope and the illusion that Hitler's appointment would 'tame' him, and make him more respectable. Many people believed that the mere responsibility of government would force Hitler to become more moderate and more rational because he no longer had the luxury of being in opposition. It was not an unreasonable expectation; many other politicians who were radical firebrands in opposition have turned temperate and restrained once in power.

Hitler acted swiftly to exploit this latent support for his government. On 3 February, just days after being appointed chancellor, he told the *Reichswehr* leadership that he 'respected' their 'neutrality' and that he did not expect or require them to fight 'domestic' battles. He assured them that he would build his state upon two pillars: the Nazi Party (his ideological following) and the (neutral) Army.

He also promised to 'exterminate' Marxism – which from the point of view of both the *Reichswehr* leadership and the Weimar constitution was little more than an act of self-defence. The KPD had openly declared its intention of destroying the Weimar Republic and, indeed, all parliamentary democracy in Germany from the day it was founded. Its self-proclaimed goal was the replacement of democracy with a 'dictatorship of the proletariat'. By 1933, the KPD was taking its orders directly from Stalin. The elimination of the KPD was not in itself anti-democratic; all democratic regimes reserve the right to outlaw those organisations that advocate the use of force to destroy them. Hitler's methods were something else again, but that lay in the future.

In early February 1933, Hitler promised only things that the *Reichswehr* wanted to hear. In addition to giving it a 'special status' within the state and eliminating the Marxist enemy, Hitler promised the *Reichswehr* that he would restore Germany's military honour, reintroduce compulsory military service, and tear up the '*Diktat*' or 'ultimatum' of Versailles. The *Reichswehr* leadership would have been forgiven for thinking they had all died and gone to heaven.

It is, therefore, not really so surprising that Hitler's violations of the Weimar constitution, which started almost immediately, did not arouse strong opposition from the *Reichswehr* leadership. On the contrary, the overall attitude of the *Reichswehr* can best be described as 'understanding' the need to make changes in a constitution that had so obviously failed because, from the point of view of the *Reichswehr* leadership, the last years of Weimar had shown that the constitution was unworkable. It appeared obvious to everyone that if there were to be any kind of national rebirth or renewal, it could only come from constitutional change, not from clinging to a bankrupt political system.

To make things particularly easy for the *Reichswehr*, one of the first things Hitler did was to close down all the opposition parties. Since the *Reichswehr* had always been 'apolitical' and prohibited from participating in party politics, it was hardly going to defend an institution in which it had no stake. The *Reichswehr* was thereby turned into an instrument of the National Socialists *without* having to give up its neutrality – and very many officers appear not even to have recognised what had happened to them. While they continued to see themselves as servants of the state, they had in fact become servants of Hitler and his Nazi regime *without consciously choosing* this fate.

And when reservations about Hitler's increasing power, policies, or ideology *did* unsettle the officers and leadership of the *Reichswehr*, then it was easy for them to reassure themselves that as long as the *Reichswehr* itself retained its position of power in the country, and as long as *Feldmarschall* von Hindenburg remained Head of State, it would be possible to stop things from going 'too far'. They blithely overestimated both their influence in the nation as a whole and their ability to manipulate the 'Austrian corporal'. They allowed themselves to be blinded by what they wanted to see and seduced by promises of what they wanted to hear. The result was a 'honeymoon' in which the vast majority of officers and leaders of the *Reichswehr*, including many who later participated in the Resistance, became supporters of National Socialism.

It is therefore both surprising and extremely significant that Friedrich Olbricht did *not* welcome Hitler's appointment as chancellor. On 30 January 1933, when Olbricht learned of Hitler's appointment over the radio, he was 'outraged, that such a dilettante with such an unsavoury past could become chancellor of the German Reich'.[3]

Olbricht's negative opinion of Hitler appears to stretch back to 1923 and Hitler's first coup attempt. Olbricht, then fighting the KPD uprising in Saxony, was infuriated that other opportunists would try to tear the Republic apart during its period of weakness. His opinion of Hitler was further reinforced two years later when he heard Hitler speak at a political rally in Dresden. Olbricht's widow remembers that she and her husband were appalled both by Hitler's style and his content. They were also horrified to discover that so many – and so many otherwise intelligent and educated – people were taken in by the 'Austrian waiter'. Perhaps motivated by the need to understand his appeal, Olbricht had then taken the trouble to read *Mein Kampf*. Indeed, he was able to quote from it extensively. In short, Olbricht had on the one hand developed an early aversion to Hitler, and on the other read enough to know that Hitler's ideology was far from harmless. Olbricht, perhaps because he had read *Mein Kampf*, did not delude himself about what Hitler was or what he wanted, and he did not indulge in fantasies about where Hitler would lead Germany. He recognised from the start that Hitler was both dictatorial and aggressive, and that he would lead Germany into a war it could not win.

Yet while he despised Hitler and was appalled by his appointment as chancellor, Olbricht was in no position to prevent it. Nor was it reasonable to expect him to resign his commission. Hitler was the legal head of government, and to start with there was every reason to believe that his term in office would be as short-lived as that of all his predecessors in the Weimar Republic. What followed was a systematic dismantling of the Weimar constitution and the creation of a totalitarian dictatorship, and yet the process was one of many small steps. None of these was so grave that it would in itself have triggered such a drastic response on Olbricht's part. Olbricht was now middle-aged, too young to retire and too old to learn a new profession. He had no other education or training beyond his military career, but he had a wife and two school-age children. It is only natural that he stayed at his post.

This is not to say that he was silent. His opinion of the new government in Berlin was expressed bluntly enough for Olbricht quickly to gain a reputation in Saxony as a non-Nazi. Likewise, Olbricht soon knew which of his fellow officers were enthusiastic about the new regime, and which weren't. Friendships began to be formed – and ended – based on the degree of political accord. The Olbrichts only became close friends with those who shared their negative view of the Nazis.

It was shared opinions about the National Socialists that strengthened the bonds of friendship with Witzleben, Thomas, and Oster. And it was the shared views of Hitler and his policies that brought the mayor of Leipzig, Carl Goerdeler, into Olbricht's circle of friends in the first place. What was initially only a group of friends became, as a result of the increasing criminality of the Nazi regime, first an opposition group and then a 'treasonous' conspiracy. But in 1933, when Hitler first came to power, Olbricht must have felt very lonely in his uncompromising rejection of National Socialism.

The First Confrontation: Olbricht and the So-called 'Röhm Putsch'
On 1 October 1933, Olbricht was posted chief of staff of the 4th Infantry Division. While he was pleased to be able to remain in his beloved Dresden, he was sorry to exchange a command for a staff job. To make things even more difficult, his new job was much more political, and Olbricht landed in the middle of a crisis. By October 1933 the *Reichswehr*'s honeymoon with Hitler was over, and the Army found itself heading for a direct confrontation with Hitler's paramilitary organisation, the SA.

As mentioned above, at the time Hitler was appointed chancellor the SA numbered an estimated 500,000 men – although some estimates put it as high as 700,000. Roughly one-third of that force was composed of unemployed young men, for whom the SA provided an identity and a sense of belonging. In addition, many men were drawn to the SA by the camaraderie, the pseudo-military training, and not least the uniforms and free meals. A surprisingly high proportion of recruits came from the working class, young men whom one would normally have expected to join Communist or Socialist youth organisations. But there can be no question that the Nazi ideology appealed strongly to these youths, as it also did to young men of lower-middle-class backgrounds. Altogether, the SA was a vital component of Hitler's movement. Indeed, it had long served both his image and his power. It impressed and awed with its torchlight parades and goose-stepping marches, and it provided the muscle-power for confrontations with the KPD and backstreet terror. It is impossible to imagine a Nazi movement without the SA.

The *Reichswehr* looked down on the rowdies and thugs who characterised the SA, and despised the largely homosexual leadership. At the same time, the *Reichswehr* could not overlook the fact that the SA represented a paramilitary organisation which by early 1934 numbered no fewer than 3 million men. As such, it represented a vast reservoir of manpower that the Army needed to draw on if it was to fulfil its own dream of expansion. It was not unreasonable to think that the brutish thugs of the SA – the men responsible for the murders, brawls, and terror – were just a small percentage of the total force, and that the bulk of the young men who had donned the SA uniform were 'normal'. The *Reichswehr* leadership believed that if they could just get control of SA training and organisation, they could turn that pool of manpower into a genuinely valuable military reserve, without technically violating the stipulations of Versailles.

The SA leadership, which consisted largely of a clique of homosexual, former *Freikorps* fighters under Ernst Röhm, hated the *Reichswehr* even more than the *Reichswehr* hated the SA. Röhm had long dreamed of a violent revolution that would sweep away not only the Weimar Republic, but also the 'treasonous' and 'reactionary' *Reichswehr*. His ambition was a new armed militia led (obviously) by himself and his friends. He had got this goal written into the Nazi Party programme; Article 22 promised to replace the 'mercenary' Army with a 'people's' Army.

While the *Reichswehr* leadership and many ordinary Germans interpreted this clause as nothing more than the intent to tear up the military clauses of Versailles and reintroduce conscription, Röhm interpreted it as the complete dissolution of the *Reichswehr* and the creation of a new Army based on the SA. Röhm expected to be appointed either *Reichswehrminister* or C-in-C of the *Reichswehr* in a Hitler government. He was therefore intensely disappointed when Hitler retained 'reactionary' generals in these positions instead. Although in the early months of Hitler's chancellorship a cautious cooperation between the SA and the *Reichswehr* developed, in which the *Reichswehr* provided 'training' for the SA, the situation was untenable in the long term. Certainly the excesses of the SA in the so-called 'wild Concentration Camps' – those illegal and improvised political prisons organised and run by the SA after the *Reichstag* fire – alarmed the *Reichswehr* leadership. Continued street violence, murders, and public arrogance on the part of the SA made the

Army increasingly nervous and uncomfortable, particularly after Röhm demanded that SA officers and NCOs be commissioned into the *Reichswehr*. Although this request was dismissed out of hand by President von Hindenburg, the *Reichswehr* leadership was only too aware that Hindenburg was an old man in failing health. Clearly he could not be counted on to keep Röhm's ambitions in check forever, and Hitler appeared to side more and more with his old 'friend' Röhm, one of the few men with whom he used the familiar form of address.

On 1 December 1933, Hitler appointed Röhm minister without portfolio in the National Socialist government. On 1 February 1934, Röhm handed the *Reichswehrminister* a memorandum in which he outlined their future relationship. The *Reichswehr*, according to Röhm, was to serve as the 'training cadre' for a larger, conscript Army. The SA would have responsibility for leadership, mobilisation, and operational control. The *Reichswehr* leadership began to suspect that Hitler had deceived them one year earlier when he promised that they, the *Reichswehr*, would be one of the two pillars of his state. They believed that their entire legacy – the traditions they had carefully and selectively preserved from the old Imperial Army, and all their arduous work of creating a first-class cadre for a new Army – was at risk. They feared that Germany was about to be placed in the hands of a clique of corrupt and perverse men who had already demonstrated their utter disrespect for the rule of law.

What the *Reichswehr* leadership did not know was that Röhm's relationship with Hitler was nowhere near as close as appearances suggested, and it was becoming increasingly tense. In fact, they were probably unaware that his relationship with Hitler had, in fact, always been very ambivalent. Röhm had helped Hitler to gain access to men of power and money when Hitler was still an obscure political activist in Bavaria. Röhm, however, had broken with Hitler in 1925 when, after Hitler was released from prison following his coup attempt in 1923, Hitler demanded that the SA subordinate itself unconditionally to the Nazi Party. Röhm flatly refused to do so, and chose to resign from the SA and the Party instead. Three years later, Röhm left Germany altogether to accept a commission in the Bolivian Army. Although he returned to Germany at Hitler's request in January 1931, he remained sceptical about Hitler's strategy of gaining power legally; Röhm preferred a revolution. After Hitler's appointment as chancellor, Röhm continued to call for a 'second revolution' and often made remarks critical of Hitler in private. More significantly, Röhm continued to exercise power through his rapidly growing paramilitary organisation and pursued strategies and tactics that were no longer consistent with Hitler's policies. There is clear evidence that Röhm used his 'storm troopers' not just to shore up the power of the Nazis and to terrorise their enemies, but also to carry out personal vendettas.

By now other intimates of Hitler, including Hermann Göring, who was Minister of the Interior, and Josef Goebbels, Minister of Popular Enlighten-ment and Propaganda, complained to Hitler about Röhm's misuse of power and increasingly opposed him. Furthermore, Röhm now had an arch-rival in the leader of the *Schutzstaffel* (Protective Squadron or SS), Heinrich Himmler. These were powerful men and close intimates of Hitler. As more and more loyal Nazis joined in the chorus of protest against the SA already taken up by the Army, Hitler was pushed into a corner. It became increasingly evident that he was going to have to choose between the SA and the others.

In the provincial capital of Dresden, events reflected developments at national level. As late as November 1933, orders signed by Olbricht suggest that the *Reichswehr* and the SA were, in fact, still cooperating at the local level in training matters. By March 1934, however, the situation had deteriorated so dramatically that the *Reichswehr* command in Dresden was trying to prevent arms and equipment from falling into the hands of the SA. The tone of correspondence suggests a particularly intense hostility towards the SA on the part of *Wehrkreis* (Military District) IV in Dresden.

Meanwhile, in Berlin Röhm had succeeded unwittingly in forging an alliance between Himmler, Göring, and the *Reichswehr*, at least inasmuch as the latter was represented by the Minister of Defence, General von Blomberg. These three factions inside the government with little else in common were now united in the single goal of eliminating Röhm and the SA. The strategy was simple. First, these three disparate elements assured Hitler at every opportunity of their own devotion and loyalty to him personally. Then they planted doubts in his mind about the competence and loyalty of Röhm and the SA. Finally, they either actively participated in or, in the case of the *Reichswehr* leadership, knowingly acquiesced in the creation of false evidence against the SA that purported to prove that the SA was about to carry out a putsch – a coup d'état – against Hitler.

Historians have documented the fact that the *Reichswehr* leadership knew perfectly well that the SA was not in fact planning any such putsch against Hitler in the summer of 1934. Furthermore, Hitler himself most probably did not need to be persuaded of such a threat; he only needed to be convinced that the time had come to get rid of Röhm and his clique. The entire fabrication of a putsch was thus more for public consumption than for Hitler. It provided the excuse and a justification for action, while the actual execution of the 'preventive strike' against the SA reveals clearly that those carrying out the action knew that there was no imminent threat.

The alleged putsch was quite simply a pretext for eliminating *all* enemies of those carrying out the action, including people patently innocent of any kind of collaboration with the SA, such as the former chancellors Papen and Schleicher. The *Reichswehr* did not bloody its own hands, but its complicity is unquestionable. Shortly before the murder bands were dispatched like mafia hit squads to gun down roughly 100 people,[4] the troop commanders of all the *Reichswehr* units received orders to stop leave and keep their troops on alert. They were then very carefully confined to barracks while around them armed bands acting on the orders of the government eliminated 'inconvenient' personalities without trial.

Exactly what happened in Dresden on 30 June 1934 is to this day unclear. It is not even known with certainty exactly how many SA leaders were gunned down in the Saxon capital. Heinrich Bennecke, in his excellent study *Die Reichswehr und der Röhm-Putsch*, claims that five senior SA leaders were executed, while Prinz Ernst Heinrich von Sachsen, one of the men arrested who escaped with his life, says only four senior SA leaders were shot. It remains completely unclear how many non-SA men were among the victims of the government-sanctioned assassinations in Saxony or elsewhere. Bennecke argues that the SS officers entrusted with the actual killings often exceeded their vague instructions, particularly in Saxony, Silesia, and East Prussia. Heinz Höhne, in his study of the alleged putsch, likewise provides evidence that the entire action rapidly deteriorated into an opportunity for personal revenge. The executioners thereby imitated the men they were killing, while allegedly punishing their victims for their lawlessness. There are quite simply no reliable sources for what happened.

Olbricht's widow, who was with her husband in Dresden on 30 June 1934, claimed that he personally saved the lives of several individuals who were marked out for execution. Although Eva Olbricht insisted that her husband saved the lives of 'a number of people', after nearly sixty years she could remember the names of only two: a retired officer with the name of Ulbricht (she remembered the name because it was so similar to her own married name) and the above-mentioned Prinz Ernst Heinrich von Sachsen.

Prinz Ernst Heinrich von Sachsen, to be sure, ascribed his survival rather to the local SS leader, a certain Herr von Alvensleben. In his memoirs, Prinz Ernst Heinrich claims that Alvensleben ignored his orders from Berlin with the 'classic' remark: 'Alvenslebens are not Jacobins.'[5] But the prince adds in his account that 'It is probable that the SS at KZ Hohenstein [the concentration camp where Prinz Ernst Heinrich and the other individuals singled out for execution were brought] intended to eliminate us anyway – under the motto "shot while trying to escape".'[6] The prince thus corroborates the fact that there were several men 'arrested' with him and taken to the concentration camp Hohenstein where, he is convinced, they were to be shot without trial. Alvensleben's scruples about killing a prince of the Saxon royal house would hardly have saved the lives of these others, who most certainly were not all princes.

Eva Olbricht's version of events, in contrast, is completely credible, if no longer verifiable. She points out that the headquarters of the 4th Infantry Division was located directly beside the '*Heller*', an open field used for exercises and where, without any doubt, at least four SA leaders were shot on 30 June 1934. It is reasonable to assume that the sound of nearby gunfire attracted the attention of the divisional staff, already on alert, and that the news that the SS had rounded up a number of other personalities, including Prinz Ernst Heinrich, aroused concern for the safety of those 'arrested'. At this point, according to Eva Olbricht, her husband reached for his telephone.

From his duties, Friedrich Olbricht was well acquainted with the local SS leader, Alvensleben. He called Herr von Alvensleben and argued that 'there had to be some mistake' – at least with respect to those individuals known to him personally, such as the retired officer Ulbricht and the Saxon prince. Annedore Leber, the widow of the SPD member of parliament and courageous opponent of Nazism, Julius Leber, wrote in her account of the events on 30 June 1934 that Olbricht 'was able to protect men threatened with execution by claiming that the already arrested men had military functions and were under Army protection'.[7]

Conceivably Alvensleben was only too happy for the intervention. It is possible that he had indeed felt serious reservations about murdering a prince of the blood. Olbricht's intervention made it easy for him to avoid becoming a 'Jacobite' while at the same time shielding him from blame for disobeying orders; he could always claim that 'the *Reichswehr*' had interfered.

Nor did Olbricht's unequivocal opposition to the murders end with his energetic intervention. Along with his commanding officer, General List, he drafted a sharp protest against the entire action, which was sent the very same day by officer courier to *Reichswehr* headquarters in Berlin. It was delivered personally and by hand to General von Reichenau, who read it without comment and dismissed the courier. Only one other general is known to have protested against these government-ordered assassinations: General Adam, the commander of Military District VII (Munich).

In contrast to these outraged officers, the *Reichswehrminister* officially thanked 'der Führer' for his 'soldierly decisiveness and exemplary courage in striking down the traitors'.[8] The government, the Ministry of Justice, and the *Reichstag* all retroactively 'approved' and 'legalised' the illegal murders, and even officers such as Generals Beck and Fritsch, whose ethics were otherwise unimpeachable, were apparently relieved that the threat of the SA had been eliminated, even if they were uncomfortable with the methods employed. Stauffenberg, by this time a cavalry *Oberleutnant*, is said to have considered the murder of the SA leadership, two retired generals (Schleicher and Bredow), two former chancellors (Schleicher and Papen), and an unknown number of civilians as a surgical act similar to lancing a boil – in short, an act of healing. In contrast, both List and Olbricht refused to sign the official order circulated in all military districts declaring the Army's 'solidarity' with the action. The order was signed by a junior officer.

The Röhm Putsch was for Olbricht an important landmark on the road that led to the coup attempt of 20 July 1944. Even today, it is extremely difficult to feel great sympathy for the majority of the victims of the murder squads of 30 June 1934. Röhm himself and his closest companions were responsible for the merciless humiliation, torture, and murder of literally thousands of opponents of the Nazi regime. It is completely understandable that the vast majority of the German people, including the officers and men of the *Reichswehr*, were relieved that the offensive and increasingly dangerous elements of the regime concentrated in the SA had been eliminated. Even the inmates of the concentration camps are said to have been relieved to see the SS take over from the SA; the SS had a reputation for being 'orderly and rational', while the SA was completely arbitrary and unpredictable. In their relief over the results, most people were prepared to turn a blind eye to the methods. For the average citizen, the murders of 30 June 1934 put an end to the SA 'reign of terror'. For the *Reichswehr* leadership, the killings of that day eliminated a dangerous rival that had threatened the very existence of the Army itself.

But for Friedrich Olbricht, the entire incident was about the rule of law, not about power. Olbricht's sense of justice was deeply offended by the events of 30 June 1934. While the rest of the *Reichswehr* stood by and watched people gunned down without even a pretence of due process, Olbricht used what influence he had to prevent as many murders as he could. While more senior officers than Olbricht excused their inaction with the pitiful claim that they would have needed orders from President Hindenburg to intervene, Olbricht acted without orders. He furthermore protested vigorously up his own chain of command. And the result? Not just silence, but retroactive approval of these gangster methods.

Thus the so-called Röhm Putsch was for Olbricht a kind of watershed. It was a lesson with double impact. First, it proved beyond any doubt his worst fears about the lawlessness and the brutality of the Nazis; but because Olbricht had never deluded himself about the criminal character of the Nazis, this lesson was not so hard as the second. The second, however, was that either the leadership of the *Reichswehr* was already so corrupted by the Nazis that it no longer recognised the magnitude of the crimes committed in the name of 'law and order', or else it lacked the courage to protest. In either case, Olbricht realised that he was more alone than ever. He also learned that if he were to be true to his own code of ethics, he would have to act alone and without orders or support from his superiors.

The Transformation of the Reichswehr *into the* Wehrmacht
The elimination of the SA leadership in the period 30 June–2 July 1934 was a victory for 'order', although not for 'law', and for the *Reichswehr*.

A dangerous rival had been made harmless, and Hitler's dependency on the *Reichswehr* and its leadership appeared to have grown correspondingly. On the other hand, the *Reichswehr* now owed a huge debt to the 'Führer' for his decisive action against the SA. And just at this critical psychological moment, President von Hindenburg died.

In a unanimous resolution on 4 August 1934, the puppet *Reichstag* passed a law uniting the offices of chancellor and president. The last truly independent, non-Nazi government institution in Germany was thus silently eliminated without a whimper of protest from any direction. With this constitutional change, Adolf Hitler, as president, also assumed the role of supreme commander of the German armed forces. To underline the point, the *Reichswehrminister*, General von Blomberg, ordered the entire *Reichswehr* to take a new oath. In contrast to the previous oath, in which the officers and men of the German armed forces swore their loyalty to 'my people and nation' (*meinem Volk und Vaterland*), the new oath was worded as follows: 'I swear before God this holy oath: that I will give to the leader of the German nation and people, Adolf Hitler, the supreme commander of the Armed Forces, unconditional obedience, and as a brave soldier will at any time be prepared to risk my life for this oath.'

The importance of this oath was twofold. It was a personal oath to Hitler – not to the people or nation or even to an abstract institution such as 'the president' or 'the commander-in-chief'. And it was 'unconditional'. It recognised no reservations for 'illegal' or 'unconstitutional' orders on the part of 'the leader of the German nation and people'. The chief of the (reinstituted) German General Staff, Ludwig Beck, recognised the dangerous and unconstitutional nature of the oath at once. He wanted to stop it. Indeed, he felt so strongly about it that when the commander of the *Reichswehr*, General Fritsch, refused to follow his advice about stopping the administration of the oath, he offered his resignation. Fritsch talked him into staying on in his job – and swearing the oath. Many other officers, however, were not allowed even to see the text of the oath before being asked to take it. Rudolf Christoph Freiherr von Gersdorff remembered vividly being ordered to attend a military ceremony in honour of the late Field Marshal von Hindenburg, and then, without warning, being told to raise his right hand and repeat the oath. Officers and men expected to re-swear the old oath, as no one had hinted at something new. Only after repeating the oath in chorus, while still in parade formation, was the full import clear. Some men, like Freiherr von Gersdorff, felt uneasy at once; but for the vast majority of officers the oath was like a time bomb. They were perfectly content in August 1934 to view Hitler as an *'Ersatz-Kaiser'*, a kind of substitute king, and so to accept the oath without thinking about it. Not until much later did the full significance of the oath become clear to them – and start to torment them.

Certainly, Hitler made no move to take advantage of his new power immediately. On the contrary, he seemed completely content to leave the running of the *Reichswehr* in the hands of the professionals, the conservative generals who had served the Kaiser and fought in the First World War. Indeed, at this stage Hitler interfered very little in internal military matters. Furthermore, this was the period in which Hitler's policies, particularly his foreign policies, were completely in tune with the goals and deepest wishes of the military leadership. Leaders like Generals Ludwig Beck, Wilhelm Adam, and Kurt von Hammerstein were no supporters of Hitler. They abhorred his style, his methods, and many of his domestic policies, but they could hardly oppose Hitler's military aims, which in fact reflected their own dearest dreams, namely the end to the restrictive military provisions of the Versailles 'Treaty'.

Within the short years 1934–7, Hitler flouted Versailles in a series of actions. He reintroduced conscription and between 1934 and 1936 increased the Army more than fivefold beyond the 100,000-man limit set in the 'Treaty', from 100,000 to 520,000 officers and men. He furthermore established a German Air Force and modernised the Army by equipping it with armour, motorised units, and heavy artillery. These were all goals that the Weimar governments, even those including the SPD, had pursued, and they were goals that the vast majority of the German population, regardless of political party affiliation, supported. The pre-Nazi governments had secretly approved an expansion of the *Reichswehr* from 12 to 21 divisions. The pre-Nazi governments had approved the secret testing of forbidden weapons and the training of German officers on tanks and aircraft. Likewise, the pre-Nazi governments had pursued openly at every international conference the goal of 'fair treatment' and 'parity'. Germany had, from Versailles onwards, consistently demanded an Army commensurate with its size, population, and position in the middle of Europe. Documents prove that the greatest pressure for withdrawal from the Disarmament Conference in 1933 came not from Hitler's Chancellery but from the conservative and aristocratic Foreign and *Reichswehr* Ministers, Baron von Neurath and General von Blomberg.

Once the German government had 'broken free of the bonds of Versailles', however, the *Reichswehr* had what amounted to a blank cheque from Hitler to build the Army of their dreams. It was in Hitler's self-interest to let the *Reichswehr* build the best Army possible. He had plans for using it. If the *Reichswehr* leadership had bothered, as Olbricht had, to read *Mein Kampf,* then they might have become uneasy about the blank cheque Hitler had given them. They might have wondered if it was such a good thing to place the best imaginable weapon in the hands of a man who believed in 'racial warfare' and the need to conquer 'living space'. But contrary to a plethora of leftist and pacifist allegations, there is absolutely no evidence that the generals of the *Reichswehr ever* shared Hitler's aggressive, much less racist, policy goals. Rather, like children with a box of toys, they did not question why someone had given them so many pretty things or what the price for them would be.

Nor should it be forgotten that 1934–7 were the years in which Hitler enjoyed his highest level of popularity among the population at large. Although without free elections such popularity is very hard to measure or document, there can be little doubt that Hitler's approval ratings in these critical years would have equalled if not exceeded those attributed to Vladimir Putin in Russia in 2007–8. Hitler had eliminated the hugely demoralising unemployment, and the economy appeared to be booming. Roads were being built, the Volkswagen was introduced, prices were fixed artificially thereby giving consumers a sense of security, and the outlawing of the unions had put an end to strikes and industrial strife in general. To many, not just German, observers, Hitler appeared to have created a highly stable and successful economic model that could challenge the economic systems of both Stalin and the Anglo-Saxon world.

And Germany was enjoying international successes as well. In a referendum in 1935 the Saarland, taken from Germany by the 'Treaty' of Versailles, voted overwhelmingly (by more than 90 per cent) to return to

Germany. In 1936, against the advice of the *Reichswehr* leadership, Hitler ordered the German Army to reoccupy the 'demilitarised' Rhineland and met with no opposition. Later the same year, Berlin hosted the Olympic Games and dazzled the entire world with the apparent success of the National Socialist experiment.

Hitler's years of success had implications internationally, domestically, and especially on his relationship with the *Reichswehr* and the officer corps. The reaction of the Great Powers to Hitler's unilateral and provocative violation of the provisions of Versailles was bafflingly feeble. But then, both the USA and Great Britain had long since become embarrassed by the draconian terms imposed after their conference at Versailles. Elites in both these countries realised that it was unreasonable for a country the size of Germany to have an Army smaller than Czechoslovakia's. They recognised that it was only 'fair' that Germany be allowed to have an Army, in terms of both size and equipment, that was proportional to its economic power and potential. As for the reoccupation of the Rhineland, British intellectuals generally agreed with George Bernard Shaw, who compared it to the Royal Navy sailing into Portsmouth; it was self-evident that Germany ought to be able to station troops on its own territory. At the same time, German rearmament automatically made those nations that were closer to its borders, particularly France, Poland, and Czechoslovakia, nervous. These countries did not share the revisionist tendencies of the Anglo-Saxon nations, and felt that the terms of Versailles had been too weak in the first place. German rearmament, therefore, sparked an arms race in Central Europe.

Domestically Hitler's successes won him not only the increasingly blind and mindless adulation of his long-time supporters, but the respect, support and even enthusiasm of former opponents. Even Socialist historians such as Hans Mommsen concede that by the late 1930s the majority of former SPD and KPD voters supported the Nazi regime. Hitler had succeeded where Bismarck had failed. He had united Germans from all social classes behind him, and the German working class no longer viewed the government as an instrument of 'class oppression', but rather as an expression of their own success.

But perhaps the most significant aspect of Hitler's successes was the effect the remilitarisation of the Rhineland had on his relationship with the commanding generals of the *Reichswehr*. In advance of the action, the generals knew that their newly expanded force was a paper tiger, and they feared that if the Western Allies responded with force, the *Reichswehr* would be at best humiliated and at worst bloodily defeated. The armies of France, Poland, and Czechoslovakia, the countries directly on Germany's borders, could together field 90 divisions without mobilisation. The *Reichswehr* had just 36 divisions – on paper. In reality there were more like 26 divisions, and even these were skeletal organisations, short on equipment, NCOs and officers, whose new conscript soldiers lacked any kind of training. What equipment the Army did have was a mixture of things left over from the Weimar period and products just starting to come out of Hitler's ramped-up armaments industry, and they were not always compatible. Furthermore, the generals recognised that the reoccupation of the Rhineland was a violation not only of the hated 'ultimatum' of Versailles but of the Treaty of Locarno, which Germany had signed not under duress, but of its own free will. The generals believed that France could not and would not allow Germany unilaterally to break this treaty as well as Versailles. They expected armed resistance that they knew they could not successfully break, and so they advised strongly against the entire action.

The effect of their protests was not to stop Hitler, or even give him pause. Rather it convinced him that his military advisers were not as clever as he had given them credit for, and it disappointed him that they lacked the aggressiveness that he had expected. Hitler is reputed to have said that before he came to power he had thought the General Staff was like a mastiff, which had to be held back from attacking everyone; but after he came to power he learned that it was like a poodle, which had to be prodded into attacking anyone.

So Hitler trusted his 'intuition' rather than the military professionals, and he was proved right. He marched into the Rhineland with his paper tiger Army and the Western powers reacted with feeble diplomatic protests. He had won his first bloodless victory, and ever after the professionals in the General Staff and the *Reichswehrministerium* secretly doubted their own judgement when it conflicted with the 'Führer's intuition'. These self-doubts could and would only grow deeper and more dangerous as Hitler's intuition brought him success in the Sudetenland,

Czechoslovakia, Scandinavia, Poland, France and the Low Countries, the Balkans, and even, initially, in the Soviet Union.

But those victories lay in the future, and Friedrich Olbricht was still a relatively unimportant staff officer in Dresden in 1934–7. The expansion of the *Reichswehr* had brought him rapid promotion. He was promoted *Oberst* on 1 February 1934, and on 1 October of the same year he moved from being chief of staff of the 4th Infantry Division to chief of staff of the newly formed IVth Corps, encompassing three divisions, and simultaneously became chief of staff of Military District IV (Dresden). His responsibilities included the organisation and training of these ballooning units, incorporating the creation, training, equipping, and planning for the mobilisation of a further six 'reserve' divisions.

Clearly these duties represented a tremendous challenge for a professional officer. Olbricht had always enjoyed the educational dimension of his profession, and he had long taken a keen interest in the support and supply aspects of keeping a military apparatus functioning at peak efficiency. He enjoyed his role in this period, particularly since he remained based in Dresden; but reports from several of the young officers then serving under him suggest that a change had come over him as well. The officer who had once been known for his charm, his humour, and his ability to break up monotony with amusing interludes was now a 'feared' superior. He had a reputation for 'asking difficult questions that put a junior officer on the spot'.[9] Others describe him as 'by no means a desk general; rather a practical man, even a strategist', but also 'an officer of the old school, polite but very reserved'.[10] And a third remembers him being: 'a hard-working and ambitious officer (in the positive sense) ... characterised by precise, logical thinking and decisiveness combined with a distant and brusque manner'.[11] Clearly the man who had been 'the life of the party' in the freer atmosphere of Weimar had withdrawn behind the convenient façade of the stern general. The department head to whom every subordinate could bring his problems had become the 'feared' superior.

Yet for all that, a young lieutenant of the time remembers that after the official part of an inspection was over Olbricht took the time to ask what he was reading. The lieutenant admitted he was *trying* to read Clausewitz's *On War* but finding it heavy going. Olbricht smiled and advised that, while he had to 'bite his way through the good Clausewitz', he ought also to take a look at Kant's *On Eternal Peace*.[12]

Olbricht was not really a different man, but the times had changed, and in a nation that adored their Führer, Olbricht was isolated in his political opinions. He could not afford to let down his defences, least of all with junior officers who had not served in the last war and had come of age and into service *after* Hitler had taken power. Olbricht was now a man hiding his opinions and feelings behind the mask of the correct, reticent, and professional senior officer. By refraining from personal exchanges, he avoided the necessity of pretending an enthusiasm he did not feel for the new regime, or revealing his disapproval and reservations to people who might not have understood them.

It was only in his private life that he allowed himself to be himself – with his dry sense of humour, intellectual curiosity, and love of socialising. He exploited the rich cultural offerings of Dresden to the fullest, frequenting the art galleries and never missing an opera premiere. Unsatisfied (not to say disgusted) with the rigidly controlled and self-censored German press, he relied for his news on foreign, particularly Swiss, newspapers. His circle of friends was determined by personal affinity, not policy. Olbricht did not distance himself from his Jewish friends and was, in fact, loyal to them in a way that was considered 'demonstrative' or even 'provocative', although Eva Olbricht claims it was 'just normal'. The circle of friends was notably not restricted to military groups. It included, for example, the director of the Dresden Opera, and, more importantly, the Mayor of Leipzig, Carl Goerdeler.

Goerdeler was undoubtedly one of the most courageous opponents of Hitler in this period in history, when the vast majority of the German people, and even many foreign observers, were very taken with the astonishingly successful dictator. Goerdeler was the son of a Prussian judge, brought up in a conservative and God-fearing family typical of the class of educated civil servants that dominated Europe in the late nineteenth century, in England no less than Germany. He himself studied law, did his compulsory military service, and then returned to his studies to earn a PhD in law and complete his qualifications as a lawyer. He was apprenticed in a bank before starting a career in the civil service. Goerdeler began his career with the firm belief that talent, competence, and education were not personal possessions to be used for one's own benefit. Rather, he had been raised to believe that it was the duty of the privileged classes to use their talents and education in the service of the nation.

Goerdeler's career was interrupted by the First World War, in which he served exclusively on the Eastern Front, including a significant secondment to the government of White Russia and Lithuania, where he was responsible for restoring a functioning financial system and turning it over to local administrators.

Germany's defeat in the First World War was a severe blow to Goerdeler, a loyal subject of the Kaiser; he found it very hard to accept the loss of the war and, more importantly, the loss of large portions of his Fatherland. But already in 1920, the 36-year-old Goerdeler was Deputy Mayor of Königsberg, a position he held for the next 10 years. It is significant that throughout the Weimar period he was active in municipal rather than national politics. His focus was more on issues of practical administration than on policy, much less political intrigue.

Undoubtedly influenced by the chaotic conditions in the *Reichstag*, he favoured strict majority (not proportional) representation and more power for the executive. This was a conservative but very practical perspective, and it should not be confused with or demonised as 'anti-democratic' or 'reactionary', as some younger historians are wont to do. Goerdeler's principal concern was that power ought to be concentrated in the hands of rational professionals, such as himself and other well-educated and experienced civil servants. He saw clearly the danger of demagogues and populists like Adolf Hitler.

Economically, Goerdeler was a liberal in the best sense of the word. He believed that competition allowed the most proficient to be successful and in so doing to ensure progress and prosperity. But he also believed that the competitive losers in a society – the unemployed, the handicapped, widows, and orphans – should receive social support from society at large. This is not paternalism, but enlightened capitalism. Thus, although Goerdeler belonged to the conservative *Deutschnationalen Volkspartei* (DNVP), over time he won the respect of many leaders in the SPD.

In the final stages of the Weimar Republic, Goerdeler served as price commissar in the Brüning government. He was considered for the position of economics or foreign minister in a cabinet under Chancellor von Papen, but he turned down the offer. Indeed, his expertise in finance was so highly valued that even Hitler asked him to join the Nazi government as price commissar in late 1934 (Goerdeler turned him down), and as late as the summer of 1936 turned to him for economic advice when the Reich (despite its outward successes) was in fact facing severe financial difficulties. Goerdeler replied with a comprehensive written recommendation, which effectively demanded a complete change of course by Hitler. Not surprisingly, his advice was ignored.

These contacts with Hitler and his ministers had nothing to do with political sympathy. Goerdeler saw in Hitler's government one more distasteful government in a long line of governments since the end of the *Kaiserreich*, but as mentioned earlier he saw it as his duty, as a loyal German citizen, to put his talents at the disposal of the nation. Furthermore, even while Goerdeler retained contacts with the highest levels of government and had several personal meetings with Hitler in the early years of the latter's government, he never compromised his ethics or his sense of justice. He had from the very start taken a firm and uncompromising stand against the racism and brutality of the regime. He personally intervened to stop the vandalism of Jewish shops in Leipzig by the SA in early 1933, and later that year he emphatically refused to join the Nazi Party, although Hitler personally advocated it. Goerdeler was outraged by the murders of 30 June 1934, and it was after this that he categorically refused to enter the Nazi government. The economic reforms that he suggested in 1936 were clearly incompatible with preparing the country for war within the next four years, as Hitler had ordered internally. Goerdeler neither knew of Hitler's firm intention to go to war, nor would he have supported it.

On 1 April 1937, Goerdeler publicly and demonstratively resigned as Mayor of Leipzig because the memorial to the composer Mendelssohn, which had previously stood in front of the Leipziger Concert House, had been removed in his absence and nothing he could do, despite his position as mayor, could restore it. His resignation was both a protest against the absurdity of anti-Semitism in a country that had so demonstrably profited from Jewish citizens and a protest against the growing impotence of all professionals. By April 1937, after the rejection of his economic proposals,

Goerdeler recognised that the Nazi government was not open to reason. It was not a government looking for solutions to problems at all. Rather, it was a clique of self-serving fanatics convinced that they could master all aspects of government simply by trusting in the 'intuition' or 'genius' of their nearly illiterate Führer.

Once he had broken with the Nazis, Goerdeler moved irrevocably from opposition to resistance. Goerdeler wrote to the *Deutsche Rundschau* in early 1938: 'Freedom of the individual, freedom of the nation is the decisive prerequisite for honourable courage and high achievement.'[13] He had recognised that the Nazis were irrational and immoral and that their government was ultimately illegal. Only freedom from these criminal madmen could restore German self-respect and secure the future of the nation. Once Goerdeler understood this, he felt it was his duty to work towards that goal, because it was for the good of the nation.

In the two and a half years between his resignation and the start of the Second World War, Goerdeler travelled extensively. His trips took him not only around Europe but to North and South America, North Africa, and the Near East. He solicited contact with leading politicians and businessmen, seeking both to learn from them and to represent non-Nazi Germany, i.e. to carry the message that there *were* Germans who did not support Hitler or subscribe to National Socialism. The problem was that there were very few of these 'other Germans', and there were certainly no grounds for overthrowing the successful and immensely popular Nazi government.

Under the circumstances, it is no wonder that Goerdeler came frequently to the Olbrichts, if only to blow off steam and enjoy an evening with people who shared his assessment of the regime. When he was in Germany, he visited the Olbrichts at least once a month, and the frequency of these occasions increased from 1937 to 1938. Eva Olbricht remembers Goerdeler as a very temperamental man who expressed himself with passion and often had to be calmed down. From her observations it seems that Friedrich Olbricht served primarily as Goerdeler's sounding board, giving him a sympathetic audience for his feelings and his (sometimes entirely unrealistic) plans for deposing Hitler. Olbricht himself, however, had not yet crossed the Rubicon. It was not until the so-called Fritsch Crisis that he moved from opposition to resistance.

The Decapitation of the Reichswehr

The reluctance of the *Reichswehr* leadership to reoccupy the Rhineland, and above all their nervous behaviour during the operation itself, had caused Hitler to lose confidence in his military advisers. His successes, both foreign and domestic, had increased his self-confidence – never in short supply – and so by 1938 Hitler had convinced himself that he no longer needed the services of men who did not believe in him unconditionally. To be sure, neither the *Reichskriegsminister*, *Generalfeldmarschall* Werner von Blomberg, nor the C-in-C of the Army, *Generaloberst* Werner Freiherr von Fritsch, had ever been opponents of Hitler or even particularly critical. But they had lost Hitler's trust and so their utility to him. Hitler did not want 'advisers' any more; he believed utterly and completely in himself.

As with the Röhm affair, when Hitler was ready to dispense with someone, he readily found willing and able helpers. In this case Hermann Göring, Minister of the Interior, and Heinrich Himmler, commander of the SS, were all too eager to help eliminate the 'reactionary' and independent leadership of the *Reichswehr*. And as in the Röhm affair, they were not above using false or manufactured evidence to obtain their ends. Or, sometimes, it is possible to simply set a trap and let your victim walk into it. This is what happened to *Generalfeldmarschall* von Blomberg.

Blomberg had been widowed for some time and, as often happens, he found comfort with a young woman, who came from an admittedly 'humble' background. He dutifully reported his desire to marry this young woman to his superior, Adolf Hitler. Hitler indulgently granted the request and even offered, along with Göring, to serve as witness at the wedding. The *Reichskriegsminister* then set off on his honeymoon, and pictures of the happy couple appeared in the press. A young corporal serving in Infantry Regiment 9 in Potsdam proudly pointed to the field marshal's new bride and announced to his lieutenant: 'I know that girl.' Not only that, he had photos of her, very scantily clad, to prove it. His discomfited lieutenant suggested he keep his mouth shut.[14] But, of course, the woman in question had known more than one Army corporal. The honeymoon was not over before the sordid details of the new Frau von Blomberg's past – well placed by Göring and Himmler – started to surface in the press. Blomberg had no choice but to resign.

The resignation of a minister of defence would normally have resulted in his replacement by a senior general. The most senior general in the *Reichswehr* at this time was *Generaloberst* Freiherr von Fritsch. Fritsch, with his monocle, his baron's title, and his emotionless demeanour, seemed to embody the spirit of independence, the cold rationality, and the disdain of the old elite for the upstart Hitler. He represented the traditions of the *Reichswehr* that Hitler was trying to drown in the flood of new recruits and new officers who were rapidly swamping the *Reichswehr* in his new *Wehrmacht*. Hitler wanted to get rid of Fritsch more than he had ever wanted to be rid of Blomberg. Therefore, in order to avoid Fritsch succeeding Blomberg, Hitler turned to his loyal lackeys, Göring and Himmler again. They promptly produced completely bogus 'evidence' of Fritsch's homosexuality – at that time a criminal offence.

The decent, dedicated Fritsch was indeed an officer of the old school, which meant he was totally unprepared to face trumped-up charges of homosexuality. He was offended, hurt, flabbergasted, and hobbled by accusations that were abhorrent to him. He appears to have been so appalled by the allegations that he never entirely grasped their significance for the *Wehrmacht* as a whole. He shied away from a confrontation because he knew his personal life would be dragged through the mud and the doctored photographs would be published in the press. He rightly foresaw that no matter how innocent he was eventually proved, for many people doubt would always remain and his reputation would never be the same again. He also wished to avoid a confrontation because it was clear that Hitler was more popular than ever and if the Army backed him (Fritsch) against Göring and Himmler, it might find itself on the losing side. In a worst-case scenario, it might even come to bloodshed. Fritsch did not think his personal reputation was worth such risks.

The Chief of the General Staff, General Ludwig Beck, whom Fritsch had four years earlier talked into taking the oath to Hitler, again saw the dangers more clearly than his commander. The head of Counter-Intelligence, Admiral Canaris, and his subordinate, Hans Oster, as well as the military lawyer, Dr Karl Sack, recognised the intentions of the Nazi leadership in fabricating evidence against the C-in-C of the Army as an effort to discredit him in the eyes of the common soldier. They saw that Hitler's goal was not just the removal of Fritsch, but direct control of the

Army itself. But none of these men was in a position to take action that might induce Hitler and his minions to back down.

They believed that the only chance of intimidating Hitler would be if a commanding general could be persuaded to offer credible, if vague, threats of 'marching' in defence of Fritsch's honour. The most obvious candidate for a credible threat to use force was the commanding general of the Berlin military district, General von Witzleben. Witzleben was later to prove his willingness to stand up to Hitler, and he would lose his life in the bloody purges that followed 20 July 1944. But at the time of the Fritsch Crisis he was in hospital, and nobody seemed to think his deputy would do the job. So three men set out from Berlin, each with the task of trying to talk a commanding general of a corps into intimidating Hitler. They went to the three generals deemed most receptive to such a move. Hans Oster went to Hanover to seek out General Ulex, commander of the XIth Corps. Hans Bernd Gisevius went to Münster to try to win over General von Kluge of the VIth Corps. And Carl Goerdeler went to talk to his friends, Generals List and Olbricht, at the IVth Corps.

Because the allegations against Fritsch were at this time still a tightly held secret, none of the three commanding generals approached by the three conspirators from Berlin had heard anything about them. All were shocked. Gisevius felt that Kluge was 'too shocked' to be asked for action – an incomprehensible argument, but Gisevius is such a notoriously unreliable source that nothing he reports can be taken at face value. All that can be said with certainty is that Kluge did not act, but apparently was not *asked* to act, either. Oster suggested to Ulex a joint démarche by all the commanding generals of the military districts; but Ulex demurred, pointing out that they would never be able to get *all* of them to agree to such a move. He felt specifically that General von Reichenau would refuse to act in tandem with the others. Goerdeler, true to his character and due to the fact that he had progressed inwardly from opposition to active resistance, demanded of List and Olbricht that they take their troops to Berlin and seize Gestapo headquarters by force.

The staff officer present at this meeting between List, Olbricht, and Goerdeler, Edgar Röhricht, remembers vividly that Olbricht answered Goerdeler. He did not reject in *principle* a coup against the Gestapo and so indirectly against Hitler's regime, but he insisted that such a coup needed to have a chance of success. Aside from the fact that such military action would require planning and aside from the simple logistical nightmare of trying to get his corps from Dresden to Berlin, Olbricht's key objection was that there was no *political* component to the planned action. The Army, he argued, could not act unless there was some political basis on which to build their action – and this was completely absent, since the German people overwhelmingly supported Hitler.

Olbricht's reaction was very characteristic and telling. He was not shocked to hear that the Nazis were fabricating evidence to try to frame one of the nation's most respected and honourable leaders. He was not outraged by the idea of using military force against the police. But he, as a soldier, wanted political leadership in an action that was to have political consequences. He wanted to know what would come *after* the coup. And he wanted the coup to have a chance of success, which could only come from proper planning. Olbricht was not a mere 'desk general', lacking initiative or daring – he had proved that in the First World War – but he was enough of a staff officer to reject ill-conceived, spur-of-the-moment suggestions. The fact that Goerdeler often had such short-lived, crazy ideas was no doubt something Olbricht had learned from listening to him over the last years. He found it easy to dismiss the impractical suggestion without rejecting the need for action as such.

On the contrary, General List and Edgar Röhricht immediately set out for Berlin to consult with General Beck. Olbricht meanwhile contacted Oster, whom he knew well from their early service together, and they discussed the idea of a joint action by all the corps commanders, but had to conclude that General Ulex's objection was well founded. At least two generals were viewed as unreliable, from the perspective of those anxious to oppose the dismissal of Fritsch: Generals von Reichenau and Dollman. In the end even Beck rejected the idea of a joint action. In light of the fact that Beck was to advocate exactly such collective action less than a year later, it is hard to credit that he objected to action on the grounds that it was 'mutiny'. More likely he recognised, as did Fritsch himself, that any action on the part of the Army would be viewed by the vast majority of German people as a reactionary coup and would only discredit the military leadership.

So *Generaloberst* Freiherr von Fritsch resigned 'for personal reasons'; and though he was later exonerated, Hitler had effectively and silently decapitated the Army. That is to say, Hitler did not replace Minister von Blomberg; he took over the defence portfolio personally. Henceforth there was no independent ministry – only his personal staff for military matters, or Joint Forces Command, the *Oberkommando der Wehrmacht* (OKW). Subordinated to this were the commands of the three armed services: the *Oberkommando des Heeres* (Army High Command), the *Oberkommando der Marine* (Navy High Command), and the *Oberkommando der Luftwaffe* (Air Force High Command).

Significantly, Hitler did not stop at the dismissal of Blomberg and Fritsch. In the wake of the reorganisation triggered by the intrigues against these senior officers, Hitler, as acting minister of defence, dismissed 16 additional senior generals and moved 44 more to secondary commands. Hitler was, to be sure, less ruthless than Stalin. He did not have the officers he did not trust executed, but he very effectively removed from all positions of power any senior Army officer whom he felt was insufficiently enthusiastic about National Socialism and, above all, his plans to 'win living space' for the German people in the East. The officers he promoted in place of those dismissed or transferred out of positions of power were those Hitler viewed as enthusiastic supporters or ambitious careerists, willing to do whatever would secure them advancement.

Hitler, clearly feeling it was time to make a clean sweep, also dismissed without pretext the aristocratic and professional Foreign Minister von Neurath. He replaced him with the completely incompetent Joachim von Ribbentrop. A number of ambassadors were also recalled and retired, including Ulrich von Hassel, then serving as ambassador to Rome.

The significance of the so-called Fritsch Crisis for the anti-Hitler opposition was that it brought together several of the men who would later form the core of the conspiracy against Hitler: General Ludwig Beck, Admiral Canaris, Hans Oster, Dr Karl Sack, General Olbricht, and Carl Goerdeler. They learned at this early juncture that a coordinated action by the commanding generals was very difficult to organise. They recognised, too, that it was impossible to organise any effective action without advance planning. The crisis brought home the importance of the political dimension as well. Clearly, as long as Hitler remained successful and popular, a few dissatisfied military men had no hope of altering the course the nation was on.

Chapter 7

THE FORMATION OF AN ANTI-HITLER CONSPIRACY

In the Sudeten Crisis of 1938

On 13 March 1938, Hitler ordered the German Army to occupy his homeland, Austria. Austria, as it existed in 1938, was a product of Versailles. It was a small, powerless, and pathetic remnant of the once proud Habsburg Empire. Stripped of all its former possessions from Hungary to the Balkans, it had not yet established an independent identity. It is generally agreed that most Austrians would have opted for union with Germany in 1918, had they been given a choice. In fact, the victorious powers of the First World War were so certain that the Austrian people would choose to join Germany if given the opportunity that the 'Treaty' of Versailles and the League of Nations both prohibited such a union. This was in violation of the Allies' own proclaimed policy of 'self-determination' – and furthermore made union with Germany, like forbidden fruit, all the more attractive.

By the late 1930s, the apparent successes of Nazi Germany under the Austrian corporal Adolf Hitler had further increased the appeal of unification. Germany was apparently prospering and, since the 1936 Olympics, even enjoyed international respectability again. By the time Hitler marched his *Wehrmacht* into his former homeland, sentiment was so strongly in favour of unification that his troops were greeted with wild enthusiasm. Allegedly even Hitler was surprised by the intensity of it. Certainly no one who witnessed the reception of Hitler's soldiers could be in doubt about the popularity of the move. Postwar attempts to describe it as an 'invasion' or 'occupation' fall wide of the mark. Legally it may have been a violation of international law, but so were the reoccupation of the Rhineland and the creation of the Luftwaffe. The point remained that these violations of 'international law' represented a revision of a body of law imposed upon the defeated peoples of the First World War without their consent.

Significantly, the peaceful revision of the unpopular 'Treaty' of Versailles was not something the world community was willing to oppose, certainly not with arms, and this had fateful consequences for the opposition to Hitler and for world history. With the incorporation of Austria into the German Empire under Hitler, the dictator achieved a German dream stretching back more than a century to the period before Bismarck. In contrast to the *'Klein-Deutschland'* of Bismarck, dominated by Prussia and excluding the significant German population of the then Austro-Hungarian Empire, Hitler's Germany was approaching the *'Gross-Deutschland'* vision of uniting all German-speaking peoples in a single state.

But there was a catch. The Versailles system had created a patchwork of small Central European countries, which were supposed to reflect the ethnic composition of their population – with one exception. German minorities were not given the same rights as other minorities. Hence there remained a very large German minority in the artificial country of 'Czechoslovakia'. That Czechoslovakia *was* artificial has been proved by subsequent history when it fell apart as soon as the international community stopped forcing it to remain united. In 1938, however, not only was it an uneasy alliance of Czechs and Slovaks, but it also had a large and discontented minority population of ethnic Germans. This minority German population for the most part wanted to be part of a German-speaking and German-controlled country. Hitler's dream of unifying all German people could, therefore, not be complete until these roughly 3 million ethnic Germans, who lived in Czech territory bordering on Germany to the south-east, were also incorporated into Germany.

Already on 22 April 1938, the first military plans for seizing the ethnically German portions of Czechoslovakia, the so-called Sudetenland, were laid. By 20 May 1938, Hitler's personal military staff, the OKW, had worked out detailed plans for an occupation of the Sudetenland. On 28 May 1938, Hitler announced his intentions to 'solve' the 'Sudeten problem' to leaders of the armed forces and members of his government. Meanwhile, Hitler was carefully laying the groundwork for invasion, using political agitators inside the ethnically German parts of Czechoslovakia to stir up the feelings of the German population. A Nazi-friendly political party started making ever-greater demands of the central Czech government.

The international community was torn between feelings of guilt because the principle of 'self-determination' had been crudely violated when drawing the border between Germany and Czechoslovakia in 1919, outrage over a possible violation of Czech territorial integrity that had been guaranteed in various treaties, and a growing unease with Hitler's aggressiveness. Despite the recognition of the fact that a degree of 'injustice' had occurred when the Sudetenland was ceded to Czechoslovakia in the first place, discomfort with Hitler's international ambitions started to raise international tension. It was by no means clear in the summer of 1938 that the Western powers would accept unilateral action on Hitler's part.

Olbricht, a man who had specialised in Balkan affairs while working for military intelligence, was very uneasy with the situation. He confessed to one of his former commanders, General Falkenhausen, that he (Olbricht) found Hitler's foreign policy 'completely incomprehensible'. Hitler, Olbricht complained, acted as if he had an armed nation behind him, but that was nothing but bluff. 'To be sure', Olbricht told Falkenhausen, 'the country is overrun with uniforms, but that won't do the trick.'[1] Olbricht expressed the fear that Hitler had become a victim of his own propaganda, and worried that the Western powers would do Hitler the favour of 'believing the exaggerations of agents and journalists'.[2]

Olbricht's assessment of Germany's military weakness was, obviously, based on first-hand knowledge that one would expect of a general and General Staff officer. His assessment of the foreign reaction, or rather his fears, reflect the fact that he had travelled abroad in the previous decade and still read the international press. But he attributed the indecisiveness in the West to fears of German power, underestimating the genuine discomfort of many in Great Britain and the USA with the provisions of Versailles itself.

When Olbricht received the first military orders for an attack on Czechoslovakia in late summer 1938, he was outraged. He burst out: 'But this is madness! Dismember Czechoslovakia, OK. Agreed. But this is war! And not just against Czechoslovakia! This is like throwing a spark into a keg of powder!'[3]

But as was so often true at this stage of his life, Olbricht was largely alone in his opinion. The bulk of his colleagues suppressed any reservations they had about the operation and 'did their duty'. They retreated behind the argument that soldiers should not mix in politics. They claimed that it was not their 'job' to set foreign policy, but rather to obey orders. Many junior officers, like Stauffenberg, were absolutely delighted and inspired by the verve and courage of their civilian leadership in righting the wrongs of Versailles and uniting all German people in accordance with the principle of 'self-determination'.

These pervasive attitudes deeply angered and frustrated Olbricht, who expressed himself in unambiguous words, notably to his first General Staff officer (Ia), Edgar Röhricht, and his secretary at the time, Elisabeth von Metzler. Olbricht was among the chiefs of staff who took part in a meeting with Hitler at the Obersalzberg on 10 August 1938. It is known that at this meeting a few of those present dared to draw attention to the deficiencies in Germany's defences on its Western borders and to the incomplete nature of its rearmament. Although the names of those who dared speak up are not recorded, it is certain that they aroused Hitler's wrath. After his return to his own headquarters, Olbricht called Metzler into his office to take down a memo on the meeting. She vividly remembered that he complained bitterly about the 'cowardice' of his fellow generals, who were 'afraid to open their mouths and contradict Hitler'.[4] This suggests that he was one of the few who did open his mouth, and felt he was left in the lurch by his colleagues.

Röhricht, who was also a witness of Olbricht's anger, furthermore had the distinct impression that his objection to the war was more than a cold calculation of the military risks involved. He felt that Olbricht was distressed by the entire idea of attacking a neighbouring country, and Metzler confirms this impression. She could tell from the tone of the discussions between Olbricht and Röhricht that both men 'distrusted Hitler and the entire National Socialist movement profoundly'.[5]

But Olbricht, as the chief of staff of an infantry corps, was hardly in a position to stop Hitler from pursuing his foreign policy objectives. The situation of the chief of the German General Staff, *Generaloberst* Ludwig Beck, should have been different. Although he commanded not a single unit and did not have direct and regular access to Hitler, his influence within the officer corps and particularly with his fellow generals was immense. Beck was a man of great moral authority.

Indeed, Ludwig Beck was arguably the last chief of the General Staff who deserved the title. He represented the very best in the tradition of advancement by merit, intellectual brilliance, and unemotional analytical ability wedded with a strong sense of public responsibility, independence of thought and, above all, strength of character. He was a thinker and strategist more than a dashing troop commander. Yet while he warned against following impulses and demanded that officers carefully think through alternatives, those who took part in training exercises under his leadership quickly recognised that this did not mean that he favoured, or himself tended towards, hesitation or excessive caution. Beck was known for preferring daring choices, provided they had been well thought through and planned. Unlike Olbricht, he was not known for his humour and charm, yet Beck emitted warmth and a humanity that instantly won trust and respect. He had a sharp and disciplined mind, a sophisticated manner, and strong moral principles that made him, with time, an uncompromising opponent of Hitler.

Ludwig Beck was born in June 1880, the son of an intellectual industrialist who made a fortune in the steel industry. He was the second son of the family and was brought up in a strict but liberal tradition. His father sought to set an example of devotion to duty and responsibility by his actions, rather than merely preaching these ideals. Furthermore, Beck's father was more interested in reading the classics and in classical music than in politics. Ludwig Beck was himself an amateur musician and he attended a liberal gymnasium. In 1898 he graduated with excellent marks, and, as with Olbricht at the same point in his life, the world was open to him. He, too, chose a military career not out of 'militaristic' tendencies (it is recorded that at the time he believed there would never be another war), but because he saw a career in the military as one of service to the nation he had been raised to love. Probably on account of his superior mathematical ability, he was accepted in an artillery regiment, and ten years later, in 1908, he was admitted to the General Staff College. From the start Beck reminded instructors of the legendary Moltke, the consummate General Staff officer, and Beck too excelled in staff rather than troop work.

In 1913, Ludwig Beck met a young lady at an officers' ball and fell in love with her almost at once. It took him three years, however, to overcome her father's resistance to the idea of her marrying a professional officer, and so it was not until 1916 that he married. A daughter was born to the young couple in January 1917, but his wife, already ill with tuberculosis, died before the year was out. Beck received the news while serving as a staff officer on the Western Front. People who knew him at the time say that from that point on he became introverted and still. He never remarried and from this time onwards, his work was his whole life.

A year later, Beck suffered another blow: the defeat of Germany in the First World War and the abdication of the Kaiser. Although by 1941 Beck was able to analyse with merciless sharpness the errors made by the German military leadership in the First World War, he, unlike Olbricht, never warmed to the Weimar Republic. Because it was *ipso facto* the government of Germany, he served it throughout its existence with loyalty, but never with enthusiasm. Beck took his oath very seriously – and it had been given to the German nation and people, not to the Weimar constitution or government organs. At no time did Beck, any more than the Weimar government, accept the justice or legality of the military provisions of Versailles. And he differed from Olbricht again in his initial reaction to Hitler's appointment to the office of chancellor. Beck was one of the many German officers who allowed himself to believe that Hitler would bring about a national renewal and restore Germany's proper place in the world.

It is very important to distinguish between Beck's hopes and goals and Hitler's. Although Beck, like Hitler, wanted to see the *Reichswehr* expanded and rearmed with modern equipment, he never shared the dictator's goal of adjusting Germany's borders by force of arms, let alone winning new 'living space' by conquest. On the contrary, Beck was very concerned that the rearmament (which he wanted) might provoke Germany's neighbours (which he did not want). He therefore strongly advocated a cautious foreign policy. Yet it was a domestic crisis that gave Beck his first serious doubts about the regime: the so-called Röhm Putsch. Beck was appalled by the methods employed and uncomfortable with the Army's passive complicity. It was because Beck had recognised Hitler's nature in June–July 1934 that he was so distressed by the introduction of a personal and unconditional oath to Hitler shortly afterwards.

Over the next several years Beck, observant and analytical as he was, saw with clarity what was happening in Germany. He may once have looked upon the prohibition of party politics with relief and, as the son of an industrialist, he may not have mourned the passing of the labour unions, but he did object to 'muzzling the free expression of opinion'. He saw the Church endangered by the progressively more heathen tone of the Nazis and especially the SS, and he saw through the intrigue against *Generaloberst* Fritsch. Beck became increasingly and acutely conscious that the 'rule of law' so essential to civilised society was threatened, if not already shattered, by the Nazi regime.

But in the end, despite these deep reservations about the domestic policies of the Nazis, it was Hitler's foreign policy that provoked Beck's resistance. Beck's cool General Staff training made it clear to him that given Germany's geopolitical position, the country could not afford – and so could not risk – war. War would inevitably threaten the very survival of the nation. Beck was tireless in stressing that there had to be a clear relationship between a nation's political goals and its capabilities: or, more precisely, between its foreign policy goals and its military capabilities. Beck was convinced that any attempt to break out of the borders set by Versailles by the use of force would necessarily involve Germany in a two-front war that he firmly believed it could not win.

When, therefore, on 5 November 1937 Hitler revealed to a select circle of military and government leaders that he expected to have to conquer 'living space' in the East by force of arms, Beck was absolutely horrified. Although he had not personally been present at the meeting and had only learned of it from a memo, Beck responded with a detailed refutation of all of Hitler's theses and conclusions. Significantly, he explicitly rejected Hitler's notion that Germany had any right to take territory from anyone else. Beck did not share Hitler's goals any more than his means. Beck's objections to Hitler's policies were fundamental and ethical, not merely tactical.

On 9 March 1938, Beck was confronted by Keitel with Hitler's orders to prepare the military occupation of Austria. Less than three years earlier, Beck had been told personally by the chief of the Austrian General Staff, Alfred Jansa, that the Austrian Army would resist any attempt by Germany to march into Austria. Beck therefore expected resistance to a German invasion, and flatly refused to formulate plans to take the smaller German nation by force.

Keitel declined to be the bearer of bad news to his Führer, and told Beck he would have to confront Hitler personally with his refusal. Hitler agreed to see Beck immediately and opened the meeting (at which Keitel and the later *Generalfeldmarschall* von Manstein were also present) by describing the political parameters that made it imperative that he act quickly to occupy Austria. He furthermore assured Beck that the Austrian Army would not resist, nor would the other powers intervene. Beck still refused to take responsibility for such a foolhardy action. Hitler countered by saying that if the Army would not act, he would turn the whole operation over to the SS and SA. Beck was trapped. That was the last thing he wanted. He and Manstein withdrew and within two days had worked out the orders for the occupation of Austria. The plans worked flawlessly, but it was the last time Beck allowed himself and his outstanding organisational and strategic talents to be misused by Hitler.

Hitler's announcement in summer 1938 that it was now time to 'solve' the Czechoslovakian problem at first provoked Beck into writing a series of ever more desperate memos outlining the risks of the proposed action. Even after a General Staff study in early summer 1938 suggested that Hitler and the OKW might be right, and the *Wehrmacht* would indeed be able to crush Czech resistance within five days and reinforce the Western borders before the Western Allies could react, Beck's opposition to the invasion only intensified. Beck did not object to the timing or tactics of the operation; he objected to the operation *as such*.

By mid-July 1938, Beck had despaired of persuading Hitler to change his mind, and he directed his appeals for reason to his military colleagues instead of the dictator. In a memo dated 16 July 1938, Beck appealed to the conscience of his fellow generals:

The very existence of the nation is at stake. History will attribute a blood guilt to leaders who do not act in accordance with their professional expertise and political conscience. Your military duty to obey ends where your knowledge, your conscience, and your responsibility forbids the execution of an order. If in such a situation your advice and warnings are ignored, then it is your right and your duty before the nation and history to resign from your positions.[6]

Beck's goal was the collective, simultaneous resignation of all commanding generals. This, he believed, would prevent Hitler from pursuing his aggressive aims. Not that Beck believed Hitler would meekly back down and that would be the end of the story. Rather, Beck warned that the Army must prepare for a domestic confrontation with the Nazi apparatus and the SA/SS. Beck's aims were clearly not an end to Hitler's foreign adventurism alone, but a complete 'cleaning' of the domestic filth as well. He urged the commander-in-chief of the Army, General von Brauchitsch, to use the inevitable confrontation 'to restore the rule of law' in Germany. Beck even recommended the slogans the Army should use to explain their actions to the population. He suggested: 'Stop the War!', 'Peace with the Church!', 'Free Expression of Opinion!', and 'Down with the Secret Police!' (More exactly, 'Down with the *Tscheka* Tactics!' – referring thereby to Stalin's secret police and their methods.) And last but not least: 'Restore law to the Reich!'

A more succinct summary of Beck's political agenda could hardly have been compiled. What is more, these objectives – formulated in the summer of 1938 when Germany was not even at war, much less defeated – clearly belie all the claims by foreign historians that 'the generals' acted on 20 July 1944 only in order to evade defeat and unconditional surrender.

But Beck's proposed collective resignation, and an open confrontation between the Army leadership and the National Socialist regime, would and could be successful only if the senior generals acted unanimously. It required that none of them were prepared to serve as Hitler's henchmen, thereby advancing their careers at the expense of their fellows. But there were, in fact, several German generals, starting with Brauchitsch himself, who proved more than willing to sacrifice their conscience and their expertise for the sake of power.

Beck resigned alone. He offered his resignation to Hitler on 15 August 1938, and it was accepted three days later. Beck even agreed to Hitler's condition of not making his resignation public. Unlike the flamboyant Goerdeler, Beck did not make a public display of protest, but departed silently and with immediate effect. Opponents of the regime, such as Olbricht's first General Staff officer Röhricht, raged that Beck and his resignation had achieved absolutely nothing.

This is not true. Beck's attempt to mobilise collective and open opposition based on rational argument and responsibility for the nation was a necessary precondition for the creation of a conspiracy. Only when all legal and peaceful methods had been exhausted could mature and responsible men be moved to take the difficult step of contemplating illegal action against their own government. Furthermore, it was in the last phase of Beck's aegis as chief of staff that the first contacts between military and civilian opponents of Hitler, with the objective of forging joint action against the regime, took place. There is also considerable evidence that Beck requested a staunch opponent of Hitler, General Carl Heinrich von Stülpnagel, to work together with the commander of the Berlin military district, General von Witzleben, on the development of plans for an Army coup against the SS/SA and Nazi organs in Berlin.[7]

Significantly, Beck's departure did not bring a halt to these preparations. On the contrary, Beck's immediate successor, General Franz Halder, was if anything more vigorous in pursuing *clandestine* opposition to Hitler's plans. A loose coalition of diverse people formed with the common goal of removing Hitler from power. In addition to Generals Halder, von Stülpnagel, and von Witzleben and the intelligence officer Hans Oster, there were a number of civilians involved in the conspiracy. Notable among these were the chief of the Berlin police, Wolf Heinrich Graf Helldorf, and his deputy Fritz-Dietlof Graf von der Schulenburg, the diplomat Ernst Freiherr von Weizäcker (father of the later president of the Federal Republic of Germany, Richard von Weizäcker), and the *Reichsminister* Dr Hjalmar Schacht. The degree and intensity of the opposition to National Socialism varied from participant to participant, and only a few of the members of this 'September Conspiracy' would prove unflagging opponents of Hitler. Yet many of the men who later laid down their lives in the attempt to bring down Hitler's government in July 1944 were indeed among the conspirators of September 1938.

Halder's plans for the removal of Hitler by military coup were designed to be set in motion by Hitler's own order to the Army to violate Czech territory. The plans were based on the assumption that such an action would trigger a declaration of war by the Western powers. The reasoning was quite simple because the fact that Hitler was still hugely popular, the Army leadership recognised that no coup would succeed unless a substantial portion of the population could be convinced that a move against Hitler was necessary and desirable. The only chance the conspirators felt they had of persuading the population that Hitler had to be removed from power was clear evidence that he was taking the country to war. The

German population in 1938, despite all its adulation of uniforms and pride in the military, did not want *war*. What had made Hitler so hugely popular up to that point was that he had achieved so much *without* war. The conspirators had good reason to believe that *if they could prove that Hitler was taking the country into a world war*, popular opinion would swing against him sufficiently to give the coup a real chance of success.

The plans called for General von Witzleben, as commander of the Berlin military district – supported by the commanders of the local troop units, the 23rd Infantry Division in Potsdam under General Graf von Brockdorff-Ahlefeldt and the 50th Infantry Regiment under *Oberst* von Hase – to arrest Hitler. Stülpnagel worked out plans for the occupation of the Chancellery, the radio stations, and the headquarters of the SS and Gestapo to support this arrest.

There was controversy within the conspiracy, however, over what to do with Hitler after his arrest. Beck is said to have insisted that Hitler be taken alive and put on trial. His objective was to reveal to the German people the full measure of his crimes. Beck and his faction also wanted to avoid the risk of a new 'stab in the back' legend, in which all subsequent humiliations were blamed on the conspirators while Hitler remained an unblemished hero. To support this action, members of the conspiracy, notably Dr Karl Sack, had collected considerable documentary evidence of Hitler's crimes, which they believed would hold up in a court of law – or at least courts governed by the rule of law as understood in Germany prior to the National Socialist 'seizure of power'. The gentlemen from Counter-Intelligence, however, favoured having a medical panel under Prof. Dr Karl Bonhoeffer (father of the famous theologian) declare Hitler mentally ill. A small radical minority of the conspirators felt it would be better not to let Hitler remain alive at all. They believed that an 'incident' could be staged in which Hitler was 'accidentally' killed. Halder was against this proposed action, however, on the grounds that it would too obviously stain the hands and reputation of the German Army. Halder did not, however, object to an assassination; he simply favoured the use of a bomb attack, which could be blamed on 'foreign agents'.

Furthermore, regardless of what happened to Hitler personally, it was clear that the Army would have to seize control of all key installations in and around Berlin and wrest control of the nation from the hands of the Nazi

Party officials. Halder depended for these key functions on military units that were *not* party to the coup planning. Obviously, to keep the plans from coming to the wrong ears and to reduce the chances of betrayal, the circle of conspirators had to be kept to a minimum. To seize control effectively of a country, however, a large number of troops were needed. Halder solved this dilemma by relying on his authority as chief of the General Staff to be able to move units without first securing political consent to his intentions. Military coups around the world and throughout the centuries have operated in the same manner: very limited numbers of insiders, who know the objectives of orders, and a wider circle of 'useful idiots' who are just obeying orders.

Several historians, notably Klaus-Jürgen Müller in his seminal work *Das Heer und Hitler*, argue that General Friedrich Olbricht was one of the insiders in the September 1938 conspiracy. This is particularly surprising because Olbricht's corps had already been deployed to the Czech border and earmarked to move into Czechoslovakia as part of Hitler's invasion plans. However, Olbricht hinted to his first General Staff officer Röhricht that no matter what Hitler ordered, the IVth Corps would not violate international borders. According to his own account, Röhricht objected to the coup plans, arguing that the Luftwaffe would proceed into Czechoslovakia anyway and there would be sheer chaos. Olbricht replied that that was precisely why they needed to be prepared to make very difficult decisions quickly and with a cool head.

But, tragically, it never came to that. The British government sought to come to a political agreement with Hitler in order to prevent war. This had little to do with weakness or even naivety – although it is no shame to say that Britain's leaders were not Hitler's equals in deceit, hysteria, or irrational behaviour. The tragedy was that the British *people* were just as vehemently opposed to war – possibly more so – than the German people. A large portion of the British population in 1938 was pacifist. An even larger portion conceded the need for war in the abstract, but was under no circumstances prepared to go to war to prevent people from obtaining the 'self-determination of peoples' that the last war had allegedly secured. Young British men were definitely *not* willing in September 1938 to die for the Czech right to retain ethnic Germans inside their artificial borders. Prime Minister Chamberlain, as a democratically elected leader of a parliamentary democracy, could not very well afford to ignore popular opinion.

Nor could a British prime minister ignore the reality of Britain's military preparedness. Britain in September 1938 was in no position to go to war with the German *Wehrmacht*. Just one example: Britain at that time did not have any fighter squadrons outfitted with monoplane aircraft; RAF fighter squadrons were equipped with biplanes that were slower than most of Hitler's bombers. The situation in the Army was not much better. Only the Royal Navy was in any way prepared for a major conflict in 1938.

Lastly, although the British were aware of Halder's coup plans, the British government at the time preferred Hitler's government to one led by 'reactionary' German generals. The British Conservative government positively liked Hitler's 'anti-Bolshevism', and they distrusted the generals, whom they unfairly associated with Ludendorff and Hindenburg.

So the British government accepted the 'mediation' of the Italian dictator Mussolini and, without a fight, gave Hitler what he wanted. Chamberlain called it 'peace in our time', but what it really did was guarantee that war was unavoidable.

The concrete prospect of war was the absolute prerequisite for the planned coup against Hitler. If Hitler attained another bloodless victory, then it was obvious that popular opinion in Germany would not support his removal. He could hardly be portrayed as 'mad' if he had just pulled off another brilliant foreign-policy success. The moment the Western powers backed down and buckled under Hitler's demands, the September Conspiracy dissolved. The coup with perhaps the best chance of success never took place. Hitler had yet another victory that bolstered not only his popularity, but his self-confidence as well. Opponents were forced yet again to doubt themselves and their judgement.

Olbricht's assessment of the situation in October 1938 was telling. He remarked to his first General Staff officer: 'What a mad world ... I have hated that man from the moment I first encountered him. I'm not about to change my opinion. And yet I must admit that if he were to die today, then based on his objective achievements, his name would belong among the greatest in German history.'[8]

Unfortunately for the people of Europe, Hitler did not do them the favour of dying in 1938.

Chapter 8

HITLER'S GENERAL?

Olbricht's Short but Successful Career as Divisional Commander

Olbricht Assumes Command

In accordance with the General Staff tradition of alternating staff and troop assignments, Olbricht was once again given an active command on 15 November 1938. Commensurate with his rank and branch of service, he was given command of an infantry division, the 24th. This was a component part of the IVth Army Corps and headquartered in Chemnitz in Saxony.

On the occasion of his new posting, Olbricht received a routine letter of congratulation from the chief of the General Staff, Franz Halder. Curiously, in this letter Halder promised explicitly to 'preserve the traditions' of his predecessor – i.e. none other than *Generaloberst* Ludwig Beck, the man most insistent upon the moral necessity of resisting Hitler's dangerous policies. While the phrase can be dismissed as a mere courtesy, it is more likely (given the fact that Halder himself had been actively involved in a coup attempt against the regime only two months earlier) to be the disguised assurance of one conspirator to another that the spirit of independence that Beck represented was still alive, if now covert rather than overt.

Meanwhile, life went on. The Olbricht family moved to Chemnitz, arriving shortly after the Nazi pogrom of 10 November 1938, in which Jewish properties had been vandalised across the whole country. The family was horrified to find that their own quarters looked out upon the burnt remains of a synagogue. But there was nothing they could do about it.

Olbricht threw himself into his new job with enthusiasm. He loved command work, and was delighted to be away from a desk more than had been possible in his last posting as chief of staff. He soon won the respect and affection of his troops, something still evident half a century later when people were asked to contact the author with anything they could remember about Olbricht during this period. An appeal via the 24th Infantry Division's newsletter, *Der Eisbär*, produced enthusiastic

119

reports from soldiers, NCOs, and secretaries – all full of fond memories of their former commander. Notably, what remained in the mind of one of his regimental commanders from this period was not only his 'excellent leadership' but his 'warmth, honesty, and decency'.[1] In National Socialist Germany, referring to someone as 'decent' was a code word meaning that the individual was *not* a Nazi.

The political loyalties of all officers of the division must have been revealed very rapidly after Olbricht assumed command, because just months after he joined the division it was ordered to prepare for the invasion of Czechoslovakia. This invasion marked the first time since Hitler had come to power that Germany planned to occupy territory that was neither traditionally part of Germany (as with the Rhineland) nor ethnically German (as with Austria and the Sudetenland). It was a blatant violation of Hitler's own promise, made at Munich just a few months earlier, that the Sudetenland was his 'last' territorial demand. It was, in short, a blunt and rude slap in the face to the Western powers, most especially Britain and France.

But this time no one in the German General Staff protested, resigned, or forged secret plans to bring down the government. Neither the chief of staff, Halder, nor lesser players such as Friedrich Olbricht had changed their minds about the criminal nature of the regime or the madness of its foreign policy, but profound demoralisation had seized the opposition.

Olbricht is a case in point. He described the coming action against what was left of Czechoslovakia as 'a clear violation of treaty obligations and an open adoption by the Nazi government of illegal force as policy'.[2] But having been prepared to commit high treason for the sake of preventing war in the previous autumn, and then having seen the Western Allies crumble and eat out of Hitler's hands, Olbricht, like the rest of the German opposition, had become cynical. If the Great Powers were not prepared to stand up to Hitler, then there would be no war; and if Hitler could obtain whatever unreasonable territorial gains he wanted without war, then there could be no popular basis for a coup d'état against him. Individual opponents and critics of Hitler might still see how evil and dangerous he was, but they could take no action against him as long as he still commanded the boundless admiration of the vast majority of his subjects. Olbricht resigned himself to his fate.

The 24th Infantry Division was designated to be one of the first German units to cross the border into the remnants of Czechoslovakia. Their mission was to rush forward and seize control of Prague without consideration of what was happening on their flanks. To obtain this objective, a motorised advance guard was created, followed by bicycle and mounted troops, with the real 'foot soldiers' bringing up the rear. On 15 March, the president of Czechoslovakia – his Army outnumbered, lacking natural defences and effective allies – capitulated to Hitler's demands for submission, and the German *Wehrmacht* marched into the country without facing any resistance. Despite very icy conditions, Olbricht's 24th Infantry Division reached the Czech capital on the same day.

The following day, Hitler flew to Prague to review his victorious troops. He stood directly beside Olbricht on the reviewing platform at Wenzelsplatz while the 24th Infantry Division passed in review. Hitler thanked Olbricht personally for his rapid execution of his orders and the outstanding performance of his division. There is some memorable film footage of General Olbricht, in steel helmet and looking very serious, beside a smiling Hitler in his brown Nazi uniform. Olbricht can be seen identifying the various units while Hitler smiles and flaps his arm as they march by. Olbricht's troops return his 'German greeting' with a very smart and precise *military* salute.

As we shall see, right until late in the evening of 20 July 1944, Hitler would continue to see in Olbricht only the dutiful and competent subordinate. Olbricht managed to disguise his true feelings without either arousing the dictator's suspicions or engaging in conspicuous acts of flattery or hero worship. This was to be one of Olbricht's most valuable assets to the Resistance: that the man they were trying to kill trusted him.

In March 1938, however, many of those who would later join the Resistance were full of enthusiasm and praise for Hitler. He had done it again. He had expanded German influence and power without a drop of blood being shed! Stauffenberg was one of Hitler's admirers at this time. He was only a junior officer on garrison duty, a cavalry captain, but he expressed confidence that Hitler would 'never' do anything to risk war. He expressed no reservations about the legality of this act of open aggression and breach of faith, apparently comfortable with success regardless of means.

And so the stage was set for the war that Beck had tried to prevent by legal means, the war that many other senior generals had been prepared to commit high treason to prevent, and which Stauffenberg thought would never come. While the German people became even more mesmerised by Hitler's invincibility, and their faith in his 'genius' lulled them into a sense of security bounding on hubris, the British people grimly faced the fact that Hitler could not be appeased and would have to be stopped by force. Chamberlain's bargaining with Hitler at Munich had bought the RAF time to deploy first-rate fighter aircraft – and time for a democracy to come to its senses. By August 1939, young men and women all across Britain were volunteering to serve their King and Country, and no one was shouting 'Hell, no, we won't go' in the streets any more. Britain was no longer prepared to sit by and watch Hitler reshape the face of Europe. War had become inevitable.

The Polish Campaign, 1939

The rapid defeat of Poland in 1939 has tended to obscure the fact that a victory was not, in fact, inevitable. The Polish Army at mobilisation numbered 2½ million men. The German invading forces numbered roughly 1½ million. Much has since been made of the fact that Germany attacked cavalry with panzers and flew its modern aircraft against obsolete biplanes. The Polish lack of modern weapons is used to suggest that Poland was yet another innocent peace-loving country set upon by the ravenous and unjustly powerful Germans. A closer look at Polish postwar policy belies this fairy tale. Furthermore, it was Germany, not Poland, that had been forbidden by Versailles to possess armour, aircraft, and an Army commensurate with its size and population. Poland, in contrast, was free to build an Army as large and modern as it wanted. If Poland went to war in 1939 with cavalry, obsolete biplanes, and virtually no air defence, then it was the Polish postwar government and the Polish General Staff that were to blame for this deplorable lack of readiness. It is the duty of every country to have the forces necessary for self-defence.

Yet as *Generalfeldmarschall* von Manstein wrote in his memoirs, *Verlorene Siege*, the victory in Poland was largely determined by three factors beyond Poland's control: geography, allies, and the Molotov–Ribbentrop Pact. Looking first at geography, in the post-First World War restructuring of

122

European borders, Poland had been given access to the sea by cutting East Prussia off from the rest of Germany. Poland, as a result, had a border with Germany in both the East and the West, which meant that Germany was in a position to attack from two directions simultaneously. Poland was bound to be caught in the 'pincer' from the first day of the war. Furthermore, Poland's total border with Germany was roughly 3,000 miles long (now that Germany had occupied Czechoslovakia), and it had a comparably long border with the Soviet Union, technically a neutral country but certainly no friend. This was a formidable defensive challenge even in the best of circumstances.

Secondly, Poland's allies were unprepared for the war. Although sentiment had definitely swung from pacifism to belligerency in Britain, in France public opinion was more divided and uncertain. And no matter how great British *determination* to stop Hitler, Britain did not have the means to intervene in Central Europe at short notice in September 1939. France, on the other hand, had promised the Poles that it would launch an attack on Germany's western border *within 14 days* of a declaration of war. This suggests either that the French General Staff vastly underestimated the effectiveness of the *Wehrmacht* or that they were simply incapable of mobilising and concentrating their own forces more rapidly. This evident lack of preparedness on the part of the Western Allies enabled the *Wehrmacht* to take the huge risk of concentrating the bulk of their combat-ready units on the invasion front. The German Army left their own western borders virtually denuded of effective troops, banking on slow, or no, response from the West. Had the Western Allies been in a position to attack Germany in force sooner, the war might have ended very differently and very rapidly – in German defeat.

Thirdly, the Soviet Union had entered a non-aggression pact with Hitler's Germany on the very eve of the German invasion of Poland. This pact included secret terms for the division of Poland between the two totalitarian powers. Poland did not know it on 1 September 1939, but it was facing two enemies, not one, and the Red Army was vastly superior to the Polish one in numbers of everything from troops to tanks.

Ultimately, it was the Soviet decision to share the spoils of Poland with Hitler that sealed Poland's fate. The Soviet Union had no enemy at its back to fear. Thus even if the *Wehrmacht* had been bogged down and failed to attain its ambitious objectives of encircling and destroying the bulk of Poland's armed forces in the first days of the war, the Soviet Union stood ready to crush Poland. In other words, even if the Germans had been stopped long enough for the Western Allies to attack Germany from the rear and defeat it, Poland would still have been lost – to the Soviets.

The German plans called for Army Group North under *Generalfeldmarschall* von Bock to cross into Poland from East Prussia, heading west to cut off the Polish forces from the sea (and any reinforcements that might come from Britain over the Baltic), and then swinging south to advance on Warsaw. Army Group South was to advance rapidly from Silesia, heading north-eastwards towards Warsaw, and meet up with Army Group North, thereby encircling the main forces of the Polish Army, which were concentrated in western Poland. Most significantly, the bulk of the Polish Army was to be destroyed or forced to surrender west of the Vistula–Narev line. To prevent any large numbers of Polish units from escaping to the east across this line, a second, more far-flung encirclement was planned along but behind the line of the River Bug.

Army Group South was divided into three armies: the 14th under *Generaloberst* List, the 10th under *Generaloberst* von Reichenau, and the 8th under *Generaloberst* Blaskowitz. (Blaskowitz was later to distinguish himself by his vigorous efforts to stop the atrocities committed by the SS in occupied Poland, and for presenting a sharp protest demanding that Hitler order an end to the racist policies and a restoration of law and order.) The 14th Army had the task of moving rapidly to the east to form the second, outer pincer beyond Lublin and heading towards Brest-Litovsk and the River Bug. The 10th and 8th Armies were to press forward towards Warsaw. The 8th Army was positioned on the northern and most exposed flank of the Army Group. It was expected that when the Polish armed forces realised they were at risk of being encircled, they would try to break out to the south-east, i.e. through the 8th Army.

The German plan worked brilliantly. Just over two weeks later, on 17 September 1939, the two German Army Groups met, trapping the bulk of the Polish Army inside the encirclement. The same day, the Soviet Union declared war on Poland and invaded from the east. The Polish government fled to exile in Romania. Meanwhile, Polish forces trapped by the Germans were engaged in determined efforts to break out to the south-east. They failed, and by 24 September 1939 the bulk of these had surrendered. Except for the troops defending Warsaw, the Polish armed forces no longer offered cohesive resistance. On 28 September 1939, the Warsaw garrison sought and received an armistice. The next day, Germany and the Soviet Union signed a treaty partitioning Poland between them. Exactly one month after the start of the war, on 1 October 1939, German troops paraded triumphantly into the Polish capital. Their casualties had been less than 11,000 German dead, compared to an estimated 50,000 Polish casualties.

Olbricht's division was attached to Army Group South, as part of Blaskowitz's 8th Army. As mentioned above, this army was positioned on the extreme left (northern) wing of the Army Group. Olbricht's division crossed the Polish border in the early hours of 1 September 1939, and on the very next day encountered determined resistance from the Polish 10th Division, which was situated on the east bank of the Prosna. The division broke through this resistance in the afternoon, and advanced over the next two days to the banks of the River Warta.

The Warta formed a serious barrier to further advance. It had a number of branches that criss-crossed a broad swampy basin. The entire region could only be crossed by motorised units by means of a causeway, roughly 2km long. This in turn crossed five bridges, each about 80m long. Determined resistance in this area would inevitably result in heavy casualties. Most importantly, by destroying the bridges on the causeway, the Polish Army could slow down the advance of the Germans for days. Fully aware of this vulnerability, Olbricht kept his units hot on the heels of the retreating Polish units, in the hope of capturing the bridges before they could be demolished.

On the evening of 4 September 1939, after heavy hand-to-hand fighting, the 24th Infantry Division succeeded in seizing all five bridges intact. During the evening, the Poles then made repeated attempts to recapture the bridges, but failed. Olbricht's division was able to gain a foothold on the eastern shore of the Warta the following day. On 6 September the Polish were forced to recognise their defeat at this location and withdrew, the 24th Infantry Division still in hot pursuit.

On 9 September 1939 the division reached their interim goal of Lowicz. By now the Polish armed forces were in a headlong retreat, apparently anxious to take up defensive positions before Warsaw. The haste of the enemy's withdrawal, combined with the audacity of the advancing troops, enabled Olbricht's division again to seize strategic bridges – this time over the Bzura – before they could be destroyed by the enemy. Once in control of Lowicz, the division sent one motorised unit to take the important rail junction at Sochaczew. Meanwhile, Polish trains were still rolling peacefully into Lowicz, unaware that the Germans had assumed control of the city. Thousands of prisoners with all their arms and equipment were taken and 2,800 ethnic Germans, who had been rounded up and detained by the Poles, were freed.

It was here in Lowicz on 10 September 1939 that the division received unsettling reports of a major Polish build-up in their rear. The large Polish forces, which had been bypassed by the German pincer movement, were now in the rear of the division and were apparently attempting a breakout to the south-east. The division immediately to the north of the 24th, the 30th Infantry Division, was being pushed back to the south, and the 24th Infantry Division received orders to give up its own bridgehead on the north shore of the Bzura and take up defensive positions in Lowicz.

On 11 September the division participated in a counter-attack against the Polish units to the north-west, but the division was repulsed and soon under heavy attack itself. Only with great effort was the 24th Infantry Division able to hold its ground. On the following day, the situation became so critical that the division was forced to abandon Lowicz. By now, however, Army Group HQ had recognised just how serious the situation was and brought up strong reinforcements. The desperation of the entrapped Polish units, however, made the attacks of 14 September 1939 the most intense and dangerous that the 24th Infantry Division had faced in the entire campaign.

By 15 September, these efforts by the Polish forces to break out of the encirclement died down. On 16 and 17 September the Germans were able again to go on the offensive. The 24th Infantry Division, however, was detached from the 8th Army on 17 September and sent to reinforce the 10th Army, which was concentrating for an attack on Warsaw.

Together with the 18th Infantry Division, the 24th was supposed to drive forward to the Weichsel and cut the lines of communication between Warsaw and Modlin. The attack that was launched on 21 September, however, failed to reach its objective despite heavy casualties. The attack had to be repeated the following day. Only then, after adequate artillery preparation, did the 24th Infantry Division manage to reach its objective, and thereby end its part in the Polish campaign.

For its achievements, the division was allowed to participate in the victory parade before Hitler, staged on 5 October 1939. The war against Poland had cost the 24th Infantry Division 54 officers, 135 NCOs, and 1,300 men. For his part in the campaign, Olbricht became one of the first 14 men ever to receive the 'Knight's Cross', a new military honour invented by Hitler and available only to men who were already in possession of the Iron Cross First Class. At the time, October 1939, it was the highest military order awarded in Germany. The citation read: 'After the Führer and commander-in-chief of the *Wehrmacht* on 30 September ... decorated the responsible senior commanders of the Polish campaign, he granted on Friday the Knight's Cross of the Iron Cross to officers who *by their personal actions* had decisively contributed to the success of the operation' (author's italics).[3] Olbricht, along with the other initial recipients, was awarded the decoration by Hitler personally. The *Völkische Beobachter* explained Olbricht's selection with the words: 'With his lightning response and unsparing personal engagement, he more than once brought about decisive situations with far-ranging consequences for the army of General Blaskowitz.'[4] Neutral America still had a military attaché in Berlin, and he echoed this praise, reporting back to Washington that Olbricht had earned his medal with 'unusual personal bravery in hand-to-hand conflict in several important battles in the Polish campaign'.[5]

Olbricht, however, told the press that his own achievements were completely insignificant beside the 'truly heroic' accomplishments of his officers and men. Four days later, Olbricht issued a Daily Order to his division in which he declared that the decoration was *not* given to him personally at all, but to the entire division. He promised: '... to wear the Knight's Cross full of gratitude for the fact that in the decisive hours, the officers and men of this division gave me their full trust and fulfilled their tasks without reservations. Most especially I remember with particular gratitude our Best: those who gave their lives for the victory of the division.'[6]

Olbricht as Divisional Commander

Olbricht's performance as a divisional commander is well recorded. Indeed, this is the only period of Obricht's life that attracted extensive press coverage and for which a personal diary has survived. In addition, several of his subordinates from this period have recorded their memories of events. All these sources are flawed in their way. The press was writing in a chauvinistic, censured totalitarian state. Olbricht's diary of the Polish campaign was typed up by the divisional clerical staff and was at no time intended to be a secret document. And his former subordinates were writing in some cases many years after the events described. Nevertheless, all these sources together provide an astonishingly well-rounded picture of Olbricht as a divisional commander.

For the press, it was Olbricht's military competence that attracted attention, and what captured media enthusiasm most was the seizure of the bridges over the Wartha. Newspaper reports praised his military success on the Wartha as a 'brilliant infantry coup [*eine infanteristische Glanzleistung*]',[7] and the *Völkische Beobachter* described the incident as follows:

> [General Olbricht] rushed forward personally to lead the attack from the front. On the market square of Wartha, he overtook the leading infantry units and continued onward with his first general staff officer to the first of the bridges on the eastern edge of the town. He found it intact and unoccupied. Without hesitation, he sent his first general staff officer back to bring forward reinforcements immediately. Hastily improvised units rushed forward at the double to seize and secure the first of the bridges. Then, led forward with unprecedented daring by the divisional commander himself and under increasing machine-gun fire from the enemy on the opposite bank, they seized two more bridges.[8]

While it was certainly in the interests of the *Völkische Beobachter* to portray the achievements of German soldiers in a dramatic and positive manner, the praise of a divisional commander in this fashion was not daily fare – certainly not for an old *Reichswehr* soldier like Olbricht with no Nazi connections or past. Nor was the *Völkische Beobachter* the only contemporary account that focused on Olbricht's personal role in the decisive engagement. The official divisional history reported, 'The divisional commander rushed forward with his Ia, Major Feyerabend, into the captured city and then beyond with the leading units of infantry to the east shore of the Wartha.'[9]

Olbricht's own description of the action not only reveals the qualities that earned him press adulation and the Knight's Cross, but also provides insight into Olbricht's own leadership style and emotions. In his semi-official diary, Olbricht wrote of the action on the very evening of the occurrence as follows:

> Afternoon we approached and took the town of Wartha, and I went forward with our leading units and *Oberstleutnant* Feyerabend to discover that the Poles, for the first time, have not blown the bridges [in our path]. No less than five bridges over the branches of the Wartha! Is it possible that they do not intend to offer any kind of resistance here? I quickly load the first troops I can grab into a car and on the vehicles of the anti-tank company and rush forward. We reach the first bridge. The enemy opens fire from the far bank. All afternoon we attempt to seize the bridges. I send forward a captain of engineers, who crawls forward courageously and finds that all the bridges have been wired for demolition. The enemy had simply lacked the time to carry out the actual detonation! A huge success for us. Unfortunately the captain of engineers severely wounded.[10]

Olbricht's enthusiasm for his profession clearly comes across in the above account, but also his acute consciousness of the costs.

Just five days after Olbricht's first dramatic military success in the Polish campaign, he achieved a second brilliant military coup. Again he took a strategically important bridge, the one at Lowicz. Again he acted in a decisive and swift manner. In his own words:

> Corps ordered the division, in cooperation with the task force Büchs, to attack Lowicz on 9 September. I suggested that the 24th ID should exploit the lead of the 31st IR to put together a motorised group which could open the attack on Lowicz at 7am on the 9th. The corps commander agreed to my suggestion. I was given command of the task force Büchs ... [W]e created a motorised unit and threw it forward at Lowicz. ... Although we're not a motorised division as such, the operation went well, all things considered.[11]

From the newspaper reports it is clear that Olbricht didn't 'throw' the improvised unit forward at all – he led it. The newspaper account describes this action as follows:

> After Olbricht had loaded his infantry on every kind of motorised vehicle he could find, he stormed *with his troops* into Lowicz, causing a huge panic. In the railway station the occupants of several enemy troop transports were simply 'arrested'. … In Lowicz as in Sochaczew, Olbricht's division – far in advance of the main body of our Army – held the Bzura bridgeheads in the face of exceptionally heavy Polish counter-attacks for three full days.[12]

While the seizure of Lowicz underlines Olbricht's leadership from the front and proves that his behaviour on the Wartha was no isolated incident, the defence of the city reveals another, equally important, side of his military capabilities. Throughout the defensive battle, Olbricht kept an eye on developments by driving forward to the units directly under attack. In this way he formed a personal impression of both the strength of the enemy and the weaknesses of his own units. He consulted with his subordinate commanders and ensured that no friction developed between them.[13] Olbricht summarised these days as follows:

> These were perhaps the most critical days for me, since the responsibility of a divisional commander in such a situation is immense. And it is a special situation here in Poland. We have advanced with exceeding daring on the heels of the enemy, but not really with the strength necessary to maintain the breadth and depth essential for battle. … The consequence is that great gaps develop and the enemy – kept well informed by the local population – knows where these are. … The casualties among officers are severe. Officers have to recklessly take action, since individual engagements develop all over the place that can only be won if one is personally there on the spot. As a result, one has no choice but to drive forward from regiment to regiment and inspire them.[14]

Olbricht's successes won him not only the adulation of the press, but recognition from his superiors. On 18 September 1939 he was awarded the Iron Cross First Class (again). In his diary he noted: 'I think I got it in

1914 on exactly the same day. I am very proud that my division – since that is who it honours – has been decorated so early. General Felber informed me that General Blaskowitz was particularly impressed by the achievements of the division.'[15] Even the chief of the General Staff, Franz Halder, noted in his diary for 14 September 1939 under the heading 'Leadership': '24th ID [Infantry Division] – very good'.[16] It was the first of only two divisions whose leadership was thus praised.

Yet from the perspective of Olbricht's subordinates it was not his daring and successes that were most important, but rather his calm and cheerfulness. Major Ernst Friedrich, a staff officer with the 24th ID, described the following incident:

> Just before the Battle on the Bzura the tension was almost unendurable. A neighbouring division had temporarily lost its combat capability … Glowno had to be held.
>
> The divisional command post was located in a school on the edge of the city. In front of it was only a thin line of defence. This was no place for a divisional commander. But the general remained, conscious that his presence alone could ensure our perseverance. He took a conscious personal risk to show the division how much he trusted it – and how much it could trust itself. Neither staff nor fighting troops noticed any particular unease on the general's part. He could even crack jokes. When it was reported that the support headquarters in our rear was threatened by Polish cavalry, he replied that the divisional chaplains would have to reach for divine weapons, as he had no earthly ones left.
>
> If one knew him well, one noticed only one indication of uneasiness: that he twice went up on to the roof of the schoolhouse, where an officer on his orders was keeping watch on the immediate vicinity, and asked if there was anything new to report. The general never did that otherwise, because he knew he could rely on his staff. … Only after the danger was past did the general remove operational headquarters to a place where we could conduct operations in a more orderly manner.[17]

But being successful and praised was not, in Olbricht's case, synonymous with being an easy subordinate. In the attack on Warsaw the following incident occurred, according to Olbricht:

I was supposed to attack again today, and the XI Corps thought, as always, that they could order from the rear. It would have required a lengthy discussion to convince them that you can order anything you like, but that in itself achieved nothing. I promised to go forward at first light and speak to my commanders. At 5am I went … and met with the commanders. We could all see that we could not possibly attack immediately with the forces we then had deployed. … The troops had to be properly positioned. … That takes time. Just as I had warned the corps commander, it would not be possible to launch an attack before 10am.[18]

In fact, Olbricht refused to order the attack before 11:15 – but then it was successful and carried out almost without casualties. Olbricht, as usual, was with the leading units, and by noon was already standing on the Weichsel.

From the perspective of his subordinates, the incident was remembered and recorded as follows:

Before Warsaw the division received orders to break through to the Weichsel in order to cut the enemy's lines of communication and supply between Warsaw and Modlin. The attack was set by our superior headquarters for 7am. The task, as the general knew, was difficult. He was convinced that the action could not be sufficiently well prepared by 7am and would therefore fail with severe loss of life. He was unable, however, to persuade his superiors of this fact. He therefore ordered his regimental commanders to his headquarters and explained the situation to them. He told them that the attack was ordered for 7am, but he would not give the order until 11:15. He assured them that he alone would bear the consequences for this deviation from orders, because he knew he could expect of his infantrymen at 11:15 what he thought was questionable at 7am.[19]

In the attack that followed at 11:15, every man in the division knew that it wasn't just a matter of defeating the enemy; it was also a matter of proving their general right. And they did so gladly, because they had seen with their own eyes that he took their risks with them and that he was prepared to defy his superiors for their sake.

From the foregoing examples, it would be easy to imagine that Olbricht was always up front with the fighting troops. While this was true during the days of rapid advance and hard fighting, Olbricht nevertheless retained an exceptional appreciation for the hard work of the support troops and turned his attention to them as soon as he could. His diary from 26 September records: '... and then inspected our support units, which I was unable to visit earlier. I checked out the kitchens and the butchers and the workshops, etc, and I was so glad I had. You could tell that the troops were sincerely pleased to have their work recognised. Everything was first rate and the divisional supply officer, Major (Res) Harla is doing a fine job.'[20]

The victory parade in Warsaw gave Olbricht the opportunity for some sightseeing and again brought him together with Hitler. In his own diary, Olbricht avoids any remark that might be controversial. However, one of his staff officers had the following incident to report:

After the fall of Warsaw there was a parade for Hitler. ... Hitler was obviously in a bad mood from the start. ... After the parade, a feast had been prepared by the field kitchen at the airport for Hitler and his generals, after which he was to fly back to Berlin. ...

Hitler arrived. He walked into the tent and saw the decorated tables. With the words, 'Oh, so this is a dinner with roses,' he turned on his heel, spoke with no one, left the Army, corps, and divisional commanders standing, and boarded his aircraft. His entourage followed him without a word.

The collected generals inside the tent looked at one another in acute embarrassment. They stood behind the tables and didn't know what to make of it all after they had given Adolf Hitler such a brilliant military victory. The disconcerted silence lasted until our general found the right words. He declared: 'Gentlemen, I can't help myself. I'm hungry. I think we should sit down.'[21]

Perhaps Olbricht was less offended by Hitler's insulting behaviour because he despised the man and did not particularly want his praise in the first place. Perhaps he was even relieved not to have to sit down to eat with him. Whatever the reason, his remark broke the tension, and the generals did indeed sit down to their victory meal without the dictator and in far better humour – thanks to the common sense of a somewhat stocky and bespectacled general from Saxony, Friedrich Olbricht.

In summarising Olbricht's leadership style at this stage in his career, however, the best voice is that of Major Friedrich, one of his staff. Five and a half years after the end of the Polish campaign, he wrote passionately: 'The trust that every man in the whole division placed in [Olbricht] was limitless. His authority rested on his personality and his actions. The affection and admiration that he enjoyed was a product of his integrity, his warm heart, and the sheer aura of humanity that surrounded him.'[22] Olbricht would have wanted no better praise.

Olbricht and the War in Poland
Olbricht's diary from the Polish campaign does more than reveal his leadership style; it also provides insight into many of his attitudes. Admittedly, given the quasi-official nature of the document, it is unreasonable to expect political opinions, much less criticism. Yet even things that Olbricht did not feel he needed to hide can strike the modern reader as odd or even alienating.

It is striking, for example, that the diary contains not a hint of shock, regret, or disapproval with regard to the unprovoked attack on Poland. Although we know that Olbricht was appalled by the planned assault on the Sudetenland to the point of contemplating treason, and that he condemned the attack on Czechoslovakia, nothing in his legacy or in the memory of those who knew him at the time hints at objections to a war against Poland.

It appears that for once Olbricht was in harmony with his fellow generals. The German Army felt that Poland was bloated with the spoils of the First World War and that in its then form (cutting Germany in two) it posed a serious long-term threat to the security of Germany. A defeat of the Polish Army and a renegotiation of the borders in Germany's favour was, therefore, something that nearly all German officers advocated.

As for any fears about a wider war, such as had inspired the coup plans in 1938, these were largely laid to rest by the Hitler–Stalin Pact. The assurance that, even if things went poorly, the Red Army stood ready to pour into Poland undoubtedly silenced opposition to the war based on pure tactical concerns. It must have been clear to everyone in the General

Staff that Germany would rarely have such a favourable opportunity to 'solve the Polish problem'. Neither Olbricht nor the other generals could know that Hitler's plans for Poland were far more draconian than their wildest dreams of new borders and political domination.

Another aspect of Olbricht's diary that strikes a discordant note in modern ears is the enthusiasm it exudes for military operations and achievements. Very clearly, despite all his serious objections to National Socialist foreign policy, he was still with heart and soul a soldier. From the moment when he himself had to act, professional pride took over from political reservations. He positively revelled in the military successes that his troops were able to attain in such a short space of time.

Nevertheless, despite this enthusiasm for his own profession and the accomplishments of his unit, Olbricht never fell victim to a glorification of war itself. On the contrary, his diary is punctuated with descriptions of the horror of war, and he repeatedly expresses distress over the consequences. For example, on 14 September 1939 he wrote:

> The attacking IR [Infantry Regiment] 31 … had to pass through the minefield we had laid. … [They discovered that] the divisional commander of the [Polish] division opposite us had driven down the road in the direction of Glowno in a staff car. … He had driven on to a mine, and the auto was completely gutted. The divisional commander was completely burned and only recognisable by his papers (very interesting operational orders, family photos, etc.). … The adjutant was also badly mutilated, and it hit me hard. … Our engineers were understandably proud of their success, since the Polish unit had been dealt a serious blow, but for the individual it is horrible.[23]

On 21 September 1939 he wrote:

> In Laski on the Laski–Sierakow road we came upon an entire convoy of Polish troops … that had attempted to break out in the direction of Warsaw. They had been caught on the 20th by the Air Force … and subjected to attacks by dive-bombers and fighters. It was a grisly sight. One was reminded of the quote: 'Horses, chariots, and men – the Lord destroyed them all.' [*Mit Mann und Ross und Wagen, hat sie der*

Herr geschlagen.] Wherever one looked: dead men, dead soldiers, dead officers, dead horses, shot-up vehicles, and guns. I saw some terrible things in the last war, but something as gruesome as this destruction – never. My escort, Lt von Götz, and I were hit hard ... I was even more moved when I met up with the adjutant of the 15th Rangers, who was burying their dead. It was roughly 100 officers and men, laid out in rows.[24]

And again, on 25 and 27 September respectively, Olbricht recorded the following observations: 'In the direction of Warsaw one sees an incredible inferno. The Air Force has carpeted Warsaw with several thousand firebombs. It is an appalling sight.'[25] And: 'The sight of shattered, burning Warsaw is profoundly upsetting.'[26]

Indeed, despite all his pride in the accomplishments of his troops, he had no desire for the conflict to be drawn out or for his division to be confronted with any more heavy fighting. On 27 September 1939 he wrote:

General Blaskowitz informed me that the original intention was to throw the 24th Division in, but thank God it was not necessary. We were naturally delighted, because despite the unprecedented artillery preparation and the heavy bombing, it was as to be expected: as soon as the infantry went in, they encountered all sorts of resistance and took serious casualties. The casualties would only have increased in house-to-house fighting. You can't destroy a city from the air. The houses are too strong for that. It is a great blessing that we were spared this fight. ...[27]

Olbricht was never indifferent to casualties.

Another feature of Olbricht's diary that strikes one as odd from today's perspective is his frequent reference to *Polish* atrocities. In hindsight we know that the Nazis were about to commit far more horrible, indeed heinous, crimes. In retrospect, the actions of the Polish population in defence of their country seem comparatively harmless, if not actually heroic. But this is the beauty of diaries: written down in the heat of the moment without the benefit of hindsight, reflection, or comparison, they show us how people really felt *at the time*. Olbricht's diary entries, therefore, reflect his own innocence – indeed, the innocence of an entire generation accustomed to the civilised world that had not yet been witness to the depths of depravity that Hitler, Stalin, Pol Pot, and the Lord's Liberation Army, etc., would lead us to in the next half-century.

Thus on 5 September 1939, Olbricht could still write with self-righteous indignation: 'The partisan warfare is appalling. The Poles have been incited to abandon their villages [when we approach], but come back by darkness to shoot us perfidiously – particularly individuals – in the back.'[28] Later in his diary he recorded the treacherous actions of Polish troops that pretended to surrender, only to attack Olbricht's unsuspecting troops when they got nearer.[29]

Just ten days into the campaign, Olbricht and his division were confronted with an even more serious example of Polish war crimes.

One of the half-tracks sent forward by me on reconnaissance … stumbled upon 2,800 German hostages in a village north-west of Lowicz. The German civilians had been rounded up in the area of Posener and Bromberg, herded forward by night, and mistreated in a bestial manner. There were 200 women among them and prominent Germans including Dr Kohner, the leader of the German Association; the German consul Wegner; and Senator Busse. Because the Poles had had too few police for the task, they armed youths of the Polish youth organisation. These behaved particularly brutally, gunning down those who could not keep up the pace. The Germans were overjoyed [to see us]; they had hardly eaten in 11 days.[30]

This may sound relatively harmless to our Auschwitz-hardened ears; but at that time Auschwitz had not yet been conceived, much less built. Nor were *Einsatzkommandos* yet operating behind the German lines, and Germany was not yet populated by armies of forced labourers. Indeed, even the German atrocities against Russian prisoners of war lay in the future.

On 17 September Olbricht reported with indignation the neglect of Polish wounded by their own Army:

In Boczki we came upon a Polish field hospital, located in the manor, with over 200 severely wounded Poles. It must be stressed that the hospital was in a deplorable state. The Polish medical personnel had abandoned it and the wounded were being looked after by a few women. They had only improvised bandages and had had nothing to eat for days. ... I told the wounded that I would deploy my medical company at once and ensure that they were brought this very night to a German field hospital, where they would see how Germans care for wounded – even the enemy.[31]

The last sentence reveals the pride Olbricht then felt in German humanity and civilisation. In light of what was to come, it sounds ludicrous, and yet this is the tragedy of the Opposition: they truly believed – until confronted with evidence to the contrary – that they were a *civilised* people, incapable of systematic brutality or mass murder.

Olbricht's sense of superiority was so great at this point that he even called for a so-called propaganda company (embedded press corps) to come and photograph the appalling conditions in the Polish field hospital. He also gave orders to his troops to report any Polish field hospitals captured, so that medics could be sent to them as rapidly as possible. Olbricht was determined to live by his own standards of humanity in warfare.

Yet despite his national pride and his pride in the accomplishments of his own troops, Olbricht was never a chauvinist. Again and again his diary reflects respect for the enemy, especially where they were fighting most doggedly. Olbricht knew personally some of the senior Polish officers he was fighting against, and he remembered them with admiration. He was impressed particularly by the daring efforts of already shattered units seeking to break out of the German encirclement. On 23 September 1939 he wrote: 'It is often regimental commanders, who with the remnants of their regiments, maybe 200–300 men, try to fight their way to freedom in daring night thrusts through the woods. One has to admire them – something I always express to them when they are brought to me.'[32] Olbricht went on: 'I'm sorry that the press reports give the impression to people at home that the Poles just run away. Since the division first withstood counter-attacks at Glowno ... the division has continuously encountered worthy opponents. In fact, I'd go so far as to say that the Poles have fought heroically.'[33]

Altogether, Olbricht's account of the Polish campaign reveals a great deal about his personality. It shows his humanity even in the midst of war, his concern for civilians caught in the middle, and his concern for the wounded, regardless of uniform. He is never indifferent to the costs of success, and he is full of praise for others, whether it is his own troops or the enemy. Above all, his diary and the press accounts of his actions decisively destroy the image created by historians of the German Resistance that Olbricht was a timid, passionless 'desk general'.

Olbricht was, as his career in the First World War and Poland shows, an almost recklessly daring commander, who led from the front and won the hearts of his troops with his leadership and his warmth. He took personal risks to seize chances if these offered themselves, but he defied his superiors for the sake of his troops if necessary. He cared about his soldiers – and they knew it. When he was posted away, his division resented it so much that they made life difficult for his successor, hardly giving him a fair chance to earn their respect and affection.[34]

Farewell to the Troops

By the end of the Polish campaign, Olbricht was one of the *Wehrmacht*'s most successful younger generals and stood alongside 'panzer generals' like Guderian and Hoepner as one of the popular, 'up-and-coming' troop commanders idolised in the press and already earmarked for higher command. His name was more familiar to newspaper readers and schoolboys than that of the obscure general who commanded nothing more than Hitler's personal protective battalion, a certain Erwin Rommel. And the Chief of the General Staff had already pegged him for command of a corps in the upcoming campaign against the Western powers.

While Olbricht and his division were boarded on trains and redeployed directly from Warsaw to the area of the Eifel on the Rhine in anticipation of a campaign against France, Halder and other senior generals were locked in a bitter struggle with Hitler over that campaign itself. Hitler had ordered the attack on France for November 1939 – less than two months after the victory in Poland. The *Wehrmacht* leadership, even Keitel, was unanimously opposed. None of the professionals felt that the Army was ready or could be made ready to confront the much larger, better-equipped, and already mobilised French Army in such a short period of time. Added to this was the time of year: winter is the season of short, wet, and even icy days in Northern Europe. Darkness and bad visibility, fog, rain, and sleet would ground the Luftwaffe, clearly one of Hitler's greatest strengths at this stage in the war. The French, meanwhile, had had plenty of time to mobilise, deploy, and settle into their massive defensive installations along the German border, the Maginot Line. For the first time, Hitler's forces would not enjoy the advantage of either surprise or technical and numerical superiority.

For officers who were already ideological opponents of Hitler, these plans to open a premature and ill-prepared offensive against the greatest power on the Continent offered a new chance to turn the tactical opposition of their more opportunistic colleagues into a front against Hitler. Coup hopes and plans were again discussed among steadfast opponents of Hitler. Briefly, it even looked as if the commander-in-chief of the Army, General Brauchitsch, might be persuaded to join them in a move against Hitler.

But when Hitler, in one of his famous temper tantrums, screamed at Brauchitsch that he 'knew the Army had never been loyal to him' and then poured insults and accusations over Brauchitsch's head, the latter abruptly backed away from any association with coup plans. As Hans Oster, one of Hitler's bitterest enemies, worded it: 'The label of cowardice has made the brave cowardly again.'[35] More disappointing, however, was that Brauchitsch's defection took Halder out of the conspiracy as well; Halder, as chief of staff with no command authority, was not willing to act in defiance of Hitler unless the C-in-C was prepared to act with him.

Nevertheless, a 'hard core' of now bitter opponents to Hitler – Oster, Goerdeler, Witzleben, and Leeb – continued to forge coup plans. They counted on Olbricht. Olbricht knew all the principal conspirators, and he spoke in confidence with his staff officers, if obliquely, about the need for political change. Friedrich remembers that:

> The winter months of 1939–40 in the Eifel on the Rhine, while the general lived and worked with his division, provided many opportunities for discussions among comrades. All hoped that a new world war could be avoided. The general, however, did not believe it. Deep worries about the future of Germany plagued him, and he used the evenings to open his heart to trusted officers. As a side effect, he hoped to open the eyes of his junior officers to Germany's true situation in the world and to things going on inside Germany.[36]

Fritz Merker remembers: '… The period before the campaign in the West was when we had our most important discussions about the world, Adolf Hitler and all these things. That's when we got to know each other well. … Olbricht had long been anti-Nazi. We both found the whole war completely unnecessary, but Olbricht's opposition was deeper. The whole National Socialist movement didn't suit him at all.'

Merker goes on to cite Olbricht's critique of National Socialist foreign policy, the idiocy of 'fighting the whole world' and not being on good terms with anyone, and his analysis of German economic policy. According to Merker, Olbricht protested in his typically down-to-earth way, 'We can't even make a decent soap; how can we make war?'[37]

Ernst Röhricht claims that Olbricht spoke in confidence to him about the need for a change of regime and vaguely about coup plans. Röhricht maintains that although he raised all sorts of tactical objections to these plans and expressed reservations about the chances of success, Olbricht remained committed.[38]

The driving force behind the coup plans in the winter of 1939–40 was undoubtedly Hans Oster. Oster, like Olbricht, had been born in Saxony in 1888, the fifth child of a Protestant pastor. His mother was Alsatian, and he was brought up in a liberal, open-minded atmosphere. Despite an early interest in theology, Oster chose a military career, and, unable to afford the life of a cavalry officer, he chose the artillery because of his love of horses. Like Olbricht, he started the First World War as an adjutant and ended it as a General Staff officer. He was awarded the Iron Cross First and Second Class, and won the *Königlich Sächsischen Militär-St-Heinrichs-Orden* (Royal Saxon Military St Heinrich Order).

Up to this point, Olbricht's and Oster's careers had been remarkably similar, but Oster's response to the German defeat and the Revolution was completely different. Oster later described the day Germany signed the Armistice in 1919 as 'the blackest day' in his life, and he claimed the collapse of Imperial Germany had affected him 'as if you had hit me on the head with a hammer'.[39] He disdained the Weimar Republic and served it without conviction; inwardly he retained his dislike. He served with Olbricht in Dresden in the early 1920s, and then in other garrison towns as he slowly climbed the ladder in the 100,000-man *Reichswehr* until, in 1932, he was forced to resign his commission because of a love affair that was exposed.

In 1933, he was working as a civilian in the counter-intelligence department of the Ministry of War. Despite his negative attitude towards the Republic, Oster was not one of the officers who were pleased with Hitler's appointment to chancellor. He remained inwardly a monarchist and could not find enthusiasm for the Austrian corporal. Furthermore, his work gave him exceptional insight into the criminal actions of the regime, and his moral outrage against the Nazis grew correspondingly. The so-called 'Röhm Putsch', when – with the complicity of the Army – Hitler eliminated the SA leadership and other inconvenient opponents, turned Oster into an angry opponent of the regime. In March 1935, shortly after Admiral Canaris assumed the position of head of Counter-Intelligence, Oster was reactivated from the reserves with the rank of major, and soon afterwards promoted to lieutenant colonel.

By March 1936, Oster's opposition to Hitler had reached the point where he hoped the French would resist the German reoccupation of the Rhineland, because he feared (rightly, as it turned out) that success would go to Hitler's head. From this point forward, he started building up a network of like-minded men for some kind of 'action' against the regime – when the opportunity arose. Since he was a personal friend of General Werner Freiherr von Fritsch, he was particularly outraged over the slanderous campaign against Fritsch that led to his resignation.

The Sudeten Crisis was, however, the turning point for Oster. It was at this time that he became actively involved in the plans to depose Hitler the moment war over the Sudetenland became inevitable. He sent no fewer than three emissaries to Britain to strengthen British resolve to stand firm against Hitler's demands. When the British prime minister flew to Munich and effectively capitulated to Hitler, Oster was devastated. The occupation of the remainder of Czechoslovakia a few months later proceeded without opposition, and the Molotov–Ribbentrop Pact made the war in Poland inevitable. It was not until the winter of 1939–40, when the military leadership resisted the timing of a campaign in the West, that Oster perceived a new opportunity for action against the regime.

Oster and his circle of conspirators were sufficiently radicalised by this point to have stopped thinking of 'arresting' Hitler and putting him on trial. They intended to eliminate him. Explosives were secured (something that was comparatively easy for a counter-intelligence unit), and the assassination of Hitler was planned – as soon as a coup on the part of leading active generals could be organised. To this end Oster tried to influence Halder and a number of commanding generals including Witzleben, Stülpnagel, Leeb, List, and Kluge, all of whom to a greater or lesser degree were already anti-Nazi, not just opposed to the ill-timed offensive in the West.

Meanwhile, Oster was also in close contact with Beck and Goerdeler, both of whom, as retirees, were more important for post-coup planning and the formulation of political objectives than for the execution of the coup. Oster's plans, however, also included establishing contact, via the Pope, with the British government. It was vital that the opposition receive some kind of assurance that the British would negotiate with a post-Hitler government. At the same time, in order to mobilise the presumed opposition of the common man to a war with France, Oster held talks with a former leader of the German trade-union movement, Wilhelm Leuschner. Leuschner had spent much time in concentration camps since 1933, but now owned and ran a small (30-man) factory in Berlin which was, in fact, a disguised Resistance cell, inasmuch as it was manned entirely by opponents of the National Socialist regime and ideology.

Although the response of the British was cautiously encouraging, the prospects for a coup dwindled as the date for the offensive in the West receded and then, after much internal controversy, the Manstein plan was accepted. Leuschner, furthermore, had to admit that contrary to the reports of the Berlin police chief, there was no real prospect of a general strike, since the bulk of the workers had now become sufficiently mesmerised by Hitler to trust him to bring them victory yet again, even against the French and the British. The leftist opposition of the early years, characterised by a plethora of illegal cells that distributed pamphlets and newspapers smuggled in from overseas or printed in tenement basements, had largely fizzled out. The Socialist, Communist, and trade-union Resistance cells had long since been infiltrated by the Gestapo and their members arrested and sent to concentration camps, while the ordinary workers became more and more reconciled to, if not wholly enthusiastic about, the Nazi regime.

But Oster remained a bitter opponent of Hitler, regardless of the chances of success, because his opposition was ethical, not tactical. In fact, Oster was one of the few officers in the German armed forces who felt so strongly about the *immorality* of the impending war in the West that he was prepared to betray Germany's plans to the prospective enemy – not, notably, to the declared enemies, France and Britain, but to the still neutral Holland and Belgium, which were soon to be victims of German aggression. When the time came he would warn Norway and Denmark, too.

Oster's actions at this time were to remain an isolated incident in the history of the conspiracy that culminated in the coup attempt on 20 July 1944. It was the only time that one of these conspirators crossed the line between *Hochverrat* or high treason (treason against the government) and *Landesverrat* or national treason (treason against the nation or people). Oster was fully aware of the gravity of his actions, but as he worded it: 'One may call me a traitor to the nation, but that is not really what I am. I believe I am a better German than all those who follow Hitler. My plan and my duty is to free Germany and the world of this [Nazi] plague.'[40]

It is unlikely that even Oster's closest associates knew what information he passed to the Dutch military attaché in the critical months between the end of the war in Poland and the start of the offensive in the West. Certainly Olbricht knew nothing of it, and he might not have approved. Olbricht was aware only that many of the men he knew, trusted, and respected and who shared his political views – Beck, Goerdeler, Leeb, and Witzleben – were trying to find the means and occasion to bring down the Nazi regime. Although he played no role whatsoever in these plans or discussions, there can be no doubt that he supported their objective.

Olbricht may have been heart and soul a soldier, but he was never *just* a soldier, bound to orders by his 'oath' and his 'duty'. And he may have helped to give Hitler one of his greatest military victories and received a decoration from Hitler's hands personally, but he was not – even then – Hitler's general. Olbricht was already firmly in the opposition camp.

Above: Dr Emil Olbricht, Friedrich Olbricht's father. Dr Friedrich Georgi

Above: Friedrich Olbricht with his parents in about 1895. Dr Friedrich Georgi

Below: Friedrich Olbricht (left) as a secondary school pupil. Dr Friedrich Georgi

Below: Lt Friedrich Olbricht, Saxon Army, 1914. Dr Friedrich Georgi

Above: Captain Friedrich Olbricht (centre) as a staff officer in the First World War, c.1917. Dr Friedrich Georgi

Above: Eva Koeppel Olbricht, 1918. Dr Friedrich Georgi

Below: Speaker in front of the Crown Prince's Palace just one hour after the Declaration of the Republic, 11 November 1918. Landesarchiv Berlin 133979

Above: Troops loyal to the majority Socialist government of Friedrich Ebert take a tea break during the November Revolution in 1918.
Landesarchiv Berlin 136679

Below: Government troops defend a street barricade during the November Revolution. Landesarchiv Berlin 322980

Above: Karl Liebknecht, Independent Socialist leader, speaks at a funeral for victims of the December 1918 uprising in Berlin, 21 December 1918. Landesarchiv Berlin 74126

Below: Barricades in the streets of Berlin during the Spartikus Revolt, 12 January 1919. The barricade is manned by troops loyal to the majority Socialist government. Landesarchiv Berlin II-985

Above: A pro-government rally, January 1919. Landesarchiv Berlin II-5888

Below: A protest rally against the Treaty of Versailles, May 1919.
Landesarchiv Berlin II-6159

Above: The reactionary Kapp Putsch against the Social Democratic government, 13–17 March 1920. Landesarchiv Berlin II-7301

Below: Armoured train at Anhalter Bahnhof in Berlin during the Putsch. Landesarchiv Berlin 355986

*Above: President Friedrich Ebert, SPD (second from right) and Defence Minister
Dr Gessler, inspect the* Reichswehr *in 1924.* Landesarchiv Berlin II-5851

*Below: The Olbricht family in 1925. From left to right: Klaus, Friedrich,
Rosemarie, Eva.* Dr Friedrich Georgi

Above: Army manoeuvres in 1934, with Eva and Friedrich Olbricht (left).
Dr Friedrich Georgi

*Below: Major Olbricht (4th from left) while serving with the T-3 Department of
the German General Staff, 1935.* Dr Friedrich Georgi

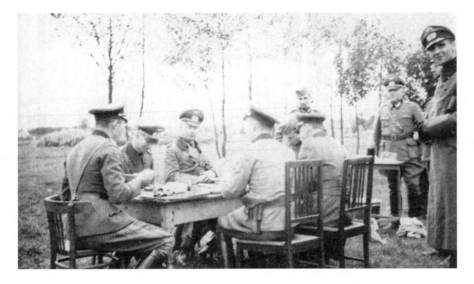

Above: General Olbricht (3rd from left) with the staff of the 24th Infantry Division during the Polish Campaign, 1939. Dr Friedrich Georgi

Right: General Olbricht and his daughter Rosemarie at her wedding to Friedrich Georgi, July 1942. Dr Friedrich Georgi

Below: General Olbricht (left), Commanding General of the 24th Infantry Division, early in 1940. Dr Friedrich Georgi

Above: General Olbricht inspecting mountain troops in training, c.1943. Dr Friedrich Georgi

Right: General Olbricht and his grandson Rudolf Georgi in December 1943. Dr Friedrich Georgi

Below: The Olbricht family in May 1944. From left to right: Eva Olbricht, Rudolf Georgi, Friedrich Olbricht, and Friedrich Georgi. Dr Friedrich Georgi

Above: Carl Goerdeler, Mayor of Leipzig 1930–6, leading civilian figure in the resistance to Hitler. Gedenkstätte Deutscher Widerstand

Right: Ludwig Beck, Chief of the German General Staff 1933–8, C-in-C of the military resistance to Hitler. Gedenkstätte Deutscher Widerstand

Below: Carl Heinrich von Stülpnagel, military governor of France, 1941–4, early and committed member of the military resistance to Hitler. Gedenkstätte Deutscher Widerstand

Below: Hans Oster, counter-intelligence officer and leading member of the military resistance to Hitler. Gedenkstätte Deutscher Widerstand

Above: Axel Freiherr (Baron) von dem Bussche, one of the young officers who offered to carry out a suicide assassination of Hitler. Gedenkstätte Deutscher Widerstand

Below: Tresckow and his staff at Army Group Centre in about 1942–3. Philipp Freiherr (Baron) von Boeselager

Above: Henning von Tresckow, a leading member of the military resistance to Hitler. Gedenkstätte Deutscher Widerstand

Below: The officers' mess at Army Group Centre, the scene of one proposed assassination attempt. Philipp Freiherr von Boeselager

Above: Members of the student resistance group 'The White Rose': Hans Scholl, Sophi Scholl and Christoph Probst. Source unknown

Right: Helmuth James Graf (Count) von Moltke, co-founder of the civilian resistance group 'Kreisauer Circle'. Source unknown

Below: Peter Graf (Count) Yorck von Wartenburg, co-founder of the civilian resistance group 'Kreisauer Circle'. Marion Gräfin Yorck von Wartenburg

Below: Claus Schenk Graf (Count) von Stauffenberg (left) at Hitler's HQ, July 1944. Gedenkstätte Deutscher Widerstand

Above: Generals Rommel (left) and Stülpnagel (right) in May 1944.
Heinrich Bücheler

Above: Hitler and Mussolini inspect the damage done by Stauffenberg's bomb.
Gedenkstätte Deutscher Widerstand

Below: Floor plan of the offices of the headquarters of the Home Army and General Army Office (GAO) in the Bendlerstrasse, Berlin. Gedenkstätte Deutscher Widerstand

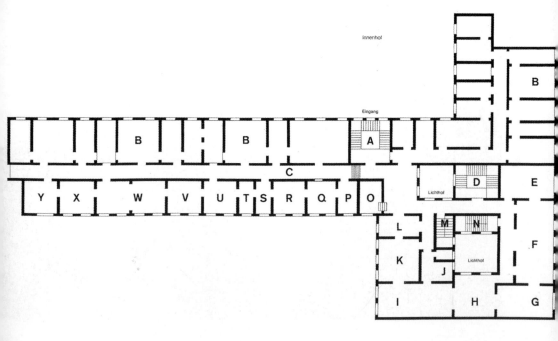

*Above: The front entrance to the office complex known as the 'Bendlerstrasse'
which housed the German General Staff in the interwar years and a number of
important army offices throughout the Nazi period.* Herbert Schrader

Below: Side entrance to the Bendlerstrasse. *The offices along the second floor were
occupied by the Home Army during the Second World War. Stauffenberg's office is
on the far left.* Herbert Schrader

Below: Entrance to the courtyard of the
Bendlerstrasse *and primary access to
the offices of the Home Army and GAO
during the Second World War.* Herbert
Schrader

Above: Courtyard of the Bendlerstrasse *where Olbricht and Stauffenberg were shot on the night of 20 July 1944.* Herbert Schrader

Left: The stairway of the Bendlerstrasse *leading from the offices of the GAO to the courtyard. Olbricht and Stauffenberg descended these stairs to their deaths on the night of 20 July 1944.* Herbert Schrader

Below: Memorial plaque on the site of Olbricht's and Stauffenberg's execution. Herbert Schrader

Chapter 9

ORGANISING HITLER'S WAR

Olbricht as Head of the General Army Office, 1940–4

The General Army Office

On 15 January 1940, Halder abruptly altered his recorded plans for giving Olbricht command of a corps in the upcoming campaign against France. Instead, he assigned Olbricht to a key position at General Staff headquarters in Berlin. There is no question that Olbricht himself was deeply disappointed and unhappy about the change. He much preferred life with the troops. The fact that he opposed a war with France had no bearing on his preference for a command over a staff job. If there was going to be a war, then Olbricht wanted to be part of it, sharing the same risks and chances as his troops. He certainly had every reason to feel that his recognised successes in Poland gave him a certain 'right' to higher command.

At the time, Olbricht might have found some consolation in the fact that his transfer to the new job was made conditional on the *absence* of an immediate attack in the West. His transfer was delayed until it was clear that a major postponement of the campaign had been effected. But then, on 15 February 1940, the reprieve was over and he was ordered to take up his new duties in Berlin. Olbricht may next have comforted himself with the thought that it was customary for General Staff officers to alternate between troop commands and staff positions. He no doubt hoped that his tenure in the massive Berlin bureaucracy would be short-lived and that he would get his corps sooner or later. It was Olbricht's great misfortune that he did his staff job too well. He soon made himself indispensable, and only his death would free him of this final desk.

The reasons for Halder's decision are not recorded. There appears to be no objective, military reason why the successful and popular infantry general should not have been allowed to join the other heroes of the Polish campaign in the campaign in the West. Nor had Olbricht in any way incurred the displeasure of his military or political masters. Olbricht enjoyed the trust and respect of everyone in his chain of command. It has been suggested, however, that Halder, although he refused to engage in treasonous activities without Brauchitsch, remained intensely pessimistic about the forthcoming campaign and wanted reliable opponents of Hitler in key positions in Berlin. Halder, who expected Germany to get bogged down in France, may even have harboured hopes that in such a situation popular opinion would turn against Hitler. He may have believed that the opportunity for a coup would eventually arise – and that when it did he would have good use for a man of decisive temperament, proven command ability, popular reputation, and unwavering opposition to Hitler in a key position in Berlin.

This is all speculation, and yet it makes sense; because whatever else one says about the new job, it was most decidedly not a demotion. It was not even a lateral move, but rather a significant promotion in terms of responsibility and influence. Command of a corps might have been more to Olbricht's *liking*. It would certainly have given him a better opportunity for greater glory. As it was, Olbricht's achievements in Poland would soon be overshadowed by the exploits of Manstein, Kluge, Guderian, and Rommel in France. But the command of a corps would not have put him in a more *important* job. There were, quite literally, scores of corps commanders in the German Army, but the head of the General Army Office (GAO) had a unique and subtly pivotal position.

The innocuous designation of the 'General Army Office' disguises its importance and scope. The GAO was the successor organisation to the Prussian Ministry of War. In peacetime it was responsible for personnel, materiel, and finances. The General Staff developed its plans based on the calculations of the GAO concerning what manpower, weapons, munitions, equipment, and other materiel could be obtained with the financial resources available. Significantly, the GAO was responsible for reserves and replacements of both materiel and men. In wartime, the duties of the GAO changed only slightly. It was still expected to recruit, assign, clothe, equip, feed, discipline, and comfort the troops as they came into the military system, but not for the operational deployment and use of the troops at the front. In peace, the head of the GAO reported directly to the C-in-C of the Army. In war, the head of the GAO reported to the (newly established) commander of the Home Army, who in turn held command over all troops still inside Germany. In summary, the responsibilities of the GAO were described by one of the officers who served in it quite simply as: 'providing the Army at the front with anything that was necessary for it to retain its combat effectiveness and enable it to achieve its objectives'.[1]

More specifically, the tasks assigned the GAO were:

1 Calculation of personnel and materiel resources and development of realistic forecasts; reconciling the differences between these and the requirements of the leadership.
2 Registration, conscription, and distribution of those eligible for military service.
3 Organisation and oversight of the conscription process.
4 Organisation of units.
5 Acquisition and distribution of horses and other beasts of burden employed by the Army.
6 Development of requirements for all kinds of arms, equipment, vehicles, fuels, and munitions.
7 Development, procurement, and management of uniforms and personal equipment for troops.
8 Acquisition, construction, and management of all land and buildings necessary for the maintenance of troops in the Home Army.
9 Military justice.
10 Military medical and veterinary corps.
11 Development and distribution of military regulations with regard to:
   a   Rank and supervision,
   b   Discipline and punishment,
   c   Complaints,
   d   Leave,
   e   Social welfare,
   f   Spiritual care/chaplaincy.

Altogether the GAO was divided into between 20 and 24 departments (the exact number varied during the course of the war) and encompassed roughly 4,000 officers and 150,000 men. (That is a good deal more than a corps, and indeed more than in the entire *Reichswehr*.)

It is notable that many of the departments of the GAO (for example, those responsible for conscription, vehicles, horses, and the medical and veterinary corps) were not only Army (*Heer*) organisations, but rather Armed Forces (*Wehrmacht*) organisations. That is, the GAO was responsible for providing these services to the other branches of the armed services (SS, Air Force, and Navy) as well as to the Army. In recognition of the fact that the GAO was providing so many services for the entire *Wehrmacht*, the Armed Forces Replacement Office was created in mid-1943, and Olbricht was designated the head of this office while retaining the title and function of head of the GAO. Curiously, immediately after Olbricht's execution on 20 July 1944, the offices were separated. Olbricht was thus the only general to be entrusted with both offices at once.

Inevitably with such a complex and comprehensive body, there was much organisational overlap, confusion, and arcane command structures. The man who acted as chief of staff of the GAO longest, General Reinhardt, admits that the picture was perplexing and opaque even to those who knew it best. But there was method in the madness. Reinhardt claims that many of the apparent contradictions and duplications of function with regard to the line of command were carefully constructed defence mechanisms to prevent Hitler's dilettantish interference in the affairs of the GAO. The various office heads agreed among themselves to seek consensus and work together to avoid taking decisions up the chain of command to OKW and Hitler. They sought to replace incompetent centralised command by an arbitrary amateur with professional cooperation that expressed itself in apparent organisational chaos. The problem was that – even though letting Hitler take charge was worse – running a war by committee was still hardly ideal. It entailed a huge amount of daily friction and frequent frustration and delays.

Quite incidentally, this complicated command structure and the need for constant coordination with other offices offered Olbricht immense advantages in his Resistance activities. He had legitimate reasons for travelling extensively; for consulting military, political, and even business leaders; and for obtaining even the most sensitive of information.

One of Olbricht's official contacts was to have a significant bearing on the anti-Hitler conspiracy. Because the GAO was responsible for finding the means to meet the Army's demands for replacements of men and equipment, the GAO worked particularly closely with the Organisational Office of the Army General Staff. From June 1940 until February 1943, a certain Major, later Lt Colonel, Claus Graf Stauffenberg worked in this Army office. One of Olbricht's staff officers remembers: 'Stauffenberg was my contact. Often when I presented Olbricht with something that had to do with organisation, he would ask me: "Where did you get this?" And I would say, "Stauffenberg". And if he wasn't in agreement with something or had further questions, then he would call Stauffenberg direct, rather than making me play the go-between.'[2] Apparently, the young general staff major made a good impression on the general. When later Olbricht was looking around for someone who could perform both official and Resistance-related activities inside the GAO, he thought of Stauffenberg; and Stauffenberg's transfer to the GAO was accordingly organised, as will be described in detail later. At this point it is only of interest that the team Olbricht–Stauffenberg had its roots in this purely official cooperation in the first three years of the war. This was, in fact, true of a number of contacts important to the Resistance.

In addition to providing Olbricht with a vast network of contacts, his position as head of the GAO also provided him with certain, if limited, opportunities for influencing the leadership of the *Wehrmacht*. Olbricht's immediate superior was the chief of Army Armaments and commander-in-chief of the Home Army (*Chef der Heeresrüstung und Oberbefehlshaber des Erstzheeres*), *Generaloberst* Fromm, and Olbricht did not officially have direct access either to the C-in-C of the Army or to Hitler. However, Olbricht often accompanied Fromm when the latter reported to either OKW or Hitler or represented him when he could not attend a meeting personally. After Olbricht became head of the Armed Forces Replacement Office on 3 August 1943, he also had legitimate reasons for sometimes bypassing Fromm and reporting direct to Keitel at OKW. His access to Hitler, however, remained indirect.

Olbricht's relationship to the General Staff of the Army was more collegial. The GAO was not a department inside the General Staff, and Olbricht had no duty to report to the chief of the General Staff. But Olbricht was a General Staff officer, and the traditions of this elite corps were strong and inbred. Olbricht frequently reported to Halder and met other generals in a variety of General Staff positions to exchange information, consult one another, or simply take part in briefings, and so on.

Despite the importance of his position and the diverse opportunities it offered for gaining information and exercising influence, it was deficient in one significant respect – something that was to prove absolutely fatal to the coup d'état against Hitler. Olbricht had no command over combat troops. All combat and training units were either under the command of the various Army Groups and Armies on the front or under the command of the C-in-C of the Home Army, *Generaloberst* Fromm. Olbricht did not have command authority over a single military unit, not even a company of dragoons.

When evaluating the career and judging the actions of Friedrich Olbricht, the huge responsibilities that he carried as head of the GAO should not be underestimated or forgotten. Despite the advantages that the organisational chaos brought, it nevertheless represented an additional burden for the chief of the GAO. One particular problem was to weigh especially heavily on Olbricht, and this was the fact that from the point where Hitler assumed personal command of the Army in December 1941, there was really no one in Hitler's inner circle who represented the interests of the Army. Hitler was surrounded by Party, SS, and (in the shape of his old colleague and deputy Göring) Air Force leaders, but the Army was a 'stepchild'. As a result, Olbricht found himself in a continuous and nerve-racking 'guerrilla war' against the other armed forces for resources and men.

Olbricht's work was made even more difficult by the fact that there was both an 'Army Staff' inside the OKW and also the old, traditional, and still independent General Staff of the Army. Neither had control over the GAO, but both placed demands on it. Olbricht was in effect the servant of two masters: always forced to present his opinion to both, to obtain the blessings of both, and to reconcile any (frequent) differences between the positions of the two staffs. When Olbricht was given the position of head of the Armed Forces Replacement Office in addition to the GAO, things only got worse. Then he also had to report to and accept instructions from the chief of the OKW, *Generaloberst* Keitel – and these instructions often clashed with those of his superior in his capacity as GAO head, *Generaloberst* Fromm.

The GAO was headquartered in the so-called *Bendlerstrasse*, a block of office buildings erected in 1911 and seat of the General Staff since the end of the First World War. Olbricht's office was only down the hall and round the corner from *Generaloberst* Fromm's. Keitel, in contrast, had his headquarters in a completely different location, often far removed from Berlin, much less the *Bendlerstrasse*. This meant that Olbricht was *de facto* more under Fromm's control than Keitel's, and the relationship between Fromm and Olbricht was complex. One of the staff officers of the GAO in the early years felt that the two generals got on very well together, if nothing else because Fromm liked to think of himself as above all the day-to-day 'dirty work', and so left this to Olbricht. Officers who served in GAO later in the war, however, report a more strained relationship between the two generals, which they attribute to Fromm's own deteriorating position. There is considerable evidence to suggest that as the war dragged on Fromm lost the respect of Hitler's staff at OKW and of the Army General Staff. Olbricht, in contrast, as his appointment to be head of the Armed Forces Replacement Office suggests, was climbing in favour. Fromm resented it; indeed, he saw Olbricht's promotion as an insult to him personally. General Reinhardt remembers briefings that Olbricht had to break off abruptly because of Fromm's rude or sarcastic behaviour or comments.

To make matters even worse, some of Olbricht's subordinate departments also had bizarre dual chains of command. To name just one example, the General Inspector of Armour was subordinate to the GAO on one hand, but reported directly to Hitler on the other. This meant that some of Olbricht's subordinates could also bypass him (just as he did Fromm) and report to his superiors in OKW if they so chose.

Meanwhile, the war was going from bad to worse; and the demands for personnel and materiel came not just from the Army, but from the Air Force, Navy, SS, the police, the Hitler Youth, the Labour Organisation (*Organisation Todt*), and even the Finance Ministry with its customs and border protection troops. Furthermore, keeping the war machine running meant that the factories, too, had to be adequately manned, and farm labour available to both sow and harvest. The railways had to run smoothly, too, if all the farm produce was to get to the cities and the industrial products – the arms, ammunition, and other equipment – to the Army at the front. All these sectors and organisations needed personnel.

When Speer got a special mandate from Hitler to secure the basis of industrial production, Olbricht feared significant disruption of military conscription. Fortunately for the *Wehrmacht* (and unfortunately for

Germany's enemies), Olbricht was able to negotiate directly with Speer an agreement that ensured they both got more or less what they needed to operate effectively. More difficult to counter were the increasingly stringent and arrogant demands of the Air Force and SS for preferential access to the pool of conscripts.

Lastly, Hitler's management methods presented huge challenges to the head of the GAO, as to all his subordinates. As is well known, Hitler either took a long time to make decisions or he intentionally kept his subordinates in the dark about his plans. At all events, his orders often appeared to come out of the blue, and he was not above deceiving his own staff as well as his enemies: for example, ordering demobilisation after the French campaign, or ordering plans to be drawn up for the invasion of England and Gibraltar in 1941. For an organisation like the GAO this leadership style was particularly difficult because all of its activities were long-term in nature, requiring good preparation and planning.

As the war changed from one of lightning successes to one of dogged defence, Hitler sank deeper and deeper into a 'bunker mentality', in which he ordered nothing more subtle than to 'fight to the last man'. His psychopathic refusal to face reality and admit impending setbacks meant that again and again, commanders were prevented from taking timely action to avoid greater casualties and disasters. Likewise, Olbricht's GAO was forced to witness case after case where suggestions for the timely production, stocking, or distribution of materiel were dismissed – only to receive frantic orders to produce the needed materiel at short notice. Instead of careful planning, improvisation was the order of the day.

A classic example of this was the attempt by Olbricht to place orders for winter uniforms for the Army in the spring of 1941. His purchase orders were stopped because his superiors in OKW were insistent that only a small garrison would be required to remain in the Soviet Union after the 'victory'; the bulk of the troops were to be back in Germany *before* winter set in. When the *Wehrmacht* did get bogged down in the Russian mud and snow and the Soviet counter-offensive started in December 1941, millions of troops were caught in the Russian winter with only summer uniforms. The appeal of the Propaganda Ministry for women to turn in their fur coats 'for the troops' was nothing but a cheap gimmick. Not one of the furs was sent to the fighting troops (one wonders who profited), and it was months before the production of winter uniforms could be geared up to the levels necessary.

Olbricht was reportedly livid. He knew what the price of inadequately clothed soldiers could be. In 1812 another vast army had gone all the way to Moscow in triumph, and been utterly destroyed by the Russian winter. But Napoleon's Army did not freeze to death because of the hubris of the dictator. Napoleon *had* provided his troops with winter uniforms, but they had discarded them during the long, hot march into Russia the previous summer. In Germany in 1941, Olbricht had to stand by and watch while his commander-in-chief condemned millions of men to unnecessary suffering out of thoughtless arrogance.

And this was only one incident. Olbricht had to face these kinds of senseless decisions with cruel consequences day after day. There can be no question that although he kept fighting for what he knew was right, he did become increasingly cynical. Bit by bit his spirit was worn down by the need to fight these unnecessary battles for what should have been common-sense, even self-evident, decisions. And with each of these exhausting and depressing fights, his hatred of Hitler grew.

Yet despite having to fight for what should have been self-evident; despite the ever more difficult circumstances and the increasingly negative war situation; indeed, despite doing all he could to prepare a coup that would bring down the mad dictator, Olbricht and his GAO performed magnificently. The entire German war machine, on all its too many fronts, was dependent upon the GAO functioning – and functioning well. If the GAO had failed in its task of providing replacement troops, equipment, weapons, or munitions to the fighting units, then not all of Manstein's or Kluge's strategic genius, nor all the courage of Germany's brave fighting men, could have prevented the front from collapsing. Likewise, the increased production of German industry under Speer's leadership would have been useless, if it had not been for the successful work of the GAO in seeing that these products were distributed to units that were refilled over and over with the troops the GAO raised and outfitted. The statistics show that Olbricht's achievements were never equalled by his successors. The volume of replacements reached its peak just before 20 July 1944.

The extent, importance, and emotional burden that Olbricht's duties at GAO constituted should never be forgotten when assessing his role in the

German Resistance. Olbricht was at no point during the Resistance a *retired* general. He was not an out-of-office politician with a lot of time on his hands to reflect on events or write policy papers. Nor was he simply a tiny cog in a huge war machine and so working in an eight-to-five job, as were others such as Counts Moltke and Yorck or Adam von Trotz zu Solz.

The weight of Olbricht's responsibility for the entire Army meant that he worked without fixed office hours, without weekends, and without leave for the last several years of his life. This, too, should not be overlooked when evaluating his performance in the Resistance. Goerdeler had retired from politics in 1937. Beck resigned in 1938. Hoepner was dismissed by Hitler for 'disobedience' in January 1942. Wizleben retired for health reasons in March 1942. Oster was suspended from office in April 1943. All these Resistance leaders had time to reflect, to meet and discuss options, to draft constitutions and appeals, and to draw up plans for a coup and a post-Hitler government. Even most of the other Resistance leaders who remained on active service at least got some leave. Tresckow had six months of home leave between April and October 1943. Stauffenberg had six months of convalescence, admittedly after being severely wounded, during almost exactly the same period. But Olbricht had no regular hours and no opportunity to 'recharge his batteries', stand back from the perpetual crisis that the war had become, and gain a new perspective – or just plain rest. Undoubtedly, this simple physical fact also had a significant impact on Olbricht's perspective and behaviour. He never had the luxury of focusing exclusively on the Resistance or the coup. Devoted as he was to destroying Hitler's government and stopping Hitler's senseless war, his commitment to the troops was too great to allow him to risk neglecting them. As the statistics show, the GAO under Olbricht never let the fighting troops down – but it knew no 'close of business', either.

Head of the General Army Office: Portrait of a General
No official assessment of Olbricht's performance as head of the General Army Office survives. His personnel file was histrionically destroyed after his posthumous expulsion from the Army on 4 August 1944. On the other hand, there are irrefutable indications that his superiors valued him, starting with his promotion to *General der Infanterie* (full general in British Army parlance and three-star general in US terminology) on 1 June 1940. He was awarded

the German Cross in Silver on 1 August 1943, and two days later entrusted with the additional responsibilities of heading the pivotal *Wehresatzamt* (Armed Forces Replacement Office) without being relieved of his duties as chief of the General Army Office. It is noteworthy that Olbricht was charged with these vitally important offices and promoted and decorated accordingly *in spite of the fact* that he was widely known to be 'pessimistic' about the war and openly critical of Hitler's 'dilettantism'.

Olbricht retained the trust of his superiors although, in sharp contrast to many other military commanders, chiefs of staff, and department heads, he consistently refused to issue orders or sign letters with 'Heil Hitler!' His secretaries report that in the GAO the standard form of address was likewise 'Good Morning', 'Good Day', or even 'God's Greeting' (*Grüss Gott*), but never 'Heil Hitler!' Anni Lerche, Olbricht's secretary for more than four years, claims that Hitler was referred to as 'the carpet biter', among other derogatory titles. All this suggests that Olbricht's competence was so highly valued that the Nazi leadership was willing to tolerate his political attitudes.

Olbricht himself characterised his relationship with his superiors, most especially OKW (i.e. Keitel and Hitler's inner circle), as 'a marriage of convenience'. He said to one of his staff officers that the Nazis would 'exploit him as an indispensable and incorruptible expert to the very limits – and then eliminate him as a dangerous witness to many damning actions on the part of the Party and the military leadership as soon as his work was done'.[3]

Those who served under Olbricht in the GAO likewise unanimously attest to his competence and intelligence. He is described as 'particularly clever', as 'relaxed', and as an 'agreeable superior'. According to one of his staff officers: 'He had great self-assurance and composure. But he lacked any mark of vanity or indication that his immense power had changed him in any way. Any kind of theatrics was alien to him.'[4] Even those officers who on 20 July 1944 took up arms against him and arrested him before the arrival of the Guards Battalion under Major Remer do not cast any aspersions on Olbricht's capabilities. Fritz Harnack says that: 'My personal impression of General Olbricht was that he was a very precise, very exacting officer who led his office in a very correct manner.'[5] Bolko von der Heyde, another of Olbricht's section heads who opposed him on 20 July 1944, said of him: 'Olbricht was a very decent man. His entire manner, the way he handled his subordinates and so forth, was that of a good – really good – department head. There is no question.'[6]

Officers who got to know him somewhat better discovered the breadth of his knowledge and his humour as well. His first General Staff officer at GAO, Fritz Merker, remarked, 'It was a pleasure to work with him. ... He was a truly educated man, [who] could have been a professor [as much as a general] ... although he was a bit of a cynic, too.'[7] And Olbricht's chief of staff, Hellmuth Reinhardt, was of the opinion that: 'Olbricht had a wonderful sense of humour, and irony, too. The Latin expression *"suaviter in modo, fortiter in re"* fit him perfectly.'[8]

Regarding Olbricht's charisma, however, opinions diverge. While some of Olbricht's former subordinates claim that he was 'the soul of the entire department' and that his 'subordinates – old and young alike – hung on his words'[9] or simply that he was 'greatly loved by soldiers and officers both',[10] others found him 'colourless'.[11] While Major Lübben felt that 'You didn't need to see the Knight's Cross on his uniform to recognise that Olbricht was a troop commander of exceptional brilliance and charisma',[12] Colonel Fritz Harnack said, 'I can't imagine him as the C-in-C of an Army.'[13]

Then again, that Olbricht possessed and demonstrated warmth and understanding for others is completely uncontroversial. Everyone who knew him as chief of the GAO agreed on this. Lübben was particularly impressed by the way the general found time for the junior officers, helping them to learn their craft, and always speaking to them in a friendly manner. Olbricht, he felt, was not driven by cold rationality, but by an inner humanity.

Ernst Friedrich remembered one specific evening in which, just when everyone was ready to go home for the night, a new crisis broke that required them to stay and complete a new 'urgent' task. Olbricht called his staff together and explained the situation, told them what they had to do and the deadline, and then, fully aware of how tense and tired they all were, asked them to sit down for a moment. Within minutes, according to Friedrich, volleys of laughter were coming from Olbricht's office as he got them all to relax. Then they all went back to their offices and 'once again' produced top-quality work for the 10:00 deadline the next morning.[14]

Equally indicative of his character, General Olbricht found the time and means to help those who turned to him. The mother of one of his daughter's friends gave birth to a mentally handicapped child. By this time – and far in advance of the mass murders of Jews, Gypsies, and gays – the helpless patients of mental institutions were already being systematically exterminated. The private protests of the Protestant Bishop of Württemberg, Theophil Wurm, and the Minister of the Interior Dr Wilhelm Frick, and the public protests of the Catholic Bishop of Münster, August Graf von Galen, had no impact on the government. Between the issuance of the so-called 'Euthanasia Orders' in January 1940 and the end of the war, more than 150,000 handicapped people – all Germans – were systematically gassed to death in the name of racial purification. The families of the murdered received bills for the costs of extermination and burial. In the case brought to Olbricht's attention by his now 20-year-old daughter, the woman's husband was granted a divorce on the grounds that the mother of a mentally handicapped child was in some way genetically deficient. The husband rapidly remarried, and the woman was left without any alimony or child support, since support for a mentally handicapped child was against the eugenics policies of the state. General Olbricht 'managed' somehow to pay the woman a 'pension' that kept her, and her children, from destitution.

Another picture of Olbricht from this period of his life is particularly interesting because it originates from Axel von dem Bussche, the young officer who later volunteered to use a primitive suicide bomb to assassinate Hitler. He first met Olbricht in the spring of 1942, and this meeting left such an impression on Bussche that 44 years later he could still remember the encounter with great detail and enthusiasm. Axel von dem Bussche related:

> He came into my office: a medium tall, and as I remember it, somewhat stocky man, who began talking about all sorts of unimportant things in a lively, humorous manner.
>
> I've always retained a very warm place in my heart for Olbricht. Without ever forgetting the rules of military courtesy, he was a *delightful* conversationalist, a likeable man. And that's not always what one expects in the Army – any army! – of a superior officer. Furthermore, he was clever, witty, and – one has to say ironically – grimly determined to bring down the [Nazi] regime at the earliest opportunity.[15]

At a later point Olbricht's determination to bring down the Nazi regime will be discussed; but returning to his style as head of the GAO, there is one last account of him from this period, published in 1954, that is based on first-hand remembrances now lost to us. Eberhard Ziller wrote: 'To the simple soldier, Olbricht had the reputation of a "fine" general. They appreciated that beside his official correctness there was also always something accessible and affable about him. Now and then one noticed in his speech and irony a slight Saxon cadence – he came from Dresden – but on the whole a Berliner nature dominated in his refreshingly rapid repartee, his generosity, his sociability, and his courteous tone.'[16]

It is noticeable that the only partially negative comments about Olbricht as head of the GAO come from those officers who were to oppose the coup on 20 July 1944. It is most probable that Olbricht had quickly discerned their loyalty to Hitler and the Nazi regime and intentionally kept his distance from them, long before the coup attempt was made. This would best explain the fact that so many other witnesses found him warm, accessible, and winning, while the men who were to arrest him and turn him over for execution found him 'colourless'.

Olbricht and the War

Before turning to Olbricht as a Resistance fighter, it is important to examine his attitude towards the war in general, and most especially the war against the Soviet Union. As is widely recognised today, the unexpectedly easy, rapid, and complete (except for that annoying little island north of the English Channel) victory in the West in 1940 shattered virtually all opposition to Hitler and his regime inside Germany. Up to this point, among an older generation that remembered all too vividly the horrors of the last war, fears of a war with France had intermittently inhibited enthusiasm for Hitler. Now these people also adored the Führer, who had given them the victory that they had been 'robbed' of 20 years earlier. And the military leadership that had doggedly opposed the war in the West had been proved wrong yet again, as during the occupation of the Rhineland, during the annexation of Austria, during the Sudeten Crisis, during the occupation of Czechoslovakia, and during the war in Poland. What was the point of having one's own opinion any more?

As for younger officers, men like Major Claus Graf von Stauffenberg, they were positively intoxicated with this series of victories and Hitler's 'genius'. Stauffenberg is supposed to have said to a fellow General Staff officer: 'Hitler has a sense for military matters. He knew, against the advice of his generals, that the Maginot Line could be breached.'[17] In fact, as Stauffenberg should have known, the plan to outflank the Maginot Line came from one of 'the generals', not Hitler. But Stauffenberg clearly didn't care for details at that time. He was too busy brushing away the dust of pessimism and 'reactionary' thinking that he found in the General Staff, filling it instead with his optimism and vision for a new Germany under the brilliant leadership of Adolf Hitler.[18]

To be fair, as some of his biographers point out, Stauffenberg did seem to feel that a peace of reconciliation with France was preferable to one of oppression, although he favoured the 'destruction' of Britain if the British didn't have the sense to make peace with Hitler. Obviously it would be wrong to impute any real co-alignment of values or goals between Stauffenberg and the Nazi government; but there can be no question that by the summer of 1940, any doubts about the value of the National Socialist 'renewal' that Stauffenberg had occasionally entertained in the past had now been swept away by the victory in the West.

Olbricht, as we have seen, was one of those 'pessimistic' and 'defeatist' generals whom Stauffenberg dismissed for failing to recognise Hitler's genius – or at least his 'sense for military affairs'. While Stauffenberg with awe insisted that Hitler's father was 'no tradesman' but rather 'War', Olbricht continued to be a pessimist and an opponent of Hitler's next war – the war against the Soviet Union. With this opposition he was more isolated than ever before.

The war against the Soviet Union was quite simply a war that the bulk of the German population applauded and supported. For many Germans, the enemy had always been on the Left. Nationalists had blamed the Left, particularly the Communists, for 'stabbing Germany in the back' in 1918 and so causing the entire disaster of armistice, abdication, 'Versailles Ultimatum', Republic, inflation, economic depression, and widespread unemployment: in short, everything evil that had befallen Germany since 1914. And for those elements of the population that did not naturally vilify the Left and Communism, Nazi propaganda had been at work, in a greenhouse environment without opposition parties or a free press, for eight years now. A war against the Soviet Union was sold as a crusade against 'Bolshevism' and, incidentally, a way of winning Germany's allegedly needed 'living space'.

In the officer corps, always more right wing than the population at large, the war against the Soviet Union was greeted with enthusiasm. Even General Hoepner, an opponent of Hitler, saw the war against the Soviet Union as a 'defence of European culture against an Asiatic [sic] flood'.[19]

Not only was there widespread approval of war against the Soviet Union (there had been little opposition to the idea of a war with France, either), but, unlike with France, there was general consensus that a war against the Soviet Union could be won, and won easily. This attitude was the result of overconfidence bred of so many easy successes reinforced by the Soviet difficulties in conquering little Finland. Furthermore, the General Staff was aware of the purges of the Soviet officer corps that had been carried out so mercilessly in the last couple of years. Thus the consensus was that any competence that had been left in the Russian Army after the Revolution had now been exterminated in the purges. Halder confidently predicted that the campaign against the Soviet Union could be won in 14 days – although not ended that rapidly: 'The wide geography and the obstinacy with which resistance would be offered was bound to drag out the conflict for several weeks [sic].'[20] If the chief of the General Staff was so confident of a swift victory, it is hardly surprising that less experienced junior officers, who had known nothing but victory in their entire careers, already imagined themselves settling down on estates in the Ukraine and having a retirement home on the Black Sea.

But Olbricht had tasted defeat before in his life, and he had been to Russia, twice. On the evening before the attack on the Soviet Union the officer on duty found General Olbricht working late. The young General Staff officer handed to Olbricht the very first map of the Russian campaign, which had just been delivered by courier. The young officer took the opportunity to ask the experienced general if the Russian troop concentrations depicted on the map represented any kind of threat. At first Olbricht didn't answer; he just considered the map. And then he said with a sigh, 'Lübben, I know Russia. I fought there in the First World War. I was in the T-3 Department. I have travelled there and I know the people. You and I, Lübben, know the Army which is now about to cross the border. I tell you today: our Army is nothing but a breath of wind upon the wide Russian steppes.'[21]

Other officers of Olbricht's staff likewise noted the general's lack of confidence in an early victory. Major Friedrich reported that Olbricht viewed the war against the Soviet Union as a 'crime against Germany'. Indeed, according to Friedrich, Olbricht was equally unimpressed by Rommel's successes in Africa and referred to the 'Atlantic Wall' as a 'bluff'. More than a year before Stalingrad, Olbricht complained about the lack of defensive positions behind the lines to facilitate a withdrawal. Albert Speer rapidly discerned Olbricht's pessimistic attitude towards the prospects of victory – and his negative opinion of Hitler's military leadership – as soon as he started working closely with him in 1943. Fromm confessed to the Gestapo interrogators, after his arrest on 20 July 1944, that Olbricht felt that 'militarily they were stumbling from one crisis to the next ... and questioned the efficacy of long-term actions, since the situation was bound to be worse two weeks from now'.[22]

In short, Olbricht never believed in the possibility of a German victory. Unlike many other generals, or young officers like Stauffenberg, he was never blinded by the brightness of Hitler's early victories. From the Sudeten Crisis onwards, Olbricht believed that war could only lead to a German defeat. And because of that, he viewed the war as a *crime*.

So why did he stay on, contributing to the war he viewed as criminal? Why not provoke a confrontation with the dictator or his direct superior that could only end in his dismissal? Olbricht clearly was not afraid to die; he had exposed himself to risk and death from the time he was a regimental adjutant dashing on horseback through the artillery fire until, as a divisional commander entitled to stay in the rear, he instead loaded troops on to his staff car to rush forward and seize the bridges over the Wartha a quarter of a century later. And Hitler was not Stalin. When he dismissed a general, even one with whom he was furious, such as Hoepner or Graf Sponeck, he did not kill them. He sent them into retirement 'in disgrace', or at worst confined them in a fortress prison. Olbricht had nothing to fear from a confrontation except loss of uniform and influence.

The idea that one stayed in a job in order to 'prevent worse from happening' is a notion that often comes up in memoirs of Nazi Germany. Many Germans later justified the fact that they were Party members and/or accepted posts and promotions and honours from the Nazis with this excuse. It has been misused so often that it is tainted. And yet it is not entirely absurd. In some cases, decent men really could do a great deal more good by staying in their jobs, or even by moving up to positions of greater power. There are countless instances of German judges, doctors, and bankers helping the persecuted from their positions of relative privilege – something they could not have done had they resigned or emigrated.

Based on what we know about Olbricht's attitudes and his actions, Olbricht did indeed endure in his position for this reason, twice over. On the one hand, he considered the leadership at OKW so 'dilettantish' that he must have feared that German soldiers would suffer unnecessary deprivations if he were to leave his official duties in the hands of less qualified and less dedicated men. On the other hand, he used his key position to further the cause of the Resistance against Hitler.

For Olbricht, the fate of Beck must have been a constant reminder of the consequences of honourable resignation. Beck had protested forthrightly, honestly, and courageously. His opposition to the Nazi regime and, above all, to the war was consistent and unwavering. But once he had resigned, he was no longer a public figure and had no influence on anyone who didn't already know him. He could only effect change *in*directly, by persuading others to act. Furthermore, this influence was worthless unless the men he inspired and advised were themselves in positions of power. Beck and Goerdeler alone could not have made a coup. Only the participation of *active* officers in senior positions made it possible for them to take part in a coup, even indirectly.

Olbricht used his position in the GAO and *Wehrersatzamt* to further Resistance aims in three distinct ways, any one of which would have justified staying on in office. First, he attempted via official channels to minimise the impact of Hitler's sometimes mad leadership decisions. Secondly, he attempted to help those in danger from the regime or already persecuted by it. And thirdly, he exploited his position to create a conspiracy network and, as we shall see, a blueprint for the destruction of the Nazi regime.

Olbricht's efforts via official channels to have an impact on Hitler's military decisions were a component part of his official duties and do not need to be described at length. A couple of examples, however, do throw light on Olbricht's character and his motives.

Olbricht, for example, consistently fought against the creation of new units and in favour of the replacement of casualties in existing units. New units – particularly the so-called Air Force Field Divisions, which were nothing but infantry units dressed in Air Force uniforms and under Air Force officers – consistently had higher casualties than old units. Old units always retained a core of well-trained, experienced, battle-hardened veterans. These 'old-timers' and 'leathernecks' were the men best suited to showing the replacement troops the unwritten laws of survival. New units, however, generally lacked these priceless individuals, and that meant that everyone had to learn everything themselves but all too often didn't have time before they were killed.

The fight for prepared positions in the rear to enable orderly withdrawals was another of Olbricht's almost continuous and usually futile battles. What is interesting about this particular tussle was that it was obviously outside his competence as chief of the GAO. Such preparations belonged in the realm of operational decision making, not to the duties of the GAO. Olbricht was involved only because commanding generals at the front begged him to keep nagging OKW, since no one else appeared to have the courage to do so.

At another point, OKW tried to transfer 500,000 troops from the Home Army to the front. Such a vast number, however, could only be raised if all the training establishments across Germany were gutted. Olbricht responded to the request by saying that since all training would have to stop, he could only give up the 500,000 men if OKW could guarantee him that the deployment of these 500,000 men to the front would lead to an immediate victory, or, in the absence of victory, if the leadership were prepared to make immediate peace. Apparently, even OKW recognised that the suspension of all training was too risky.

Having been persuaded that the *Wehrmacht* troops attached to the Home Army were contributing to the war effort in their own way, the OKW next decided to re-examine all those males in Germany who had been exempted from the draft for one reason or another. Olbricht confirmed without hesitation the exemption of pastors and priests (over the protest of the Party and SS), but did not feel that hairdressers for the film industry deserved the same protection. Here, however, he made a miscalculation. Goebbels protested vehemently, and Hitler personally screamed and insulted Olbricht and his responsible subordinates in one of his infamous rages.

The man most directly attacked in this fit of rage was a certain General von

Unruh, who had been asked to reassess the exemptions. He at once offered his resignation to Olbricht, who talked him out of resigning with the telling argument: 'Only by staying on can we one day hope to prevent the worst from happening to Germany.'[23] A clearer expression of Olbricht's motives for soldiering on in a difficult, thankless, and inglorious job is hard to imagine.

Humanitarian Resistance

While the above activities were strictly within the boundaries of loyal service and in no way constituted any kind of 'resistance' to the Nazi regime, Olbricht used his position in the GAO for a number of activities that were *not* consistent with loyalty to the regime. These activities were not directed towards the elimination of Hitler and his government, but rather sought to counter or circumvent specific Nazi policies. Such activities were much more common in Nazi Germany than direct attempts to bring down the National Socialist state. Although not completely unproblematic, most historians would agree today that such activities constituted a form of 'resistance' within the context of a totalitarian state.

Olbricht was, in consequence of his position, exceptionally well placed to render such acts of humanitarian resistance. Obviously, everything he did in this direction had to be done in secret, often without even the beneficiaries being aware of whom they had to thank. If Olbricht had openly defied the Nazis on humanitarian and racial issues, he would have risked dismissal from his post, which, as we shall see in the next chapter, would have made it almost impossible for the conspiracy against Hitler to function. Indeed, with each year, Olbricht and his GAO became more central to the hopes for a successful coup d'état against Hitler. Consequently, when trying to reconstruct what Olbricht actually did with respect to humanitarian resistance, we are confronted with only fragmentary evidence for those cases of aid that have subsequently come to light. It is reasonable to assume that Olbricht did far more than we can now prove.

Starting with the most inconsequential but telling acts of humanitarian assistance for victims of the regime, we know that Olbricht helped a young woman of 'non-Aryan' background to obtain the necessary permission to marry an officer, although this was strictly against the racial policies of Nazi Germany. In another case, when a woman was interrogated by the Gestapo for possession of Bishop Galen's sermons against the so-called 'Euthanasia Programme', Olbricht allowed her to warn her husband, to whom she had forwarded the sermon, using GAO post (which was faster than the normal field post). When Graf Sponeck was put before a kangaroo court martial, Olbricht helped him with legal assistance, which had been officially denied him. When Hitler 'pardoned' Graf Sponeck and commuted his death sentence to imprisonment, but specifically prohibited the condemned and his family from ever receiving a pension, Olbricht made sure that Graf Sponeck's family got the pension due to a *Generalleutnant* anyway. He then continued to ward off repeated attempts by the SS to get control of Graf Sponeck, and also successfully fought off the SS campaign to dismantle the entire institution of 'fortress imprisonment' (*Festungshaft*). This was an anachronistic form of military punishment in which the condemned was confined to a fortress, but had freedom to move anywhere within it. Clearly this was much more humane than being locked in a single cell – enabling exercise, contact with the entire garrison, and even visitors. No sooner was Olbricht's protective hand removed than Graf Sponeck was murdered. Himmler ordered his execution on the morning of 23 July 1944, although he had been imprisoned since early 1942 and could in no way have contributed to the coup attempt of 20 July 1944.

But in other cases Olbricht's protection was effective even after his own demise, and lives were saved. When Joachim Müller, the director of the Protestant missionary organisation Light in the East, was arrested for 'fraternisation with the Jewish racial enemy', Olbricht arranged for the immediate conscription of this reserve officer to the Army. In the Army he was beyond the reach of the Gestapo, and to this day he believes that only Olbricht's action prevented his certain death in a concentration camp.

All in all, the Military Justice Department was one of Olbricht's most important tools for humanitarian resistance. This department was under Olbricht's authority; and in close cooperation with the military justice Dr Karl Sack, Olbricht was able to protect many soldiers and officers who were accused of political crimes. He was able to warn many on the brink of arrest for political crimes, enabling them to destroy incriminating evidence or alter their behaviour. In other cases he was able to influence directly the trials, or at least the sentencing.

To understand the magnitude of Olbricht's service in this regard, it is important to remember that political trials in Nazi Germany were usually remanded to the infamous *Volksgerichtshof*, or People's Court. This court had been established in April 1934 with the mandate to try all cases of high and national treason (*Hochverrat und Landesverrat*). The court was explicitly instructed *not* to dispense justice, but rather to exterminate the enemies of National Socialism. Both professional and lay judges of the court were selected for their loyalty to the National Socialist regime rather than for their understanding or training in the law. There was no appeal against a decision of the *Volksgerichtshof*, and the punishments were notoriously draconian. To give just a few examples: in 1940 a man received a year in prison merely for saying that German workers were being lied to. The sentence was nine months' imprisonment for saying that Hitler was responsible for the war. But 1940 was a year of victory and benevolence. By the end of the war, such remarks were punished with the death sentence. The death penalty was used for jokes against the leaders of the regime, and by then even diary entries that reflected a lack of faith in final victory could be used as evidence of 'defeatism' – a capital crime. As a result, the number of people sentenced to death increased dramatically in the course of the war, from 926 in 1940 to 5,336 in 1943 – the year before the coup attempt of 20 July 1944 and the explosion in the number of judicial murders that followed it. By 1945 there were so many arrests without warrants and executions without trials that statistics became meaningless. Somewhere between 5,000 and 10,000 political prisoners fell victim to the last spasms of 'retribution' on the part of a dying totalitarian regime.

Olbricht's efforts to keep military personnel out of the hands of the *Volksgerichtshof* were therefore extremely important, but far from uniformly successful. In 1943 the local authorities acted too swiftly to give his office time to intercede on behalf of the military members of the 'White Rose' Resistance cell. The White Rose was a small, intellectual Resistance group composed primarily of medical students at the University of Munich, many of whom were *Wehrmacht* NCOs. The leaders were the students Sophie and Hans Scholl (sister and brother). The soldiers in this group, including Hans Scholl, had witnessed German atrocities and racial policies on the Eastern Front and were so morally outraged that they felt compelled to try to inspire a protest movement. They clandestinely produced pamphlets calling on the German people to rise up against the corrupt and criminal regime of Adolf Hitler. The first of these pamphlets appeared in the spring of 1942. This pamphlet cried out: '... Offer passive resistance – *resistance* – wherever you are. Stop the continuation of this atheistic war machine before it is too late – before the last of our cities lies in ruins like Cologne and the last of our youth has been bled dry for the hubris of a subhuman. Never forget that every people deserves the government which it tolerates!'[24]

It appeared at first that this pamphlet had been an isolated incident, because none followed it until early 1943. The explanation was simple: the active soldiers in the group had been sent on a routine rotation to the front. In early 1943 the pamphlets appeared again: a second, a third, and then a fourth. In this, the last pamphlet of the White Rose, the idealistic students wrote:

> We wish to expressly draw attention to the fact that we are not in the service of any foreign power. Although we know that National Socialist power can only be broken militarily, we are trying to achieve a renaissance of the badly wounded German spirit from within. This rebirth must, however, include a clear recognition of the guilt the German people has laid upon itself, and it must be preceded by a ruthless fight against Hitler and his all-too-numerous henchmen ...
>
> We will not remain silent! We are your guilty conscience! The White Rose will not leave you in peace!
>
> Please copy and pass on![25]

These pamphlets were clearly the work of idealistic young people, largely out of touch with the bulk of the population and unschooled in the methods of effective propaganda. Their idealism and inexperience led to their rapid demise.

By February 1943, the defeat at Stalingrad had started to turn public opinion against Hitler. Believing that the time had come for an uprising of the conscience, the students overplayed their hand in a very bold, not to say foolhardy, distribution action. On 18 February 1943, they went into the main lecture building of Munich University and started laying pamphlets in the halls and stairways in broad daylight. They attracted the attention of the watchman when they dumped a suitcase full of pamphlets from the second-storey landing of the stairway into the inner courtyard. Outraged, the orderly and correct watchman alerted the Gestapo and personally arrested the two Scholls. They and an accomplice, Christian Probst, were charged with treason, tried, sentenced to death, and beheaded within just four days. The executions took place on the same day as the sentencing: 22 February 1943. A further fourteen members of the group were tried in a second trial on 19 April 1943. Of these, three – Professor Huber, Alexander Smorell, and Wilhelm Graf – were likewise sentenced to death, while the others received prison sentences ranging from six months to ten years.

But to return to General Olbricht: Olbricht's efforts to assist those accused of political crimes was not a purely humanitarian affair. It was vitally important to the coup planning that the active conspirators had a degree of 'immunity' from political arrest. This was best provided by the Military Justice Department under Olbricht, which rigorously defended its 'independence'. The Nazi Party was well aware of the Army's 'political unreliability', and for this very reason made repeated efforts to tear all 'political crimes' out of the jurisdiction of the courts martial. There were also continual attempts to create 'special courts' to deal with political crimes *within* the armed forces. Olbricht, as always, had to be very cautious in his actions, because excessive zeal in any one case might just give his enemies in the SS the ammunition they needed to gain jurisdiction over political prisoners and trials within the armed forces generally. It is very much to Olbricht's credit that as long as he lived, he succeeded in retaining a degree of independence for the military justice system. Many hundreds of men who might otherwise have been turned over to the *Volksgerichtshof* or a military equivalent owe him their lives without even knowing his name.

Yet probably the most important humanitarian service Olbricht achieved was the moderation of an order drafted by Nazi fanatics for the treatment of Soviet prisoners of war in the jurisdiction of the Home Army. It is one of the most shameful pages in the history of the German Army, even in this debased era, that Soviet prisoners of war were not treated in accordance with the Geneva Conventions. It is immaterial that the Soviet Union had not signed those conventions. The German Army had a proud tradition of 'correct' behaviour towards prisoners of war, which it maintained by and large, even in the Nazi period, with respect to the

Western Allies. Not so with respect to Soviet prisoners. Just as the Commissar Orders and the Barbarossa Instructions issued before the start of the invasion of the Soviet Union symbolise the intention to fight the war in the East by different rules, so the treatment of Soviet prisoners was from the start characterised by degradation, mistreatment, and neglect. Many thousands of Soviet prisoners were allowed to starve, freeze, and die of thirst. Others were treated hardly better than the concentration camp inmates. Soviet prisoners were used as slave labour in the areas just behind the front, and on the home front.

This is where Olbricht had a small but significant opportunity to exert humanitarian influence. One of his staff officers, Hermann Lübben, remembers vividly that a draft order was forwarded to the GAO from OKW and landed on his desk. It was supposed to be issued to the Home Army over General Fromm's signature. Lübben was appalled to find the order 'an expression of the total inhumanity of the NS system' and full of violations of international law with respect to the treatment of prisoners of war.[26] Lübben immediately informed Olbricht about what he had on his desk, and started trying to find out via the back door just what kind of leeway the GAO had for changing the orders. He was told that it was a *'Führerbefehl'* – i.e. an order directly from Hitler and as such absolutely immutable. Olbricht requested that Lübben brief the already retired generals Beck and Hoepner on the orders. Shortly thereafter, Lübben received routine orders to take up a staff position with the troops fighting to relieve Stalingrad, and soon found himself a prisoner of war in the Soviet Union.

Lübben was shown a copy of the actual order regarding the treatment of POWs in the Home Army issued by Fromm 43 years later. Lübben reacted emphatically:

The orders that came down to us from OKW with respect to the treatment of Russian prisoners of war was inhumane and a violation of every law of humanity and all international law. The consequences would have been terrible damage to the image of the German people and for German prisoners in the hands of our enemies. The actual order issued by the Home Army is a perfect example of how Olbricht managed to transform an order initially characterised by the National Socialist obsession with extermination into something more tolerable. Olbricht was in no position to prevent the violations of the Geneva Conventions, but he certainly removed some of the sting, and that is very much to Olbricht's credit.[27]

Apparently, Olbricht wriggled out of using the OKW draft by adapting the orders already issued in the Field Army. These were bad enough and also clearly in violation of the Geneva Conventions, but not quite so characterised by 'the obsession with extermination' as the OKW draft. Even here Olbricht managed to insert the key phrase: 'Every form of torture and cruelty is beneath the dignity of a German soldier and is to be avoided.'[28] Thus countless Soviet prisoners of war undoubtedly owe immeasurable thanks to the 'obscure' general working at a thankless job in GAO, without ever having heard his name.

Chapter 10

RESISTANCE TO HITLER

Review and Summary of the German Resistance to Hitler, 1933–44

Before examining in detail Olbricht's role in the military conspiracy that culminated in the coup attempt of 20 July 1944, it is useful to review the total landscape of Resistance activity inside Nazi Germany. This will help to put the efforts of the conspirators into better perspective.

Communist Resistance
The German Communist Party (*Kommunistische Partei Deutschlands*, or KPD) deserves some credit for arguably being the first party to offer organised resistance to the Nazi regime, although this resistance is somewhat tarnished by the fact that the KPD had also opposed the Weimar Republic. Thus, although the KPD called for a general strike almost immediately after Hitler was named chancellor, this did not represent any particular change of tactic or tone from its shrill abuse of all the elected governments that had preceded Hitler since 1 December 1930. Indeed, the last three governments of the Weimar Republic were routinely derided as 'fascist', and the KPD had called for general strikes against them as well.

Furthermore, the KPD consistently advocated violent revolution against the Republic, and even after Hitler had dissolved the unions and started on his path to dictatorship, the Central Committee of the KPD continued to see the Socialists and the independent unions – not the Nazis – as the most dangerous enemies of the working class. Thus the Central Committee called for the 'destruction' of the Social Democratic Party (SPD) rather than perceiving in it an ally in a struggle against Nazi oppression.

Yet while the KPD focused its hatred on the SPD, the Nazis were busy rounding up and imprisoning (in the 'wild' concentration camps) German Communist leaders, intellectuals, members of parliament, journalists, and others. Because the KPD had already been banned and all the Communist members of the *Reichstag* had already been put in

171

concentration camps or gone into hiding, the KPD was not represented in the *Reichstag* when Hitler introduced the 'Enabling Law', which granted him indefinite dictatorial powers. In addition, the centralised structure of the KPD, in which the leaders were effectively appointed from above and (as in the NSDAP) seen as 'infallible', made it relatively easy for the NSDAP to shatter the organisation of the KPD. The massive arrests of KPD leaders left the party membership largely headless.

Yet with surprising speed, the remaining members of the KPD reorganised into illegal cells and prepared to fight on for their cause. The problem was that the party line was dictated in Moscow; and so the KPD, even underground and in exile, 'resisted' Hitler only to the extent that Stalin ordered it to do so. Initially, the KPD was only concerned about establishing an underground party organisation. A secondary activity was the production and distribution of leaflets condemning the Nazis and their policies, much as the KPD had condemned the government of Weimar, and often in virtually identical language. The lack of any real attempt to bring down the Nazi government is explained by the fact that in Moscow the NSDAP government was seen as a step in the right direction: a step nearer to revolution and the dictatorship of the proletariat.

Then during the half decade from late 1934 to 1939, Stalin started to worry about possible German and Polish aggression, and so Soviet policy changed and now advocated a 'Red Front' against Fascism. However, the conclusion of the Molotov–Ribbentrop Pact in August 1939 meant another about-turn. Abruptly all opposition to Hitler, Stalin's partner in the aggression against Poland, had to cease. German Communist leaders who, persecuted in Germany, had fled to the Soviet Union soon disappeared into Stalin's gulags, many never to appear again. Only Germany's invasion of the Soviet Union turned the tables yet again.

Henceforth, 'resistance' to Hitler's government became the sacred cause of all Communists. The problem for those Communists still at liberty in Germany was that their resistance automatically became 'national' and not just 'high' treason, because they were now openly and unabashedly supporters of one of Germany's military enemies. The fact that they reported all their activities back to the leadership in Moscow, and so to Germany's bitterest enemy, made the Communists very suspect in the eyes of other patriots – even, and most especially, the Socialists.

The latter, furthermore, had had bitter experience with betrayals on the part of the KPD in earlier years.

Most significantly, at no time in the history of the KPD did it advocate democratic government. The goal of the KPD was always the establishment of a dictatorship and the replacement of one infallible leader (Hitler) with another (Stalin). Thus while KPD policies sometimes took the form of 'resistance' to Hitler, in fact the KPD was always the handmaiden of Stalin and the Soviet Union. As such, long before this was made explicit by the state of war between Germany and the Soviet Union, their activities were more those of agents in the service of a foreign power than those of a genuine domestic opposition to the National Socialist government.

Socialist Resistance

The SPD, in contrast, was one of the pillars of the Weimar Republic. Hitler's thugs had been opposed in countless street brawls by members of the SPD's youth organisations and other SPD members. Hitler's appointment as chancellor was met with mass demonstrations. More importantly, the SPD was the only party that voted unanimously against Hitler's 'Enabling Law'. To be sure, the SPD also underestimated Hitler at first and believed they could oppose him using legal (indeed, parliamentary) means, but it was not alone in such naivety. Furthermore, it remained a staunch and consistent opponent of the National Socialist regime even after it was forced underground and into exile.

However, a major problem for the SPD was that its power had traditionally rested on its popular appeal to voters. The SPD had been a successful *mass* party which had survived persecution at the hands of Chancellor Bismarck, essentially because Bismarck was a Prussian aristocrat who respected the rule of law and Friedrich the Great's prohibition of torture and the misuse of power. By 1933, the SPD was no longer revolutionary (despite its rhetoric), and it had neither the means nor the aptitude for seizing power illegally. Its only 'weapon', apart from winning elections, was the general strike. But a general strike also depended on *mass* support, and even in the years of the SPD's greatest popularity it had proved a dull and ineffective weapon.

After the 'Enabling Law' was passed, parliamentary opposition became impossible. Meanwhile, many of the more outspoken critics of National

Socialism, such as the Socialist member of parliament from Lübeck, Julius Leber, had already been thrown into concentration camps. Indeed, at the time the 'Enabling Law' was brought before the *Reichstag*, no less than 25 SPD members of parliament had already been arrested. The courageous vote against the 'Enabling Law' – carried out despite the threats of the SS and the Nazi Party – led to further arrests, and in June the SPD itself was outlawed.

Henceforth, like the Communists, the SPD could only continue to operate illegally. This it did, like the Communists, by forming cells and printing and distributing leaflets that drew attention to the evils of National Socialism and its policies. As more and more of the workers and intellectuals who had once voted SPD became increasingly seduced by Hitler's successes, however, the remnants of the SPD leadership had to give up any dream of bringing down Hitler's government. The best they could hope for was to keep their ideology alive, to retain their contacts with one another, and to provide assistance to those who were persecuted for their beliefs by the regime.

However, unlike the KPD, the SPD had no supreme leader giving orders and dictating policy, and no foreign power whose interests had to be pursued. This meant that Social Democratic opposition rapidly splintered. The cells of resistance became ever more separated from one another as the Gestapo struck or members fled into exile. These various groups, largely isolated from one another, either had or soon developed their own visions of Socialism – or at least of the tactics that needed to be pursued in the fight against the Nazi dictatorship. These views and tactics often deviated from what the party leadership in exile propagated. In short, there was no single 'Socialist' resistance movement, but rather many people or groups that had belonged to, or voted for, or merely sympathised with, the SPD in the past, and now these hoped for a future in which Socialism would play a role.

It was, above all, these Socialist cells that, used to helping those of their members who were wanted by the Gestapo, supported Jews, pacifists, deserters, and many other individuals persecuted by the regime. Many Socialists paid for their courage with their freedom and their lives, but they were on the whole engaged in humanitarian acts of resistance, not actively trying to topple the Nazi government. Only a few leaders of the Socialist or union movements succeeded in establishing contact with other centres of opposition and through these promoted the activities of the conspirators centred around General Beck.

Intellectual Resistance: The Kreisauer Circle

Finally, there is one last group of opposition leaders that needs to be mentioned, although they are harder to define and even their modern designation, 'the Kreisauer Circle', was invented by the Gestapo. The Kreisauer Circle was really little more than a loose network of like-minded people who, convinced that National Socialism was evil and would one day be destroyed, consciously set out to develop ideas of what a future German state *ought* to look like. Unlike the KPD or SPD, the Kreisauer Circle had no ready-made answers or ideology, and it is to their credit that they did not simply want a restoration of something that had gone before and been proved wanting, whether that was the monarchy or the Weimar Republic.

The Kreisauer Circle was established by two young men, Helmuth James Graf von Moltke and Peter Graf Yorck von Wartenburg, but its composition was never fixed or formal. The two founders simply consulted friends and friends of friends, and contacted people that they felt were experts in one field or another, to help them address the various aspects of creating a future post-Nazi regime. On the whole, the dynamics and energy for the group came from the younger generation, but much of the expertise in specific fields (constitutional law, economics, foreign policy) came from an older generation.

Many of the members of the group were religious socialists: men who rejected the Marxists' contempt for religion and believed that true Christianity led to a kind of socialism. It was one of the group's goals to bring the Church and the working class together for the sake of national renewal. But it would be wrong to suggest that there was any single ideology that united the group. The Kreisauer Circle shared an abhorrence of National Socialism and the desire to work towards a better future, at least in theory, but not a dogma.

These loose ties of friendship, based on a shared perception of
Socialism, first started to coagulate into a more coheren
same time as the first coup plans began to develo
Although the two central figures in the Kr
civilians with legal backgrounds, they

famous military families. Moltke was a great-nephew of the *Feldmarschall* von Moltke who had been so influential in the General Staff and in winning Germany's wars in the second half of the nineteenth century. Yorck was descended from the Prussian general who had forced the Prussian king to abandon Napoleon in 1812 by – without orders – pulling his Prussian corps out of Napoleon's Army. Both men had many ties of friendship and kin to the officer corps.

It was in the second half of 1940 that the first effort was made to bring 'everyone' together in a joint meeting. This took place over a weekend at the estate of Graf Moltke, Kreisau in Silesia. The decision was taken at this meeting to seek contact with leaders of the two dominant faiths in Germany – the Lutheran and the Catholic Churches – and with leaders of the SPD and the unions. Likewise, in early 1941, contact was established with two retired chiefs of the German General Staff, Ludwig Beck and Franz Halder. Contacts eventually reached all the way to the KPD and other Communist circles, such as the so-called Red Orchestra, a tiny cell that passed secret military information to the Soviets. In the interests of security, however, only the two leaders, Yorck and Moltke, knew about all the contacts. Most of the 'networking' was done in very small groups, and mostly in Berlin itself. However, there were a series of larger meetings devoted to specific themes that took place on country estates outside Berlin, predominantly those owned by either Moltke or Yorck.

At these meetings degree of consensus was attained on such themes as the need t itarian or monopolistic parties and unions and replace listic structures, enabling free choice and co Circle can be said to have generally favoured ottom up to the creation of central organs the Circle favoured a kind of European Europe'. In conjunction with this goal, ith the resistance movements in the n effort to lay the foundations for

emphasis the Kreisauer Circle edoms. It was in this context tutional law and economics. eed in a constitution, the

Kreisauer Circle was acutely aware that economic realities often effectively robbed people of their theoretical freedoms. Desperation for food and work, above all, could drive men to extremes, and hence a degree of economic security was a necessary precondition to individual freedom. The Circle, therefore, gave economic policy a great deal of attention and sought ways to ensure minimum standards of living.

None of these concepts are particularly radical. They were, rather, the common denominators that united the group without representing any particular innovation. And, of course, the devil is in the detail. By early 1944, in part due to the arrest of Helmuth Graf Moltke, the Circle started to disintegrate. Some of the members, notably Peter Graf Yorck, sought closer ties to Stauffenberg and the conspirators of 20 July. Some advocated closer cooperation with the Communists. Almost all wanted 'the Army' – or rather, those few generals in the Army with shared enmity to Hitler – 'to act'.

In short, everyone associated with the Kreisauer Circle was acutely aware that they – the Circle – had no means to bring down the Nazi government. They knew that all their planning could only have meaning if the Nazi government were either defeated militarily or toppled in a coup.

An Allied victory, especially after the declaration of a policy of 'unconditional surrender' in January 1943, offered little real opportunity for the Kreisauer Circle to exercise any kind of influence over the shape of a future Germany. A coup, in contrast, was the very best means for them to have a say in a post-Hitler regime. Nevertheless, several members of the group, most notably Helmuth Graf Moltke himself, opposed the idea of assassination, as it was feared that Hitler's murder would create a martyr legend around which future National Socialists would rally. It was also argued that Germany had to be completely and utterly defeated in order to teach the majority a lesson about the consequences of their earlier adoration of Hitler and acceptance of totalitarianism. However, the bulk of the members of the Circle recognised that the assassination of Hitler was a necessary prerequisite to a coup d'état; only Hitler's death would free the men of the *Wehrmacht* of their oath to him. It could, furthermore, be expected to have the added benefit of simultaneously demoralising Hitler's adherents.

In summary, it is fair to say that the Kreisauer Circle was more an opposition group than a Resistance organisation. For actual resistance, for deeds, it was dependent on those few men in Germany who still had a weapon with which to fight Hitler: i.e. the anti-Nazi elements inside the upper echelons of the German Army. Ultimately, all German opposition elements interested in actually ending the National Socialist dictatorship from within, rather than waiting for delivery from abroad, were dependent on these men. This is the reason why those conspirators working actively on plans to assassinate Hitler and replace his regime with one based on principles of law remain the focus of any study of German opposition and resistance to Hitler. Let us return and focus on the Military Resistance.

Military Resistance

As described earlier, the military leadership had, sporadically and in differing constellations, considered taking action against Hitler from the moment it became apparent that he might actually be entrusted with the government. The issues at stake, the Army's independence, the honour of a commander, the risk of war, had varied over time. In the late summer of 1938, however, things had reached a point where the second most senior officer in the German Army, the chief of the General Staff, felt compelled to resign in protest against the military plans and foreign policy of the civilian government.

Then, having exhausted all legal means of protesting against the impending war, a select group of senior officers actively planned a coup d'état against the civilian head of state. However, when this coup had to be aborted because of the Allied capitulation to Hitler at Munich, the military opposition largely disintegrated. Not that the opponents of the regime were in any way reconciled with National Socialism or co-opted by the regime; but they saw no opportunity for action against the government, and their official duties scattered them.

In the next year and a half, Hitler's military plans met with varying degrees of opposition on the part of military commanders for largely tactical reasons, but no further coordinated efforts to plan or work towards the removal of the Nazi government were undertaken by military leaders. Nevertheless, the deposition of Hitler remained an imperative objective for retired *Generaloberst* Beck.

Beck saw clearly that Hitler's war aims were neither reasonable nor limited and that they *must* lead Germany into a world war, which it could not possibly win. Such a world war, he reasoned, could only end in disaster for Germany, and so Beck argued passionately, in his own intellectual manner, that the officer corps had the duty to eliminate the cause of Germany's impending catastrophe: Hitler and the Nazi regime. It is wrong to suggest that this opposition on Beck's part had anything in common with supporting Hitler's policies 'only as long as they were victorious'. Beck did not turn against Hitler only after he had been defeated. He turned against Hitler at the very height of his success and popularity, and he abhorred Hitler, his policies, and his regime.

As a soldier and former chief of staff, it is only natural that Beck focused on and justified his opposition most passionately and extensively in military terms, but he soon gathered around himself a network of civilians who shared his views of Hitler and the regime. These were men like Goerdeler; Johannes Popitz, a former Prussian finance minister; Hjalmar Schacht, a former economics minister; and Ulrich von Hassel, a diplomat and former ambassador to Rome – in short, men of proven competence in a variety of fields. They were men of an older generation, bound by a sense of responsibility and by a code of honour. They were all men who were as convinced as Beck was himself that action had to be taken against the Nazi regime, even if this was technically high treason. They sought not merely to end the war, but also to end the dishonour that was besmirching their beloved country. Again and again, Beck worded his appeal for action against the regime in terms of duty: the duty of honourable and responsible men to eliminate criminals and madmen. It was an attitude shared by all in his circle of friends and co-conspirators.

Yet Beck could not take direct action. He was no longer in a position of power. But he still had influence, immense influence, within the Army based on the respect that an entire generation of still-active officers had for him. It was probably due to Beck's influence with Halder that Olbricht was denied his place among the up-and-coming divisional commanders on the Western Front and sent to take over the GAO. He was most probably sent there because Beck wanted to have a proven non-Nazi in a key position in the Home Army.

When Olbricht assumed his double duties as chief of the General Army Office and Beck's man in the Home Army, Germany was on the brink of going to war with the modern, well-equipped, larger French Army supported by an elite expeditionary force from Great Britain. The efforts of senior commanding generals to postpone this confrontation had been successful; incrementally the timing for the offensive was pushed back until the spring. Those generals who had opposed the offensive merely for tactical reasons had been appeased and co-opted. Beck, however, anticipated a repeat of 1914: a war of high attrition with no clear winner at best and a rapid German defeat at worst.

Beck's calculation was that as soon as the German Army got bogged down in the West, Hitler's popularity would plummet. This in turn would create the political environment necessary for a successful coup d'état against the dictator. Olbricht's secret job – from the moment he took over his post at the General Army Office – was to prepare plans for a future coup that could be implemented as soon as the 'right' political situation developed.

From the start, Olbricht worked very closely with Hans Oster. Both men recognised that while a lone man might theoretically successfully kill Hitler, this alone would not bring down the Nazi regime. There were too many in the Nazi hierarchy able and willing to exploit their powerful positions and control of troops, media, and finance to retain power for themselves, at least for a period. Thus, these two conspirators never considered an assassination in isolation. For the Beck–Olbricht–Oster group, assassination was always perceived as the first and necessary precondition for a coup, but not the end in itself.

Oster, working as he did in counter-intelligence, had access to explosives and a variety of other dubious tools useful for planning, and executing, an assassination. He was in consequence responsible for planning the assassination: the trigger for a coup. Olbricht's job, on the other hand, was to exploit his access to information and people in the GAO both to gain insight into the dictator's apparatus and to create lines of communication between like-minded opponents of the regime.

Obviously, neither Olbricht nor Oster commanded troops. They could not simply order the arrest of leading Nazis or seize control of the apparatus of the state by force of arms. In order to carry out a coup, even after a successful assassination, Oster and Olbricht needed a senior troop commander who was willing to order the troops under his command to take over physically those installations critical to control of the state. Olbricht could plan, but only a commanding general could act. And so both Olbricht and Oster were condemned to inaction until two conditions were met. First, the political and/or military environment had to be altered sufficiently for the popular mood to turn against Hitler; and secondly, a senior commander with troops under his command had to be willing to take part in the coup.

In the months leading up to the invasion of the Soviet Union, two orders were released by OKW for distribution to the senior officers of the Army. These orders, the Commissar Order and the Barbarossa Instructions, were clear violations of the Geneva Conventions and Germany's own military code. The Commissar Order stated that all captured commissars (the political officers of the Soviet armed forces) were to be 'eliminated' immediately. In short, they were not to be treated as prisoners of war, even if they surrendered. Nor were they to be accorded any kind of trial, but simply murdered. The Barbarossa Instructions were a much lengthier and vaguer document that, among other things, authorised the taking and execution of hostages and exempted German troops from punishment for 'acts of retribution'. Both these orders were signed not by Hitler but rather by the commander-in-chief of the Army, *Generaloberst* von Brauchitsch. They effectively ordered the German Army to engage in atrocities and granted impunity for crimes against international law.

Many senior officers, including several field marshals and Army Group commanders, were outraged by the orders. Olbricht tried to use the orders as a recruiting tool for the conspiracy. Beck and Goerdeler likewise contacted senior officers, acquainted them with these orders, and tried to persuade them that the time had come to 'put an end' to Hitler's criminal activities.

The response of the senior commanders is telling. They *did* protest. They sent staff officers to OKW to tell Keitel and Brauchitsch that the orders were 'unacceptable' or would have detrimental effects on discipline and morale. A variety of first-hand accounts corroborate that the orders, when issued, were accompanied by verbal counter-orders *not* to follow these illegal orders. But such anecdotal evidence only shows that here and there, in specific instances, commanders chose to distance themselves from these orders. The behaviour of German troops in the Soviet Union belies the myth that the *Wehrmacht* consistently repudiated these orders.

Thus it was with these orders, if not before, that any clear distinction that might previously have been drawn between the 'criminal Nazis' and the 'decent' or 'upright' military was lost beyond recall. Certainly, looked at in retrospect, it is true that the greatest atrocities – the death camps and concentration camps, the 'Euthanasia Programme', and the forced labour – were Nazi inventions. On the whole, the German armed forces fought a conventional war. But as Beck, Goerdeler, Olbricht, and Oster tried to make clear to the responsible commanders before it was too late, with these orders the German Army became accomplices in Hitler's illegal policies. With these orders, the Army abandoned any claim to morality.

By September 1941, the German Army was mired deep inside Russia, and the SS had been hard at work carrying out Hitler's racial policies. At Army Group Centre a group of staff officers had become witnesses to atrocities at Babi Yar near Kiev in the Soviet Union in which close to 34,000 Jewish civilians were massacred on 29–30 September 1941. They were so horrified by what was being done in Germany's name that they came to the conclusion that Hitler and his regime had to be deposed.

The driving force in the Army Group Centre Resistance cell was the relatively junior staff officer Henning von Tresckow. Tresckow was born in January 1901, more than twelve years after Friedrich Olbricht and almost seven years before Claus Graf Stauffenberg. He was, and was proud to be, a Prussian 'junker': that is, a member of the more or less impoverished gentry of Prussia, which had served their King and Country as officers for generations. He was raised in a devout Protestant tradition, and he always saw his duty to God and country as central to his life. His father was a retired general, already 51 at the time of his birth, and his mother was the daughter of a Prussian minister of culture, Graf Robert Zedlitz-Trützschler.

The First World War started before Tresckow had completed gymnasium. In 1917, still only 16 years of age, he volunteered for service and was accepted by the prestigious First Guards Infantry Regiment in Potsdam. On 5 June 1918, at only 17 years of age, he was commissioned a lieutenant in the Imperial Army. He was sent immediately to the Western Front and took part in the last disastrous German offensive and the fateful retreat. During these short six and a half months on the front, he earned the Iron Cross. After his regiment returned to Potsdam, he took part as a volunteer in the suppression of the Spartacus uprising in Berlin in January 1919.

However, Tresckow was not fighting for the new and struggling Republic (as Olbricht was at this time), but rather *against* the parties of the extreme Left, which he blamed for Germany's defeat and humiliation. Although he was accepted into the elite *Reichswehr* in the 9th Infantry Regiment in Potsdam, he was uncomfortable serving the Republic. He was further disillusioned by the dilettantish Kapp Putsch, and by the *Reichswehr*'s role in putting it down. He was also increasingly conscious of his inadequate education, and so at the end of October 1920 he resigned his commission and enrolled in university.

He studied law, political science, and finance. After just three terms, however, he was offered a job with a bank, and he jumped at the chance. It was here that he experienced the Great Inflation and the introduction of a new currency. He was able, in these volatile times, to make himself a small fortune. This enabled him to accept the invitation of an acquaintance to embark on a trip round the world. The experience was enlightening. He was confronted, for example, with rabid anti-German feeling in both Paris and London: something that astonished him and left a lasting impression. He travelled next to Brazil, Argentina, and Chile, but it was here that news reached him that the family estate was in danger of being lost as a result of the currency reform. He decided to put his fortune at his father's disposal in order to save 'the farm'. He broke off his travels and returned at once to Germany.

Having achieved his objective, he took a job as the managing director of a small factory, and roughly a year and a half after his return to Germany he married. His bride was the daughter of the former minister of war and chief of the General Staff during the First World War, Erika von Falkenhayn. Perhaps it was due to her influence that he decided to reapply to the *Reichswehr* and resume his military career.

On 1 February 1926, Tresckow was once again a lieutenant in his old regiment. It was a regiment in which the aristocrats so dominated the officer corps that it was known as Infantry Regiment Graf 9. In this regiment the tradition was not only *Kaiserlich* (i.e. focused on the defeated German Empire), but *Königlich* (i.e. focused on the Prussian monarchy from the period before German unification in 1871).

As the worldwide economic crisis brought the good years of the Weimar Republic to a close and unemployment, bankruptcy, and unrest grew, Tresckow saw in the National Socialist movement many positive elements. Ignoring the ugly aspects – the anti-Semitism, the crude racial theories, and the demands for territorial expansion – Tresckow, like so many other essentially conservative officers, allowed himself to be deceived. He welcomed Hitler's appointment as chancellor and was willing to defend him energetically against his more conservative colleagues, who were appalled by Hitler's rise to power.

Tresckow was particularly delighted by Hitler's rapid moves to rearm. He appears to have ignored all the indications of the regime's lawlessness – one presumes because, like so many other officers, he didn't particularly care about Communists or Socialists or unions or even freedom of the press. But when on Hitler's orders two *Reichswehr* generals, von Schleicher and von Bredow, were murdered on 30 June 1934, Tresckow started to look at the National Socialist regime more critically. He was still far removed from Olbricht, however, who by this time was already engaged in confronting and protesting against Nazi actions.

On 1 October 1934, Tresckow started General Staff training. Two years later he graduated top of his class, and was at once appointed to the War Ministry and put to work on the plans to invade Czechoslovakia. Here he became better acquainted with Generals Beck, Fritsch, and Manstein. The Nazi intrigues against Generals Blomberg and Fritsch shocked him so deeply that Tresckow, despite his brilliant career, seriously considered resigning his commission. He was talked out of it by *Generalfeldmarschall* (GFM) von Witzleben, who told him bluntly that the Army needed officers who shared his own outrage over the National Socialist regime. Witzleben, of course, was at this time one of the officers approached by Goerdeler and Oster with a mind to using the affair as the pretext for an anti-Nazi coup.

Tresckow apparently, like Olbricht, knew about, but was not actively involved in, the coup plans surrounding the Sudeten Crisis. He was deeply depressed by Hitler's bloodless victory at Munich, and completely horrified by the pogrom against the Jews that followed on 9 November 1938. In the last months before the start of the Second World War, Tresckow came to the conclusion, just as Beck, Olbricht, and Oster (but not Stauffenberg) did at this time, that Hitler had to be eliminated in order to prevent a new world war.

But once the war had started, Tresckow's upbringing and heritage made it impossible for him to stand aside or fight against German victory. Although aware of the paradox that each victory strengthened Hitler,

Tresckow, like Olbricht, could not help but actively work for German victory. But as the preparations for the attack on the Soviet Union took shape and the barbaric Barbarossa Instructions made it clear what kind of war Hitler was preparing, Tresckow did manage to collect around himself, in his new position as first General Staff officer (Ia) of Army Group Centre, a group of like-minded officers. And it was these already anti-Nazi officers who became witnesses to the brutal massacre carried out by SS *Einsatzkommandos* against Jews at Babi Yar in relative proximity to the HQ of Army Group Centre.

Tresckow decided that Hitler and his regime could be tolerated no longer. He had to be eliminated, like a mad dog. So he sent one of his closest associates, Fabian von Schlabrendorff, to Berlin with the task of finding out if there was anyone left in Berlin as determined as he was to eliminate the Nazi dictatorship. Logically, Schlabrendorff went first to *Generaloberst* Beck. Beck, of course, put Schlabrendorff (and so Tresckow's entire group) in touch with Olbricht and Oster. Henceforth, the conspiracy had three central operative cells: Oster in the *Abwehr*, responsible for the assassination; Olbricht in GAO, responsible for planning the coup that would follow the assassination; and Tresckow in Army Group Centre, responsible for recruiting a reliable active field marshal who would lend his name and troops to the coup.

The Soviet counter-offensive that opened on 6 December 1941 represented the first reverse suffered by Hitler's *Wehrmacht* since its inception in 1934. To be sure, the Luftwaffe had failed to win air superiority over the British Isles in the summer and autumn of 1940, but, from the German perspective, Hitler hadn't really wanted to invade Britain anyway, and the German *Army* wasn't even engaged. To this day, few Germans have ever even heard of the Battle of Britain, and they attribute to it no significance whatsoever.

But the Russian counter-offensive not only stopped the *Wehrmacht* in its tracks, it threw the *Wehrmacht* back. This brought the first faint flicker of hope to the German opposition that the mood in Germany itself might soon change: the first hope that a coup, if carried out, might find resonance among the population. Almost as important, Army Group Centre got a new commander. The ineffective GFM von Bock was replaced by GFM Günther von Kluge.

Kluge was a brilliant strategist who had already proved his competence as an Army commander in Poland, France, and Russia. In France it was his 4th Army that carried out the audacious attack through the Ardennes, a feat that the Western Allies had not believed possible. It was his 4th Army that forced the crossing of the Meuse just five days after the start of the war. It was likewise Kluge's 4th Army that cut off the British Expeditionary Force with its back to the sea, and Kluge received the orders from Hitler personally to stop the panzers under his command just 10 miles short of Dunkirk. The plan for the campaign in the West stemmed from Manstein, but its brilliant execution was largely to Kluge's credit. It is one of the bizarre ironies of history that the name of one of his subordinate divisional commanders, Erwin Rommel, is better known today than Kluge's own.

More important from the perspective of Olbricht and Tresckow in December 1941, however, was the fact that Kluge had been an active participant in the plot to depose Hitler during the Sudeten Crisis, and Kluge had opposed the war in the West as well. Kluge was, in fact, firmly in the anti-Nazi camp.

Thus the winter of 1941–2 was a pivotal turning point for the Military Resistance to Hitler. It is the point at which concrete coup plans started to be formed under the codename 'Valkyrie'. As will be described in detail later, Olbricht at this point developed official General Staff plans ostensibly intended for purely military purposes and adapted these plans for his clandestine activities. Thus Valkyrie was *both* an official military plan for dealing with a crisis inside the Reich set off by, say, an uprising on the part of forced labourers, a commando raid by the enemy, or the death of Hitler, *and* the blueprint for the military aspects of a coup against the Nazi regime. At the same time, the 'political wing' of the conspiracy – the experienced civilians of Beck's circle – started to look at the political requirements of a coup. In March 1942 the first 'shadow government', or post-Hitler government, was drawn up on paper, and drafts of radio announcements and so on started to circulate among the conspirators.

But within a few months, the German Army had stabilised the situation on the Eastern Front. Meanwhile, the German U-boats in the Atlantic were racking up huge successes and robbing Churchill of his sleep, while Rommel was enjoying breathtaking victories in his little sideshow. Most importantly, however, by summer 1942 the German Army was on the offensive again on the Eastern Front. The popular mood swung back to adulation of Hitler, and no field marshal in his right mind was going to move against him. The coup plans had to be shelved again, but not by any means abandoned. The conspirators all firmly believed that the war *could not* be won, and that when the inevitable reverses on the front came, that public opinion would turn more anti-Nazi than ever. After all, by now Bomber Command was regularly attacking German cities by night and the USA, now in the war on the Allied side, was starting its own daylight bombing campaign. Thus, added to any future setbacks at the front, the situation on the home front was gradually deteriorating.

But despite Tresckow's best efforts, Kluge had so far failed to commit himself to the conspiracy, even though he fundamentally agreed with Tresckow's assessment of Hitler as mad and his regime as criminal. Many who knew Kluge well, most notably one of his personal adjutants (*Ordonnanzoffizier*) at this time, Philipp Freiherr von Boeselager, believed that Kluge simply could not bring himself to commit an act of treason in the middle of a war.

By the autumn of 1942, Olbricht was so frustrated by lack of support from a senior front commander that he suggested that the Home Army (rather than one of the front armies) must be hitched to the wagon of the coup d'état. At the same time, excessive interest on the part of the Gestapo and SS in the activities of the Counter-Intelligence Office made it advisable for Oster to suspend his Resistance activities. Olbricht was compelled to reduce his official and personal contact with Oster to avoid endangering his own position. Tresckow took over responsibility for the assassination planning.

At last, the winter of 1942–3 brought the anticipated reverse in Germany's military fortunes. At once the anti-Nazi conspirators in the military intensified their activities. The tragedy of Stalingrad was already in the offing, and the military conspirators wanted to be ready to exploit the inevitable shock and outrage on the part of the population that was due to follow. Olbricht explicitly asked Tresckow to give him eight weeks to get the coup plans (which had been much neglected during the summer of German victories) up to date. At the end of February 1943, Olbricht passed the word to Tresckow via Schlabrendorff: 'We're finished. The trigger can be pulled.'[1]

Tresckow was ready. First, he had at last succeeded in winning over the support of GFM von Kluge. Kluge, in despair over Hitler's dilettantish and stubborn command style during the disastrous winter of 1942–3, was ready to put himself at the disposal of the coup *on condition* that Hitler was killed first. Kluge was never to waver from this position – as would prove fateful for both the conspiracy and the field marshal himself in July 1944. But in early 1943, his prerequisite was completely in line with the desires and expectations of the entire active military conspiracy. And Tresckow had both the means and the opportunity to act.

Tresckow had lobbied hard with OKW to persuade Hitler's staff that the dictator should personally visit Army Group Centre. Once Hitler was committed (unwittingly) to walking into the lion's den (of the anti-Hitler staff at Army Group Centre), it was only a matter of deciding exactly how to go about killing him. Various plans and methods were discussed. Individual officers, notably Georg Freiherr von Boeselager, were extremely good marksmen, and were prepared to shoot Hitler with their pistols at close range. But cooler heads prevailed and pointed out that Hitler would be surrounded by loyal staff and bodyguards. It would be comparatively easy to disrupt one man's aim, either by overpowering (or just jostling) the assassin or by pushing or pulling the dictator out of danger at the right moment. The idea therefore evolved into a joint assassination, with all those members of the conspiracy who would be present at the planned luncheon for Hitler collectively shooting him: a modern version of the assassination of Caesar. But in the end this plan, too, was dropped. Hitler ate his meal in the midst of officers determined to murder him without suffering any harm, or even becoming suspicious. Why? Kluge is alleged to have objected to the idea of shooting a man at dinner, but the bottom line was that Tresckow had a far better idea.

Tresckow had obtained captured British plastic explosives, and he fashioned this material into the shape of a bottle, wrapped it up like a gift, and then – having watched Hitler board one of the two planes that always transported him from place to place – asked another officer about to board the same plane to take the package to a friend back in Berlin. The explosive had a 30-minute fuse, which Tresckow had already set off before turning the package over to the innocent 'courier'.

This was truly the perfect assassination plan. If all had functioned, the bomb would have exploded while Hitler's plane was in the air over territory controlled by Soviet partisans. The aircraft would have crashed deep inside partisan territory, and it would have taken days to recover the pieces. Hitler would have been dead, and the official 'Plan Valkyrie' would have been set in motion completely legally. Because the explosives used were British, the initial suspicion would have fallen on foreign saboteurs rather than domestic opponents. Meanwhile, the Military Resistance would have gone into action, executing the prepared coup – the secret aspects of 'Plan Valkyrie' – while the SS and Nazi Party would have been taken by surprise, stunned by the loss of the 'infallible leader', and very likely in the midst of bitter infighting over who should succeed Hitler. (There was never any love lost between Himmler, Goebbels, and Goering.) While the Nazis bickered among themselves, the population at large, given the recent loss of an entire army at Stalingrad and the increasing devastation of the Anglo-American air offensive, would most likely have lined up behind the military provisional government. This was because the Army at the time still enjoyed immense prestige, and because the increasing corruption and draft evasion of low-level Nazi officials had undermined support for the Nazi regime as a whole.

But although the detonator worked, the explosives failed to ignite. The explosion did not take place. Hitler's aircraft landed safely. Tresckow had to send Schlabrendorff rushing back to Berlin by train to collect the package before it was delivered to its unsuspecting alleged recipient. (Tresckow called ahead, saying that there had been a mistake and packages had been mixed up.) Incredibly, even though the assassination attempt failed, Tresckow managed to cover it up in time, and the conspiracy was not exposed to its enemies.

Nor did Tresckow despair. Just eight days later, on 21 March 1943, a new opportunity presented itself. Hitler was scheduled to visit an exhibit of captured Soviet equipment and weapons at the Armoury in Berlin. A representative of Army Group Centre staff was to be there to explain anything the dictator wanted to know. One of the conspirators, Rudolf-Christoph Freiherr von Gersdorff, volunteered to sacrifice himself in order to kill Hitler.

Gersdorff's initial plan was to attach the explosives to the speaker's podium. To this end, Gersdorff spent hours in the Armoury on the day before the event trying to find an opportunity to lay his bomb, but there were still workers everywhere. Unsure where else Hitler would stop or when, Gersdorff decided instead to carry the bomb in his pocket as he escorted Hitler about the exhibition. But Hitler rushed through the exhibition without stopping to look at anything. Gersdorff tried to attract his attention to one thing or another, but the dictator, as if sensing the danger, would not be detained. Although Gersdorff used only a 10-minute fuse, Hitler was out again into the street (where Gersdorff was not authorised to follow and where the effect would have been lost) before the fuse was burnt up. Gersdorff rushed to a toilet and defused the bomb just in time.

There are some very interesting aspects of this assassination attempt. It was by no means as ideal as the aircraft plan from the week before. The assassin would immediately have been identified as an officer of Army Group Centre's staff, and so suspicion would have fallen on a key Resistance cell. Since some kind of investigation would have been necessary, even if the conspirators succeeded in gaining control of the government it would have been more difficult to carry out a cover-up, and the Nazis would have been better placed to fight back. But perhaps most significantly, because Olbricht himself had to attend the event and was seated close to the speaker's podium, he fully expected to be killed in the explosion. (He had not been informed of Gersdorff's change of plan at the last minute.) Had he been killed, there would have been no one in the GAO who was involved in the coup. No one back at Home Army HQ in the *Bendlerstrasse* would have ensured that the orders went out as planned; there would have been no one to ascertain that the conspirators were informed and that Kluge was alerted immediately so that the anti-Nazi shadow government could seize control of the state.

Olbricht's deputy at this time, his chief of staff, was Hellmuth Reinhardt, and Reinhardt was *not* part of the conspiracy. Reinhardt knew very well what Olbricht thought of Hitler, and he was not likely to inform on him, but he had also made it clear that he wanted no part of any treasonable activities. Thus, had the bomb succeeded in killing both Hitler and Olbricht on 21 March 1943, the coup would have been in the hands not of the conspirators, but of the official recipients of the Valkyrie orders – essentially, the neutral Army apparatus under the self-interested *Generaloberst* Fromm.

Would Beck and Oster have been able to exert sufficient influence on Fromm and other neutral officers to ensure that the SS and other Nazis did not retain control of the government despite Hitler's death? Would Kluge have been able to rapidly line up the front commanders behind an opposition government? It all seems highly doubtful; and this is probably what prompted Olbricht to express dissatisfaction with his own planning as soon as these two near-assassinations were over.

The most reasonable explanation of the situation is that the coup plans that Olbricht completed in February 1943 presupposed his presence in the *Bendlerstrasse*, but when the opportunity for an assassination at the Armoury came up, Olbricht agreed that the attempt should go ahead even if the coup plans at that time were not designed for this eventuality. Clearly, the priority was eliminating Hitler and then worrying about how to deal with what came afterwards. Once the immediate opportunity was passed, however, Olbricht wanted to rethink his own plans.

Another factor also contributed to a reassessment of the situation at this time. Oster had been suspended from duty, and an investigation of one of his closest associates had begun. Although the charges against this associate, Dohnanyi, were related to currency violations rather than treason, Dohnanyi knew too much about the military conspiracy for comfort. The risk was high that the Gestapo would turn up evidence of the conspiracy. In short, one of the three Resistance cells of the military conspiracy had been shattered. Only Olbricht and Tresckow remained.

To make matters worse, it was at this critical point that Ludwig Beck's stomach cancer became so acute that he had to be operated on – a total of five times. For weeks he was in a critical condition. The moral and intellectual leader of the military conspiracy was thus taken completely out of action for an indefinite period of time. Beck's illness weakened the entire conspiracy. Goerdeler did not enjoy the same respect even among the civilians, much less the military. It is doubtful that the temperamental former mayor could have successfully led a coup without the moral authority of Beck behind him.

All these factors together resulted in a clear crisis of confidence in the military conspiracy. Tresckow, deeply depressed by the two successive failures in March, returned to Berlin on leave, and a series of meetings took place between the conspirators in various constellations. The coup plans were discussed in detail between Tresckow and Olbricht. While Olbricht was being burdened with new official duties as head of the Armed Forces Replacement Office, Tresckow used his leave to review and improve the secret aspects of Valkyrie. It was also agreed between them and a gradually recovering Beck that – in the absence of Oster and his Resistance cell – Olbricht needed a reliable Resistance deputy. In short, he had to replace Reinhardt with a man who was as committed to the coup d'état as Olbricht was himself. He needed a chief of staff who could both perform his military duties *and* promote the coup.

The problem was not, in fact, new. Reinhardt had been Olbricht's chief of staff since 1 March 1941, and it was clear that he was due for transfer and promotion in March or April 1943. Olbricht was keen to replace him with someone who would be prepared to work as his deputy in both an official and an unofficial capacity. A diary entry by Hermann Kaiser, one of the conspirators, from 2 February 1943 proves that Olbricht had already selected a likely successor, namely Claus Graf von Stauffenberg.

Stauffenberg was born in Bavaria on 15 November 1907. He was the third son of a Swabian count who had served for many years in the court of the King of Württemberg. His mother was a lady-in-waiting to the Queen. In short, the family was very conservative, monarchist, and Catholic. Due probably to the influence of their mother, all three Stauffenberg sons were very artistic; they played musical instruments, put on concerts, and attended and put on plays, and they soon came under the influence of the poet Stefan George. The boys also became very involved in the romantic Youth Movement of the interwar period, despite their father's contempt for so much emotionalism. Claus initially expressed an interest in becoming an architect. Of his elder brothers (who were twins), one became a professor of history and the other studied law. Because Claus had been weak and sickly as a child, his mother had often kept him home from school, and he did not attend a gymnasium or boarding school. He sat exams as an 'external candidate' and received mediocre grades. Perhaps this discouraged him from applying to university. At all events, after passing his exams he applied to and was accepted in the 17th Cavalry Regiment, a Bavarian regiment that carried on the traditions of those regiments to which Stauffenberg's ancestors had belonged in their time.

Before examining Stauffenberg's military career, however, it is important to look at the influence of Stefan George. Stauffenberg maintained a close relationship with the poet for roughly 10 years, starting in 1923. Thus Stauffenberg was only 16 years old when he first came under the poet's spell, and the effect was lasting. Even later in life, Stauffenberg is said to have referred to the poet as his 'master', describing his relationship to George as one of a disciple and comparing his master to Socrates. To the end of his life Stauffenberg could quote verbatim from George's poems, and possibly his very last words were a reference to the George poem 'Secret Germany'. Certainly, George wrote and preached about a 'New Empire', a new Germany, even a Thousand-Year Reich. The Nazis found much inspiration in George and claimed him for their own, although he was not ever part of the National Socialist movement and certainly never a follower or admirer of Hitler. George did, however, believe in a spiritual elite that would lead the masses; and all his disciples, including Claus von Stauffenberg, viewed themselves as members of this elite. George also believed and taught that each individual had a destiny, and a duty to fulfil that destiny. He is also alleged to have believed that the physical attributes of a person reflected inner character: the more beautiful the exterior, the more beautiful the soul. Stauffenberg was a very handsome youth and man, and many witnesses attest that George had great hopes for him – something that would obviously deeply flatter and influence an impressionable teenager such as Claus von Stauffenberg. At all events, he retained his close ties to the poet until the latter's death in 1933, following which Stauffenberg kept a vigil.

Meanwhile, however, Stauffenberg had started his military career. Having entered the *Reichswehr* as a recruit/officer candidate in 1926, it was 1 January 1930 before he was commissioned, and another three years before he was promoted to first lieutenant on 1 May 1933, by which date Hitler had come to power. The degree of Stauffenberg's enthusiasm for the new regime is controversial. Some accounts attribute genuine enthusiasm, others insist he was simply 'trying to be fair' and refused to insult and sneer at the Nazis (as was common in some aristocratic circles). But one thing is clear: Stauffenberg had never really liked the Republic. Equally certain is it that he felt Germany needed some form of 'renewal'. Like Tresckow and Beck, he may well have let himself hope that National

Socialism would bring the national revival he longed for. He naturally welcomed the expansion of the armed forces, as did all the rest of the officer corps.

From 1 May 1933 until 1 October 1936 Stauffenberg attended the cavalry school, where he excelled at dressage. Although in this discipline he was superior to members of the German equestrian team that took the gold medal at the 1936 Olympics, he was not selected for the team, apparently for deficiencies in stadium or cross-country jumping. He was, however, selected for the War Academy and so tentatively for the General Staff. His performance at the General Staff College, as in his entire military career, was good but not – as historians and biographers with admiring hindsight allege – truly outstanding. He did not, like Tresckow, graduate at the top of his class and get assigned straight away to the Operations Department of the Ministry of War to work on the most urgent plans. Instead he was sent to a division, and there posted *not* to the prestigious position of first General Staff officer but rather assigned as second General Staff officer, with responsibility for logistics. No amount of apologia from biographers should obscure the fact that in the General Staff of 1938, the most brilliant staff officers were always assigned to operations, not logistics; and that the more competent or brilliant an officer was considered, the higher the level of command to which he was assigned. A divisional post was the lowest level for staff officers, even if it often proved to be the most challenging and rewarding of positions.

Stauffenberg remained in the position of a divisional second General Staff officer with the First Light (later 6th Panzer) Division through the occupation of the Sudetenland, the Polish campaign, and the start of the French campaign. He did his work well and was highly respected, but he was not promoted to first General Staff officer when that position fell vacant. It is also important to note that neither during this period, nor during the short interlude when he served with an active division (again as a staff officer) in Africa, was Stauffenberg decorated. In fact, at no point in his entire career did Stauffenberg ever command troops in wartime. The enthusiasm of his later admirers for his 'decisiveness' should not obscure the fact that Stauffenberg is one of the few leading members of the Military Resistance who, in fact, never proved himself in combat and never demonstrated courage in the face of the enemy sufficient for official recognition. Perhaps this was just poor luck. In the middle of the campaign in France, while he was still rushing forward with one of the leading panzer divisions that created the very term 'Blitzkrieg', he received orders to report to the organisational (not the more prestigious operational) department of the General Staff in Berlin. On the other hand, this transfer also suggests that although he was doing a good job, no one felt that he was indispensable or his presence with the division imperative for its success.

As already mentioned, at this time Stauffenberg was enthusiastic about Hitler and his 'genius' for war. He found the attitude of staff officers in Berlin unnecessarily pessimistic, and attributed it to class prejudice and blind conservatism. Despite some recorded remarks that indicate Stauffenberg did not like *everything* the Nazis did, nothing up to this point in his career suggests that Stauffenberg was in any way exceptional, either in terms of military competence or in terms of political insight.

For the next two years Stauffenberg worked in the organisational department of the General Staff. Here he engaged closely with Halder, who had planned the coup of 1938, and with Olbricht's staff. Halder certainly exposed Stauffenberg to the point of view of the military conspirators, but Stauffenberg was not entirely receptive to opposition thinking even if he kept an open mind. Olbricht, meanwhile, came to appreciate the junior officer's organisational talent, and Stauffenberg undoubtedly possessed exceptional skills in this area, First-hand accounts also attest to Stauffenberg's devotion to duty, his energy, his sense of humour, and his charm. However, his advance during this period continued to be average; he was a major throughout his tour of duty at the Organisational Department.

Over these critical two years Stauffenberg was, however, confronted with Hitler's unreasonable demands and his illogical decisions, and he became increasingly disillusioned with the dictator. Whereas in early 1942, Stauffenberg applauded the fact that Hitler had taken over personal command of the Army and still believed Hitler could win the war, by August of the same year Stauffenberg was according to some (albeit very weak) sources hotly calling for Hitler's elimination *because* he stood in the way of victory.[2]

It is certain, however, that Stauffenberg had a personal conversation with GFM von Manstein in January 1943, shortly before the surrender of the 6th Army at Stalingrad. In this meeting, the newly promoted lieutenant colonel tried to persuade Manstein to 'do something' about 'changing the command structure': i.e. stopping Hitler from making the military decisions. Manstein's answer disappointed Stauffenberg (as it did all the military opposition, who expected more backbone from Germany's leading military strategist). Apparently, once Stauffenberg became convinced (as the Military Resistance had long ago) that the field marshals were on the whole too cowardly to oppose Hitler openly, he moved rapidly to seek a more radical solution.

It is highly significant that although Stauffenberg's official work included organisation of Russian volunteer units and he clearly objected to their deplorable treatment, there is nothing to indicate that he shared Olbricht's, Beck's, or Tresckow's abhorrence of the Nazis' criminal tactics and policies. The mafia-like murders of the SA leaders had not opened his eyes to the nature of Hitler's regime; nor had the intrigue against Fritsch, nor the atrocities in Poland and the Soviet Union. It was simply the fact that Hitler was losing the war of aggression that he himself had started that at last drove Stauffenberg into the opposition camp.

To be fair, once Stauffenberg had changed his colours, he was fanatical about it. But now his military career got in his way. After more than two years in a staff position in Berlin it was time, in accordance with standard General Staff practice, for Stauffenberg to go back to active service. He was promoted *Oberstleutnant*, effective 1 January 1943, and posted (finally) as first General Staff officer to the 10th Panzer Division in Africa. But his change of heart about Hitler and his organisational talent had already made him Olbricht's choice as Reinhardt's successor. Stauffenberg did not know this, and he went to Africa apparently content to get away from all the infighting and frustration in Berlin.

Stauffenberg arrived in Africa after just eight days' leave, in early February 1943. Roughly two months later, on 7 April, while retreating with the rest of his division before the British 8th Army, he became the victim of a low-flying Allied aircraft. He was found alive in his shot-up staff car by the next vehicle to come along the road. He had lost his right hand, two fingers of his left hand, and the sight in his left eye. At first it was not certain he would recover, and he was hospitalised for three months.

During this time, his determination to 'do something' against Hitler grew. Precisely because Stauffenberg had been taken in by Hitler for so long, it appears that he now felt betrayed. Stauffenberg, it is said, was particularly keen to emphasise how Hitler had 'betrayed' the 'original ideals' [sic] of National Socialism.[3] Filled with Stefan George's notions of elites and destiny, Stauffenberg was convinced that he would have to act himself. He told his wife: 'I have the feeling that I must now do something to save the Reich.'[4] In short, he had come to the conclusion that he – a severely wounded lieutenant colonel of the General Staff – would have to 'go into action', since 'the generals' were not doing anything.

Apparently, Stauffenberg was completely unaware that at least some generals had indeed done a great deal more than he ever had to try to stop Hitler. But that speaks for their discretion and should not be held against Stauffenberg. Nevertheless, his dismissal of 'the generals' for their inactivity included his future immediate superior, General Olbricht. Stauffenberg hadn't the faintest idea what was expected of him in the GAO until he made his first courtesy call on Olbricht in August 1943.

Based on reports from other conspirators, Olbricht was now confident that Stauffenberg's political sympathies coincided with those of the opposition. At their first meeting he asked Stauffenberg directly about his willingness to contribute to the coup planning already in progress. What is more, Olbricht made it very clear in this first interview that he was himself too burdened by official duties and commitments to micro-manage the coup planning, and that he *expected* Stauffenberg to shoulder the bulk of the work with respect to Resistance activities. Stauffenberg, to his credit, declared himself willing and ready to start immediately. The leading surgeon treating Stauffenberg, however, insisted that he needed two additional operations, and so Stauffenberg did not take up his duties at GAO straight away.

Meanwhile, Beck had recovered his strength and determination to proceed with a coup, and Kluge had reiterated his commitment to the conspiracy. Olbricht announced his intention to act even if Fromm would not: that is, he was willing to issue the Valkyrie orders *illegally* if Fromm could not be persuaded to issue them legally. Olbricht even indicated that he would arrest Fromm if necessary. Tresckow, who was still in Berlin, worked with Olbricht to get the plans up to date yet again. In short, the military conspirators were determined to act, as soon as they could find a way to kill Hitler.

On 1 October 1943, Stauffenberg took up his duties as chief of staff of the General Army Office in Berlin. His position here was deputy to General Olbricht. He had exactly the same function and position inside the conspiracy – not, as some biographers of Stauffenberg would have one believe, the other way round. Stauffenberg and Olbricht worked very closely together. In the conspiracy, the best traditions of the General Staff ruled: every officer, no matter how junior, was encouraged to voice his opinion. There was no rigid hierarchy, and discussions were open, honest, and full of controversy. But at no time did Stauffenberg question that Olbricht was his senior in both military and Resistance matters. Nor did Stauffenberg attempt to usurp Olbricht's, Beck's, or Tresckow's leadership role in the Military Resistance. No decision was made, no action taken, no contact established by Stauffenberg without first consulting Olbricht and, very often, Beck.

Nevertheless, Stauffenberg did start to take an informal leading role in the conspiracy, because Olbricht had delegated it to him. Olbricht's official duties required his presence at meetings, conferences, briefings, and inspections all over the Reich. In consequence, Olbricht could not devote the time necessary to coup planning. That was now Stauffenberg's job.

That Stauffenberg attacked these duties with invigorating élan and energy is certainly to his credit – but there was also a reason for this. Stauffenberg had wasted a lot of time. Until his fateful meeting with Olbricht in August 1943, Stauffenberg may have *said* a lot about how Hitler ought to be shot (by someone else), or urged that the command structure be altered (by the field marshals), but he hadn't actually *done* anything. He had been aware of the Kreisauer Circle since early 1942, but he had indicated to Moltke and Yorck (a distant relative) that he 'wasn't interested'.

By October 1943, Goerdeler, Beck, and Olbricht had been seeking ways to bring down Hitler's regime for a good five years, but Stauffenberg had only just discovered his calling and mission in life. Naturally, like any new convert, he was particularly zealous. Almost as importantly, he had not experienced the failures, setbacks, and disappointments that the others had endured. He had not seen Britain collapse before Hitler at Munich and rob the conspiracy of its chance for action. He had not watched a ticking bomb go aboard Hitler's plane and waited breathlessly for the chance to set the coup in motion, only to have the bomb fail. He had not taken his seat beside a podium he thought was rigged for demolition for the sake of seeing Germany freed of a dictator. Stauffenberg was not worn down by the years of futile hope, and he was not yet cynical from the many failures. We will never know how the romantic, emotional, and volatile Stauffenberg would have reacted to the repeated disappointments of the previous years; but no doubt it was for the good of the conspiracy as a whole that he was not yet as jaded or weary as the other, older conspirators were.

In any case, more or less simultaneously with Stauffenberg's arrival at GAO, Tresckow was given command of a regiment on the Eastern Front. As a result, the staff of Army Group Centre could no longer serve as a Resistance cell. Of the three Military Resistance cells that had existed in late 1941 – Counter-Intelligence, Army Group Centre, and GAO – only the GAO cell was still operative by October 1943.

Before looking at the activities of Olbricht/Stauffenberg in the last nine months of the military conspiracy, it is useful to go back and examine Olbricht's motives and positions on key Resistance issues.

Chapter 11

THE REASONS WHY

Olbricht's Motives for Resistance, 1940–4

Crossing the Rubicon

Active planning of a military coup d'état against a popular government is qualitatively very different from many other kinds of anti-regime attitudes and behaviour. Many opponents of Hitler failed to transform feelings of disgust and hostility towards the regime, and oppositional attitudes, into actions. Most significantly, many of Germany's senior military leaders – men of integrity, courage, and intelligence such as GFM von Manstein – could not bring themselves to take this final step of committing treason. It is important, therefore, to ask the question: why was Olbricht so different from the others, and what motivated him?

What stands out most when contrasting Olbricht to his fellow generals are two points: first, that he supported the Republic; and secondly, that he was never taken in by Hitler. These two facts are interrelated.

Looked at from the other perspective, for many in Germany in the 1920s and 1930s, the rejection of Weimar led to an almost blind or desperate longing for something better. They saw in Hitler what they wanted to see, closing their eyes to indications that he was something else. Meanwhile, Hitler's initial attacks against the institutions of the Republic – the constitution, competing political parties and trade unions, freedom of the press – aroused no hostility among this segment of the population. On the contrary, the years of prosperity and triumph under Hitler healed wounds left by the humiliation of the lost war, but at the same time eroded moral and ethical standards. Tolerance for Hitler's early illegalities and acts of force bred unconscious acceptance for ever-greater acts of injustice. A gradual and slow process of escalating immorality on the part of the regime produced a slow and gradual decline in the moral standards of the ordinary man. It should never be forgotten that Hitler did not start with Auschwitz. Nobody was confronted in January 1933 with a choice between Weimar and 'Total War' or 'Death Camps'. But by the time the death camps were being erected, the vast majority of the German population had already compromised their own code of honour in so many ways that there was no going back.

Olbricht's support for the democratic Weimar regime was largely what made him so unreceptive to Hitler's rhetoric and style. Thus Olbricht was lucky to have been free of any kind of illusions about Hitler. Because he supported the Republic, he saw the very first violations of the Weimar constitution for what they were. He likewise recognised illegal actions and dictatorial behaviour for what they were. At no point did he compromise himself by justifying, even in his mind, the illegal and immoral acts of the regime. In consequence, Olbricht's own moral standards were not eroded or corrupted.

Likewise, his fundamentally republican sentiments made him immune to the longing for a 'replacement Kaiser'. This, in turn, had a significant impact on his attitude towards the oath to Hitler. Fundamentally monarchist officers, men who had sincerely seen themselves as personally bound to the supreme commander as young officers of the German Empire, often reverted to this sense of personal bondage after they had sworn themselves – no matter how unintentionally – to Hitler. (Many modern readers find it hard to believe that German soldiers and officers 'really took an oath seriously', which, I submit, is a very poor commentary on modern attitudes towards oaths.)

But Olbricht's loyalty to the Weimar Republic does not explain his readiness to work actively against the Nazi government. The easy road, even for the most outraged opponents of the National Socialists, was to condemn Hitler and his minions in the safety of silence, but to keep their own hands clean of any wrongdoing by doing nothing and letting 'history' take its course. Millions and millions of basically 'decent' Germans did exactly this. They deplored Hitler in private, in their diaries and letters and in their homes, but in public they did whatever was necessary to retain their jobs, their status, and their standard of living. After the war they were anxious to explain: they had never voted for Hitler, they had never supported him, they had never joined the Party, and so on. Many could even point to tiny acts of nonconformity, to gestures of defiance or small acts of humanitarian resistance. And these same people looked down on the men of 20 July 1944 as 'traitors'.

Olbricht and many of his co-conspirators knew it would end like this. They recognised that they would be despised as traitors and as murderers – even by those they were giving their lives to save. In the grey dawn of 21 July 1944, Henning von Tresckow said calmly to a fellow conspirator: 'Now the whole world will attack and insult us.'[1]

That the conspirators of 20 July acted despite the fact that they knew they would be reviled by their countrymen is revealing. These men were not motivated by expectations of fame or power, as are most men who bring down one government in order to set up one of their own. Furthermore, the conspirators of 20 July 1944 knew that the unconditional surrender demands of the Allies would in all probability result in their own dismissal within days, if not hours – if they survived at all. Olbricht, if no one else, was perfectly aware that he might well not live long enough to fill the exalted positions the conspiracy assigned him. When the various civilian groups were busy drawing up the shadow cabinet of a post-Hitler government, Olbricht was heard to say that they were welcome to plan whatever they wanted, but first something had to happen and then they would 'see who is left over'.[2]

In today's context it is also important to point out that the conspirators of 20 July 1944 were not motivated by expectations of martyrdom or rewards in the afterlife. Not one of the conspirators of 20 July 1944 subscribed to the kind of religious cult that motivates suicide bombers today.

Nor did the core conspirators such as Olbricht and Beck act in order to end a lost war, as the Western Allies claimed and many in the USA and Britain believe to this day. Certainly, the senseless sacrifice of young soldiers at the front and civilians in the air raids was something that weighed heavily on the hearts of the Military Resistance leaders, Olbricht included. Stauffenberg talked of 'not being able to look the widows and orphans in the eye' if he did not do something to stop the war.[3] Tresckow was reputedly 'tortured' by the 'loss of life on all sides in this unholy war'.[4] But this was not the motivation for the conspirators. After all, the key conspirators – Beck, Olbricht, Oster, Stülpnagel, and Goerdeler – started working on a coup before the war even started, or at a time when Germany was victorious on all fronts. This conspiracy had nothing to do with defeated generals trying to avoid the humiliation of a new surrender, even if it can be argued that some famous latecomers to the conspiracy, such as Stauffenberg or Rommel, joined the conspiracy for this reason.

What did motivate the principal conspirators was a sense of responsibility for their fellow man, particularly their fellow citizens. Forty years after the end of the war, the young assassin Axel von dem Bussche could still quote verbatim the paragraph of the German military code that defined self-defence as any action necessary to prevent immediate harm to oneself *or others*. Bussche believed that since Hitler's policies – most especially the death squads and death camps – were threatening millions of innocent lives, killing the dictator was not only justified but, according to the German military law, his duty.

In Olbricht's case, it is fair to say that he was motivated by a combination of moral outrage over a criminal regime and a sense of responsibility towards his country and countrymen. Olbricht never lost sight of the fact that the regime had seized dictatorial powers illegally; and he recognised the truly criminal nature of the Nazi regime at the latest by June 1934, when Hitler had the SA leadership murdered without due process. He shared this moral outrage and vehement condemnation of the criminal character of the Nazi regime most clearly with Ludwig Beck, Hans Oster, and Henning von Tresckow. These were men who consistently focused on the moral perversion of the National Socialist system and justified action against it as the imperative of eliminating absolute evil in a moral and religious sense. Beck, the intellectual, argued that unusual times required unusual measures. Tresckow, more bluntly, spoke of shooting Hitler like a 'mad dog'.

And all these men gradually came to the same conclusion: that the coup itself was not about stopping the war (whether it was lost or not), nor about ending the bloodshed, much less changing the cabinet or even the constitution. The coup was a gesture, a symbolic gesture, to save not German territory, but German honour. The comparison was made to Sodom and Gomorrah, to the need to find ten good men if the city (read Germany) were to be spared utter retribution. In Beck's words: 'It doesn't matter what happens to one person or another, nor even what happens to the nation. What matters is that it is our moral duty to put an end to the crimes and murders committed in Germany's name.'[5] Tresckow urged his co-conspirators to act despite all setbacks with the reasoning: 'The practical effect is unimportant. All that matters is that the German Resistance demonstrates before the world and history that it was willing to risk the final throw.'[6]

In the remaining hours of 20 July 1944, Olbricht told his son-in-law that he did not know how he would be judged in the future, but he knew for certain that he had not been driven by personal gain, but rather by 'endless distress over our Fatherland and the fate of our nation'.[7] He added: 'I am dying for Germany.'[8] And then, echoing Tresckow's message quoted above, he added: 'We have risked the final throw.'[9]

In other words, Olbricht was motivated by patriotism: not the sort of patriotism that wants to see one's nation expand its territory or dominate its neighbours politically and economically. Those kinds of patriots were found in Hitler's camp. Olbricht's patriotism was directed, much like that of the idealistic students of the White Rose, towards saving Germany's soul. He sought to restore German honour by showing to the world and history that there were Germans who abhorred and rejected such a regime and were willing to sacrifice their lives in an attempt – however hopeless – to destroy it. He worded it this way: 'So many brave soldiers are dying on all fronts, ultimately for nothing. We too must be prepared to die for Germany – in order to free it.'[10]

Assassination

It is one of the greatest paradoxes of the military conspiracy against Hitler that an opposition based on moral outrage over the criminal character and actions of the Nazi regime favoured another heinous crime: the assassination of a head of state. But this was the tragedy of the German Resistance: the only effective means of stopping the worst crimes, whether in the death camps or on the front, was with another crime – murder. The Nazi regime was a dictatorship with a 'supreme leader' who was no figurehead, but rather the very source of the most barbarous and inhuman of ideologies and policies. Nothing short of Hitler's removal could cripple the regime, and his removal could realistically only be effected by assassination.

During the early stages of the conspiracy other alternatives had seemed possible and been considered: namely, the arrest and trial of Hitler for his various crimes or his confinement in a mental institution. Goerdeler maintained right to the end that Hitler must be tried for his crimes after a successful coup. Still others, such as Graf Moltke, opposed the coup itself because he felt it would be better if Hitler were forced to drink the bitter dregs of Germany's utter defeat and surrender. Certainly many conspirators, despite their moral outrage over the behaviour of Hitler and his minions, nevertheless retained moral scruples about murder. They asked sincerely whether by committing this act, they did not lower themselves to the level of their enemy. Could an act of murder serve as the basis for a legal and ethical government?

But the reality was that as long as Hitler was alive, he commanded the support of a fanatical and unscrupulous minority of active Nazis and an even larger portion of a gullible and self-interested public as well. As a result, some conspirators came relatively rapidly to the conclusion that Hitler would have to be killed if the coup were to have a chance of success.

On the whole, the military conspirators were more comfortable with killing. They had been raised and trained to see killing under defined circumstances (war) as morally justified. They had, as Axel von dem Bussche knew by heart, a military code that defined a duty to kill in self-defence, and defined 'self-defence' as the defence not just of oneself but of others: namely, defenceless and innocent civilians. Lastly, men like GFM von Kluge were realists, men used to calculating risks and prospective casualties, and they saw that it was necessary to kill Hitler if they were to free many potential supporters from the bonds of the oath they had taken to him.

Nevertheless, after the defeat at Stalingrad and the announcement of the Allied 'unconditional surrender' policy, some military conspirators who had previously supported the assassination of Hitler started to question the wisdom of this course. They argued that if a post-Hitler government signed an unconditional surrender, then it would be blamed for defeat and so be tainted from the start, just as the Weimar Republic had been by Versailles. Some conspirators, such as General Georg Thomas, wanted the conspiracy to secure a promise of something less drastic than unconditional surrender from the Western Allies before taking action against Hitler – or else leave Hitler alive to sign the damning surrender himself. They wanted Hitler to take the blame for the disaster he had brought upon Germany.

All of these positions have value. No one has a monopoly on morality. We cannot know what would have happened if the Military Resistance had succeeded in killing Hitler and a post-Hitler government had been forced to sign an unconditional surrender. We cannot know for certain if a credible, respected, and ethical government could indeed have been built upon the foundation of murder, even if the victim was a criminal madman. While it is not completely inconceivable that a respected government might have emerged despite its murderous roots, it is just as possible that such a murder would have proved an insuperable handicap to the new government and ultimately led to a revival of Nazism and a new conflict in Europe.

Olbricht's position, however, was clear. The testimony of those who knew him indicates that like most of his fellow conspirators, Olbricht initially favoured putting Hitler on trial. Indeed, *Feldmarschall* Erwin von Witzleben insisted before the *Volksgerichtshof* on 7 August 1944 that right up to 20 July 1944, Olbricht intended to arrest, not assassinate, Hitler. However, this allegation is not credible, and only attests to Witzleben's desperation to save his own life by distancing himself from the assassin Stauffenberg. In fact, we know that in the autumn of 1941, Olbricht and Tresckow started their collaboration. Since Tresckow was committed to assassination by this time, it is reasonable to assume, in the absence of evidence to the contrary, that Olbricht shared his views. More importantly, the secret aspects of Valkyrie – all worked out in Olbricht's office and under his guidance, if not drafted by him personally – were based on the presumption that Hitler was dead, the victim of an assassination. Valkyrie had been turned into a secret plan for the coup by the summer of 1942 at the latest, so it is fair to conclude that Olbricht supported the assassination of Hitler by that time.

However, the reasons that Olbricht favoured the assassination changed over time. In the beginning, Olbricht saw the assassination of Hitler as the necessary precondition for the success of the coup. According to his son-in-law: 'Olbricht believed from 1942 to 1944 that a military revolt had a chance of success only if Hitler – and if possible, Himmler and Göring – were physically removed.'[11] The logic is twofold. Hitler's death would free basically sympathetic but more hidebound officers from their oath to Hitler and at the same time throw the Nazi enemy into disarray: the adoring idiots would be devastated by the loss of their beloved leader, while the self-serving criminals would be at each other's throats in a desperate power struggle.

But as early as Tresckow's second assassination attempt, when Olbricht expected to be killed in the same blast that eliminated Hitler, Olbricht's priorities had shifted. Whether it was the effect of Stalingrad or the 'unconditional surrender' policy, Olbricht had become committed to the assassination of Hitler *regardless* of the impact on coup success. The assassination had become a goal in itself and a means of 'freeing Germany'.

Thus the assassination took on a double importance for Olbricht. It was *still* very much a necessary precondition for the success of a coup, but it was also – even if the coup could not succeed – an act of affirmation. It was necessary in order to prove that the Resistance existed, that it recognised Hitler for what he was, and that the Resistance was prepared to sacrifice itself for what it believed in: a better, post-Hitler world.

Domestic and Foreign-Policy Issues

Exactly what that world was supposed to look like, on the other hand, was not something Olbricht actively attempted to influence. He scrupulously held himself out of political discussions and planning. He clearly felt that political and constitutional issues were the preserve of the professionals, whether the experienced men who had gathered around Beck or the selected experts of the Kreisauer Circle. His son-in-law remembers him laughing at the various shadow-cabinet lists – not because he lacked respect for what the civilians were trying to do, but because he felt there were too many unpredictable variables that could not be calculated in advance. As the remark quoted earlier underlines, he knew that as the Elder Moltke had insisted 'no plan survives contact with the enemy', and in consequence much would have to be improvised after they found out who was 'left over'.

Nevertheless, it is to Olbricht's credit that the civilian conspirators saw him as sufficiently competent and politically savvy to assume the post of minister or deputy minister of war in a post-Hitler cabinet. In part, this was a tribute to the work he had been doing all along, but it was also an acknowledgement of the fact that Olbricht was a political officer, even if he wasn't a politician. Had he not been politically engaged, he would not have been involved in the military conspiracy at all, but rather one of the majority of German officers who justified carrying out Hitler's criminal orders because it was his 'duty'.

Olbricht had a clear political opinion: that the Nazi regime was illegal and immoral and had to be replaced. Whether it was replaced by a federalist or centralist republic, by a constitutional monarchy or a parliamentary democracy, was something he had, literally, no time to debate. As the war dragged on and Germany's military situation deteriorated, Olbricht realised – long before the civilians who worked so diligently on constitutional plans – that it was not the conspirators, but the victors, who would write Germany's next constitution.

With respect to international affairs, Olbricht was even more reticent. He knew about the various efforts on the part of the conspiracy to establish contact with the Western Allies, whether via the Pope, Switzerland, or Sweden, but such initiatives did not originate with him. Likewise, although he recognised the complications that the demand for unconditional surrender brought to the conspiracy, he does not appear to have ever given up hope that the Western Allies might be moved to some concessions short of this uncompromising position.

There are highly unreliable sources which suggest that Olbricht, along with a long list of other personalities including Rundstedt and Zeitzler (who were not even members of the conspiracy!), favoured a 'Western solution'. This was a proposal that called for a post-Hitler government to obtain a ceasefire on the Western Front and redeploy troops to the East, or even to order the troops in the West to lay down their arms to admit the Western Allies into Germany while the German Army continued to fight the Soviets on the Eastern Front. There are some indications that GFM von Kluge – who *was* a member of the conspiracy – tried to make contact with Field Marshal Montgomery on 20 July 1944. Kluge commanded the Army Group facing the Normandy invasion. If anyone could have negotiated an armistice in this sector, it would have been he. But Kluge was a field marshal and Army Group commander, and he did not need Olbricht or even Beck's sanction for a military course of action he thought correct.

While it is completely unclear whether or not Olbricht favoured this 'Western solution', it is safe to say that he did *not* seek contact with the Communists. Only historians in the former East Germany have made this claim for Olbricht, and all other sources suggest rather that Olbricht was very sceptical about the utility of ties to the Communists. This can most probably be traced back to his experience in the immediate post-First World War era. In the volatile years of the German Revolution and the Spartacus uprising, Olbricht had moved between the fronts – changing uniforms, acting as a liaison, or collecting intelligence. Very likely it was this familiarity with the Communists and their dogmatism that convinced him that they were neither useful allies nor trustworthy co-conspirators. When in the last months before the coup attempt Stauffenberg became increasingly intrigued with various 'Eastern' solutions and sanctioned contact between SPD and KPD Resistance cells, Stauffenberg was very much perceived as being the initiator of these contacts. Olbricht apparently remained sceptical about the Communists, without actually forbidding Stauffenberg from proceeding. Olbricht's widow believes her husband made no efforts to rein in Stauffenberg at this juncture because he had reached the point where all that mattered was that an attempt was made: 'regardless of what came afterwards'.[12]

Chances of Success

An estimation of the chances of success was likewise an important factor in Resistance motivation and behaviour. Whether one was planning on distributing forbidden information, hiding a victim of persecution, or planning a coup, it was always necessary to balance the prospective good that might be achieved with the risk of discovery and death. While low prospects for success might be an excuse for inaction on the part of the less committed or cowardly, hopeless gestures of resistance were not the actions of responsible and serious Resistance leaders, either.

Olbricht was described by his contemporaries as the 'perpetual realist'. His 'realistic' assessment of Germany's military chances had long since earned him the reputation of a 'defeatist' in OKW, a reputation he could only afford because he was too competent to be dispensable. With respect to the chances of success for the coup, his assessment varied. He was acutely aware that external factors had a huge impact on the prospects for success, and that the mood of the population at large was subject to dramatic swings based on the war situation. Nevertheless, Olbricht never believed that the coup had no chance of success. He was not on a suicide mission, but rather one that he hoped to complete successfully, even if the chances were considerably below 50–50.

By July 1944 all the principal conspirators were convinced that, although the chances of success had dwindled dramatically since March 1943 (much less September 1938), the attempt must be made regardless. At the same time, all the conspirators knew that the consequences of failure would be death and retribution against family and friends. Yet they steadfastly refused to make any attempt to escape in the event of failure.

Olbricht's son-in-law, a staff officer with the Luftwaffe stationed at an airbase on the outskirts of Berlin, had on his own initiative looked into the possibility of flying his father-in-law and other conspirators out of Berlin after a failed coup. Olbricht would not even discuss it. He explained his position to his son-in-law with the following words: 'An evasion or escape from the responsibility for what we are about to do does not exist. We are standing with our backs to the wall. For more than four years, so many decent people have died both at home and on the front for nothing. It is high time that we act and, if necessary, make the ultimate sacrifice for the sake of history.'[13]

Chapter 12

THE CONSUMMATE CONSPIRATOR

Olbricht's Role and Methods in the Military Resistance, 1940–4

Chief of Staff of the Anti-Nazi Military Conspiracy

The tradition of the German General Staff was more than 100 years old by the time the Third Reich came into being. In General Staff tradition, staff officers have no names. The motto of the General Staff was 'be more than you appear to be'; staff officers were to work in the background – not lead from the front. When originally conceived by Scharnhorst and Gneisenau, the duty of every staff officer was to ensure that the right things happened, but to let the royal figureheads reap the harvest of glory.

An officer who internalised this code was obviously well suited to participation in a conspiracy. Olbricht was the consummate General Staff officer. He had proved his capabilities over nearly three decades, and his competence is documented in the career described here. It is his misfortune that his competence as the chief of staff of the conspiracy has largely been ignored in the historical record, precisely because he lived by the General Staff code of being more than he appeared to be. Many historians, not to mention film-makers, have been deceived by Olbricht's self-effacing style of operation and misled by the self-serving accounts of survivors into underestimating Olbricht's importance.

The Gestapo was not so naive. Even if we now know that the Gestapo, especially in the early stages of the investigation, did not know the extent of the conspiracy – and even taking into account that many people lied to the Gestapo, particularly under torture, to place blame on those already dead – it is nevertheless fair to say that the Gestapo investigation started at the heart of the conspiracy and worked outwards. At the heart of the conspiracy was Olbricht. Thus the infamous judge of the *Volksgerichtshof*, Roland Freisler, described Olbricht as the 'most agile' of the conspirators and the 'central figure' in the *'Putschzentral'*, i.e. the centre of the coup.[1]

The chief SS investigator of the coup attempt, SS *Obersturmbannführer* Georg Kiesel, was more precise; he described Olbricht as 'Beck's closest associate; in effect, the chief of staff of the conspiracy'.[2]

But just what does the chief of staff of a conspiracy do?

Olbricht's principal Resistance activities can be divided into three categories. First, and particularly in the beginning, was the establishment and maintenance of a Resistance network. Secondly, he made use of that network to try to ensure that he had reliable people (in the Resistance sense) in key places, something that could be described as 'human resources management'. And last of all, he was responsible for developing the military plans for carrying out the coup d'état.

Networking

Turning first to networking, the key factor to remember is just how delicate the balance was between having too many and too few participants. Each new person drawn into the conspiracy was a risk. He or she was one more person who might be blackmailed, tortured, or bribed into betrayal. He or she was one more person who might make an unwitting mistake which could lead to the premature discovery of the conspiracy by the Nazi police apparatus. But if there were too few conspirators, then it would be impossible to carry out an effective coup at all.

In practice, this meant that the number of completely initiated conspirators – those who understood the full extent of goals, plans, membership, and structure – had to be kept to a minimum, while the number of partially initiated conspirators could be substantially larger. The idea was that each new conspirator knew only as much as was necessary for his or her designated role in the conspiracy, while only a tiny core group had an overview of the entire network. Olbricht was one of the few members of the inner core.

Today it is impossible to gain a complete picture of the comprehensive and complex network of contacts that Olbricht maintained with both military and civilian opposition circles. We know, however, that Olbricht had two assets that greatly assisted him in his networking. First, his official position as head of the GAO gave him perfectly legitimate reasons for corresponding with and meeting not only Army leaders but also officers from other services, representatives of civilian ministries and organisations, and business leaders. Secondly, his open, friendly, and cheerful personality enabled him to turn official contacts into personal ones. The hospitable atmosphere in the Olbricht home and Olbricht's active social life, in which he was superbly supported by his wife, likewise provided an excellent cover for meetings that were neither business nor pleasure, but treason.

Naturally, it was easiest for Olbricht to maintain ties with those conspirators whom he had known over a long time. Men like Beck, Oster, Thomas, Stülpnagel, and even Goerdeler were men he'd known for more than a decade. It aroused not the slightest suspicion if they were frequent visitors to his family home. Even Hoepner was such an old friend and near neighbour that Olbricht could meet him freely despite his disgrace and dismissal from the Army. Likewise, the officers of Olbricht's and Fromm's staff could be, and were, frequent guests of the Olbrichts without the slightest risk of awakening mistrust on the part of the authorities or overzealous neighbours. Meetings with men like Berlin Commandant General von Hase, Chief Military Justice Dr Sack, or the Berlin chief of police, Graf Helldorf, with whom Olbricht had to work closely in his duties, could likewise take place without risk or deceit.

Most significantly, perhaps, Olbricht's official position was important enough and his rank high enough for it to arouse no suspicion even if a *Generalfeldmarschall* such as Kluge agreed to call in for an evening. This was how Olbricht succeeded in organising several meetings between the active Kluge, still an Army Group commander, and the presumptive head of state and head of government (chancellor) of a proposed post-Hitler government, the retired Beck and Goerdeler respectively.

In the same way, there was nothing inherently suspicious about GFM von Manstein attempting to contact Olbricht in late May 1944. Manstein's adjutant at the time, Alexander Stahlberg, although himself one of the partially initiated conspirators, believes Manstein only wanted to talk to Olbricht about things related to his official duties, such as replacements, reserves, and weapons development. But Olbricht's son-in-law, Georgi, who took the call, believes that Manstein was interested in the coup plans. The fact that Olbricht refused to see Manstein supports Georgi's thesis. Olbricht had no reason to keep official information from a field marshal who still enjoyed Hitler's complete confidence even if he had been temporarily moved to the 'leadership reserve'. He did have a reason to want to avoid a discussion of Resistance plans.

Manstein had been given multiple opportunities to throw in his lot with the conspiracy, and through Stahlberg, who was a cousin and friend of Tresckow, he kept his ear to developments within the Military Resistance without being initiated in the conspiracy. Yet Manstein had never had the courage to join the conspiracy; or, more plausibly, he had always overestimated his own genius. Up to his very dismissal, Manstein had believed that somehow the mastermind of the victory in France and captor of Sebastapol would eventually talk 'sense' to Hitler. For someone whose only concern was winning the war, or stopping the senseless slaughter, such a solution might have seemed sufficient. For Olbricht, who wanted to end the regime, not just the war, it was not. In short, Olbricht had no real common ground with Manstein. An active field marshal with popular support, such as Rommel, might still be useful to the conspiracy; but not a retired military genius who had still not learned just how immoral the Nazi regime was. So Olbricht refused to receive GFM von Manstein in May 1944.

In contrast, Olbricht always had time for those field marshals and senior generals, no matter how disgraced, who shared his moral values. Olbricht's widow reported that on those evenings when Beck was expected at the Olbricht residence, her husband, in violation of all security regulations, brought the situation map home with him. Witzleben testified before the *Volksgerichtshof* that Olbricht showed him the situation map whenever he (Witzleben) visited Olbricht in the *Bendlerstrasse*. One of Olbricht's secretaries, Delia Ziegler, likewise remembered 'frequent' visits by both Witzleben and Hoepner, who came to Olbricht's office in order to obtain uncensored information about the progress of the war. One of Olbricht's staff officers, Hermann Lübben, recalls visits by the 'retired generals' to Olbricht's office happening every three to four months. In retrospect it is amazing that these visits did not arouse suspicion, but apparently the Nazi apparatus thought these retired generals were harmless.

Olbricht did not, however, maintain ties to the military only. He had frequent meetings with Albert Speer, for example – although this was purely official. Other contacts were quasi-official, such as his continued association with the military attachés of Central Europe, whom he had known since his days in the T-3 department. These and legitimate civilian contacts made it easier for him than for, say, Tresckow, to include civilian conspirators in his circle without arousing suspicion. It was particularly easy for him to maintain the friendship with Goerdeler and Hassel, since both of these were men he had known for decades.

Likewise, it was Olbricht who arranged a meeting between Tresckow and the former ambassador Friedrich Werner Graf von der Schulenburg in 1943, although it is no longer clear how Olbricht himself came to know Schulenburg. Hans-Bernd von Haeften and Adam von Trott zu Solz, two civilian conspirators whom Olbricht had no official reason for meeting, were also frequent guests at the Olbricht villa, for conspiratorial purposes.

While Olbricht made it possible for Beck to meet some active officers to whom he might otherwise not have had access and also gave the former chief of staff regular briefings on the war situation, Beck in return gave Olbricht access to the prestigious 'Wednesday Society' (*Mitwochsgesellschaft*). This was an exclusive club for men deemed 'leading' in their particular field. Beck, as a former chief of the General Staff, was their military member. Other members were prominent academics, artists, physicians, scientists, bankers, and men of industry and commerce. The society had been established in 1863 and met on the second Wednesday of every month. Beck and Hassel were both members during the Second World War, and Beck took Olbricht along with him as a guest on more than one occasion. This enabled Olbricht to become acquainted with several other members of the Society, such as the leading surgeon of the time, Dr Ferdinand Sauerbruch, and the former Prussian finance minister, Prof Dr Johannes Popitz. It is to Olbricht's credit that he was welcome in this exalted intellectual circle.

It is also notable, although not surprising, that Olbricht maintained friendly ties with important union leaders such as Wilhelm Leuschner and Jakob Kaiser. In fact, Olbricht provided Leuschner with documents that facilitated travel and so enabled him to keep up and extend his network of contacts with other former union leaders. Olbricht also became friends with the former Social Democratic member of parliament, Julius Leber, and the SPD politician was a welcome guest at the Olbricht villa.

All in all, the Villa Olbricht on the Wildpfad in Grünewald was a central point of contact for members of the conspiracy. So many different kinds of people – active and retired military, civil servants and diplomats, businessmen and scholars – were guests there that no one seemed 'out of the ordinary'. It was here that meetings between Beck, Goerdeler, Olbricht, Stauffenberg, and Hoepner usually took place. It was here that a key meeting between the man who controlled communications at Hitler's HQ, General Fritz Erich Fellgiebel, and Beck, Goerdeler, and Schulenburg took place in 1943. It was here that the newcomer to the conspiracy, Stauffenberg, was introduced to the 'old hands' in the late summer and early autumn of 1943. And it was here that the crucial meeting between Kluge, Goerdeler, Beck, Tresckow, and Olbricht took place in September 1943. Charmingly, according to the records of the Gestapo investigation, the assurance of support for the coup from the workers' movement (the SPD and unions) was conveyed symbolically to the sceptical Field Marshal von Kluge by the union leader Jakob Kaiser tipping his hat to the generals on the balcony as he walked past the Olbricht residence. More than any other single place, the Olbricht villa in Grünewald was the central meeting place of the anti-Nazi conspiracy.

Human-Resources Management

As was mentioned earlier, it was essential to keep the circle of truly informed conspirators as small as possible, while at the same time positioning as many sympathisers (with only limited knowledge of the conspiracy) in key jobs. Some historians have argued that Olbricht's greatest contribution to the entire conspiracy was that he: ' ... with unprecedented mastery of Army organisation, procedures, and personnel structures, combined with persuasive powers, conviction, and negotiating skills, carefully but steadily succeeded in building up a network of conspirators and semi-conspirators in the important military posts and key positions'.[3] Olbricht's recruiting tactics were circumspect and focused on winning over key generals, while placing junior officers with known opposition sentiments – but not necessarily knowledge of any organised conspiracy – in key positions at lower levels. He made particular efforts to win over commanding generals such as Reinhardt and Henrici. Although he was not always successful, one of his most significant successes was the recruitment of General von Hase. As the city commandant of Berlin, Hase commanded the only combat troops stationed inside the city. Hase thus became a completely initiated and vitally important member of the conspiracy once he had been recruited by Olbricht.

With junior officers the tactic was often more a matter of exposing the individual to the real military situation, something that many junior officers had no opportunity to grasp from their low-level jobs. Olbricht thereby awakened them to the hopelessness of the situation – unless 'something' changed. Thus, without even hinting at anything like plans to remove Hitler, he sought to make these young officers more receptive to a coup by shattering their naive faith in the infallibility of Hitler's leadership.

One of Olbricht's most important and successful works of personnel management was the selection and successful recruitment of Stauffenberg himself. As we have seen, Olbricht knew that his previous chief of staff, Reinhardt, was not willing to engage in treason and was due for promotion and transfer in March or April 1943. Olbricht was therefore on the lookout for a replacement who would be both good at his official duties and supportive in Resistance activities.

Stauffenberg's years of experience in the organisational department of the General Staff made him an obvious candidate from the official perspective, but by no means the only candidate. There were undoubtedly dozens of highly talented General Staff officers in the German Army in 1943 who could have carried out Stauffenberg's official duties at least as well as he did. More to the point, there were many wounded and mutilated General Staff officers with experience from the front who had earned a 'tour of duty' in Berlin. Likewise, there were a number of senior officers who knew and appreciated Stauffenberg's talents, and who showed an interest in having him for their staffs after his wounds made him available for central-staff work again. The fact that Olbricht won out over the others suggests that on the one hand, he had more clout with the Army personnel office, and, on the other, he knew Stauffenberg would also be of use to him in his treasonous activities.

That Olbricht was aware of Stauffenberg's change of heart is another clear example of his masterful human-resource management. It is well documented that Olbricht and Stauffenberg met for the first time in August 1943. All sources agree that Stauffenberg had no idea until this first meeting that Olbricht was involved in a conspiracy against Hitler, and less that Olbricht would ask him to participate actively. But Olbricht knew what he wanted from Stauffenberg by April 1943 at the latest, when he had to ask Reinhardt to stay on in his current duties until the severely wounded Stauffenberg was fit enough to take over Reinhardt's job. But how could he be sure that the former ardent supporter of Hitler and believer in the Führer's military genius had changed his mind?

The answer appears to be Tresckow who, according to Manstein's adjutant Stahlberg, organised the meeting between Stauffenberg and Manstein in early 1943. It appears that Tresckow had wind of Stauffenberg's change of heart and recommended to Olbricht that they take a closer look at him. Moreover, they gave him a little test. As Stahlberg recounts, Stauffenberg's trip to Manstein was carefully prepared by Tresckow. Furthermore, after the meeting, Manstein was asked by the then chief of the General Staff, *Generaloberst* Zeitzler, for his 'opinion' of Stauffenberg. So much interest in a freshly promoted lieutenant colonel is not ordinary and cannot be considered routine. It appears that Stahlberg was expected to report to Tresckow on how well Stauffenberg argued with Manstein, while Manstein's report to Zeitzler was expected to provide another perspective on the candidate's discretion.

The following sequence of events tells its own story. On 26 January 1943, Stauffenberg had his meeting with Manstein. On 27 January, Zeitzler asked for Manstein's opinion of Stauffenberg, and Manstein suggested that Stauffenberg had been in Berlin too long and needed to get out with the troops. On 2 February, the conspirator Hermann Kaiser recorded in his diary that Stauffenberg had been selected as Reinhardt's successor at an unknown future date. On 7 February, Stauffenberg received orders for Africa. In short, Stauffenberg's transfer to the 10th Panzer Division in Africa was a necessary precondition for his transfer to GAO, since it would have been completely contrary to General Staff policy for an officer of such junior rank to have two successive tours of duty in Berlin. Stauffenberg had to do troop duty *before* he could be appointed to GAO.

Another example of Olbricht's human-resources management is provided by Axel von dem Bussche. The significance of this example is not, as with Stauffenberg, the effect, but rather that it conveys an idea of how Olbricht worked in case after case trying to get the 'right' people into the right jobs. Bussche described in a personal interview with the author how he suddenly found himself the adjutant of the Infantry

Replacement Regiment 23, although he was actually too junior for the job and did not want it.

He reconstructed his appointment as follows. At this time, after the serious military setbacks of winter 1941–2, General Olbricht was working on coup plans. He was therefore reviewing which troops were stationed in and around Berlin. Of key importance here were the garrison towns of Spandau and Potsdam, both located on the outskirts of Berlin and connected to the capital by commuter trains and excellent roads. One of the troop units stationed in Potsdam was Infantry Replacement Regiment 23. This regiment could rapidly reach Berlin to support a coup, if it were led by the right officers. It was also the replacement regiment for Tresckow's own IR 9. The older officers of the regiment were reliable, but each year the new recruits coming in were more and more the products of National Socialism. It was important to keep an eye on them and know the exact political colours of each. The adjutant of the regiment was ideally situated to know about the political leanings of the junior officers, and to control who was where. So Olbricht asked his friend and fellow-conspirator Fritz-Dietlof Graf von der Schulenburg to be sure that the adjutant of IR 23 was 'reliable', i.e. anti-Nazi.

Graf Schulenburg, who knew his officers well, selected Axel von dem Bussche, using as a pretext for his transfer back to the Replacement Regiment a new decree that said that if a soldier or officer was the last living son in his family, he was exempt from front-line service. Since Axel's brother had just been killed, Axel qualified for this protection, even though he himself protested that he 'didn't want to be a memorial'.[4]

Once Bussche was back in Potsdam, Schulenburg, whom Bussche knew personally and trusted, told the younger Bussche that he should 'do whatever he was ordered to do by a certain General Olbricht', a man Bussche had never heard of before. This warning alone was a signal to Bussche that whatever it was that Olbricht ordered, it had nothing to do with ordinary duty; German officers could be expected to follow military orders without being told to do so by friends. Bussche describes what happened next:

One day I got a call from the adjutant of the deputy commander of the Replacement Office, a man I didn't know, informing me that General Olbricht was already on his way to visit my regiment. Now the commander of the Replacement Army was as far removed from me as the dear God is from earth. There was a division in between, and a corps, and the personnel department, and various other offices. And I thought to myself: if this Olbricht himself is coming to see me, then no red carpet. Better wait and see what happens instead.[5]

Indeed, Olbricht spoke only of unimportant official business – things no three-star general needed to discuss personally with a subaltern – and then suggested a walk across the wide exercise fields, where no one could hear what was said. On this walk, Olbricht explained to Bussche just what his duties were – his unofficial duties, that is. Namely: to keep his regiment as free of Nazi sympathisers and Hitler adherents as possible. Bussche candidly admitted to the general that he didn't know how to do that; and the patient Olbricht explained 'with a certain Saxon charm' that the Replacement Army had a whole variety of training courses of varying length to which officers could be sent for additional training. So it was 'relatively easy', the general suggested, to get rid of any officers Bussche didn't particularly like. In short, the conspiracy worked by trying to put 'reliable' officers in key positions, who then at their own level perpetuated that policy of finding 'reliable' officers.[6]

Yet another example of Olbricht human-resources management, again, a single case study of the kind of thing he had to do over and over again, was the appointment of Fritz Merker to the GAO in 1942. Merker had been Olbricht's first General Staff officer in the 24th Infantry Division. Olbricht knew his anti-Nazi sentiments and so trusted him in the dual sense of professional and conspiratorial work. He brought Merker first into his own staff, and then, as he was later to do with Stauffenberg himself, moved him over on to Fromm's staff as a means of hemming in the fickle C-in-C of the Home Army with trustworthy (in the sense of the conspiracy) staff officers.

The Gestapo interrogations in connection with the 20 July Plot brought the Gestapo to the conclusion that the GAO (i.e. Olbricht) systematically sought to place 'treasonous' officers into all the subordinate military district commands. The goal, according to the Gestapo, was 'a living tie to the military districts in order to avoid unnecessary and lengthy correspondence and to make it unnecessary for the commanders to travel too often to Berlin. These officers were to be of particular value in "critical situations".'[7] To give just one of many examples, in 1942 the conspirators won over to their cause the chief of staff of Military District VI (Kassel), *Generalmajor* von Nida. He vaguely informed his first General Staff officer, *Oberst* Vethacke, about the coup, and together they tried to collect around them officers who shared their views of the regime. Although a difficult task given the ever-changing composition of any staff, Nida was so successful that his staff proved one of the most loyal to the conspiracy on 20 July 1944, although he himself had been transferred away from the military district. This was in part because his originally scheduled transfer at the start of 1944 was delayed by GAO until a 'reliable' replacement could be located and appointed. Another successful example of Olbricht's personnel policies was the appointment of the reliably anti-Nazi Graf Schwerin to the important Brandenburg Division on 1 March 1943.

Olbricht's concern for 'reliable' officers was not focused exclusively on those of the General Staff. As always, he valued the ordinary soldier, too. When a former clerk from the 24th Infantry Division stopped to see him in Berlin, Olbricht realised that this soldier shared his political views and so decided he could use the man in the GAO. He made every effort to effect the clerk's transfer, but this time he bit into granite in the form of General Model's resistance to the move.

Since the conspiracy also relied upon the cooperation of comrades and subordinates who were not in any way initiated into the coup plans, it is useful to see how this personnel policy worked. The man who had accompanied Olbricht on his trip to the Soviet Union, Hans-Joachim von Horn, served as Beck's adjutant in 1935–6. Later, when serving with the staff of the XIIth Army Corps in Poland, an officer of Counter-Intelligence visited him to reveal to him the atrocities committed in Poland by the SS. This officer ended his briefing by declaring that 'We have to clean up', to which Horn replied without hesitation: 'If you need me, I am at your disposal.'[8] After that, Horn didn't hear anything more from the conspirators. In fact, he didn't even know there was a conspiracy. But suddenly in early 1944 he was visited on the front by General Schmundt, Hitler's personal adjutant. Schmundt explained that Horn had to go to Bern as military attaché because the current attaché, General von Ilsemann, had 'gone native' and was no longer a good National Socialist. Horn became the German military attaché in Bern, Switzerland, in time for the 20 July coup.

The entire conspiracy appears to have collaborated on this appointment. On the one hand, Olbricht, Beck, and Oster (via his messenger to Poland in 1939) could all vouch for Horn's credentials as anti-Nazi, but it took Tresckow's friendship with Schmundt to effect the transfer to Bern. Bern was critical to the conspiracy, because this was where Allen Dulles and many other members of the Allied intelligence services had their offices. In the event of a coup, the conspirators wanted to communicate with the Western governments through these channels and plead their case for something other than unconditional surrender. The conspirators had up to this point relied upon the uninitiated but clearly anti-Nazi Ilsemann; but when it became evident that he was untenable, they scrambled to find a 'reliable' replacement who appeared completely unsuspicious to the Nazis. Horn was a particularly good choice because of his facility with languages, including Russian, and his personal friendship with both Beck and Olbricht.

Lastly, Stauffenberg's transfer from Olbricht's staff to Fromm's must be cited as one of Olbricht's master strokes in the field of personnel policy. The Valkyrie orders were officially designed to put down a domestic crisis and were to be signed by Hitler himself, unless he was incapacitated. In the event of Hitler's incapacitation, then (and only then) the commander of the Home Army, *Generaloberst* Fromm, was authorised to issue the orders. The chief of staff of any German military unit, however, was automatically the deputy of the commander, and as such often signed orders in his name. Olbricht, on the other hand, was *not* authorised to do so. To be sure, this situation wasn't all that obvious, even to the subordinate commanders. Olbricht's position was in some areas parallel to Fromm's, and by summer 1944 he was such a powerful and familiar figure that his orders – as we shall see – were largely followed without authorisation. But officially, only Fromm, or his chief of staff, was authorised to issue Valkyrie if Hitler himself was prevented from doing so. Hence it was a small coup in itself to position the fanatical conspirator Stauffenberg in the direct chain of command for the Valkyrie orders.

Although Fromm initiated the transfer of Stauffenberg from Olbricht's staff to his own, he could only do so with Olbricht's and Stauffenberg's explicit cooperation. Both men willingly approved the move because of the advantages it offered the conspiracy. But it also brought a fateful complication. As Fromm's chief of staff and deputy, Stauffenberg was required to travel to Hitler's HQ with considerable frequency. After all other assassination plans had failed and the situation deteriorated on the front, Stauffenberg could not resist the temptation to play the assassin. Yet in so doing, he jeopardised the very benefits that his position as chief of staff to Fromm had brought. If Stauffenberg (as Bussche or Gersdorff had planned to do) blew himself up with the dictator, then there would still be no reliable member of the conspiracy legally authorised to issue Valkyrie. Hence all of Stauffenberg's assassination attempts were based on the almost schizophrenic need to be in two places at once.

Coup Plans

Olbricht's principal task as the chief of staff of the military conspiracy against Hitler, however, was to develop the military coup plans. Despite a bizarre persistence of the myth that Stauffenberg was the originator of the secret aspects of Valkyrie, the evidence is overwhelming that it was Olbricht who initiated Valkyrie planning and adapted this official plan for Resistance purposes.

General Reinhardt remembers that shortly after the start of the campaign against the Soviet Union in 1941, all divisions had already been committed, and the Home Army faced the dilemma of scraping together new divisions for the emergency that they knew would inevitably come. Olbricht's staff worked on a variety of mobilisation plans for the units of the Home Army, which were given Wagnerian names such as 'Rheingold' and, yes, 'Valkyrie'.

The date at which 'Valkyrie' became a plan for the suppression of internal unrest is not precise. The Gestapo investigations of the failed coup point to a conversion date for these plans of somewhere in the winter of 1941–2 – at exactly the time when the military conspiracy was regrouping after the years of Hitler's victories and becoming active again. The Gestapo files indicate further that Olbricht was the driving force behind the discussions about needing plans to suppress 'inner unrest'. It appears from the interrogation of Canaris and Oster that Olbricht talked Canaris into sending a series of reports to Hitler outlining the risks to the security of the Reich posed by large numbers of forced labourers inside Germany. Canaris's reports had the desired effect, and in due time orders were issued from Hitler's HQ to the Home Army to work out military plans to counter internal unrest.

In short, Olbricht recognised that official plans designed to suppress a revolt by slave labourers would be the ideal mechanism for planning a military coup, and he told Canaris this. Canaris used his position as head of Counter-Intelligence to persuade Hitler that there was a (completely fictitious) risk of a forced-labourer uprising. The paranoid dictator obligingly ordered one of his bitterest domestic enemies to start making plans that could, and would, be used as the blueprint for a coup against him.

Other surviving members of the conspiracy can verify that Valkyrie was already the blueprint for the coup by mid-1942, more than a year before Stauffenberg joined the conspiracy. First, Friedrich Georgi remembers that his father-in-law first spoke to him about the real purposes of Valkyrie shortly after his wedding. A man does not mistake the date of his own wedding, and this was July 1942. Georgi was at this time asked to help type up some of the secret orders associated with Valkyrie, including, as he remembered vividly because it excited him so much at the time, the orders to close down the concentration camps.

But without doubt, the most convincing of all witnesses is Axel von dem Bussche. Bussche, as noted above, was appointed adjutant of the 23rd Infantry Regiment and only held this position for roughly half a year in early 1942, before being sent back to the Eastern Front that summer. He met Olbricht only once during this period, and the meeting made such a deep impression on him that he could still describe it in lively and enthusiastic detail more than 40 years later. During this brief meeting, Bussche says that Olbricht lectured him about Valkyrie. In Bussche's own words: '"Valkyrie" was a well-organised plan of the Home Army that was supposed to be used in the event that the millions of forced labourers revolted. It was a plan, as Fritz Schulenburg had told me, that in the event of a coup would be used to seize control of the radio stations, the barracks of the SS and Gestapo, etc. So much I knew, so that Olbricht – who was kneedeep in these preparations – didn't have to give me remedial education.'[9]

Since Bussche left Potsdam in the summer of 1942, he cannot have mistaken the timing of his meeting with Olbricht.

Clearly Valkyrie was a coup blueprint more than a year before Stauffenberg joined the conspiracy, and it is almost certain that it was these plans Olbricht was thinking of when he told Tresckow in November 1942 that he needed eight weeks to get his planning up to date. The activities of Hans-Bernd Gisevius, who at Oster's request worked in the GAO on these plans, represented a reworking and updating of the existing official and secret aspects of Valkyrie.

We know from officers of Olbricht's staff who were loyal to Hitler on 20 July 1944 that the official Valkyrie plans were constantly being updated to reflect troop movements, bomb damage to installations, the creation of new organisations, and alterations in command structures, among other things. Altogether, they were reworked at least 220 times. The plans dated 31 July 1943 – before Stauffenberg had even heard about the conspiracy – were already the eighty-third version of Valkyrie. As for the secret plans, these too were updated, albeit more irregularly, as the conspirators had time for them. Hence there is nothing odd about Tresckow working on the secret plans in the late spring and early summer of 1943, or Stauffenberg looking them over again during his own convalescence in August and September 1943. These actions do not in any way contradict or alter the fact that Valkyrie had been designed for use as a coup blueprint in the winter of 1941–2, and that the originator of the very idea to use an official plan for suppressing domestic unrest as a coup blueprint was Friedrich Olbricht.

Olbricht also worked closely with the senior general of the signal corps, Fellgiebel, to work out a means for the conspiracy to obtain a monopoly on telecommunications during the critical hours of the coup. Fellgiebel, however, rapidly came to the conclusion that it would not be possible for the coup to completely cut off Hitler's HQ without first occupying the relay stations, something that would arouse suspicion. Olbricht chose, as a less satisfactory alternative, the occupation by troops loyal to the conspiracy of all radio stations in and around Berlin. Olbricht ordered one of his subordinate department heads, *Oberst* Hassel, to list all radio stations in and around Berlin and make an estimate of how many troops would be needed to 'protect' these vital communication centres from 'sabotage'. Olbricht specifically asked for a listing of not just military but also SS, SD, Foreign Ministry, Propaganda Ministry, and police radio and telegraph installations. The sheer number of such installations must have been daunting to the conspirators. With the troops available, it was virtually impossible to secure them all.

But to return to Valkyrie, the key aspect of this scheme was that it was a completely legitimate and official General Staff plan. As such it was designed to exploit the existing military apparatus, and it depended upon military discipline and obedience rather than inciting rebellion or revolt. The plan assumed that the vast majority of officers receiving the Valkyrie orders would *not* be conspirators – not even partially initiated ones. Indeed, the assumption was that a significant portion of the officers and men carrying out the Valkyrie orders would be completely loyal followers of Hitler and National Socialism!

The fatal flaw in the plan was that neither Olbricht nor Stauffenberg were legally authorised to initiate it as long as Hitler lived. Olbricht was not authorised to issue Valkyrie at all, even if Hitler were dead; and Stauffenberg, after he became chief of staff to Fromm, was only authorised to issue the orders in Fromm's name. If Hitler survived the assassination or if Fromm failed to cast his lot with the conspirators, then Olbricht and Stauffenberg could only act in violation of the established chain of command. This instantly put at risk the entire plan, since it was by no means certain that regime-loyal German officers and soldiers would follow orders coming from an unauthorised source. The conspirators could try to bluff their way through a coup, hoping that people further down the chain of command would not ask too many questions; but they knew that if they issued the orders without authorisation and something went wrong, they would have no second chance.

Olbricht's Methods

Thus the ultimate success of the coup was dependent not only on good planning, but also on intense secrecy and discretion to prevent premature discovery. The conspirators were at constant risk of discovery, and discovery meant arrest, interrogation, and death – not just for the individual initially exposed, but for all the fellow conspirators, whose names would be torn from the victim by torture, and for the victims' families and friends.

For those of us living in a post-totalitarian world, it is almost inconceivable just how careful the conspirators had to be and to what extreme measures they had to go in order to keep their activities hidden from the agents of the police state they were trying to depose. Allen

Dulles tried to explain the situation saying: 'In Nazi Germany telephones were tapped, mail was censored, and every servant, taxicab driver, or messenger was regarded as a possible Nazi agent. All the key conspirators used codenames in conversation and correspondence. Meeting places changed constantly.'[10]

Frau Dr Sack remembers that her husband warned her not even to look in the direction of the Olbricht villa when they were walking around the neighbourhood, to avoid seeming too interested. Frau Olbricht reported that although her husband had a direct military telephone connection from his office (i.e. a line not controlled by the German Post Office, which was always subject to tapping), he nevertheless liked to make some of his calls from his son-in-law's equally secure military lines. When Beck came to visit the Olbrichts, he didn't come directly. Instead, he went to the railway station and entered by the entrance that suggested he was heading in the opposite direction. Then he would go through the tunnel and out of the other door, to be picked up by a Luftwaffe (not Army) staff car. He was brought back in the same manner. Other visitors were collected, again usually by a Luftwaffe car, at different public places around the city and returned to yet others. Such are the necessary ploys of any conspirator in a totalitarian dictatorship.

Olbricht's position was unique in so far as his importance and rank enabled him to be 'above suspicion' by the vast army of unofficial and low-level spies and informers. The average block warden and ardent Hitler Youth leader was awe-struck by the three-star general who openly consorted with some of Nazi Germany's most prominent leaders, from field marshals to Albert Speer and Heinrich Himmler. On the other hand, the fact that Olbricht had to do business with the Speers and Himmlers of the world also meant that he had to keep a very tight rein on his tongue and manner at all times. Beck is known to have reminded more temperamental and impatient conspirators that Olbricht was in an extremely difficult position, and his position deteriorated as the other Military Resistance centres closed down. Particularly after Oster's Resistance cell had aroused Gestapo misgivings, it became imperative that Olbricht not come under suspicion. For the sake of the conspiracy, Olbricht could not afford to take too many chances, or the Military Resistance would have lost its very last platform for action.

One of the worst impediments to Olbricht's Resistance activities was the personality of his immediate superior, *Generaloberst* Fromm, who was accused by his own staff of laziness, cowardice, and greed for glory or a craving for recognition. He was furthermore alleged to be an alcoholic. But when Georgi once referred to him as 'a stupid pig', Olbricht quickly corrected him, saying: 'Stupid is the one thing he's not.'[11]

However, because he was Olbricht's immediate superior *and* the only officer authorised to issue Valkyrie in the event of Hitler's incapacity, Olbricht had no choice but to get along with him. Certainly Olbricht and other conspirators tried to win Fromm over to the conspiracy, but Fromm very intentionally remained ambivalent. He told Halder in November 1939 that he would not take part in a coup; and more than three years later, when Olbricht described the catastrophic war situation in a particularly dramatic briefing designed to make him see the need for replacing Hitler, Fromm responded with a dry: 'That was very interesting. Well, then, Heil Hitler!'[12] On the other hand, Fromm is alleged to have said point-blank to Olbricht: 'When you plan your coup, be sure not to forget Wilhelm Keitel.'[13] By which he meant: be sure you get rid of Keitel, Fromm's most-hated rival, at the same time as Hitler. To sum up Fromm's position, he wanted no part in the conspiracy, unless it was already successful.

Olbricht had to work with Fromm daily, and it is recorded that as the war situation deteriorated, so did the relationship between the two men. Officers of the staff were witness to one particularly violent clash between the generals in which Fromm told Olbricht that one had to obey orders 100 per cent of the time, and Olbricht retorted that in 100 cases, one had to be able to say no at least once. It is also a matter of record that General Schmundt on two occasions had to ask Fromm to give Olbricht 'official reprimands' for remarks he had made that had reached Hitler's ears. Although we do not know exactly what these comments were, they clearly fell in the category of 'defeatist' rather than 'disloyal', or they would have resulted in much greater unpleasantness than an official reprimand.

Yet not only was Olbricht's direct superior difficult, so was his first deputy and closest associate, his chief of staff. Not that Reinhardt was unpleasant or incompetent, but he was completely 'unreliable' from the conspiracy's point of view. This meant that until the arrival of Stauffenberg, Olbricht had to hide his conspiratorial work not only from his immediate superior (who was round the corner and down the hall a bit) but from his closest associate, sitting just one office away. And many other officers of Olbricht's staff were equally 'unreliable'. Some were even outright adherents of Hitler, who 40 years after the end of the war justified their loyalty to Hitler with all the good the dictator had done in the 1930s.

Very likely it was this environment that schooled Olbricht to be very cautious indeed. Those officers who knew Olbricht's true feelings, those who had served with him in the 24th Infantry Division, for example, admired his ability to disguise his feelings. Hermann Lübben, for example, attests that: 'Olbricht was incredibly careful in his choice of words and never used a phrase on which one could have nailed him down.'[14] In another instance, he once caught a young officer slipping out of the auditorium where Goebbels was about to speak. The frightened young man thought he was about to be reprimanded by the senior general, and couldn't believe his luck when Olbricht remarked, 'Don't worry. I wouldn't be here if I didn't have to be.'[15] But Olbricht's widow was shocked to hear of the incident and said that such a remark was 'going very far' for her husband. He didn't usually risk revealing his sentiments to strangers. Indeed, even men who had known him for years, such as General and Frau von Tettau, claim never to have known he was part of the Resistance until he was executed on 20 July 1944.

The very manner in which Olbricht 'lectured' Bussche about Valkyrie is likewise extremely revealing, showing his cautious and indirect methods of communicating. In the already mentioned visit by Olbricht to Bussche while the latter was the adjutant of the 23rd Infantry Regiment in Potsdam, Olbricht only talked to Bussche about Valkyrie after they were alone in the middle of a broad field – although Valkyrie was a completely official General Staff plan. And then, as Bussche describes it, the following happened:

> He [Olbricht] said to me: 'Now, Valkyrie: that is for when the forced labourers strike and we have to restore order, you understand?' I said: *'Jawohl, Herr General.'* 'And if it gets really bad, then we'll have to take control of the radio stations and the ministries in Berlin, you understand what I mean?' And I said: *'Jawohl, Herr General.'* 'And then we will need very reliable people, so make sure you don't have any fickle National Socialists in this regiment.' Olbricht did *not* say what

Valkyrie was really about. First, I knew that already; and second, no conspiring general puts himself at the mercy of some possibly indiscreet *Oberleutnant*. … He didn't say: 'We need to seize the Chancellery.' At most he would say, 'We must defend the Chancellery – you understand what I mean?' If I had been hauled up before a court of law, I would never have been able to testify against him, because not once did he say anything like 'We'll throw the Nazis out.'[16]

Olbricht's style was thus radically different from that of many other conspirators. Oster was notoriously blunt, and Olbricht was reportedly furious about his lack of circumspection. The Gestapo interrogations reveal that Olbricht ordered Oster to maintain 'absolute silence' and speak about his views of the Nazis to no one who was not *already* initiated into the coup. Dr Sack was likewise ordered by Olbricht to be more careful. Even Stauffenberg's style, when he finally joined the conspiracy, was very different from Olbricht's. One need only contrast the way Olbricht spoke to Bussche, whom he knew from trusted friends to be anti-Nazi, with Stauffenberg's discussion with a complete stranger, *Oberleutnant* Urban Thiersch. Thiersch remembers that the first words Stauffenberg spoke to him when he reported for duty in the staff of the Home Army were: 'Let's get right to the point. I am engaged in high treason with every means at my disposal.'[17] After that, Stauffenberg went on to explain the war situation and why Hitler had to be eliminated in order to stop the slaughter on all fronts.

It was the essential difference in methodology and style between the careful and professional Olbricht and the flamboyant and temperamental Goerdeler and Hermann Kaiser that have had a devastating and unfair impact upon Olbricht's historical reputation. Both Goerdeler and Hermann Kaiser, who was essentially a high-school teacher but as a reserve officer was on General Fromm's staff in the *Bendlerstrasse*, kept diaries. These documents fell into Gestapo hands. Their opinions have therefore coloured the entire image of Olbricht in the postwar literature.

Hermann Kaiser (not to be confused with the union leader Jakob Kaiser) was the same age as Olbricht and, like Olbricht, an opponent of Hitler from very early on, in Kaiser's case from 1933 onwards. But Kaiser had a completely different personality from Olbricht. Those who knew him described him as passionate and impulsive. The Gestapo records reveal that Olbricht had to warn him more than once to be more careful, and that his tendency to express his opinion of Hitler and the Nazis to anyone and everyone led to his denunciation for treason. Olbricht and Sack had to go to a great deal of trouble to get the charges dropped.

Hermann Kaiser was also an impatient man, and he kept trying to pressure Olbricht into 'doing something'. He introduced to Olbricht an (unfortunately unnamed) civilian opponent of Hitler, and thereby aroused Olbricht's wrath because he considered the man a 'dilettante'. Olbricht gave Kaiser a sharp ticking-off for endangering the entire conspiracy and the chances of a successful coup by bringing people 'like this' anywhere near the conspirators. He continued the dressing-down by informing Kaiser that he took his orders from Beck only, and ended the reprimand with the words that he was doing all he could 'for the liberation of Germany' but that such dilettantes would only 'ruin everything'.[18]

Olbricht's emphasis in this and later actions was always on taking only calculated and responsible risks. Kaiser, in contrast, tended to act impulsively, and so endangered all the careful planning of Olbricht and the other professionals. Yet a single diary entry of this impetuous, fervent, and often irresponsible man has become one of the most commonly quoted epitaphs for General Olbricht. On 20 February 1943, in a diary entry reflecting Kaiser's own frustration and despair at that one moment in time, Kaiser wrote: '[Olbricht] wants to act when he gets the order, and [Fromm] wants to give the order when something happens.'[19]

Historians and film-makers have taken this momentary, petulant judgement of a temperamental amateur and treated it like a sober summary of Olbricht's entire Resistance attitudes and activities. The absurdity of this is underlined by the fact that Hermann Kaiser himself changed his assessment of Olbricht, and later diary entries reflect his own irritation with other dilettantish, impatient, and unprofessional civilian conspirators, including Goerdeler. Moreover, other entries from this same diary testify to Olbricht's willingness to act *without* orders from Fromm (notably the entry from 29 July 1943). But for those commentators and historians who prefer to lionise Stauffenberg, it is convenient to quote the earlier entry and not the later ones. That way Stauffenberg can be the hero of the Military Resistance despite his late arrival and his more dubious motives.

The differences between Olbricht and Goerdeler pose another problem for Olbricht's image. Goerdeler deserves credit for his unwavering opposition to the National Socialist regime. Furthermore, because he left such a rich legacy of written material about his Resistance activities and was interrogated by the Gestapo for a comparatively long time, he greatly enhanced the historical record. Goerdeler made it easy for future biographers and historians to reconstruct his motives, goals, and positions. By contrast, Olbricht – the consummate conspirator – was extremely careful *not* to write anything down that might incriminate him or endanger fellow conspirators; and since he was executed before falling into Gestapo hands, he was never interrogated or brought before a judge.

In consequence of this uneven distribution of source material, Goerdeler's view of things has had a disproportionately significant impact on the entire image and understanding of the German Resistance to Hitler, or at least the conspiracy culminating in the coup of 20 July 1944. We know much more about what Goerdeler thought of Olbricht than the reverse. While serious historians have drawn attention to many of Goerdeler's faults – his tendency to simplification, his 'exaggerated optimism',[20] and his 'grotesque carelessness'[21] – nevertheless, his opinion of others is (at least in the case of Olbricht) widely quoted and credited without the slightest reflection on the source.

A closer look at Goerdeler, however, shows that he appears to have lived in an ivory tower of sorts, fully disconnected from the grim and bloody world in which Olbricht had to operate. Goerdeler was still suggesting in May 1943 that 'the generals' should collectively protest against Hitler's leadership, even though this method of opposing the dictator's policies had failed repeatedly in 1938 and in 1939. In February 1943 Goerdeler, but not the SPD or union leaders, imagined that the German workers were already in a 'revolutionary' frame of mind; history shows us that they were not revolutionary in February 1945 even after two full years of the Allied bombing offensive. The civilian Goerdeler, who did not fight even a single day on any front in the Second World War, repeatedly tried to lecture officers with extensive front-line experience on what soldiers really thought and felt. It is not surprising that Goerdeler infuriated many senior officers. Perhaps most fatal of all, Goerdeler refused to recognise that men like GFM von Keitel and Heinz von Guderian had long since sold their souls to the Nazis.

Goerdeler's weaknesses make him more human and appealing in many ways. He would be well suited to the role of tragic hero in the hands of a modern Shakespeare. But Goerdeler's impatience, his overestimation of his own powers of persuasion, and his underestimation of the evil around him were highly dangerous for the conspiracy. Goerdeler was comparable to a loose cannon, always in danger of smashing something vital as it crashed about in undirected activities and initiatives. His continuous nagging at the active conspirators to 'act' without the least consideration for the consequences tested the patience of even the most sympathetic. Olbricht reputedly was one of those who bore Goerdeler's inappropriate suggestions and pressure with the greatest patience. Stauffenberg was allegedly often angered and embittered by the civilian meddler. Hermann Kaiser, although so similar to Goerdeler in temperament, had by July 1944 come to doubt whether Goerdeler was even suited to the post of chancellor. Shadow-cabinet lists increasingly favoured the more cautious and stable Julius Leber to the volatile Goerdeler.

Yet again, a single snapshot from Goerdeler's voluminous legacy has cast a gigantic shadow over the image of Olbricht in the postwar literature. In the midst of a documented crisis of doubt for this otherwise excessive optimist, Goerdeler allegedly wrote a letter to Olbricht and Zeitzler. This combination is itself highly intriguing, as it puts Olbricht on the same level as the chief of the General Staff and suggests that, at least from Goerdeler's perspective, they were working closely together. (Something not entirely irrelevant to the aforementioned constellation of facts surrounding Stauffenberg's meeting with Manstein and his subsequent postings.) Unfortunately, it is not this that has attracted the attention of historians, but rather the fact that Goerdeler found it necessary to urge Olbricht to action.

The letter is a passionate appeal not to 'await the right psychological moment' but rather to 'create' it. It argues that by revealing the horrible crimes of the Nazis, one would cause the popular mood to change (overnight) from pro- to anti-Nazi. The letter ends with the suggestion that if no other solution could be found, Goerdeler himself was prepared to talk to Hitler personally – and 'tell him that his resignation is required for the good of the nation'.[22]

It is hard to know whether to weep or laugh at so much naivety, and yet, rather than being used as proof of Goerdeler's hopeless alienation from reality, this letter is repeatedly cited as proof of Olbricht's 'indecisiveness' or 'hesitancy'. At a time when Olbricht, together with Tresckow, was updating Valkyrie, had already identified Stauffenberg as his chief of staff, and had taken over responsibility for the assassination as well as the coup, he was 'indecisive' and 'hesitant'? In fact, no one else in the entire conspiracy was doing anything at all. Stauffenberg was recovering from wounds and filled with vague notions of 'saving Germany', while Tresckow was on leave and Oster was under Gestapo observation. Goerdeler's frustration is understandable, but his naivity is tragic – and the willingness of historians and film-makers to generalise about Olbricht's entire behaviour on the basis of this letter is reprehensible.

The absurdity of using a nagging letter of Goerdeler's as proof of the absence of decisiveness on the part of the recipient is underlined by Goerdeler's letter to Stauffenberg on 12 July 1944. Apparently Goerdeler felt it was necessary to urge Stauffenberg to action the day after his first assassination attempt and three days before his second. There really can be no doubt about Stauffenberg's commitment to act at this point in time.

Furthermore, there are serious reasons to doubt whether this oft-cited letter was even directed at Olbricht at all. Given the years of friendship between the two men and the fact that Goerdeler was a frequent guest at the Olbricht home, one wonders why Goerdeler would address him, first, in a letter at all, and, secondly, with *'hochverehrter Herr General'* (essentially, 'Your Excellency'). Even if Goerdeler in his despair and frustration was trying to emphasise his displeasure by stressing distance rather than friendship, the use of the formal style of address and the last name would have been sufficient to convey this.

The written legacy of these two men, Hermann Kaiser and Carl Goerdeler, has done immense damage to the image of Friedrich Olbricht in the postwar literature. Both men were friends and co-conspirators of Olbricht, and it was probably never their intention to let momentary personal crises obscure the years – even decades – of consistent, diligent, and committed opposition that Olbricht brought to the Resistance. It is not to their discredit that they had moments of doubt or expressed impatience with a situation that drove all the opponents of Hitler to the brink of despair. It is, however, a sad commentary on modern historians that they have been so quick to quote these documents out of context and expand their meaning beyond all justification.

Returning to the objective record, it is a fact that while both Hermann Kaiser and Goerdeler aroused the suspicions of the Gestapo by their incautious behaviour, Olbricht managed to keep his far more significant activities hidden. What is more, at the same time that Olbricht's became the only active cell of the Military Resistance, responsible for coup and assassination plan, he was still rising in Hitler's favour and gaining new responsibilities as the chief of the Armed Forces Replacement Office. No one in Hitler's circle doubted Olbricht's loyalty, and it was because of this that he was able to remain in a key position at the heart of the Home Army. It is only because Olbricht did not arouse the suspicion of the Gestapo that the Military Resistance had any chance of taking action at all. If Olbricht had lost the trust of his Nazi superiors, there would never have been any coup attempt, no 'final throw', and the German Resistance would be an obscure footnote in the history of the Second World War.

The clearest proof of Olbricht's success as a conspirator is the fact that late in the evening of 20 July 1944, Keitel sent a cable addressed to Olbricht personally. In this cable, Keitel ordered Olbricht to stop following the orders issued by Fromm, Witzleben, and Hoepner. Not only did Keitel never dream that Olbricht had written most of the orders going out over the names of the others, Keitel actually believed that he could stop the coup simply by ordering Olbricht to disobey Fromm. In short, in Hitler's HQ Stauffenberg and Fromm were perceived as the source of the revolt, while Olbricht – more than six hours into the coup he had set in motion – was still trusted. His role was not recognised until after he was dead.

Not only had Olbricht almost single-handedly kept the conspiracy viable until the 'final throw' had been made, he was also not discovered until after his death. There could hardly be any higher tribute to Olbricht's skills as a conspirator.

Chapter 13

THE CONSPIRACY FAILS

October 1943 to July 1944

The Last Nine Months of the Military Conspiracy

When Stauffenberg finally took up his new duties at the GAO, the coup plans had just undergone a review and update at the hands of Tresckow and the responsibility for the assassination had been turned over to Olbricht. Thus the most pressing Resistance task for Olbricht's new chief of staff was organising the trigger for a coup – the assassination.

The key problem with assassinating Hitler was access to the dictator with a weapon. Hitler was very well protected by methods now familiar to us in a terrorist-plagued world. The days when Hitler bathed in the adoration of his subjects were long since over. He did not drive about in open cars, making himself a target for sharpshooters. Instead, whenever he drove somewhere it was in a darkened vehicle, and there was always a second, identical vehicle in the escort convoy to confuse would-be assassins. A double often sat in the other one, or in both. SS guards surrounded Hitler wherever he went. Access to him was extremely limited and strictly controlled. Even officers invited to the dictator's headquarters for briefings were required to remove their sidearms before entering Hitler's presence. Hence it was clearly a rare opportunity when the GAO learned in November 1943 that Hitler wanted to see the new winter uniforms modelled before him personally. When modelling a combat uniform, the man wearing it would have to wear all his equipment, including his arms.

There had never been a shortage of volunteers to act as assassins. Ewald von Kleist, Eberhard von Breitenbuch, the already mentioned Georg Freiherr von Boeselager, and Rudolf-Christoph Freiherr von Gersdorff were all such men. But for one reason or another, their efforts had come to naught. In November 1943, Stauffenberg easily recruited yet another willing suicide bomber: the long-since anti-Nazi officer Axel Freiherr von dem Bussche. Bussche, a tall, athletic officer who had come to the Resistance after witnessing a massacre of Jews in the Soviet Union, felt he would be able to pull the pin on a hand grenade and then hold on to Hitler, regardless of what the SS did to or around him, until both he and the dictator blew up.

Bussche went to Hitler's headquarters and waited there for several days for the arrival of the uniform he was supposed to model. Instead, the uniform was destroyed in an Allied air raid. Bussche had to return to the Eastern Front, where he soon lost a leg and won a Knight's Cross. Another assassination attempt had failed.

Throughout the next six months, Stauffenberg continued to work tirelessly toward the goal of removing Hitler from power, searching ever more desperately for ways to get assassins into Hitler's presence. He also took an increasingly active role in post-coup planning and efforts to expand the network of conspirators, notably to Communist circles. But the military situation, which had once hampered the conspirators because German arms were too successful, now thwarted them by its rapid deterioration.

The Military Situation in July 1944

By July 1944 it was obvious that Germany had lost the war. Germany was fighting on three fronts, and on all of them it faced enemies with far greater reserves of troops, munitions, armour, and aircraft. Everywhere divisions were deployed that had the strength of peacetime battalions. Panzer divisions with a paper strength of several hundred tanks actually possessed between ten and twenty that were serviceable. Strategically, the Luftwaffe was not able to stop the bomber streams that pounded German cities by day and by night, grinding down civilian morale and shattering German infrastructure and industry. Likewise, the tactical superiority of the Allied air forces was so great that the mobility of the German Army was severely restricted, and commanding officers found it almost impossible to gain accurate intelligence.[1] On the Eastern Front, 28 divisions had been completely wiped out, along with 300,000 men, in the Soviet 'summer offensive'. Army Group North was surrounded and Army Group Centre had ceased to exist. Soviet panzers were only miles from the East Prussian border. On the Western Front, Germany had suffered 113,000 casualties since the Normandy invasion on 6 June 1944, and had been able to make good only 15,000 of those losses. The German commanders were in agreement that it was only a matter of weeks, or at most months, before the Anglo-Americans broke through the German defences and reached the German border. In short, Germany appeared on the brink of military collapse in July 1944.

This hopeless military situation has induced many, particularly foreigners, to conclude that the coup attempt of 20 July 1944 was precipitated by the impending defeat. While the military situation was not the root of the military conspiracy, nor the conspiracy motivated solely by the desire to avert surrender, it is nevertheless true that the military situation had a powerful influence on the conspiracy. This was particularly pronounced in the months immediately leading up to the coup attempt. There is no doubt that the leading military conspirators – notably Beck, Olbricht, and Stauffenberg – firmly believed that they had only a matter of weeks in which to attempt to liberate Germany from within.

And it wasn't the military situation alone that was pushing the conspiracy towards a crisis. The Gestapo, too, was closing in on the conspiracy. On 4 July 1944, the important civilian conspirator Adolf Reichwein was arrested. On the following day, the man increasingly seen as the presumptive chancellor in a post-Hitler government, Julius Leber, was taken into Gestapo custody. On 17 July, a warrant for the arrest of Carl Goerdeler was issued. Rumours of an imminent coup attempt reached the ears of the conspirators. A Counter-Intelligence officer, who knew far too much, threatened to 'expose the whole shop in the *Bendlerstrasse* [GAO]' if the Gestapo got their hands on him.

It was before this background of impending military disaster and Gestapo arrest that the mood among the conspirators reached the fatalistic point where action was preferred to inaction – regardless of the consequences. Convinced that their enemies were closing in on them in any case, Stauffenberg, with the acquiescence of Olbricht and Beck, insisted on attempting the assassination himself. The inner circle knew that in taking on the role of assassin, Stauffenberg weakened his chances of 'legally' issuing Valkyrie. But that seemed a small price to pay for getting a bomb into Hitler's immediate proximity after so many frustrating failures over the previous two years. After all, until 1 July 1944, the conspiracy had relied on Fromm, or Olbricht acting illegally, to set Valkyrie in motion. In a way, they were back to their old plans, with only one modification: Stauffenberg would *not* intentionally blow himself up with

Hitler as the more junior officers had planned. Instead, he would at least try to get away with his life and return to help with the coup.

Stauffenberg's First Assassination Attempts

Stauffenberg assumed his duties as chief of staff to the C-in-C of the Home Army on 1 July 1944. As early as 6 July he was ordered to attend a briefing at Hitler's HQ (which at this time was located in the Berghof near Berchtesgaden, Bavaria) and took explosives with him. However, it is not clear whether Stauffenberg intended to attempt an assassination or merely hand the explosives over to another conspirator, *Generalmajor* Hellmuth Stieff. The modelling of the new winter uniform, postponed repeatedly since the planned assassination attempt of November the previous year, was scheduled for the next day, 7 July, and many sources suggest that Stieff intended to use this opportunity to make an assassination attempt of his own.

Yet no such attempt was made. On 11 July 1944, Stauffenberg was again ordered to report to Hitler's HQ, and this time there is no question that Stauffenberg intended to use the opportunity for an assassination attempt. Olbricht alerted both Hoepner and Witzleben on 10 July 1944 that they needed to be in Berlin the next day. In addition, 20 signals officers were put on alert for 'special duties'. The commander of Military District II was warned that martial law was likely to be declared in the near future. It is important to note, however, that according to Gestapo interrogation reports, only a very small circle of insiders was alerted prior to 11 July 1944. The reason given is that 'Stauffenberg had decided on this course of action very suddenly.'[2]

On Tuesday, 11 July 1944, Stauffenberg flew to Hitler's HQ near Berchtesgaden. However, it had been decided in advance of this meeting that Stauffenberg would only make the assassination attempt if Himmler and Göring, Hitler's most likely deputies or replacements in the event of his sudden demise, were also present at the briefing and could be eliminated at the same time. It is unclear who had set these preconditions, but most likely they had been laid down by Beck, or Beck and Olbricht together, because these were the two men from whom Stauffenberg took his orders in Resistance matters. When Stauffenberg realised that neither Himmler nor Göring would be present at the briefing, he turned to his fellow conspirator Stieff and asked, 'My God! Shouldn't we do it anyway?'[3] Stieff advised against it.

But Stauffenberg didn't take his orders from Stieff. At roughly 13.00, Stauffenberg put a call through to Olbricht. In this conversation either – as related in the Gestapo report of 24 July 1944 – Stauffenberg did so to inform Olbricht that he had not been able to act because of the absence of Himmler and Göring, or – as historians prefer to describe the situation – he asked for Olbricht's guidance and was advised against action. In any case, Stauffenberg returned to Berlin without having attempted the assassination. In consequence, a variety of preparatory actions had to be cancelled. It is important to note this sequence of events, because in much of the literature an identical description of events often appears under the date 15 July 1944.

However, we know that in the very centre of the conspiracy, namely between Stauffenberg, Olbricht, and Beck, it was mutually decided that there would be *no* repeat of the events of 11 July 1944. Instead, it was agreed that the next assassination attempt against Hitler would be made *regardless* of whether Himmler and Göring were present. Thus, as soon as Stauffenberg knew that he was expected at Hitler's HQ on 15 July, the conspiracy viewed that date as 'D-Day'.

This time much more comprehensive preparatory measures were undertaken, and a much larger list of conspirators and partial conspirators was alerted of upcoming events. Furthermore, because the SS and Luftwaffe had considerably more troops located inside Berlin itself, while Army units were stationed farther away on the outskirts of Berlin, it was decided that everything should be done to ensure that the 'reliable' Army units got a head start. The best way to effect this was to issue the lowest level of preparedness for Valkyrie, Alarm Level One, for the Berlin military district roughly two hours *before* the earliest possible time for an assassination attempt.

This decision was extremely risky. Since Valkyrie could only be issued by Fromm in the event of Hitler's incapacitation, the issuance of Valkyrie, even at Alarm Level One, two hours before the anticipated time of Hitler's demise, was not authorised even for Fromm. Furthermore, since Fromm was flying to Hitler's HQ with Stauffenberg, Olbricht was committing himself to the illegal issuance of the Valkyrie orders. Since the issuance of orders of this nature was a highly visible act involving hundreds of troops and could never be kept secret, it was clear that should the assassination fail, suspicion would fall immediately on Olbricht – no one else. Such a risky course of action could only be justified if everyone agreed in advance that there would be no conditions, no uncertainties: Stauffenberg *would* set off the bomb on 15 July 1944.

In the early morning of 15 July 1944, Stauffenberg and Fromm flew to East Prussia, where Hitler had meanwhile moved his headquarters. They landed at the nearest airfield at about 9:30 and passed into the inner security zone at the so-called *Wolfschanze*, the massive high-security complex housing Hitler's HQ, at approximately 11:00. At 13:10 the daily briefing began, with both Stauffenberg and Fromm attending. This briefing lasted only until 13:40, but directly afterwards Stauffenberg was required to take part in a second briefing that lasted until 14:20. As Stauffenberg explained the situation to his brother and co-conspirator Berthold Graf Stauffenberg, 'Suddenly a second briefing was called at which [he] had to make a presentation, so [he] had absolutely no opportunity to attempt the assassination.'[4] It has been suggested that Stauffenberg may not even have had the opportunity to pack the explosives in his briefcase, much less set the fuse.

In the meantime, however, as agreed in advance, the Valkyrie orders, Alarm Level One, had been issued for the Berlin military district. Alarm Level One required that the designated units go on alert and await further orders. Various officers and troops who belonged to the Valkyrie units remember having leave cancelled and being confined to base. Others report that they were required to put live ammunition into their tanks and line them up ready for immediate departure.

When Stauffenberg got out of his second briefing in the *Wolfschanze* without having had a chance to do what he had promised, he at once got in touch with Olbricht to report what had happened. This conversation was witnessed at both ends: in East Prussia by Stauffenberg's escort inside the inner security zone of the *Wolfschanze*, *Oberleutnant* Giesberg, and in Berlin by General Hoepner, who was with Olbricht when he received the call. Both men survived 20 July 1944 long enough to be interrogated by the Gestapo. Both confirm that the conversation took place, and Hoepner further stated that the content of the call was only that Stauffenberg had been unable to take action.

In the literature about 15 July 1944, however, another telephone call is often described. People who were nowhere near the two men involved in the conversation have written accounts using verbatim quotes of what was said, as if they had personally been tapping the telephone line or at least taking notes.[5] According to these sources, Stauffenberg called Olbricht *before* going into the first briefing to report that Himmler and Göring were again absent and to *ask* if he should still go ahead with the assassination. Why he should do so when it had been agreed in advance that he would act 'regardless' is either not addressed at all, or it is suggested that Stauffenberg lost his nerve. To make the account even less logical, it is then claimed that although the Valkyrie orders had already gone out illegally and Olbricht had thereby already exposed himself, Olbricht suddenly changed his mind and advised against taking action. Adding a final absurdity to the whole story, Stauffenberg is then supposed to have asked his own adjutant for advice and on the recommendation of a subaltern (but against the advice of his superior), decided to do what he had promised to do before leaving Berlin.

The same source claims that Stauffenberg called back only 15 minutes later to say he hadn't been able to carry out the attempt and that Olbricht reacted 'as if a stone had fallen from his heart'.[6] The source of this account was not a witness to this call either, nor does he cite a witness. It is hard to imagine that someone who had just issued orders illegally over his own signature would be relieved to learn that his action was about to be discovered. Furthermore, the entire conspiracy stood in imminent danger of being discovered – despite the fact that the assassination had not been attempted. How could Olbricht have been relieved to learn that four years of careful planning, always at the risk of his life, had come to naught or that he, his friends, family, and colleagues were at severe risk of being arrested for treason? It is hard to understand why so many historians give credence to this illogical and unsubstantiated account.

Another oft-cited account suggests that before the briefing Stauffenberg telephoned Olbricht, Beck, and 'other generals', all of whom discussed 'the situation' among themselves indecisively before telling Stauffenberg *not* to act. Again, the issue of why Stauffenberg should have called in the first place, when it had been agreed before he left Berlin that he would act 'regardless', is not explained. Again, there is absolutely no logic for Olbricht and 'the other generals' telling Stauffenberg *not* to act *after* the Valkyrie orders had already gone out. And to add the last piece of absurdity to this version of the story, according to this account it was Stauffenberg's replacement as chief of staff to Olbricht, Albrecht Ritter Mertz von Quirnheim (again an officer junior to Stauffenberg), who urged him to go ahead anyway. Notably, the source of this version of events is the widow of Mertz von Quirnheim, a man who had come to the conspiracy only two weeks earlier.

There is yet a third version of this telephone call. Olbricht routinely took his midday meal at home with his wife. His chief of staff, formerly Stauffenberg and now Mertz, often came with him. The daily briefings of Hitler routinely took place at 13:00, and had Stauffenberg wished to reach Olbricht immediately prior to the briefing, he would have placed the call directly to the Olbricht villa or the call would have been redirected there. It was because Olbricht was at home when he received the call from the *Wolfschanze* that Hoepner was also present when the call was placed, as is testified to by the Gestapo interrogations of Hoepner. Thus unlike Frau Mertz, who was not even in Berlin in July 1944, Frau Olbricht was with her husband when he received a call from Stauffenberg at the *Wolfschanze* in which Stauffenberg asked whether he should proceed with the assassination despite the absence of Himmler and Göring. Frau Olbricht remembers that her husband very firmly and emphatically said 'yes' and then left the house with Mertz von Quirnheim *to set Valkyrie in motion.*

While this version of events at least avoids the absurdity of Olbricht telling Stauffenberg not to act, it is nevertheless still problematic. For a start, the Valkyrie orders had already been issued; and more significantly, it still begs the question of why Stauffenberg called at all, when it had been agreed in advance that he would act regardless of whether Himmler and Göring were present. If Stauffenberg did indeed waste precious time before the briefing, time that might otherwise have been used to pack the explosives and set the fuse, to ask Berlin for instructions, then Stauffenberg alone bears the responsibility for failure on 15 July 1944. The conspirators had agreed that Stauffenberg would act regardless, and the orders were issued in advance on that assurance. Olbricht did his part: he issued the orders illegally at the designated time; but if this version of events is true, Stauffenberg failed to keep his side of the bargain.

The most probable explanation of events, and of the historical confusion, is, however, that there were *not* two telephone calls on 15 July

1944, but rather on 11 July. On 11 July, when it had been agreed that Stauffenberg should only carry out the assassination if Himmler and Göring were present, Stauffenberg wanted to go ahead anyway. He asked Stieff, but he neither liked Stieff's negative answer nor took his orders from him. So he put a call through to Olbricht, reaching him at his villa, where he was lunching with Mertz von Quirnheim and Frau Olbricht. Either the two officers urged Stauffenberg to go ahead, as Frau Olbricht remembers it, or Stauffenberg was kept waiting while Olbricht telephoned Beck and possibly other conspirators such as Hoepner and Witzleben, as Frau Mertz reported. Maybe, the consensus of 'the generals' on that day (11 July 1944) was not to proceed with the assassination. Perhaps, Stauffenberg still wanted to go ahead and asked Mertz for his personal opinion, receiving the desired concurrence.

It is not entirely unreasonable that Olbricht might have opposed the assassination at this time, or at least let himself be influenced by the other generals, because on 11 July 1944 he had not yet issued the Valkyrie orders. Furthermore, since on this date Stauffenberg had decided to act precipitately, Olbricht may have felt that the preparations for the coup were not as thorough as they could have been – not as thorough as they would be on the 15th, for example. He may have initially approved the attempt, despite insufficient preparations, for the sake of killing all three top Nazis, but not if only Hitler would be killed. He might, indeed, even have been relieved on 11 July when he later learned that Stauffenberg had not acted.

In short, if one places the events frequently dated 15 July on 11 July instead, the sequence of events all fits together. On that day Stauffenberg flew to the *Wolfschanze* with instructions to act only if Himmler and Göring were present. They were not. He called Olbricht to urge action despite this fact. Olbricht, after consulting with Beck and others, advised against it. Stauffenberg, however, decided to go ahead anyway; but he no longer had time, and called a second time to say there had been no attempt. His dissatisfaction with the situation, however, resulted in intense discussions after his return. It was consequently agreed that at the next opportunity, Stauffenberg would act 'regardless', and to improve the chances for a successful coup many more preparations were made in advance – including the decision to issue Valkyrie at Alarm Level One two hours in advance of the expected time of the assassination.

If one accepts this interpretation, the events of 15 July are completely consistent with the Gestapo interrogations, without the postwar embellishments from 'witnesses' who were not present at the events described. Furthermore, the events of 15 July would no longer entail a loss of nerve on Stauffenberg's part or a suicidal indecisiveness on Olbricht's. Instead, the explanation Stauffenberg gave his brother, that he simply didn't have time to set off the bomb because of the second briefing, is sufficient to explain what happened. In this case, there was only one telephone call on that day: the call at 14:35 in which, as Hoepner told the Gestapo, Stauffenberg reported that he had not been able to act.

We know that when this call got through to Olbricht, Valkyrie Alarm Level One had already been issued three-and-a-half hours earlier. Olbricht had to find some way to back-pedal and, if at all possible, prevent discovery of the coup and save Valkyrie for use at a later date. He could not just cancel the orders, as this would have raised as many questions as the initial release of the orders; so Olbricht fled to the front, as they say in German, and immediately set off on an inspection tour of the various Valkyrie units.

He took along on this inspection tour the junior officer at GAO with official responsibility for Valkyrie, Major i.G. Fritz Harnack. Harnack was not a conspirator, and he had not been informed about the issuance of the orders four hours earlier. He was 'inwardly outraged that the officer responsible was not informed about a planned exercise until after the event'.[7]

But Olbricht did his best not only to disguise the real reasons for the Valkyrie alarm, but also to make a virtue out of necessity. He visited each of the units involved, inspected their state of preparedness, and noticed which units were really well turned out and ready and which were not. He also gave little speeches at each unit, explaining the (official) purposes of Valkyrie and trying to impress upon the soldiers how important it was: in short, to improve morale for the next time round. The tour also gave Olbricht the opportunity to meet some of the newer commanders personally and gain an impression of them. All in all, the inspection, as any inspection, turned up certain deficiencies in the planning that could be addressed in the next days.

Nevertheless, although the Gestapo expressed amazement and admiration that the entire deception functioned so flawlessly, the results of the premature issuance of the Valkyrie orders were overwhelmingly negative. The bottom line was that Olbricht was not authorised to issue Valkyrie – not even as an exercise. When Fromm learned what Olbricht had done, he was understandably furious. Olbricht was subjected to a severe dressing-down. Nor did the problems stop there. The Valkyrie alarm had also attracted the attention of both Keitel and Himmler. These men wanted to know what was going on. It is, as the Gestapo noted, truly amazing that Olbricht was not immediately relieved of his command. It is very likely that the Gestapo would have investigated the incident, if the conspiracy hadn't acted faster with the coup on 20 July 1944. But no matter how lucky Olbricht had been in the short term, the anger of his superiors and the interest of Himmler made it absolutely impossible to issue the orders a second time *unless it was absolutely certain that Hitler was already dead.*

In the meantime, however, the conspiracy had 'got away with it'. They had not been discovered, and the coup plans were still intact and in place. The conspirators made preparations for the next attempt. In addition to putting the conspirators on alert, on 19 July 1944 Olbricht managed to delay the transport of panzer troops out of the Berlin area on the pretext that another Valkyrie exercise was planned for 20 July, in which the panzers would be required.[8] It was clear to all conspirators that Stauffenberg had to act on this next occasion 'regardless', and equally obvious that this time there could be no issuance of the Valkyrie orders until it was 100 per cent certain that Hitler was dead.

20 July 1944

Early on the morning of 20 July 1944, Stauffenberg again flew to Hitler's HQ in East Prussia with the intention of killing the Nazi dictator. Nearly all the principal conspirators were informed about the imminent assassination attempt. The key actors in the conspiracy started to gather in the *Bendlerstrasse*. Junior officers from Infantry Regiment 9, all of whom had agreed without hesitation or further information to be at the disposal of an anti-Nazi action, were ordered to await further orders at the luxury hotel, the Esplanade, in the vicinity of the *Bendlerstrasse*. Even the uninitiated were put on alert: Olbricht told all his staff officers that they were to remain in their offices awaiting 'developments' from noon onwards. He told them that important decisions and orders were expected to come out of Hitler's daily briefing.

Since this briefing was scheduled for 13:00, however, no one expected anything to happen before that time. In order not to arouse suspicion, Olbricht went home at noon for lunch as usual. Mertz remained in the *Bendlerstrasse* 'just in case'. Olbricht did warn his wife, though, that he would be short of time and that everything should be ready punctually. He arrived for lunch with General Hoepner. Both generals were reportedly in a good mood and allegedly even drank a toast to the success of the coup, although the source for this is dubious. Nevertheless, a friend of Olbricht's daughter, who was a house guest at the time, noticed that for the first time since she had moved in with the Olbrichts the general took his pistol with him as he left the house. Olbricht and Hoepner left the Olbricht villa some time after 13:00. So far there had been no news from the *Wolfschanze*.

In the *Wolfschanze*, however, the daily briefing had been moved forward by half an hour due to the expected arrival of Mussolini. Stauffenberg had activated the fuses on the bomb in one of his briefcases, placed this bomb under the briefing table close to where Hitler was standing, and then slipped out of the briefing hut on the pretext of making a phone call. Shortly after 12:40, an explosion took place. Stauffenberg then bluffed his way past the guards controlling the lockdown of Hitler's HQ. He made it aboard the waiting aircraft and took off, just moments before all aircraft at the field were grounded. He had succeeded in detonating a bomb in the room where Hitler was standing and in escaping the *Wolfschanze* with his life, but he had had no opportunity to telephone Berlin. He was incommunicado until he landed.

General Fellgiebel, the signals general with responsibility for ensuring that information about the coup reached Olbricht and then cutting Hitler's HQ off from the outside world, learned, however, what Stauffenberg had not waited to find out: that Hitler had survived the blast. When Fellgiebel tried to pass this word on to the conspirators in Berlin, he discovered that someone else, namely the deputy commander of Hitler's HQ, had already taken control of all communications to and from the *Wolfschanze*. There are two versions of what happened next.

According to some sources, it was not until 15:00 that the first news of an 'incident' at Hitler's HQ reached the *Bendlerstrasse*. Allegedly, General Thiele at GAO was informed by someone at the *Wolfschanze* that a communiqué was to be expected shortly. Olbricht requested more information, and received an answer at about 15:30 that an explosion had taken place in which several officers were severely injured. No information about Hitler's condition was provided. SS investigators, however, were convinced that shortly after 15:00 Olbricht received from an unidentified source the full content of the communiqué, which reported an attempt on Hitler's life *and his survival*.

Yet other sources suggest that Fellgiebel had managed to get through a single cryptic message *before* all communications from the *Wolfschanze* were temporarily blocked. According to this version of events, Fellgiebel sent the following message to Olbricht at 13:15: 'Something terrible has happened. The Führer lives.'[9] But the source for this version of events is weak, and the earlier interpretation, based on Hoepner's testimony, appears more credible.

Regardless of which version of events one prefers, the only thing that was definite at the *Bendlerstrasse* by 15:30 on the afternoon of 20 July 1944 was that the assassination had failed. It was not clear, though, whether Stauffenberg had been killed in his own attempt or had survived the blast only to be arrested. Although with the wisdom of hindsight, historians and film-makers suggest that 'a decisive general' would have acted even on the basis of this highly unsatisfactory information and set the coup in motion, after the disaster of 15 July 1944 Olbricht would have been well justified in deciding *not* to put the whole conspiracy at risk again. After all, had Stauffenberg blown himself up in some kind of accident, it would have been madness to set the coup in motion *knowing* that Hitler was still alive. In such a situation, the coup might still have had a chance at a later date with a different assassin.

Yet it appears probable, based on the testimony of Fromm and Hoepner before the Gestapo, that Olbricht decided to go ahead with the coup despite the ambiguous news. The fact that Stauffenberg might have survived and might already be undergoing interrogation may have influenced this decision. Other sources, however, contend that Olbricht took no action until Stauffenberg's adjutant, Werner von Haeften, called him from the Berlin airfield at which Stauffenberg and Haeften had just landed. Stauffenberg and Haeften were blissfully unaware that the assassination attempt had failed. Haeften assured Olbricht that Hitler was dead.

At the latest now, after being assured by Stauffenberg of Hitler's death, Olbricht went personally to *Generaloberst* Fromm to try to get the man who was authorised to issue Valkyrie in the event of Hitler's death to do exactly that. Had Hitler been dead, Fromm might very well have cooperated in order to secure his future in a post-Hitler world. Had he cooperated, then Valkyrie would have been issued completely in conformity with the regulations. But Fromm was sceptical – especially after the fiasco of 15 July. Although Olbricht told him Hitler was dead and gave Fellgiebel as the source, Fromm wanted *proof* that Hitler was dead. Olbricht, trusting in Stauffenberg's assurances, himself picked up the phone and demanded a connection to GFM von Keitel. With Olbricht on one extension and Fromm on the other, the connection went through. Keitel emphatically denied that Hitler had been killed. Fromm consequently refused to issue Valkyrie.

From Olbricht's perspective, however, even now there were two possibilities. One was that Keitel was lying to cover up the death of the all-powerful dictator until the Nazi leadership had decided what action to take next. The other was that Stauffenberg had lied and the assassination had indeed failed. Olbricht could not know which scenario was correct, but he certainly could not be *certain* that Keitel was lying. Meanwhile, Mertz had released the first Valkyrie orders. It is possible that Olbricht had ordered him to do so while he went to talk to Fromm, but it is more likely that Mertz acted on his own initiative. Olbricht went to Fromm, hoping to talk him into signing the orders and so avoiding all the pitfalls and disadvantages of sending out the orders illegally a second time.

Between 16:30 and 16:45, Stauffenberg arrived in the *Bendlerstrasse*. He reported at once to Olbricht and assured him that Hitler was dead. Obviously, he couldn't really confirm Hitler's death, but one must try to put oneself in Stauffenberg's shoes: after two unsuccessful assassination attempts, he had finally managed to detonate a bomb in Hitler's headquarters and then, under dramatic circumstances, succeeded in escaping alive. Stauffenberg honestly didn't know that Hitler had survived the blast. Nor did he know that Fellgiebel had failed to close down communications from OKW, and that hence the entire Nazi apparatus was still fully operational.

Olbricht, in contrast, had heard nothing but ambiguous or contradictory news – most recently Keitel's point-blank denial that Hitler had been killed. So he listened to Stauffenberg and believed, or at least backed, him, but there was certainly no cause for euphoria on Olbricht's part. Olbricht was far too old, too rational, and too experienced. He simply asked Stauffenberg to come with him to Fromm. Here Olbricht told Fromm that Stauffenberg had just brought word confirming that Hitler had been killed in an explosion. Fromm told Stauffenberg that Keitel denied this, and Stauffenberg called Keitel a liar. This time Stauffenberg exaggerated even more by claiming, completely fancifully, to have personally seen Hitler's body carried out of the briefing hut. Whether Stauffenberg intentionally added this touch in an effort to convince Fromm or had talked himself into believing it, we will never know. In any case, Olbricht now informed Fromm that under the circumstances Valkyrie had been issued. Fromm exploded and wanted to know just who had signed the orders. Olbricht said (correctly) Mertz von Quirnheim. Mertz was ordered to report to Fromm, where he confirmed that the orders had been issued. Fromm told Mertz that he was under arrest.

Apparently, only at this point did Stauffenberg admit that he had himself set off the bomb – to which Fromm replied that in that case he ought to shoot himself at once, because he had failed. Stauffenberg refused, and Olbricht tried yet again to persuade Fromm to join the conspiracy. Fromm turned to Olbricht and asked, 'Then you, too, Olbricht, are part of this conspiracy?' Olbricht is said to have replied, 'Yes, but I am only on the fringes of the group which will take over the government.' Dramatic as this dialogue is, three of the four participants were dead within hours and never subjected to Gestapo interrogation. Fromm is the only source for this entire encounter.

Fromm's account continues that on learning of Olbricht's involvement in the coup, he declared him arrested too, but Olbricht replied calmly that Fromm had 'mistaken' the situation and that it was Fromm who was under arrest. Various sources say that Fromm then attacked Stauffenberg, and two junior officers supporting the conspirators entered with drawn pistols and arrested Fromm. Hoepner (as planned by the conspirators) took over Fromm's office and desk and at once started issuing orders as 'commander-in-chief' of the Home Army.

After this, the entire coup appeared to go according to plan. While Olbricht and Stauffenberg were with Fromm, Mertz had informed the staff of the GAO that Hitler had fallen victim to an assassination attempt. He informed them that *Generaloberst* Beck had been named interim head of state, that GFM von Witzleben had taken over command of the *Wehrmacht*, and that martial law had been declared. Harnack, the staff officer responsible for Valkyrie, was put to work carrying out the official aspects of Valkyrie; while the Hitler supporters, Lieutenant Colonels von der Heyde and Herber, were explicitly ordered to continue their regular duties.

Olbricht and Stauffenberg, meanwhile, went to work telephoning key offices and commands, informing them of the situation, and generally driving the coup forward. They answered questions and countered doubts voiced by both the initiated and the uninitiated. For example, Olbricht took a call from Albert Speer. Speer describes the conversation as follows:

> As soon as I left Goebbels's [office] I put a call through to the *Bendlerstrasse* and asked to speak to Fromm, in an effort to get details. 'General Fromm is not available', I was told. 'Then General Olbricht, please.' He was at once on the line. 'What's going on, Herr General?' I asked in the joking tone we often used together in difficult times. 'I have work to do, and the soldiers won't let me leave Goebbels's ministry.' 'I'm sorry; in your case that is a mistake. I'll take care of it at once.' Then he hung up before I could ask any further questions.[10]

Even now, in the very midst of the coup, neither Speer nor the uninitiated officers in the *Bendlerstrasse* suspected Olbricht of treason. According to officers who knew nothing of the coup, Olbricht's entire behaviour during these fateful hours was grave, as one would expect in such a situation, but calm and steadfast. Mertz, in contrast, was according to Heyde 'very nervous'. Heyde felt he failed to exude the level-headedness one expected of a chief of staff in a difficult situation. In the SS reports on 20 July 1944 it is likewise stated that: '[Stauffenberg] and Olbricht ... were the only ones who kept their nerves and their heads.'[11]

Meanwhile, one after another of the subordinate commands was receiving and carrying out the illegally issued orders. Beck insisted that insiders be informed at once that Keitel claimed Hitler had survived the assassination attempt, but the conspirators such as the Berlin Commandant General von Hase or the Military Governor of France, General von Stülpnagel, were committed anti-Nazis and they joined the coup attempt regardless. Surprisingly, even the uninitiated followed the Valkyrie orders at the outset, despite the fact that Olbricht or Mertz had signed them without authorisation.

The problem was simply that Hitler was *not* dead. Furthermore, the conspirators at his HQ had been unable to cut off the *Wolfschanze* from the outside world, and hence Hitler's entire staff (OKW) was fully operational. This meant that any commander who couldn't or didn't want to believe that Hitler was dead could contact the *Wolfschanze* requesting confirmation or details. Hitler's staff had initially assumed that the assassination was the act of a lone man, as in the Beer Hall assassination attempt of 1938. These calls asking for clarification of the situation, however, alerted Hitler and OKW to the fact that a coup was in progress in Berlin.

At roughly 18:00, the first counter-orders went out from OKW. Keitel decreed that all orders signed by Fromm, Witzleben, and Hoepner were null and void. Furthermore, a public announcement was now made over the radio informing the German people that an assassination attempt had been made, but that it had failed; it stated that Hitler was only slightly hurt.

Now the first calls started to come in to the *Bendlerstrasse* from confused subordinate commanders who had two contradictory sets of orders on their desks. Olbricht and Stauffenberg tried to convince all these callers that the orders from OKW were incorrect – that they were the machinations of the SS in an effort to retain control of the state despite Hitler's demise. The Army, Olbricht and Stauffenberg assured the military commanders, was taking over now that Hitler was dead. The implication was that the Army was finally 'cleaning up', something that many military men who were not conspirators nevertheless welcomed and supported.

As a result, as long as the situation remained unclear, the conspirators enjoyed a surprising degree of success. Officers of Olbricht's staff were actually initially convinced that the radio announcement proved Hitler *was* dead, arguing that because of the shock Hitler's death would cause, the Propaganda Ministry was planning to make the announcement only in stages: first that there had been an attempt and Hitler was slightly hurt, then that his wounds were more serious than initially thought, and then – tragically – that he had died unexpectedly of his wounds. But when the orders came into Olbricht's own office, ordering him personally to stop following the orders of Fromm, Witzleben, and Hoepner, doubt took root even here.

On the outside, too, doubts were growing. People started to ask themselves, 'What if Hitler is still alive?' Clearly, if he were dead there was no harm in 'following orders', but if he were alive and they followed the wrong orders it would mean arrest, possibly torture, and death. In this moment, when officers were confronted with two sets of contradictory orders, the political sentiments of each individual became decisive. A comparison between the response to the orders in Paris and in Military District II is particularly telling.

In Paris, where the military governor, General von Stülpnagel, was an opponent of Hitler going back to the conspiracy of 1938, the orders from the *Bendlerstrasse* were followed willingly and with alacrity. Despite the fact that Beck explicitly and personally informed Stülpnagel that Hitler might still be alive, Stülpnagel went ahead with the coup plans. The SD and SS leaders were arrested and confined under Army guards, with orders to kill if there was resistance. Within hours Paris was completely in the hands of the conspirators without a single shot being fired, and Stülpnagel was on his way to GFM von Kluge. Kluge had replaced GFM Rommel as the commanding general of the Army Group facing the Allied invasion. Stülpnagel hoped to persuade Kluge to join the coup and, more importantly, negotiate with the Western Allies.

In Military District II, the commander, General Kienitz, could not bring himself to follow the Valkyrie orders because these were 'clearly treasonous'. Keitel had called him personally, informing him of Hitler's survival and hinting that there were doubts about Kienitz's loyalty. When Olbricht tried to talk him into joining the coup, he was already immune to the argument. He described the situation as follows:

> I confess that, despite [fighting in] two world wars, these were the most difficult hours of my life … I remember that I said to my staff: 'It is terrible to stand with your heart on one side and your reason and duty on the other.' Without having made a decision I set off for my office, and on the way there it became clear to me that under the circumstances it was completely irresponsible as a military district commander to join the coup. There could be no doubt that Keitel's orders were correct and that the claims coming out of Berlin, that Hitler was dead, were false. To have followed these orders would have unquestionably constituted high treason.[12]

Whether one was sympathetic to the coup or not, the fact that Hitler still lived made any action directed against his government high treason.

GFM von Kluge, likewise, was only prepared to participate in the coup if Hitler were dead. This, remember, had always been his position, even back in 1943 when he gave the officers of his staff permission to shoot the dictator down during a visit to Kluge's headquarters. When on 20 July 1944 the news reached him that Hitler had survived the assassination attempt, Kluge remained true to his own principles. Since Hitler was not dead, he would not countenance the coup; but he did utter the wistful words, 'If only the pig were dead. ...'[13]

Likewise, in Berlin it was the certainty of Hitler's survival that turned the tide against the conspirators. Most spectacularly, the always suspect (from the conspiracy's perspective) commander of the *Grossdeutschland* Guard Battalion, the unit responsible for sealing off the government district of Berlin, turned against the conspiracy – but only *after* speaking with Hitler personally. Major Remer first carried out his military orders meticulously. Goebbels, however, could put a call through to the *Wolfschanze* (because the conspirators did not control the communications in and out of the *Wolfschanze*). Furthermore, Goebbels had enough power to demand to speak to Hitler personally, and Goebbels could then hand the receiver over to the awestruck Army major. Major Remer, never an insider, never even a sympathiser, became Hitler's ardent supporter at once. Hitler personally promoted him two ranks and ordered him to crush the coup with his troops. From one minute to the next, Remer went from keeping guard on the Propaganda Ministry so well that Speer had to get Olbricht's personal permission to get out, to being the man determined to put down the coup.

Had the conspiracy succeeded in having one of their own – say, Axel von dem Bussche – in command of the *Grossdeutschland* Guard Battalion on 20 July 1944, maybe even Hitler's survival would have been immaterial. But for the vast majority of German officers, just as Kluge had foreseen, Hitler's death was the absolutely necessary prerequisite for action against the regime.

Even in the *Bendlerstrasse* itself, the increasing certainty that Hitler was alive eroded the support that Olbricht and Stauffenberg had initially enjoyed among their respective staffs. When at roughly 21:00 Olbricht had to ask his officers to take over guard duty because the troops of the *Grossdeutschland* Guard Battalion had withdrawn, it was inevitable that questions would be raised. It didn't help that at roughly the same time the appointment of Heinrich Himmler as C-in-C of the Home Army was announced over the radio.

Several officers of GAO decided it was time to go to General Olbricht and find out directly from him what was going on. They confronted Olbricht at about 22:30, fully armed since they had been asked to take over guard duty. As these officers assured me personally, they did not come in with pistols drawn, and they did not threaten General Olbricht. They still trusted him, but they no longer believed that they had been told the whole truth. At this very late point, Olbricht admitted that Stauffenberg had tried to kill Hitler and had failed, but insisted that the coup was still in progress. He asked his officers to remain loyal to him.

It is noteworthy that the officers who took part in this confrontation all expressed outrage that they had been kept in the dark so long, and were then asked to sacrifice themselves in a lost cause. One of them, Fritz Harnack, went so far as to say explicitly: 'I'm certain that if we had been told what was really going on, there would have been no question – but then we would all be dead now.'[14] It was the combination of feeling they had been deceived and the knowledge that the coup had failed that turned these staff officers against Olbricht in the late evening of 20 July 1944.

At this inopportune moment, Stauffenberg sought Olbricht out. Seeing the other officers with their weapons, he decided to flee. One of the officers shouted after Stauffenberg, ordering him to halt. Stauffenberg did not. Accounts differ, but either his other adjutant, *Hauptmann* Klausing, or one of the officers confronting Olbricht, *Oberstleutnant* Franz Herber, shot first. In any case, several shots were fired – apparently the nervous reaction of over-tired and confused officers who still didn't really know what was going on or who the enemy was. Stauffenberg was wounded but made good his escape down the corridor, but not from the building.

Olbricht was escorted by several of these staff officers to where Fromm was still being held in custody by junior officers loyal to the conspiracy. Fromm was released and immediately ordered the known conspirators arrested. Without the slightest adherence to legal niceties, he summarily found them guilty of high treason and sentenced them to death. Fromm was in a hurry to get rid of these men, since he knew perfectly well that under Gestapo interrogation they might well implicate him in the conspiracy. So he ordered that Beck, Olbricht, Stauffenberg, Mertz von Quirnheim, and Stauffenberg's adjutant, Werner von Haeften, be executed immediately.

Beck asked permission to shoot himself, and was granted this right.

Meanwhile, the other four officers were taken immediately down the winding red marble stairway from the GAO into the courtyard of the *Bendlerstrasse*. A firing squad was hastily improvised, and the south wall of the courtyard was lit by the headlights of various staff cars. The four conspirators were shot one after another, starting with Friedrich Olbricht.

Olbricht's Last Hours

In all probability, Olbricht's first doubts about the success of the assassination came during the telephone call between Fromm and Keitel at roughly 16:00. Although he subsequently acted on the basis of Stauffenberg's assurances to the contrary, Olbricht could not have been blind to the increasing indications that Hitler had indeed survived. When it was announced over the radio that Hitler would speak in a couple of hours, when his own orders were obeyed more and more unwillingly or not at all, and when the troops of the *Grossdeutschland* Guard Battalion withdrew from the *Bendlerstrasse*, he knew the coup had failed. Only one thing remained: to take leave of his loved ones.

Both his wife and his daughter were spending the day in Königsbrück near Dresden. In the course of the day he made several calls to them, the last being at about 20:00. He said only that he would have no further opportunity to speak with them and that they would learn of events from public sources. At about the same time he asked his son-in-law, Major i.G. Georgi, to come to the *Bendlerstrasse*.

At this time Georgi was serving with the Air Force General Staff. He had no trouble reaching the *Bendlerstrasse*. Here he was told by Olbricht that it looked as if the coup had failed, but his father-in-law also informed him that he intended to carry on with the attempt. Interestingly, this conversation took place at about the time that Keitel sent the telegram to Olbricht personally, ordering him to put down the coup. In short, Olbricht had an alternative: had he wanted to betray his fellow conspirators and pretend innocence, he could have followed Keitel's orders and preserved his neck and even his position in the short term. Whether he would also have survived the inevitable Gestapo investigation that followed is another story. But to have done so would have been to betray himself, as well as his friends. It was not in his character. He told Georgi simply that he could not leave Stauffenberg in the lurch.

Georgi stayed in the *Bendlerstrasse*, a witness to Olbricht's ongoing attempts to talk the increasingly sceptical subordinate commanders into following the Valkyrie orders. Just nine years after these events, Georgi remembered these final hours and described them as follows: 'There was no resignation and no lethargy. Rather, there was pride and dignity such as I can only look back on with the deepest emotion. These men, standing in the Valley of Death, knew that they would have to cross that valley to immortality. They died in the firm conviction that their action, despite its apparent failure, would lay the foundation for a moral and material renaissance of their nation.'[15]

As the situation continued to deteriorate, Olbricht asked Georgi to take a briefcase full of incriminating material out of the *Bendlerstrasse* for him. Georgi's first reaction was to remain and go down with the ship that was the German Military Resistance. Olbricht convinced him that he had to survive – not just for the sake of his wife Eva and daughter Rosemarie, but also so that Georgi could pass on Olbricht's legacy, so that Georgi could explain to future generations what Olbricht had believed in and tried to achieve.

Georgi had not yet left the *Bendlerstrasse*, however, when Olbricht's staff mutinied as described above. Since these men did not recognise him, however, Georgi was able to slip out of the *Bendlerstrasse* unhindered shortly before midnight. At his own quarters, he immediately sat down and wrote a short summary of all that his father-in-law had said to him at their parting. He taped this to the top side of his desk drawer, where it could not be seen when opened. It remained there, undiscovered, throughout his arrest, interrogation, and disgrace. It was still there when, after the war, he returned and removed it himself. It is one of the most authentic documents of the Resistance that we have today, written almost precisely at the hour in which Olbricht died.

Georgi quotes Friedrich Olbricht: 'I do not know how future generations will judge our actions or what they will think of me, but I know for a fact that none of us acted from baser motives. Only the desperate situation forced us to risk everything to save Germany from complete destruction. I'm convinced that one day, posterity will recognise this and understand.'[16]

Let us hope so.

CONCLUSION

Olbricht was the first of literally thousands of Germans to fall victim to the National Socialist purge that followed the failed coup of 20 July 1944. It is fitting that he should die first, because – with the exception of *Generaloberst* Ludwig Beck, who died almost simultaneously – no other figure in the German Resistance to Hitler had been such a consistent and effective opponent of the regime.

Olbricht was an opponent of Hitler from before he came to power. This was because on the one hand, he recognised Hitler's demonic and dangerous character; and on the other, he had been one of the few *Reichswehr* officers who served the Weimar Republic with conviction and sincere loyalty. Because he did not view the Republic as a disgrace and long for some kind of national 'renewal', he never allowed himself to believe that Hitler and his movement might be a positive force for the restoration of German honour and power.

Furthermore, because Olbricht recognised the legitimacy of the Republic, he discerned the illegal nature of the Nazi regime from the very start. Nor was he enchanted by Hitler's early successes. Regardless of how much he may have welcomed an expansion of the *Reichswehr*, he saw the murders of 30 June 1934 as the barbaric acts of lawlessness that they were. He did not look the other way or rationalise what had been done. As a result, his moral standards were not corrupted by rationalisation of, much less complicity in, crimes.

By 1938, Olbricht's opposition to the increasingly dangerous and lawless Nazi regime had reached the point where he was prepared to consider a coup d'état against the government. He had already experienced intense disappointment at the lack of moral courage on the part of the *Reichswehr* leadership in the aftermath of the state murders carried out on 30 June 1934, and knew that no official *Reichswehr* protests would be forthcoming

CONCLUSION

against new Nazi outrages. He recognised, too, that there were no longer any legal means left for opposing Hitler. Thus, when Goerdeler suggested a coup in response to the smear campaign against *Generaloberst* Fritsch, Olbricht agreed in principle; he objected only to the lack of political preparation. From this point forward, Olbricht had abandoned opposition and dissent and had crossed into the camp of the Resistance.

Because Olbricht's opposition and resistance were motivated by moral outrage at the policies and methods of the Nazis, his opinion of and attitude towards the Nazi regime were never softened or tempered by internal or international successes. Olbricht's motives for advocating a coup against Hitler were the restoration of the rule of law and the end of irrational and immoral domestic and international policies. No Munich Agreement, no military victory over Poland or France – much less an invasion of the Soviet Union – could restore justice, legality, and rationality to German policy. Hence, these victories meant nothing to Olbricht. His opposition to the regime remained inflexible and undiminished throughout the years of Hitler's greatest triumphs.

From 1940 onwards he belonged to the inner core of the conspiracy centred around *Generaloberst* Beck, which actively sought to bring down the Nazi regime. Starting in early 1942, he developed the clever tactic of using a legitimate General Staff plan, Valkyrie, as the basis for a coup against the government. By then he was, as the would-be assassin Axel von dem Bussche worded it, 'grimly determined to bring down the regime at the first possible opportunity'.[1] By the end of the same year, according to the Gestapo summary of interrogations, he argued 'with increasing urgency that the military must act regardless of how difficult the coup might be, and that it was wrong to keep putting it off'.[2] After Oster was suspended from duty and following the failed assassination attempts of early 1943, Olbricht assumed responsibility for planning the assassination as well as the coup. In the summer of 1943, he recruited Claus Graf Stauffenberg for the Resistance. On 15 July 1944, he issued the Valkyrie orders two hours in advance of the first possible opportunity for the assassination.

On 20 July 1944 itself, Olbricht waited only for confirmation that an 'incident' had occurred before he set the coup in motion for a second time. Once the coup had started, he was, according to all first-hand accounts, consistently energetic and forceful in trying to drive the coup forward to success. He did not call it off the minute Keitel denied Hitler's death. He ordered the arrest of Fromm and others. He signed orders for those who wanted written orders, and he threatened others with court martial when, as the news of Hitler's survival became increasingly credible, they resisted his orders. If one gives credence to the reports of eyewitnesses – rather than the post-mortem commentary – at no time on 20 July did Olbricht hesitate or lose heart.

But precisely because Olbricht had opposed Hitler for so long, he had also experienced all the disappointments and failures of the German Resistance from 1933 to 1944. By July 1944 he had repeatedly seen how easily plans can go wrong. Already, in 1934, he had learned his lesson about the susceptibility of the Army leadership to political expediency. In 1938 he had seen how the actions of foreign powers could rob the Resistance of its basis for action. In 1940 it was the successes of the *Wehrmacht* itself that shattered all chances for a successful coup. In 1943 he waited with bated breath for two brilliantly conceived and courageously executed assassination attempts to set off the coup – only to experience failures resulting from completely uncontrollable circumstances. These events left their mark. Olbricht was not diverted or discouraged from pursuing the goal he had set, the downfall of the Nazi regime, but he was not prone to excessive optimism, either.

His style was undoubtedly affected by these repeated disappointments. And it was these earlier failures that dictated the absolute imperative of retaining his key position holding the reins of Valkyrie. Had Olbricht, like Oster, forfeited his job because he had lost the trust of the Nazi leadership, there would never have been a 20 July 1944. All of Stauffenberg's burning desire to 'save Germany' would have served him little if his next assignment had taken him somewhere other than to the GAO. After all, as a mere lieutenant colonel of the General Staff, Stauffenberg could have landed in an almost infinite number of obscure jobs. His energy and commitment would have brought no benefit to the Resistance if he had found himself serving on the staff of, say, Military District XVII in Vienna, or – as a former cavalry officer – as coordinator of the supply remounts for the increasingly horse-dependent *Wehrmacht*.

Thus it is fair to say that Claus Graf Stauffenberg very likely would never have entered history at all if it hadn't been for Friedrich Olbricht.

Had Olbricht chosen a different chief of staff, then that man would have been Olbricht's right-hand man in planning and carrying out the coup. And he, not Stauffenberg, would have been one of the heroes of the German Military Resistance.

But Olbricht *did* choose Stauffenberg, and there were good reasons. Not so much Stauffenberg's organisational talent – there were many competent lieutenant colonels in the German General Staff in 1943 – but rather his personality made him the ideal candidate for the job Olbricht gave him. Many witnesses testify to the fact that Olbricht and Stauffenberg were a team: one that worked together easily, happily, and even brilliantly.

They worked well together in large part because they complemented one another. Olbricht was disciplined and mature. He had been worn down by many disappointments. He had lost his son in a war he had tried to prevent and viewed as criminal. But he was still the canny, experienced, and highly effective mastermind behind Valkyrie. Stauffenberg, in contrast, was passionate and flamboyant, even undisciplined, but highly creative and motivated by a need to make up for lost time. The contrast between the two men is perhaps best captured by the artistic director of the Deutsche Oper Berlin, Götz Friedrich. He stressed that his father, who served for years on Olbricht's staff, had been fascinated by Stauffenberg's 'flair', but admired Olbricht for his integrity and moral courage.

Stauffenberg brought fresh energy, fresh perspectives, and new dynamism to a coup that was undoubtedly in a crisis in the summer of 1943. But the crisis was not the result of Olbricht losing heart or failing to try hard enough. Rather, it had been brought about because one after another of the *other* conspirators had been taken out of action by Gestapo suspicion, military assignments, or medical emergencies. Stauffenberg's personality was attractive, and his forthright manner won new converts where Olbricht's caution would not have dared to seek them, but he did not replace Olbricht. Rather Stauffenberg complemented and supported Olbricht, and strengthened his existing coup HQ by sharing his burden.

The impact was completely positive. Not one person who personally knew the two men at this time can remember them bickering, squabbling, or complaining about one another. And no description of the relationship between Olbricht and Stauffenberg would be complete without mentioning that they *liked* working together. The secretaries who worked in the small room between their respective offices, Anni Lerche and Delia Ziegler, both remembered how much the two men joked with one another. Anni Lerche said the atmosphere in the GAO was always cheerful, something clearly indicative of a first-class relationship. Delia Ziegler said of Olbricht and Stauffenberg: 'When the two of them are together, you hear so much laughter, just laughter.'[3]

Ultimately they went to their deaths together without either of them blaming the other for the failure of the assassination or the coup. This is why postwar recriminations against Olbricht are particularly sad. Olbricht and Stauffenberg saw themselves as a team, as comrades, working together towards the same goal. Neither of them would have wanted to gain fame and honour at the expense of the other. They respected one another for the strengths each saw in the other: Olbricht for his experience, his integrity, and his moral courage, and Stauffenberg for his energy and creativity.

Olbricht died as a direct result of the failure of Valkyrie. It was a fitting end, because no other conspirator was as closely linked to Valkyrie as he. It was to Olbricht's credit that a plan for the suppression of 'internal unrest' had been approved by Hitler. It was Olbricht's idea to use such a plan as the cover for a coup to bring down the very regime it was allegedly designed to protect. It was his caution and competence that enabled him to develop this plan over more than two years without ever arousing the suspicions of his Nazi superiors. It was certainly thanks to his competence and high standing that he was able to preserve this plan for its illicit purposes even after the fiasco of 15 July 1944. And it speaks volumes for his intelligence and skill as a chief of staff that the plan worked well until it ran up against the reality of Hitler's survival. Nor was Olbricht to blame for the failure of Valkyrie. It was not his fault that the assassination failed, so that officers were not freed of their oath. Nor was it Olbricht's fault that the *Wolfschanze* was not incommunicado and counter-orders could be issued. But it is Olbricht's tragedy that his role in the German Resistance has been overshadowed by others and his contributions underestimated, demeaned, or forgotten.

NOTES

Acknowledgements and Introduction
1 Axel Freiherr von dem Bussche, personal interview with the author, 26 November 1985.

3 The War to End all Wars
1 *Der Königlich-Sächsische Militär-St. Heinrichts-Orden, 1736–1918: Ein Ehrenblatt der Sächsischen Armee* (Frankfurt/Main, 1964), 493.
2 Friedrich Olbricht, 'Bericht über die Tätigkeit des Regiments vor Verdun', in Karl Böttger, *Das Königlich-Sächsische 7. infantrie Regiment 'König Georg' Nr 106* (Dresden, 1927), 103.
3 Ibid, 100.
4 Ibid, 101.
5 Ibid, 106.

4 Between Revolution and Reaction
1 Hans von Seeckt, in F. von Rabenau, *Seeckt, Aus seinem Leben* (Leipzig, 1940), 126.
2 *Generalleutnant* von Stolzmann, Wehrkreiskommando IV, Nr 11369 pers (Dresden, 27 August 1920, Militaerarchive der Deutschen Demokratischen Republik), R4573, 3.
3 Friedrich Olbricht, *Beurteilung der Lage*, Wehrkreiskommando IV, Abt Ia Nachr Nr (Dresden, 27 October 1920, Militaerarchive der Deutschen Demokratischen Republik), R4572, 24–7.
4 Ibid.

5 The Fragile Republic
1 Quoted in W.T. Angress, *Stillborn Revolution* (Princeton, 1963), 428.
2 Job von Witzleben, personal interview with the author, 15 November 1985.
3 Hans-Joachim von Horn, interview with the author, 13 May 1986.
4 G-2 Report, No. 11399, 'Unauthorized Photographs Taken by Foreign Officers', dated 22 April 1931.
5 Josef Stalin, quoted in Paul Johnson, *A History of the Modern World from 1917 to the 1980s* (London, 1982), 270.
6 Eva Olbricht, personal interview with the author, 8 February 1986.
7 Anna Louise Strong, quoted in Paul Johnson, *A History of the Modern World*, 275.
8 H.G. Wells, quoted in Paul Johnson, *A History of the Modern World*, 276.

6 National Socialist Peace
1 Friedrich Georgi, lecture before the Rotary Club Berlin-South, 6 November 1963.
2 Kurt Freiherr von Hammerstein, quoted in Kunrat Freiherr von Hammerstein, *Spähtrupp* (Stuttgart, 1963), 49–50.
3 Günter Wollstein, 'Friedrich Olbricht', in Rudolf Lill and Heinrich Oberreuter (eds), *20. Juli, Portraits des Widerstands* (Düsseldorf, 1984), 212.
4 Heinz Höhne, in his detailed investigation of the so-called 'Röhm Putsch', records exactly 85 known victims of the assassination campaign. Very probably there were more (unnamed) victims, but it is unlikely that the number of these nameless victims numbered in the hundreds, as many historians still claim. A death toll between 100 and 150 seems most probable. See Höhne, *Mordsache Röhm: Hitlers Durchbruch zum Alleinherrschaft 1933–1934* (Hamburg, 1984), 319–321.
5 Prinz Ernst Heinrich von Sachsen, *Mein Lebensweg vom Königsschloß zum Bauernhof* (Munich, 1969), 223.

6   Ibid.
7   Annedore Leber, *Das Gewissen Entscheidet: Bereiche des deutschen Widerstandes von 1933–1945 in Lebensbildern* (Frankfurt/Main, 1960), 263.
8   Heinrich Bennecke, *Die Reichswehr und der 'Röhm-Putsch'* (Munich, 1964), 73.
9   Job von Witzleben, interview with the author, 21 February 1986.
10 Gunther Aßmann, interview with the author, 3 March 1986.
11 Eberhard Matthes, letter to the author, 21 November 1985.
12 Job von Witzleben, interview with the author, 21 February 1986.
13 Carl Goerdeler, *Deutschen Rundschau,* April 1938.
14 Axel Freiherr von dem Bussche told this story, date forgotten.

7   The Formation of an Anti-Hitler Conspiracy
1   Edgar Röhricht, *Pflicht und Gewissen: Erinnerungen eines deutschen Generals 1932–1944* (Stuttgart, 1965), 128.
2   Ibid.
3   Ibid, 134.
4   Elisabeth von Metzler, letter to the author, 21 November 1985.
5   Ibid.
6   Memo dated 16 July 1938, signed by *Generaloberst* Ludwig Beck; quotes (among others) in Müller *Das Heer und Hitler*, 321.
7   Joachim von Stülpnagel, interview with the author, 6 June 1988.
8   Edgar Röhricht, *Pflicht und Gewissen*, 142.

8   Hitler's General?
1   Maria Rittau, widow of one of Olbricht's regimental commanders at this time, interview with the author, 13 May 1986.
2   Eva Olbricht, notes for an unpublished manuscript from 1964.
3   *Völkische Beobachter*, 28 October 1939.
4   Ibid.
5   G-2 Report from 6 December 1939. NARA, Washington, DC. Report Group 165, MID 2016-1108/68.
6   Daily Order from the commander of the 24th Infantry Division, dated 31 October 1939 and signed by *Generalleutnant* Olbricht.
7   *Völkische Beobachter*, 28 October 1939.
8   Ibid.
9   Hans von Tettau and Kurt Versock, *Geschichte der 24. Infantrie Division* (Stolberg, 1956), 17.
10 Friedrich Olbricht, diary entry, 4 September 1939.
11 Ibid, 9 September 1939.
12 *Völkische Beobachter*, 28 October 1939.
13 In Olbricht's diary he reports for 14 September 1939: 'Fortunately, I happened to be there; otherwise it would have been impossible to get the commander of the Bavarian IR 20 and Oberst Rittau [one of his own regimental commanders] to agree.'
14 Friedrich Olbricht, diary entry, 14 September 1939.
15 Ibid, 18 September 1939, 2.
16 Franz Halder, *Kriegstagebuch*, Vol. I (Stuttgart, 1964), 75.
17 Ernst Friedrich, 'General Olbricht', unpublished manuscript, May 1945, 10.
18 Friedrich Olbricht, diary entry, 22 September 1939.
19 Friedrich, 'General Olbricht', 4.
20 Friedrich Olbricht, diary entry, 26 September 1939.
21 Friedrich, 'General Olbricht', 5.
22 Friedrich, 'General Olbricht', 6.
23 Friedrich Olbricht, diary entry, 14 September 1939.
24 Ibid, 21 September 1939.
25 Ibid, 25 September 1939.
26 Ibid, 27 September 1939.
27 Ibid.

28 Ibid, 5 September 1939.

29 Ibid, 21 September 1939.

30 Ibid, 9 September 1939.

31 Ibid, 17 September 1939.

32 Ibid, 23 September 1939.

33 Ibid.

34 Georg Meyer, interview with the author, 6 September 1985, and Fritz Merker, interview with the author, 20 April 1985.

35 Hans Oster, quoted in John W. Wheeler-Bennett, *Die Nemesis der Macht: Die deutsche Armee in der Politik 1918–1945* (Düsseldorf, 1981), 497.

36 Friedrich, 'General Olbricht', 7.

37 Fritz Merker, interview with the author, 20 April 1985.

38 Harold C. Deutsch, *Verschwörung gegen den Krieg: Der Widerstand in den Jahren 1939–1940* (Munich, 1969), 216.

39 Romedio Galeazzo Graf von Thun-Hohenstein, 'Hans Oster', in Rudolf Lill and Heinrich Oberreuter (eds), *20. Juli: Portraits des Widerstands* (Düsseldorf, 1984), 226.

40 Hans Oster, quoted in Romedio Galeazzo Graf von Thun-Hohenstein, *Der Verschwörer: General Oster und die Militäropposition* (Munich, 1984), 193.

9 Organising Hitler's War

1 Hellmuth Reinhardt, former chief of staff of the Allgemeine Heeresamt (predecessor of Stauffenberg in this position), interview with the author, 19 June 1986.

2 Hermann G. Lübben, interview with the author, 19 November 1986.

3 Friedrich, 'General Olbricht', 16.

4 Hermann G. Lübben, 'Zur Vorgeschichte des Widerstandes vom 20.7.44. Im Generalstabe des Generals Olbricht', unpublished memoir, November 1986, 2.

5 Fritz Harnack, personal interview with the author, 14 May 1986.

6 Bolko von der Heyde, personal interview with the author, 16 November 1985.

7 Fritz Merker, personal interview with the author, 20 April 1985.

8 Hellmuth Reinhardt, personal interview with the author, 19 June 1986.

9 Friedrich, 5.

10 Bernhard Bechler, quoted in Kurt Finker, *Stauffenberg und der 20. Juli 1944* (Berlin (East), 1977), 176.

11 Bolko von der Heyde, letter to the author, 11 November 1985.

12 Hermann G. Lübben, 'Zur Vorgeschichte des Widerstandes vom 20.7.44. Im Generalstabe des Generals Olbricht', unpublished memoir, November 1986, 2.

13 Fritz Harnack, personal interview with the author, 14 May 1986.

14 Friedrich, 'General Olbricht', 10.

15 Axel Freiherr von dem Bussche, personal interview with the author, 26 November 1986.

16 Eberhard Zeller, *Geist der Freiheit: Der Zwanzigste Juli* (Munich, 1954), 184.

17 Claus Graf Stauffenberg, quoted in Wolfgang Venohr, *Stauffenberg: Symbol der deutschen Einheit, Eine Politische Biographie* (Berlin, 1986), 129.

18 Venohr; see also Christian Müller, *Obert i.G. Stauffenberg, Eine Biographie* (Düsseldorf, 1970), and Finker, *Stauffenberg*.

19 Gerd Überschär, 'Militäropposition gegen Hitlers Kriegspolitik 1939 bis 1941', in Jürgen Schmädeke and Peter Steinbach (eds), *Der Widerstand gegen den Nationalsozialismus: Die deutsche Gesellschaft und der Widerstand gegen Hitler* (Munich, 1985), 359.

20 Franz Halder, *Kriegstagebuch*, Vol. III, 38.

21 Hermann G. Lübben, letter to the *Süddeutsche Zeitung*, Nr 179, 7 August 1986.

22 Hans-Adolf Jacobsen (ed), *Spiegelbild einer Verschwörung: Die Kaltenbrunner-Berichte an Bormann und Hitler über das Attentat vom 20. Juli 1944. Geheime Dokumente aus dem ehemaligen Reichssicherheitshauptamt* (Stuttgart, 1961), 340. These were the daily reports sent to Martin Bormann and Adolf Hitler about the progress the Gestapo was making in their interrogations of people arrested in connection with the coup attempt of 20 July 1944. This is in the report of 2 September 1944.

23 Friedrich, 'General Olbricht', 19.

24 First pamphlet of the White Rose, printed in Inge Scholl, *Die Weisse Rose* (Frankfurt/Main, 3rd edn, 1982), 97.
25 Fourth pamphlet of the White Rose, in Scholl, *Die Weisse Rose*, 114–15.
26 Hermann G. Lübben, 'Zur Vorgeschichte des Widerstandes vom 20.7.44. Im Generalstabe des Generals Olbricht', unpublished memoir, November 1986, 14.
27 Hermann G. Lübben, letter to the author, 5 March 1987.
28 Christian Streit, *Keine Kameraden: Die Wehrmacht und die sowjetischen Kriegsgefangenen 1941–1945* (Stuttgart, 1978), 242.

10 Resistance to Hitler
1 Fabian von Schlabrendorff, *Offizier gegen Hitler* (Zürich, 1946), 69–70.
2 Joachim Kramarz, *Stauffenberg: the Architect of the Famous July 20th Conspiracy to Assassinate Hitler* (New York, 1967), 106.
3 Müller, *Obert i.G. Stauffenberg*, 348.
4 Müller, *Obert i.G. Stauffenberg*, 291. See also Kramarz, *Stauffenberg*, 121ff.

11 The Reasons Why
1 Henning von Tresckow, quoted in Bodo Scheurig, *Henning von Tresckow* (Frankfurt/Main, 1980), 201.
2 Friedrich Georgi, interview with the author, 29 April 1987.
3 Kramarz, *Stauffenberg*, 122.
4 Scheurig, *Henning von Tresckow*, 133.
5 Ludwig Beck, quoted in Nicholas Reynolds, *Beck: Gehorsam und Widerstand* (Wiesbaden, 1977), 226.
6 Scheurig, *Henning von Tresckow*, 193.
7 Friedrich Georgi's memo of 21 July 1944, written down on the night of his father-in-law's execution, to record their last meeting in the late evening of 20 July 1944.
8 Ibid.
9 Ibid.
10 Ibid.
11 Friedrich Georgi, speech before the Heeresamt der Bundeswehr, 23 April 1987.
12 Eva Olbricht, interview with the author, 15 March 1986.
13 Friedrich Georgi, speech before the Heeresamt der Bundeswehr, 11 July 1986.

12 The Consummate Conspirator
1 'Volksgerichtshof-Verhandlung vom 7. und 8. August 1944', NARA, T-84, Roll 21, XXXIII, 299.
2 'SS-Bericht über den 20. Juli: Aus den Papieren des SS-Obersturmbannführers Georg Kiesel', *Nordwestdeutsche Hefte*, vol. 1 of 2, Hamburg, 1947, 16.
3 Reinhard von Plessen, 'General Friedrich Olbricht: Im Zentrum des Widerstandes', *Information für die Truppe*, Bonn, July 1986(7), 40.
4 Axel Freiherr von dem Bussche, personal interview with the author, 26 November 1985.
5 Ibid.
6 All quotes from Bussche interview with the author, 26 November 1985.
7 Report of the chief of the Security Police and SD (Kaltenbrunner) on Bormann and Hitler, 1 September 1944. Reprinted in Hans-Adolf Jacobsen (ed), *Opposition gegen Hitler und der Staatsstreich vom 20. Juli 1944: Geheime Dokumente aus dem ehemaligen Reichssicherheitshauptamt*, (Stuttgart, 1989), 333–4.
8 Hans-Joachim von Horn, interview with the author, 13 May 1986.
9 Axel Freiherr von dem Bussche, interview with the author, 26 November 1986.
10 Allen Welsh Dulles, *Germany's Underground* (New York, 1947), 33.
11 Friedrich Georgi, interview with the author, 22 February 1986.
12 Christian Müller, *Obert i.G. Stauffenberg*, 470.
13 Peter Hoffman, *Widerstand, Staatsstreich, Attentat: Der Kampf der Opposition gegen Hitler* (Munich, 1985), 463.
14 Hermann G. Lübben, interview with the author, 19 November 1986.

15 Werner Görisch, letter to Herrn von Ponickaus, 2 December 1985.
16 Axel Freiherr von dem Bussche, interview with the author, 26 November 1985.
17 Christian Müller, *Obert i.G. Stauffenberg*, 427.
18 Hermann Kaiser, diary entry, 24 February 1943.
19 Ibid, 20 February 1943.
20 Hans Rothfels, *Die Deutsche Opposition gegen Hitler* (Frankfurt/Main, 1986), 109.
21 Hoffman, *Widerstand, Staatsstreich, Attentat*, 75.
22 Carl Goerdeler, letter to Zeitzler and allegedly Olbricht, 15 May 1944.

13 The Conspiracy Fails
1 GFM von Kluge, commanding Army Group B facing the Western Allies, makes clear in his unpublished diaries that Allied air superiority was the greatest factor inhibiting his ability to respond effectively to the invasion. The diaries were put at the author's disposal by his former adjutant Philipp Freiherr von Boeselager.
2 Gestapo report, 28 July 1944, see Jacobsen (ed), *Spiegelbild einer Verschwörung*.
3 Gestapo report, 3 August 1944, see Jacobsen (ed), *Spiegelbild einer Verschwörung*.
4 Gestapo report, 24 July 1944, see Jacobsen (ed), *Spiegelbild einer Verschwörung*.
5 This is particularly true of the account by Hans Bernd Gisevius, *Bis zum bitteren Ende: Vom Reichstagsbrand bis zum 20. Juli 1944* (Hamburg, 1961), 491.
6 Ibid.
7 Fritz Harnack, interview with the author, 14 May 1986. Harnack went on to tell that on that same evening he had vented his frustration to a fellow staff officer, Major i.G. Hayessen, saying roughly: 'This is a mess! I'm responsible for "Valkyrie" and the general goes behind my back and issues the orders and then takes Major Oertzen around on an inspection – when he doesn't even belong to GAO!' To which Hayessen replied: 'If you knew what I know since this morning, you wouldn't talk like that.' Hayessen was later condemned to death and executed for failing to report what he knew about the conspiracy.
8 Heinz Guderian, *Panzer Leader* (London, 1980), 339.
9 All of the following: Zeller, *Geist der Freiheit*, 286. Kramarz, *Stauffenberg*, 189. Hoffmann, *Widerstand, Staatsstreich, Attentat*, 506. Müller, *Obert i.G. Stauffenberg*, 487.
10 Albert Speer, *Erinnerungen* (Berlin, 1969), 394.
11 Johannes Rohowsky, 'SS-Bericht über den 20. Juli 1944 (Draft)', unpublished essay dated 27 June 1947.
12 Werner Kienitz, 'Der Wehrkreis II vor dem Zusammenbruch des Reiches, Erlebnisse und Betrachtungen', unpublished manuscript, May 1953.
13 Volker Schmidtchen, 'Karl Heinrich von Stülpnagel', in Rudolf Lill and Heinrich Oberreuter (eds), *20. Juli: Portraits des Widerstands* (Düsseldorf, 1984), 304.
14 Harnack, interview with the author, 14 May 1986.
15 Dr Friedrich Georgi, speech at the unveiling of the commemorative plaque to the Resistance in the courtyard of the *Bendlerstrasse*, 20 July 1953.
16 Friedrich Olbricht, quoted in Friedrich Georgi's memorandum, 21 July 1944, 00:10am.

Conclusion
1 Axel Freiherr von dem Bussche, interview with the author, 26 November 1986.
2 Gestapo report to Hitler, 21 August 1944, see Jacobsen (ed), *Spiegelbild einer Verschwörung*.
3 Delia Ziegler, quoted by Eva Olbricht in an interview with East German TV, 29 April 1987.

BIBLIOGRAPHY

Unpublished Sources

Interviews

Aßman, Gunther, interview with the author on 3 March 1986.

Bussche, Axel Freiherr von dem, interviews with the author on 16 November 1985 and 26 November 1985.

—, interview with East German TV on 24 April 1987.

Ebel, Klaus, interview with the author on 11 November 1985.

Friedrich, Götz, interview with the author on 3 May 1987.

Georgi, Friedrich, interviews with the author on 1 February 1986, 8 February 1986, 22 February 1986, 8 March 1986, 15 March 1986, 29 April 1987, and 17 July 1987.

—, interview with East German TV on 2 May 1987.

Georgi, Rosemarie (née Olbricht), interviews with the author on 1 February 1886, 8 February 1986, 22 February 1986, 15 March 1986, and 4 May 1986.

Harnack, Fritz, interview with the author on 14 May 1986.

Heyde, Bolko von der, interview with the author on 16 November 1985.

Horn, Hans-Joachim von, interview with the author on 13 May 1986.

Knudsen, Helge, interview with the author on 3 March 1988.

Lerche, Anni, interview with the author on 28 October 1985.

Lübben, Hermann G., interview with the author on 19 November 1986.

Merker, Fritz, interview with the author on 20 April 1985.

Meyer, Georg, interview with the author on 6 September 1985.

Olbricht, Eva, interview with Bengt von zur Mühlen on 8 April 1948.

—, interviews with the author on 1 February 1986, 8 February 1986, 22 February 1986, 8 March 1986, 15 March 1986, 4 May 1986, and 17 July 1987.

—, interview with East German TV on 29 April 1987.

Reinhardt, Hellmuth, interview with the author on 19 June 1986 and 25 May 1987.

Rentsch, Ingeborg, interview with the author on 27 March 1986.

Rittau, Maria, interview with the author on 13 May 1986.

Stauffenberg, Nina, interview with the author on 25 May 1987.

Stülpnagel, Joachim von, interview with the author, 6 June 1988.

Thomas, Dieter, interview with the author on 30 July 1986.

Voigt, Kurt, interview with the author on 16 January 1986.

Winterfeld, Alix von, interview with the author on 20 February 1986.

Witzleben, Job von, interview with the author on 15 November 1985 and 21 February 1986.

Letters

Bläck, F., letter to Ludwig Freiherr von Hammerstein from 3 July 1947.

Bödeker, Otto, sworn statement from 22 December 1959, copy in the possession of the author.

Bösch, Hermann, letter to the author from 12 December 1985.

Brunn, Hugo, letter to Hermann Kaiser from 20 September 1940.

Fink, Friedrich Karl Freiherr von, letter to the author from 9 January 1986.

Georgi, Friedrich, letter to Eberhard Klause from 11 March 1986.

—, letter to the editor of the *Frankfurter Allgemeinen Zeitung* from 29 September 1986.

Göhrisch, Werner, letter to Herrn von Ponickaus from 2 December 1985.

Heinrich, Martin, letter to the author from 28 January 1986.

Herber, Franz, letter to the author from 30 October 1985.

Heyde, Bolko von der Hyde, letter to the author, 11 November 1985.

Kähler, D. Ernst, letter to the author from 29 July 1987.

Koch, Willi R., memo from 4 April 1968.

—, letters to the author from 18 March 1986 and 4 April 1986.

Koehler, Lisa, letter to the author from 2 June 1986.

Kracklauer, Karl, letter to the author from 17 July 1987.

Lübben, Hermann G., letter to the *Süddeutsche Zeitung*, Nr 179, 7 August 1986.

—, letter to the author from 5 March 1987.

Matthes, Eberhard, letter to the author from 21 November 1985.

Metzler, Albert von, letters to the author from 21 November 1985 and 4 December 1985.

Metzler, Elisabeth von, letters to the author from 1 November 1985 and 21 November 1985.

Nölting, Waltraut, letter to the author from 23 March 1987.

Olbricht, Friedrich, letters to his mother from 28 March 1941 and 18 April 1942.

—, letter to Stefan Rittau from 31 July 1942.

—, letter to Maria Rittau from 28 August 1942.

—, letter to Rosemarie Georgi from 27 November 1943.

Pechel, Rudolf, letter to Ludwig Kaiser from 9 May 1946.

Reinhardt, Hellmuth, letter to the author from 1 May 1986.

Rittau, Hans, letter to the author from 22 May 1986.

Rittau, Stefan, letter to his wife from 19 December 1942.

Sack, Helle, letter to the author on 12 November 1985.

Speer, Albert, letter to the *Reichsjustizminister* Dr Thierack from 3 March 1945.

Stahlberg, Alexander, letter to the author dated 18 February 1986.

Winterfeldt, Alix von, letter to Ludwig Kaiser dated 5 May 1964.

Speeches

Georgi, Friedrich, 'Die politische und militärische Situation Deutschlands am 20.07.1944 and der Ablauf des Tages', speech before the Rotary Club Berlin-South on 18 July 1960.

—, 'Friedrich Olbricht: Soldat im Widerstand', speech before the Rotary Club Berlin-South on 6 November 1963.

—, 'Gedanken und Gefühle eines überlebenden Beteiligten zum 20. Juli – 40 Jahre danach', speech before the Rotary Club Berlin-South on 16 April 1984.

—, speech before the Heeresamt der Bundeswehr, 11 July 1986.

—, 'Soldat im Widerstand: General der Infantrie Friedrich Olbricht', speech before the Heeresamt of the Bundeswehr on 23 April 1987.

Rühl, Dr, 'Ansprache des Staatssekretärs Dr. Rühl', speech at the Memorial to General Olbricht in the Heeresamt der Bundeswehr in Bonn on 11 July 1986.

Wachter, *Generalleutnant*, 'Ansprache bei der Gedenkfeier für General der Infantrie Friedrich Olbricht im Heeresamt der Bundeswehr', speech at a Memorial to General Olbricht in the Heeresamt der Bundeswehr in Bonn on 11 July 1986.

Memoirs, Diaries, Essays, and Other Personal Unpublished Documents

Falkenhausen, Alexander Freiherr von, 'Bericht über meine Stellung zur NSDAP und ihrem Regime', unpublished statement from 10 January 1947.

Friedrich, Ernst, 'General Olbricht', unpublished manuscript from May 1945, in the legacy of Ernst Friedrich, copy in the possession of the author.

Hammerstein, Ludwig Freiherr von, unpublished diary from February to April 1945.

Heyde, Bolko von der, 'Der 20. Juli 1944 im OKH-AHA in der Bendlerstraße', unpublished memoir from 1948.

Heyn, Hans Günther, unpublished memoir from 1948.

Holzinger, *Oberlandesgerichtspräsident*, report on Ludwig Kaiser from 20 March 1958.

Kaiser, Hermann, diaries from 22 January 1941 to 22 November 1941.

Kaiser, Ludwig, 'Ein Beitrag zur Geschichte der Staatsumwälzung vom 20.07.1944 (Goerdeler-Bewegung) Teilbericht', unpublished and undated essay.

—, 'Aktenvermerk betr. Hermann Kaisers Kriegsgerichtliches Verfahren', unpublished *aide-memoire* from 2 February 1971.

Kienitz, Werner, 'Der Wehrkreis II vor dem Zusammenbruch des Reiches. Erlebnisse und Betrachtungen', unpublished memoir from May 1953.

Lübben, Hermann G., 'Zur Vorgeschichte des Widerstands vom 20.07.1944. Im Generalstab des Generals Olbricht', unpublished memoir from November 1986.

Nida, Ludwig von, untitled memoir about the 20 July Plot, dated 8 September 1947.

Olbricht, Eva, 'Friedrich Olbricht: General der Infantrie', unpublished and undated essay.

Olbricht, Friedrich, 'Mit der 24. Infantrie-Division im Polenfeldzug: Persönliches Kriegstagebuch vom 06.09.1939–05.10.1939', personal diaries of Olbricht from the Polish campaign.

Pridun, Karl, '20. Juli 1944: Position Paper', unpublished essay dated 30 October 1953.

Rahne, Hermann, 'Überlegungen zur Biographie des Generals Friedrich Olbricht', unpublished essay, Dresden, March 1987.

Reinhardt, Hellmuth, 'Das Allgemeine Heeresamt (AHA) im Oberkommando des Heeres/Chef H Rüst und BdE', unpublished memoir dated 1947.

Rohowsky, Johannes, 'SS Bericht über den 20 Juli 1944 (Draft)', unpublished essay dated 27 June 1947.

Schubert, Günter, 'Der 30. Juni 1934', unpublished essay.

Seelhorst, Gisela, 'Persönliche Erinnerungen an Friedrich Olbricht', unpublished memoir dated 28 March 1987.

Thomas, Georg, 'Die Opposition', unpublished memoir dated December 1945.

Weinheimer, Wilhelm, 'Erklärung', (memoir) from 7 May 1947.

Willisen, Achim Freiherr von, 'Bemerkungen zu dem Bericht des Generals der Infantrie Werner Kienitz: "Der Wehrkreis II vor dem Zusammenbruch des Reiches. Erlebnisse und Betrachtungen"', essay from 21 April 1971.

—, 'Zu der Veröffentlichung in der Beilage der Wochenzeitung "Das Parliament" B 28/65 vom 14. Juli 1965. Der 20. Juli im Wehrkreis II', essay from 1 September 1971.

Witzleben, Job von, 'Persönliches Gedächtnisprotokoll vom 20.02.1986', unpublished memoir dated 20 February 1986.

Ziegler, Delia, 'Betr.: Oberkriegsrat d.R. Ludwig Kaiser', unpublished manuscript from 3 December 1962.

—, 'Bericht über den 20. Juli 1944', unpublished and undated manuscript.

Military Orders and Intelligence Reports

Allgemeines Heeresamt (GAO) orders:
- No. 3830/43g.
- No. 17146/40.
- No. 48379/43.
- No. 45220/43.

Chef der Heeresleitung (C-in-C of the Army) orders:
- TA 1277/31 from 4 June 1931.
- TA 1349/32/VI/Ia from 11 June 1931.
- TA 1258/31 from 29 June 1931.
- TA 1562/31 from 17 August 1931.
- TA 1862/31/V/Ia from 25 August 1931.
- TA 1869/312/IV/Ia from 28 August 1931.
- TA 1929/31/IV/Ia from 25 September 1931.

Chef der Heeresrüstung und Befehlshaber des Ersatzheeres (Armed Forces Replacement Army) orders:
- 8880/42 from 10 November 1942.
- 34867/42 from 1 December 1942.

Cheston, Charles, memoranda for the Secretary of State of the US from 22 July 1944 and 20 January 1945, and memorandum for the President of the United States from 1 February 1945.

G-2 Reports:
- No. 11399, 'Unauthorized Photographs Taken by Foreign Officers' dated 22 April 1931.

- No. 10499, 'Visit of German Officers to Russia' from 19 November 1929.
- No. 15759 from 26 February 1938.
- No. D-16972 from 9 November 1939.
- No. D-16975 from 9 November 1939.
- No. 1108 from 6 December 1939.
- No. 17327 from 8 June 1940.
- No. 17746 from 23 November 1940.

Generalkommando des XIX Armeekorps orders:

- No. 277/IIa from 22 November 1916.
- No. 2884/IIa from 7 February 1917.
- No. 3103/IIa from 7 February 1917.

Generalstab des Feldheeres, order No. 55000 from 22 June 1917.

Kriegsministerium orders:

- No. 595 IVG from 17 November 1916.
- No. 12754 IV from 20 December 1916.

Oberkommando der 3. Armee order No. 12339 from 18 November 1918.

Oberkommando des Heeres, Heerespersonalamt, orders:

- No. 11751/42g from 31 October 1942.
- No. 13745/42g from 22 December 1942.
- No. 3900/43g from 29 March 1943.

Oberkommando der Wehrmacht (Armed Forces High Command) orders:

- No. 4312/40 from 4 July 1940.
- No. 12045/41 from 29 January 1941.
- No. 900/41g from 11 June 1941.
- No. 368/42g from 28 January 1942.

'Office Memorandum to General Donovan from Mr. Kimble' from 15 September 1944.

Office of Strategic Services (OSS) cables dated:

- 12 May 1944.
- 13 May 1944.
- 13 July 1944.
- 23 July 1944.
- 10 August 1944.
- 19 January 1945.
- 25 January 1945.
- 26 January 1945.
- 28 January 1945.
- 27 February 1945.

Olbricht, Friedrich, *Beurteilung der Lage*, Wehrkreiskommando IV, Abt Ia Nachr Nr, Dresden, 27 October 1920, Militaerarchive der Deutschen Demokratischen Republik, R4572.

OSS reports:

- 'Further Information on German Opposition Group; Abwehr Activities in Switzerland', undated.

– 'von Moltke, Count', dated 2 November 1943.
– 'von Moltke, Helmuth', dated 19 March 1944.
– 'For Brigadier General Thomas J. Betts', dated 21 July 1944.
– 'The Events of July 20, 1944', dated 15 September 1944.
– 'The German Coup d'Etat', dated 2 February 1945.
– 'Eye-Witness Account of the 20th of July 1944, 29 March 1945', dated 29 March 1945.

Reichsführer SS, Daily Order No. 1150/43g.

Reichswehrministerium (Defence Ministry), orders:
– No. 12.32g from 8 January 1932.
– No. 888/33 from 8 December 1933.
– No. 75/35g from 10 March 1934.
– No. 418/34 from 23 July 1934.

Stolzmann, Generalleutnant von, Wehrkreiskommando IV, Nr 11369 pers, Dresden, 27 August 1920, Militaerarchive der Deutschen Demokratischen Republik, R4573.

Truppenamt T-3 orders:
– No. 3008/28 T-3 IV from 15 August 1928.
– No. 283/34g from 13 August 1934.

4. Division orders:
– No. 395/33g Ia Op.2 from 2 December 1933.
– No. 33/34g IIb from 15 March 1934.
– No. 108/34g IIb from 22 August 1934.

24. Infantrie Division orders:
– No. 30 Ia from 21 September 1939.

Wehrkreiskommando (Military District) IV orders:
– No. 206/33 g from 8 November 1933.
– No. 913/34 IIIC Ic Abw from 31 January 1934.
– No. 1100/34 g Ic Abw/Ib/B from 3 March 1934.
– No. 144/34 g Ic Abw from 4 August 1934.
– No. 460/34 g Ia Op.2 from 5 September 1934.
– No. 4438/34 Ic Abw/IIIe from 15 September 1934.

Miscellaneous Other Documents

Bundesarchiv, Zentralnachweisstelle, 'Militärische Dienstlaufbahn des General der Infanterie Friedrich Olbricht', 16 June 1986.

Cron, Hermann, 'Die Organisation des deutschen Heeres im Weltkrieg', Bundesarchiv, Abt. VI-Militärarchiv, Freiburg, S15/5.

Gericht der Wehrmachtskommandantur Berlin, StL X Nr. 1800/43, Einstellungsverfahren zu Nr. 6708 ChHRüst u. BdH/Stab zu Nr. 1268/43, from 29 October 1943.

Heeresgruppe Süd, Kriegstagebuch (war diary) from 25–8 January 1944.

Huppenkothen, Walter, protocol of the interrogation of Walter Huppenkothen from 19 August 1947.

Infanterie Regiment 10 Jubiläumstreffen from 12/13 June 1965.

Krematorium der Stadt Berlin, Bezirksamt Wedding, letter to Frau Eva Olbricht regarding the burning and burial of the corpse of General Olbricht, dated 23 August 1948.

NSDAP Dresden, 'Bericht an Rudolf Heß über Gauleiter Martin Mutschmann', from 1 March 1935.

'Volksgerichtshof-Verhandlung vom 7. und 8. August 1944', NARA, T-84, Roll 21, XXXIII Taufbuch der Kirchgemeinde Leisnig, Auszug aus dem Jahr 1888, No. 278.

24. Infanterie Division, Abt. Ia, 'Bericht über die Kämpfe der 24. Division in Polen 1939', dated 4 December 1939.

Published Sources

Absolom, Rudolf, *Das Wehrmachtsstrafrecht im 2. Weltkrieg: Sammlung der grundlegenden Gesetze, Verordnungen und Erlasse*, Comelimünster, 1958.

Angress, W.T., *Stillborn Revolution*, Princeton, Princeton University Press, 1963.

Bennecke, Heinrich, *Die Reichswehr und der 'Röhm-Putsch'*, Munich, Olzog Verlag, 1964.

Benoist-Méchin, J., *Geschichte des deutschen Heeres seit dem Waffenstillstand*, Vols I–III, Hamburg, 1965.

Bessel, Richard, 'Militarismus im innenpolitischen Leben der Weimarer Republik: Von den Freikorps zur SA', in Klaus-Jürgen Müller and Eckhard Opitz (eds), *Militär und Militarismus in der Weimarer Republik*, Düsseldorf, Droste Verlag, 1978.

'Bis zuletzt an Stauffenbergs Seite', *Neue Zeit*, Berlin, 19 July 1986.

Bonhoeffer, Dietrich, *Letters and Papers from Prison*, London, SCM Press Ltd, 1971.

Bösch, Hermann, *Heeresrichter Dr. Karl Sack im Widerstand: Eine historisch-politische Studie*, Munich, Gotthold Müller Verlag, 1967.

Böttger, Karl et al, *Das Königlich Sächsische 7. Infantrie-Regiment 'König Georg' Nr 106*, Dresden, 1927.

Bracher, Karl Dietrich, 'Demokratie und Machtergreifung – Der Weg zum 30. Januar 1933', in Rudolf Lill and Heinrich Oberreuter (eds), *Machtverfall und Machtergreifung*, Munich, Bayerische Landeszentrale für politische Bildungsarbeit, 1983.

Bücheler, Heinrich, *Hoepner: Ein deutsches Soldatenschicksal des XX. Jahrhunderts*, Herford, Mitler, 1980.

—, *Carl-Heinrich von Stülpnagel: Soldat, Philosoph, Verschwörer*, Frankfurt/Main, Ullstein, 1989.

Buchheit, Gert, *Ludwig Beck: Ein preußischer General*, Munich, Paul List Verlag, 1964.

'Bundeswehr und 20. Juli', *Badische Zeitung*, Freiburg im Breisgau, 19 July 1986.

Carsten, Francis L., *Reichswehr und Politik 1918–1939*, Cologne, Kiepenheuer & Witsch, 1964.

Conquest, Robert, *The Great Terror: Stalin's Purge of the Thirties*, New York, New Perspectives, 1968.

Cooper, Matthew, *The German Army, 1933–1945: Its Political and Military Failure*, New York, Stein and Day, 1978.

Craig, Gordon A., *The Politics of the Prussian Army, 1640–1945*, London, 1978.

Cremer, Helmut, 'Zum 100. Geburtstag von General Friedrich Olbricht: "Wir haben das Letzte gewagt für Deutschland"', *Sächsische Zeitung*, Dresden, 4 October 1988.

Deist, Wilhelm, 'Militär und Innenpolitik im Weltkrieg 1914–1918', in Erich Matthias and Hans Meier-Welcker (eds), *Quellen zur Geschichte des Parlamentarismus und der politischen Parteien*, Zweite Reihe, Vol. 1/I, Düsseldorf, 1971.

— (ed.), *Ursachen und Voraussetzungen de Zweiten Weltkrieges*, Frankfurt/Main, Fischer Taschenbuch, 1989.

Demeter, Karl, *Das deutsche Offizierkorps in Gesellschaft und Staat, 1650–1945*, Frankfurt/Main, Bernard & Graefe Verlag, 1962.

Der Königlich-Sächsische Militär-St. Heinrichts-Orden, 1736–1918: Ein Ehrenblatt der Sächsischen Armee, Frankfurt/Main, 1964.

Deutsch, Harold C., *Verschwörung gegen den Krieg: Der Widerstand in den Jahren 1939–1940*, Munich, Beck, 1969.

—, 'Hitler and his Generals: The Hidden Crisis January–June 1938', *Bundeswehr Aktuell*, No. 80, Bonn, 21 July 1986.

Dohna, Lothar Graf zu, 'Vom Kirchenkampf zum Widerstand: Probleme der Widerstandsforschung im Brennspiegel einer Fallstudie', in *Deutschland und Europa in der Neuzeit: Festschrift für Karl Otmar Freiherr von Arentin*, Stuttgart, Franz Steiner Verlag, 1988.

Dornberger, Walter, *Peenemünde: die Geschichte der V-Waffen*, Eßlingen, Bechtle Verlag, 1981.

Douglas-Hamilton, James, *Motive for a Mission: The Story Behind Hess's Flight to Britain*, London, Macmillan and Co, 1971.

Dulles, Allen Welsh, *Germany's Underground*, New York, Macmillan, 1947.

Dupuy, T.N., *A Genius for War: The German Army and General Staff, 1807–1945*, Toronto, Prentice-Hall of Canada, Ltd, 1977.

Dyck, Harvey Leonard, *Weimar Germany and Soviet Russia, 1926–1933: A Study in Diplomatic Instability*, New York, Columbia University Press, 1966.

Ehlers, Dieter, *Technik und Moral einer Verschwörung: Der Aufstand am 20. Juli 1944*, Bonn, Athenaum Verlag, 1964.

Einbeck, Eberhard, *Das Exempel Graf Sponeck: Ein Beitrag zum Thema Hitler und die Generale*, Bremen, Schünemann, 1970.

'Eindrücke von den diesjährige Herbstübungen unserer Reichswehr in Sachsen', *Der 107er*, No. 11, Leipzig, 1925.

Einem, Karl von, *Erinnerungen eines Soldatens, 1853–1933*, Leipzig, Koehler, 1933.

Einundzwanzigster Jahresbericht des Vereins Sächsischer Realschullehrer, Großhain, 1913.

Erfurth, Waldemar, *Die Geschichte des deutschen Generalstabes 1918–1945*, Göttingen, Musterschmidt Verlag, 1957.

Erickson, John, *The Soviet High Command: A Military–Political History 1918–1941*, London, Macmillan, 1962.

Fahrenberg, Heinrich, 'Georg Maercker, 1965–1924', *Wehrwissenschaftliche Rundschau*, 4/80, Freiburg, 1980.

Federeyer, Karl, 'Die späte Ehrung des Generals Olbricht', *Frankfurter Allgemeine Zeitung*, Frankfurt, 12 July 1986.

Finker, Kurt, *Stauffenberg und der 20. Juli 1944*, Berlin (East), Union-Verlag, 1977.

Foertsch, Hermann, *Schuld und Verhängnis: Die Fritsch-Krise im Frühjahr 1938 als Wendepunkt in der Geschichte der nationalsozialistischen Zeit*, Stuttgart, Deutsche Verlags-Anstalt, 1951.

Foreign Relations of the United States: Diplomatic Papers 1944, Vol. I, Washington, Agency for International Development, 1966.

Fritzche, Hans Karl, *Ein Leben im Schatten des Verrates: Erinnerungen eines Überlebenden an den 20. Juli 1944*, Freiburg, Herder, 1984.

Funke, Manfred (ed.), *Demokratie und Diktatur: Geist und Gestalt politischer Herrschaft in Deutschland und Europa*, Düsseldorf, Droste, 1987.

Galante, Pierre, *Operation Valkyrie: The German Generals' Plot Against Hitler*, New York, Harper & Row, 1981.

'Gedenken an den Widerstand: Im Heeresamt Erinnerungstafel an General Olbricht enthült', *Kölnische Rundschau*, Cologne, 12 July 1986.

'Generalleutnant Olbricht und sein Vater Prof. Dr. Olbricht', *Der Türner von Chemnitz*, Chemnitz, 1939.

Georgi, Friedrich, 'General der Infantrie Olbricht', *Der Eisbär meldet*, No. 136, 1989.

—, *Soldat im Widerstand: General der Infantrie* Friedrich *Olbricht*, Berlin, 1989.

Gersdorff, Rudolf-Christian Freiherr von, *Soldat im Untergang*, Frankfurt/Main, Ullstein Verlag, 1977.

Geyer, Michael, 'Der zur Organisation erhobene Burgfrieden: Heeresrüstung und das Problem des Militarismus in der Weimarer Republik', in Klaus-Jürgen Müller and Eckhard Opitz (eds), *Militär und Militärismus in der Weimarer Republik*, Düsseldorf, Droste Verlag, 1978.

—, *Aufrüstung oder Sicherheit: Die Reichswehr in der Krise der Machtpolitik 1924–1936*, Wiesbaden, Franz Steiner Verlag, 1980.

Gisevius, Hans Bernd, *Bis zum bitteren Ende: Vom Reichstagsbrand bis zum 20. Juli 1944*, Hamburg, Rütten & Loening Verlag, 1961.

Goerdeler, Carl, *Deutschen Rundschau*, April 1938.

Gordon, Harold J., *Die Reichswehr und die Weimarer Republik, 1919–1926*, Frankfurt/Main, Bernard & Graefe, 1959.

Görlitz, Walter, *Kleine Geschichte der deutschen Generalstabes*, Berlin, Haude and Spener, 1977.

Graml, Hermann, 'Die deutsche Militäropposition vom Sommer 1940 bis zum Frühjahr 1943', in *Vollmacht des Gewissens*, Vol. II, Frankfurt/Main, Alfred Metzner, 1965.

Grimmarisches ECCE 1912, Vol. 33, Dresden, 1912.

Groscurth, Helmuth, *Tagebücher eines Abwehroffiziers, 1938–1940*, Stuttgart, Deutsche Verlags-Anstalt, 1970.

Grunberger, Richard, *The 12 Year Reich: A Social History of Nazi Germany, 1933–1945*, New York, Holt, Rinehart & Winston, 1971.

Guderian, Heinz, *Panzer Leader*, London, Macdonald Futura Publishers, 1980.

Haffner, Sebastian, *1918/1919: Eine deutsche Revolution*, Munich, 1977.

Halder, Franz, *Kriegstagebuch*, Vols 1–3, Stuttgart, W. Kohlhammer Verlag, 1964.

Hansen, Ernst Willi, 'Zum Militärisch-Industriellen-Komplex in der Weimarer Republik', in Klaus-Jürgen Müller and Eckhard Opitz (eds), *Militär und Militärismus in der Weimarer Republik*, Düsseldorf, Droste Verlag, 1978.

Hassel, Ulrich von, *Vom anderen Deutschland: Aus den nachgelassenen Tagebüchern 1938–1944*, Frankfurt/Main, Fischer Bücherei, 1964.

'Herbstübung unserer Reichswehr in der Lausitz', *Der 107er*, No. 5, Leipzig, October 1924.

Hoffman, Peter, 'Der militärische Widerstand in der zweiten Kriegshälfte, 1942–1944/45', in *Vorträge zur Militärgeschichte*, Vol. 5, Herford, 1984.

—, 'Motive', in Jürgen Schmädeke and Peter Steinbach (eds), *Der Widerstand gegen die Nationalsozialismus: Die deutsche Gesellschaft und der Widerstand gegen Hitler*, Munich, Piper, 1985.

—, 'Stauffenberg und die Veränderungen der außen- und innenpolitischen Handlungsbedingungen für die Durchführung des "Walküre"-Plans', in Jürgen Schmädeke and Peter Steinbach (eds), *Der Widerstand gegen die Nationalsozialismus: Die deutsche Gesellschaft und der Widerstand gegen Hitler*, Munich, Piper, 1985.

—, *Widerstand, Staatsstreich, Attentat: Der Kampf der Opposition gegen Hitler*, Munich, Piper, 1985.

Höhne, Heinz, *Canaris: Patriot im Zweilicht*, Munich, 1976.

—, *Mordsache Röhm: Hitlers Durchbruch zur Alleinherrschaft, 1933–1934*, Hamburg, Rowohlt, 1984.

Hoßbach, Friedrich, *Zwischen Wehrmacht und Hitler, 1934–1938*, Göttingen, Vandenhoeck & Ruprecht, 1965.

Hürten, Heinz, 'Zwischen Revolution und Kapp-Putsch', in *Quellen zur Geschichte des Parlamentarismus und der politischen Parteien, Zweite Reihe: Militär und Politik*, Vol. 2, Düsseldorf, 1971.

Illustrierte Geschichte der Novemberrevolution in Deutschland, Berlin (East), Dietz, 1968.

Jacobsen, Hans-Adolf (ed.), *Spiegelbild einer Verschwörung: Die Kaltenbrunner-Berichte an Bormann und Hitler über das Attentat vom 20. Juli 1944. Geheime Dokumente aus dem ehemaligen Reichssicherheitshauptamt*, Stuttgart, Seewald Verlag, 1961.

—, *Opposition gegen Hitler und der Staatsstreich vom 20. Juli 1944: Geheime Dokumente aus dem ehemaligen Reichssicherheitshauptamt*, Stuttgart, 1989.

'Jahresbericht des Gymnasiums zu Bautzen für das Schuljahr Ostern 1900 bis 1901', Bautzen, 1901.

'Jahresbericht des Gymnasiums zu Bautzen für das Schuljahr Ostern 1900 bis 1905', Bautzen, 1905.

'Jahresbericht des Gymnasiums zu Bautzen für das Schuljahr Ostern 1900 bis 1907', Bautzen, 1907.

John, Otto, '*Falsch und zu spät*'?: *Der 20. Juli 1944*, Munich, 1984.

Johnson, Paul, *A History of the Modern World from 1917 to the 1980s*, London, Weidenfeld & Nicolson, 1982.

Kaiser, Peter M., 'Herman, Ludwig und Heinrich Kaiser und der 20. Juli 1944', *Informationen*, No. 2/3 84, Frankfurt/Main, 1984.

Kardorff, Ursula von, *Berliner Aufzeichnungen aus den Jahren 1942 bis 1945*, Munich, Biederstein, 1976.

Kirchbach, Arndt von, *Lebenserinnerungen*, Ebersbach, 1985.

Kister, Kurt, 'Friedrich Olbricht – Ein Planer des 20. Juli: Idealbild eines Offiziers', *Süddeutsche Zeitung*, Munich, 19 July 1986.

Klemperer, Lemens von, 'Der deutsche Wiederstand gegen den Nationalsozialismus im Lichte der Konservativen Tradition', in Manfred Funke (ed.), *Demokratie und Diktatur: Geist und Gestalt politischer Herrschaft in Deutschland und Europa*, Düsseldorf, Droste, 1987.

Kluge, Ulrich, *Soldatenräte und Revolution*, Göttingen, 1975.

Knudsen, Helge, *Oprorere i Hitlers Borg*, Copenhagen, 1947.

Kolb, Eberhard, *Die Arbeiterräte in der deutschen Innenpolitik 1918–1919*, Frankfurt/Main, Ullstein Verlag, 1978.

Der Königlich Sächsische Militär-St. Heinrichs-Orden, 1736–1918: Ein Ehrenblatt der Sächsische Armee, Frankfurt/Main, 1964.

Kötschke, Rudolf, and Hellmut Kretzmar, *Sächsische Geschichte*, Frankfurt/Main, 1965.

Kramarz, Joachim, *Stauffenberg: The Architect of the Famous July 20th Conspiracy to Assassinate Hitler*, New York, Macmillan, 1967.

Krausnick, Helmut, 'Wehrmacht und Nationalsozialismus', in *Vollmacht des Gewissens*, Vol. I, Frankfurt/Main, Metzner, 1960.

Der Kreisauer Kreis: Zur Ausstellung der Stiftung Preußischer Kulturbesitz, Berlin, 1985.

Kriegstagebuch des Oberkommandos der Wehrmacht 1940–1945, Vol. I–IV, Frankfurt/Main, Bernard & Graefe Verlag für Wehrwesen, 1965.

Krüger, Peter, *Die Außenpolitik der Republik von Weimar*, Darmstadt, Wissenschaftliche Buchgesellschaft, 1985.

Kühn, Kirst, *Georg Schumann: Eine Biographie*, Berlin (East), 1965.

Kunze, ?, 'Andere Regimentsgeschichten', *Der 107er*, No. 5, Leipzig, May 1932.

Langewiesche, Dieter, 'Was heißt "Widerstand gegen den Nationalsozialismus"?', in *Gesellschaft und Wissenschaft: Ringvorlesungen im Wintersemester 1982/83 und Sommersemester 1983, Universität Hamburg*, Hamburg, University Press of Hamburg, 1983.

Leber, Annedore, *Das Gewissen entscheidet: Bereiche des deutschen Widerstandes von 1933–1945 in Lebensbildern*, Frankfurt/Main, Büchergilde Gutenberg, 1960.

—, *Das Gewissen steht auf: 64 Lebensbilder aus dem deutschen Widerstand 1933–1945*, Frankfurt/Main, Büchergilde Gutenberg, 1960.

Lill, Rudolf and Heinrich Oberreuter (eds), *Machtverfall und Machtergreifung*, Munich, Bayerische Landeszentrale für politische Bildungsarbeit, 1983.

—, *20 Juli: Porträts des Widerstandes*, Düsseldorf, Econ Verlag, 1984.

Loewenstern, Erno von, 'Was würdest du tun?', *Die Welt*, Hamburg, 19–20 July 1986.

Löffler, Otto, 'Mit 107 ins feld', *Der 107er*, Nos 3, 4, and 5, Leipzig, August, September, and October 1924.

Manstein, Erich von, *Verlorene Siege*, Munich, 1981.

Manstein, Rüdiger von, and Theodor Fuchs, *Soldat im 20. Jahrhundert*, Munich, 1981.

Martin, Bernd, 'Das außenpolitische Versagen des Widerstands 1933/1942', in Jürgen Schmädeke and Peter Steinbach (eds), *Der Widerstand gegen die Nationalsozialismus: Die deutsche Gesellschaft und der Widerstand gegen Hitler*, Munich, Piper, 1985.

Matthias, Erich and Hans Meier-Welcker (eds), *Quellen zur Geschichte des Parlamentarismus und der politischen Parteien*, Zweite Reihe, Vol. 1/I, Düsseldorf, Droste Verlag, 1971.

Meier-Welcker, Hans, *Aufzeichnungen eines Generalstabsoffiziers, 1932–1942*, Freiburg i. Br, Rombach, 1969.

Melnikov, Daniil, *20. Juli 1944: Legende und Wirklichkeit*, Berlin (East), 1964.

Messerschmidt, Manfred, *Die Wehrmacht im NS-Staat: Zeit der Indoktrination*, Hamburg, Decker's Verlag, 1969.

—, 'Militärische Motive zur Durchführung des Umsturzes', in Jürgen Schmädeke and Peter Steinbach (eds), *Der Widerstand gegen die Nationalsozialismus: Die deutsche Gesellschaft und der Widerstand gegen Hitler*, Munich, Piper, 1985.

—, 'Motivationen der nationalkonserfvaiven?? Opposition und des militärischen Widerstandes seit dem Frankreich Feldzug', in Jürgen Schmädeke and Peter Steinbach (eds), *Der Widerstand gegen die Nationalsozialismus: Die deutsche Gesellschaft und der Widerstand gegen Hitler*, Munich, Piper, 1985.

—, 'Außenpolitik und Kriegsvorbereitungen', in Wilhelm Deist (ed.), *Ursachen und Voraussetzungen de Zweiten Weltkrieges*, Frankfurt/Main, Fischer Taschenbuch, 1989.

Meyer, Georg, 'General Guderian zur Erinnerung an seinem 100. Geburtstag', in *Militärgeschichtliches Beiheft zur Europäischen Wehrkunde*, Vol. 3, Herford, June 1988.

Meyer-Krahmer, Marianne, *Carl Goerdeler und sein Weg in den Widerstand: Eine Reise in die Welt meines Vaters*, Freiburg i. Br, Herder Taschenbuch Verlag, 1989.

Model, Hansgeorg, *Der deutsche Generalstabsoffizier: Seine Auswahl und Ausbildung im Reichswehr, Wehrmacht und Bundeswehr*, Frankfurt/Main, Bernard & Graefe Verlag, 1968.

Möller, Horst, 'Die nationalsozialismus Machtergreifung – eine Revolution?', in Rudolf Lill and Heinrich Oberreuter (eds), *Machtverfall und Machtergreifung*, Munich, Bayerische Landeszentrale für politische Bildungsarbeit, 1983.

Mommsen, Hans, 'Verfassungs- und Verwaltungsreformpläne der Widerstandsgruppen des 20. Julis 1944', in Jürgen Schmädeke and Peter Steinbach (eds), *Der Widerstand gegen die Nationalsozialismus: Die deutsche Gesellschaft und der Widerstand gegen Hitler*, Munich, Piper, 1985.

—, 'Die Opposition gegen Hitler und die deutsche Gesellschaft 1933–1945', in Klaus-Jürgen Müller (ed.), *Der deutsche Widerstand 1933–1945*, Paderborn, Ferdinand Schoningh, 1986.

Müller, Christian, *Oberst i.G. Stauffenberg, Eine Biographie*, Düsseldorf, Droste, 1970.

Müller, Josef, *Bis zur letzten Konsequenz: Ein Leben für Frieden und Freiheit*, Munich, Süddeutscher Verlag, 1975.

Müller, Klaus-Jürgen, *Armee, Politik und Gesellschaft in Deutschland 1933–1945*, Paderborn, Schoningh, 1979.

—, (ed.), *Der deutsche Widerstand 1933–1945*, Paderborn, Ferdinand Schoningh, 1986.

—, *Armee und Drittes Reich 1933–1939*, Paderborn, Schoningh, 1987.

—, *Das Heer und Hitler: Armee und nationalsozialistisches Regime 1933–1940*, 2nd edn, Stuttgart, Deutsche Verlags-Anstalt, 1988.

Müller, Klaus-Jürgen and Eckhard Opitz (eds), *Militär und Militärismus in der Weimarer Republik*, Düsseldorf, Droste Verlag, 1978.

Müller, Wolfgang, *Gegen eine neue Dolchstoßlüge: ein Erlebnisbericht zum 20. Juli 1944*, Hanover, Das Andere Deutschland, 1947.

Nebgen, Elfriede, *Jacob Kaiser: Der Widerstandskämpfer*, Stuttgart, 1967.

Olbricht, Friedrich, 'Bericht über die Tätigkeit des Regiments vor Verdun', in Böttger, Karl (ed.), *Das Königlich Sächsiche 7. Infantrie-Regiment ‚König Georg' Nr. 106*, Dresden, 1927.

Opitz, Eckardt, 'Exkurs: Sozialdemokratie und Militarismus in der Weimarer Republik', Müller, Klaus-Jürgen and Eckhard Opitz (eds), *Militär und Militärismus in der Weimarer Republik*, Düsseldorf, Droste Verlag, 1978.

Paul, Wolfgang, *Entscheidung im September: das Wunder an der Marne*, Esslingen, Bechtle Verlag, 1974.

Pechel, Peter, Johannes Steinhoff, and Dennis Showalter (eds), *Deutsche im Zweiten Weltkrieg*, Munich, 1984.

Petter, Wolfgang, 'Deutscher Bund und deutsche Mittelstaaten', in Abschnitt IV, *Deutsche Militärgeischte 1648–1939*, Militärgeschichtlichen Forschungsamt, Munich, 1984.

Plessen, Reinhard von, 'General Friedrich Olbricht: Im Zentrum des Widerstandes', in *Information für die Truppe*, Bonn, July 1986(7).

Poelchau, Harald, *Die letzten Stunden: Erinnerungen eines Gefängnispfarrers aufgezeichnet von Graf Alexander Stenbock-Fermor*, Berlin, Verlag Volk und Welt, 1949.

Rabenau, F. Von, *Seeckt, Aus seinem Leben*, Leipzig, 1940.

Reynolds, Nicholas, *Beck: Gehorsam und Widerstand*, Wiesbaden, Limes Verlag, 1977.

Rohde, Horst, 'Hitlers erste "Blitzkrieg" und seine Auswirkungen auf Nordosteuropa', in *Das Deutsche Reich und der Zweite Weltkrieg*, Stuttgart, Deutsche Verlags-Anstalt, 1979.

Röhricht, Edgar, *Pflicht und Gewissen: Erinnerungen eines deutschen Generals 1932–1944*, Stuttgart, Kohlhammer, 1965.

Roon, Ger van, 'Hermann Kaiser und der deutsche Widerstand', in *Vierteljahreshefte für Zeitgeschichte*, 24. Jahrgang, Vol. 3, Munich, 1987.

—, *Widerstand im Dritten Reich: Ein Überblick*, Munich, 1987.

Rosenberg, Arthur, *Entstehung und Geschichte der Weimarer Republik*, Frankfurt/Main, Europäische Verlaganstalt, 1983.

Rosenhaft, Eve, 'Gewalt in der Politik: Zum Problem des "Sozialen Militarismus"', in Müller, Klaus-Jürgen and Eckhard Opitz (eds), *Militär und Militärismus in der Weimarer Republik*, Düsseldorf, Droste Verlag, 1978.

The Rote Kapelle: the CIA's History of the Soviet Intelligence and Espionage Networks in Western Europe 1936–1945, Washington, University Publications of America, 1979.

Rothfels, Hans, *Die deutsche Opposition gegen Hitler: Eine Würdigung*, Frankfurt/Main, 1986.

Ruhmreiche Sächsische Soldaten in sechs Jahrhunderten, Dresden, Verlag Heimatwerk Sachsen, 1940.

Sachsen, Ernst Heinrich Prinz von, *Mein Lebensweg vom Königsschloß zum Bauernhof*, Munich, List, 1969.

Sächsische Landesblätter: Nachrichten der Sächsischen Regiments-Vereinigung Nos 15, 18, and 19, Dresden, 1936; Nos 7, 8, 10, 12, and 13, Dresden, 1937; Nos 3, 7, 8, and 9, Dresden, 1938.

Salewski, Michael, 'Die bewaffnete Macht im Dritten Reich', in *DeutscheMilitärgeschichte 1648–1939*, Munich, 1978.

Schapiro, Leonard, *Die Geschichte der Kommunistischen Partei der Sowjetunion*, Berlin, S. Fischer Verlag, 1962.

Scheider, Wolfgang, 'Zwei Generationen im militärischen Widerstand gegen Nationalsozialismus', in Jürgen Schmädeke and Peter Steinbach (eds), *Der Widerstand gegen die Nationalsozialismus: Die deutsche Gesellschaft und der Widerstand gegen Hitler*, Munich, Piper, 1985.

Scheurig, Bodo, *Henning von Tresckow*, Frankfurt/Main, 1980.

Schimmler, Bernd, *Recht ohne Gerechtigkeit: Zur Tätigkeit der Berliner Sondergerichte im Nationalsozialismus*, Berlin, Autoren Verlag, 1984.

Schlabrendorff, Fabian von, *Offiziere gegen Hitler*, Zürich, Europa Verlag, 1946.

—, *Begegnungen in fünf Jahrzenten*, Tübingen, 1979.

Schmädeke, Jürgen, 'Die Blomberg-Fritsch-Krise: Vom Widerspruch zum Widerstand', in Jürgen Schmädeke and Peter Steinbach (eds), *Der Widerstand gegen die Nationalsozialismus: Die deutsche Gesellschaft und der Widerstand gegen Hitler*, Munich, Piper, 1985.

Schmädeke, Jürgen and Peter Steinbach (eds), *Der Widerstand gegen die Nationalsozialismus: Die deutsche Gesellschaft und der Widerstand gegen Hitler*, Munich, Piper, 1985.

Schmidt-Richberg, Wiegand, 'Die Regierungszeit Wilhlm?? II', in Part V, *Deutsche Militärgeschichte 1648–1939*, Munich, 1968.

Scholl, Inge, *Die Weisse Rose*, Frankfurt/Main, 3 edn, 1982).

Schönau, Elisabeth von, *Vom Thron zu Altar: Georg Kronprinz von Sachsen*, Paderborn, 1955.

Schramm, Wilhelm Ritter von, *Aufstand der Generale: Der 20. Juli in Paris*, Munich, Kindler, 1964.

Schüddekopf, Otto-Ernst, *Das Heer und die Republik: Quellen zur Politik der Reichswehrführung 1918–1933*, Hanover, O. Goedel, 1955.

—, *Nationalbolschewismus in Deutschland 1918–1933*, Frankfurt/Main, Verlag Ullstein, 1972.

Schultzendorff, Walther von, *Proletarier und Prätorianer: Bürgerkriegs-situationen aus der Frühzeit der Weimarer Republik*, Cologne, Markus- Verlag, 1966.

Speer, Albert, *Erinnerungen*, Berlin, Propyläen Verlag, 1969.

'SS-Bericht über den 20. Juli aus den Papieren des SS-Obersturmbannführers Dr. Georg Kiesel', *Nordwestdeutsche Hefte*, Vols 1/2, Hamburg, 1947.

Stahlberg, Alexander, *Die verdammte Pflicht: Erinnerungen 1932 bis 1945*, Berlin, Ullstein Verlag, 1987.

Steinbach, Peter, 'Der militärische Widerstand und seine Beziehungen zu den zivilen Gruppierungen des Widerstandes', in Heinrich Walle (ed.), *Aufstand des Gewissens*, Herford, E.S. Mittler, 1984.

—, 'Zum Verhältnis der Ziele der militärischen und zivilen Widerstands-gruppen', in Jürgen Schmädeke and Peter Steinbach (eds), *Der Widerstand gegen die Nationalsozialismus: Die deutsche Gesellschaft und der Widerstand gegen Hitler*, Munich, Piper, 1985.

Streit, Christian, *Keine Kameraden: Die Wehrmacht und die sowjetischen Kriegsgefangenen 1941–1945*, Stuttgart, Deutsche Verlags-Anstalt, 1978.

Tessin, Georg, *Verbände und Truppen der deutschen Wehrmacht und Waffen-SS im Zweiten Weltkrieg 1939–1945*, Osnabrück, Biblio Verlag, 1977.

Tettau, Hans von, and Kurt Versock, *Geschichte der 24. Infantrie-Division*, Selbstverlag, Stolberg, 1956.

Thun-Hohenstein, Graf Romedio Galeazzo, *Der Verschwörer: General Oster und die Militäropposition*, Munich, Deutscher Taschenbuch Verlag, 1984.

Ueberschär, Gerd R., 'Militäropposition gegen Hitlers Kriegspolitik 1939 bis 1941: Motive, Struktur und Alternativvorstellungen des enstehenden militärischen Widerstands', in Jürgen Schmädeke and Peter Steinbach (eds), *Der Widerstand gegen die Nationalsozialismus: Die deutsche Gesellschaft und der Widerstand gegen Hitler*, Munich, Piper, 1985.

—, 'General Halder and the Resistance to Hitler in the German High Command, 1938–1940', *European History Quarterly*, Vol. 18, London, 1988.

Venohr, Wolfgang, *Stauffenberg: Symbol der deutschen Einheit: Eine Politische Biographie*, Berlin, Ullstein Verlag, 1986.

'Verschwörung des 20. Juli: Beteiligte sagen aus', *Die Welt*, No. 89, Hamburg, 31 July 1947.

Versock, Kurt, 'Zum Gedenken unseres allzeit hochverehrten Divisionskommandeurs 1938–1940: Friedrich Olbricht, General der Infantrie', *Der Eisbär meldet*, No. 136.

Vogelsang, Thilo, *Kurt von Schleicher: Ein General als Politiker*, Göttingen, Musterschmidt, 1965.

Volkischer Beobachter, Munich, 16 March 1938, 28 October 1939, 22 July 1944, 24 July 1944, and 25 July 1944.

Wagner, Elisabeth (ed.), *Der Generalquartiermeister: Briefe und Tagebuchaufzeichnungen des Generalquartiermeisters des Heeres General der Artillerie Eduard Wagner*, Munich, Gunter Olzog Verlag, 1963.

Wagner, Walter, *Der Volksgerichtshof im nationalsozialistischen Staat*, Stuttgart, Deutsche Verlagsanstalt, 1974.

Walle, Heinrich (ed.), *Aufstand des Gewissens*, Herford, E.S. Mittler, 1984.

Watzdorf, Bernd, 'Generalstabsausbildung 1932–1935', *Zeitschrift für Militärgeschichte*, I/1963, Berlin (East), 1963.

Welkerling, Wolfgang, 'Ein Wehrmachtsgeneral auf dem Weg zum Antifaschisten: Zur Biographie des Generals der Artillerie Fritz Lindemann (1894–1944)', *Zeitschrift für Geschichtswissenschaft*, Vol. 9, Berlin (East), 1989.

—, 'Zum 45. Jahrestag des Sprengstoffanschlags auf Hitler: Hans Ludwig Sierks – ein aufrechter Antifaschist', *Jahrbuch 1989 zur Geschichte Dresdens*, Dresden, 1989.

Der Weltkrieg 1914–1918, documentation in 9 volumes published by the Reichsarchiv, Berlin, 1925–1939.

Wendt, Bernd-Jürgen, *München 1938: England zwischen Hitler and Preußen*, Frankfurt/Main, Europaische Verlagsanstalt, 1965.

—, 'Die Weimarer Demokratie in der Weltwirtschaftskrise: Zur kontroversen Deutung und zur Aktualität der Brüning-Ära', in *Gesellschaft und Wissenschaft, Ringvorlesungen Wintersemester 1982/83 and Sommersemester 1983, Universität Hamburg*, Hamburg, University Press of Hamburg, 1983.

Wheeler-Bennet, John W., *Die Nemesis der Macht: Die deutsche Armee in der Politik 1918–1945*, Düsseldorf, Athenäum/Droste, 1981.

Wohlfeil, Reiner, 'Heer und Republik', in *Deutsche Militärgeschichte 1648–1939*, Vol. III, Munich, Herrsching, 1983.

Wollstein, Günther, 'Friedrich Olbricht', in Rudolf Lill and Heinrich Oberreuter (eds), *Machtverfall und Machtergreifung*, Munich, Bayerische Landeszentrale für politische Bildungsarbeit, 1983.

Yorck von Wartenburg, Marion Gräfin, *Die Stärke der Stille: Erzählung eines Lebens aus dem deutschen Widerstand*, Cologne, Diederichs, 1984.

Zeller, Eberhard, *Geist der Freiheit: Der Zwanzigste Juli*, Munich, Hermann Rinn, 1954.

Ziegler, Delia, 'Der Bericht der Sekretärin des Generals Olbricht: Delia Ziegler', *Die Welt*, Hamburg, 21 August 1949.

INDEX

Adam, Wilhelm 74, 89, 92
Allied bombing offensive 232, 237
Allied intelligence services 222
Alvensleben, von 88-89
Anti-Semitism 99, 119, 157, 182-185, 237
Army Group Centre 15, 182, 185, 188, 199
Astor, Lady 72
Atlantic Wall 161
Austrian Army 112
Austrian occupation 106-107, 112-113, 120, 158
Austro-Hungarian Empire 107

Barbarossa Instructions 169, 181
Battle of Berlin 15
Battle of Britain 185
Bavaria, King of 44
Beck, Ludwig 18-19, 22, 40, 66, 89, 91-92, 102, 104-
    105, 109-114, 143-144, 169, 175-176, 184-185,
    191, 213-214, 227, 244, 250-251, 253, 259
  cancer operation 191-192
  disagreement with Hitler's policies 111-116, 119,
      178-181, 196, 198, 202
  marriage 111
  resignation from German Staff 18, 114-115, 154, 162
  suicide 22, 255, 258
Belgium 144
Bendlerstrasse (Army HQ) 19-22; 150-151, 190-191,
    214, 230, 238, 246-249, 251-254, 256-257
Bennecke, Heinrich 87
Berlin garrison 56
Berlin riots 74
Bismarck 41, 94, 107, 173
Blaskowitz 124-125, 127, 131, 136
Blomberg, Werner von 72, 86, 91, 93, 101-102, 105, 184
  resignation from ministry of defence 101
Bock, von 185
Boeslager, Georg Freiherr von 188, 236
Boeslager, Philipp Freiherr von 187
Bonhoeffer, Prof. Dr Karl 116
Böttcher 64-65
Brauchitsch, von 114, 140, 146, 181
Bredow, von 89, 184
Breitenbuch, Eberhard von 236
British Expeditionary Force 180, 186
British 8th Army 196
Brockdorff-Ahlefeldt, Graf von 116
Bussche-Steithorst, Axel Freiherr von dem 7-8, 10, 157,
    203, 205, 218-220, 223-224, 230, 236-237, 254, 259
Busse, 137

Canaris 19, 40, 102, 105, 142, 223-224
Carpenter 71
Catholic Church 176

Centre Party 51
Chamberlain, Neville 117-118
Commissar Orders 169, 181
Communist Party of the Soviet Union 63
Concentration camps 8, 21, 90, 182, 224
  Auschwitz 137, 200
  KZ Hohenstein 88
Constitutional Assembly 51
Counter-Intelligence Office 187, 199
Crown Prince, The 52, 55
Cuno, Chancellor 62
Curzon Line 15
Czech Communist Party 58
Czech Socialist Party 58
Czechoslovakia 107-108, 113
  invasion 113, 115, 117, 120-121, 134, 184
  occupation 123, 158

d'Abernon, Viscount 64
Danish Army 36
Death camps 182, 201, 203
Denmark 144
Deutsche Oper Berlin 261
Deutsche Rundschau 100
Disarmament Conference 1933 93
DNVP (*Deutschnationalen Volkspartei*) 98
Dollman 104
Dresden clashes 57
Dulles, Allen 222, 226-227

Eastern Front (WWII) 15, 166, 186-187, 199, 208,
    224, 237
Ebert, Friedrich 44, 46, 48-49, 54
Einem, von 37
Eisner, Kurt 44
Enabling Law 172-174
Euthanasia Orders 157, 165, 182

Falkenhausen, 108
Falkenhayn, Erika von 183
Federal Republic of Germany 115
Felber 131
Fellgiebel, Fritz Erich 216, 225, 247-249
Feyerabend, 128
Field Army 170
Finance Ministry 151
First World War 29-40, 42
  Armistice 42-43, 141
  Battle of the Loretto Heights 32
  Battle of Verdun 33-34
  Eastern Front 32-33, 98
  First Battle of the Marne 31-32
  Flanders 37

Somme Front 34
Western Front 32, 111, 182
Wytschaete-Bogen battle 37
Fortress imprisonment (*Festungshaft*) 165
France 144
Franco-Prussian War 36
Freisler, Roland 211
French Army 63, 139, 179
French campaign 139, 145-146, 152, 160, 194-195, 259
Freikorps 48-50, 56, 84
Maerker 49-51
Friedrich, Ernst 131, 134, 156, 161
Friedrich, Prof. Götz 9-10, 261
Friedrich II, 'the Great' 35, 173
Frick, Dr Wilhelm 157
Fritsch, Werner Freiherr von 89, 91, 101-105, 112, 142, 184, 196
Fritsch Crisis 100, 102-105, 259
Fromm 18-20, 149-151, 161, 169, 190-191, 197, 213, 220, 222, 230, 235, 238, 240, 246, 248-252, 255-256, 260
personality 228

Galen, August Graf von, Bishop of Münster 157, 164
General Army Office (GAO) 146-154, 180, 199, 255-256, 260
Armed Forces Replacement Office 148-149, 151, 155, 192, 235
General Inspector of Armour 151
tasks 147-148
General Staff 7, 34-37, 43, 59, 66-67, 95, 110, 117, 146, 150, 194-195, 221, 260-261
adaptation of plans for clandestine activities 186
College 194
forbidden 53
secret 55
traditions 54, 119, 211
Geneva Conventions 168, 170, 181
George III, Johann, Elector of Saxony 27
George, Stefan 66, 192-193, 197
Georgi, Dr Friedrich 10, 213, 224, 228, 256-257
arrest and interrogation 257
escape from the *Bendlerstrasse* 257
German Air Force (Luftwaffe) 92, 106, 185
German Army (WWI) 36, 43
defeated 52
demobilisation 47, 55
withdrawal, 1918 38
XIXth Corps 30-31, 37, 47
German Army 185
conscription reintroduced 92
modernised 92
treatment of Soviet prisoners of war 168-169, 181-182
German Democratic Republic 64
German High Command 38
German Ministry of Defence 63
German Navy
defeated 52
High Seas Fleet mutiny 43, 45
German Resistance 9-10, 20, 22-23, 40, 81, 121, 139, 143, 148-149, 154, 158, 162, 171, 204, 207, 232, 257-260, 262
German Revolution 1918-19 41, 43-49, 51, 56, 68, 141, 209
Gersdorff, Rudolf Christoph Freiherr von 91-92, 189-190, 223

Gessler 64
Gestapo 8, 21, 103, 116, 143, 161, 164-165, 168, 174, 187, 191, 211, 216, 220, 223-224, 227, 230, 232, 234, 240-241, 243, 245-246, 248, 250, 255-256, 259, 261
closing in on conspiracy 238-239
Giesberg 241
Gisevius, Hans Bernd 103, 225
Gneisenau, Wilhelm Graf von 35, 211
Goebbels, Josef 21-22, 86, 163, 189, 229, 251, 254
Goerdeler, Carl Friedrich 19, 83, 97-100, 103-105, 114, 140, 143-144, 162, 179, 181, 184, 191, 198, 202, 204-205, 213, 230-235, 259
retirement 154
visits to Olbricht 100, 215-216
warrant issued for arrest 238
written records 232-235
Goering/Göring, Hermann 16, 86, 101-102, 150, 189, 206, 239-240, 242-244
Götz, von 136
Graf, Wilhelm 168
Great Depression 1929 74
Groener, Wilhelm 53-54, 74
Guderian, Heinz von 139, 146, 232

Habsburg Empire 106
Haeften, Hans-Bernd von 215
Haeften, Werner von 248, 255
Halder, Franze 66, 115, 117-120, 131, 139-140, 143, 145-146, 149, 160, 176, 179, 195, 228
Hammerstein, Ludwig Freiherr von 9-10
Hammerstein-Equord, Major Kurt von 56, 66, 71, 73-74, 78-79, 92
Harla 133
Harnack, Fritz 155-156, 245, 255
Hase, von 116, 213, 216, 251
Hassel, Ulrich von 105, 179, 215, 225
Helldorf, Wolf Heinrich Graf 115, 213
Henrici 216
Herber, Franz 251, 255
Heyde, Bolko von der 155, 251
Heye 73
Himmler, Heinrich 8, 16, 86, 101-102, 165, 189, 206, 227, 239-240, 242-244, 246, 254
Hindenburg, von 52, 56, 76, 79, 81, 85, 90-91, 118
Hitler, Adolf 62
appointment to: chancellor 76-84, 184; president 91; supreme commander of the armed forces 91, 150
asked to form a government 78-79
close down of opposition parties 81, 111, 174
dismissal of military leaders 101-105
foreign policies 92, 109, 112; Poland 135
highest level of popularity 93
ideology and racial policies 82, 182
management methods 152
military tactics 38, 152, 161
personal security 236
purges 103, 258
speeches 8
Hitler assassination and overthrow attempts 17, 116, 142, 154, 162, 187, 191, 197-198, 202 et seq.
aircraft bomb attempt, March 1943 188-189, 191, 199, 234, 260
Beer Hall bomb 17, 252
Berlin Armoury attempt, March 1943 189-191, 199, 207, 210, 234, 260
Manstein Plan 143
September 1938 Conspiracy 115-118, 195, 210, 253

11 July 1944 attempt 239-244
15 July 1944 8, 240-242, 248-249, 259, 262
20 July 1944 Plot 8, 15-19, 22, 103, 114, 158, 165, 177, 201-202, 221, 232, 246-255, 259-262
Hitler-Stalin Pact 134
Hitler Youth 151, 227
Hoepner, 20, 40, 66, 139, 154, 161, 169, 213-214, 216, 235, 239, 241, 243-245, 247-248, 250, 252
Höhne, Heinz 87
Holland 144
Home Army 7, 17, 21, 149-150, 163, 168-169, 179, 222, 230, 235, 250, 254
responsibilities 16, 224
treatment of POWs 169
Horn, Hans-Joachim von 68, 70-72, 221-222
Hörsing 57
Huber, Prof. 168

Ilsemann, von 221
Imperial Army 48, 53, 55, 59-60, 67, 85, 182
Independent Socialist Party 41-42, 44-49, 51, 58, 60

Jansa, Alfred 112

Kaiser, Hermann 192, 218, 230-231, 233-235
Kaiser, Jakob 215-216, 230
Kaiser, The 43-44, 53-54, 61, 92, 98
abdication 44-47, 111
Kapp Putsch 55, 57, 183
Kapp, Dr Wolfgang 56
Keitel, Wilhelm von 17, 112-113, 139, 149-151, 155, 181, 228, 232, 235, 246, 249-253, 256, 260
Kellogg-Briand Pact 73
Keynes, John Maynard 53
Kienitz 253
Kiesel, Georg 212
Klausing 255
Kleist, Ewald von 236
Kluc, von 31
Kluge, Günther von 38, 103, 143, 146, 153, 185-188, 191, 197, 205, 208, 213, 216, 253-254
Kohner, Dr 137
KPD (German Communist Party) 47, 49, 51, 58, 60, 62, 64-65, 75-76, 80, 82-83, 94, 171-173, 176
intention to destroy the Weimar Republic 80, 171
resistance to Nazi regime 171-172
Kreisauer Kreis (Circle) 19, 40, 175-177, 198, 207

Labour Organisation (Organisation Todt) 151
League of Nations 73, 106
Leber, Annedore 88
Leber, Julius 88, 174, 215, 233
Leeb 140, 143-144
Leipzig riots 57
Lenin 25
ideals 48
Lerche, Anni 155, 262
Leuschner, Wilhelm 143, 215
Liebknecht, Karl 44, 49
Light in the East 165
List 89, 103-104, 143
Lotd's Liberation Army 137
Lübben, Hermann 156, 160, 169, 214, 229
Ludendorff, von 62, 118
Lutheran Church 176
Lüttwitz, Walther von 55-57
Luxemburg, Rosa 49

Maerker 49-51
Maginot Line 140, 159
Majority Socialists 45-46, 49, 51
Manstein, von 38, 113, 122, 146, 153, 184, 186, 196, 200, 213-214, 218, 233
Maunoury, Michel-Joseph 31
Max, Prince of Baden 44
Mein Kampf book 82, 93
Merker, Fritz 141, 156, 220
Metzler, Elisabeth von 109
Mierry 68-69
Military Justice Department 165, 168
Military Resistance to Hitler 66, 178, 186, 189, 194, 196, 198, 202, 206, 214, 227, 231, 235, 257, 261
Model, 221
Molotov-Ribbentrop Pact 15, 122, 142, 172
Moltke, von the Elder 27, 36, 110, 154, 176, 207
Moltke, Gräfin 40
Moltke, Helmuth James Graf von 175-177, 198, 205
Mommsen, Hans 94
Montgomery, Bernard 208
Müller, General 63-64
Müller, Joachim 165
Müller, Klaus-Jürgen 117
Munich Agreement 120, 259
Munich University 166-157
Mussolini, Benito 16, 118, 247

Napoleon 35-36, 153, 176
National Socialism (NSDAP) (Nazis) 72-85, 100, 116, 172, 184, 197, 219
propaganda 76, 86
Neruda, Pablo 72
Neurath, Baron von 93, 105
Nida, von 221
Nölting, Fritz 28-29
Normandy invasion 16, 208, 237
Norway 144
Noske, Gustav 56

Oath to Hitler 91, 111, 144, 177, 201, 205-206, 262
OKW (Joint Forces Command) 17, 105, 107, 113, 148-149, 151, 252
Air Force High Command (Luftwaffe) 105
Army High Command (Heeres) 105
Navy High Command (Marine) 105
re-examination of exempted males 163
Olbricht, Emil 25, 50
killed in accident 28, 261
Olbricht, Eva (née Koeppel) 10, 29, 37-40, 50, 55, 65, 67, 82, 87-88, 97, 100, 209, 214, 229, 243-244, 247, 256-257
Olbricht, Friedrich 7-9, 19-23 et seq.
anti-Nazi 141, 155, 157, 164, 196, 201, 219-220, 258
army career 26-28, 34, 37, 47, 55, 59, 65-66, 74-75, 83, 119, 128-129, 155, 160, 229;
promotions 28, 31, 34, 37, 96, 146, 148-149, 151, 154-155
awards and decorations 144, 155; German Cross in Silver 155; Iron Cross (2nd class) 31; Iron Cross (1st class) 33, 127, 130; Knight's Cross 127, 129; Royal Saxon Military St Heinrich Order 31
birth 24-25
charm and popularity 67, 96, 110, 213
chief of Allgemeine Heeresamt 68

citations 31, 127
competence and intelligence 155, 262
courage 34, 127-128, 133, 161, 262
courtship by mail 39
education 26
entertaining and socialising 68, 97, 213-215
execution 22, 148, 155, 158, 229, 232, 255, 262
first battle 31
foreign travels 67, 108; Soviet Union 1930 69-73, 221
friendships 82-83, 97, 213-215, 234
General Staff HQ (head of GAO) 145, 149, 154, 156-158, 162-164, 179, 185, 192, 212-213, 220
General Staff training 37; officer 47, 50-51
helping others (humanitarian resistance) 156-157, 164-166, 168-169, 201
Hitler assassination and coup plans 185, 191-192, 197-198, 206-210, 212, 216, 219, 223-235, 248, 261
homes: Chemnitz 19; Dresden 65, 75, 83, 96; Grünewald villa 215-216, 227, 243; Leipzig 46-47
human resources management 216-220
humanity 136-139, 156, 164
leadership style 129-132, 134, 139
marriage 38-40, 46
meeting Hitler 133, 144
official reprimands 228
opposition to creation of new units 162
opposition to war with Soviet Union 73, 160
outrage at Hitler's appointment 81-82
patriotism 204
personal documents and diaries 33, 128-129, 133-138, 154
political opinion 207-208, 214
posthumous expulsion from the Army 154
Russian experience (WWI) 32-33, 160
sense of humour 49, 68, 96-97, 110, 131, 156-157, 262
sense of justice 90
serving in T-3 67-68, 73-74, 160, 215
short-sighted 26
support of the republic 55, 57, 66, 200-201, 258
warmth and decency 120, 134, 139, 155-156, 158
Olbricht, Klaus 65
Olbricht, Rosemarie 65, 256-257
Olympic Games, Berlin 1936 94, 106, 194
Oster, Hans 40, 66, 83, 102-105, 115, 140-142, 154, 180-181, 184-185, 202, 213, 234
  awards 141
  interrogation 223, 230
  resistance activities suspended 187
  resignation from Reichswehr 141
  suspended from duty 191, 259-260

Papen, Franz von 76-77, 87, 99
People's Court (Volksgerichtshof) 166, 206, 211, 214
Poland 123
  partitioned 125
Polish Army 122, 124-126, 134
Polish invasion/campaign 122-127, 129, 134, 137-139, 142, 145, 158, 194, 196, 221, 259
Pol Pot 137
Pope, The 143, 208
Popitz, Prof Dr Johannes 179, 215
Potsdam Conference 52, 70
Probst, Christian 168
Propaganda Ministry 152, 225, 252, 254

Prussian Army 35
Putin, Vladimir 93

Quirnheim, Albrecht Ritter Mertz von 243-244, 247, 249-251, 255

Radio in the American Sector (RIAS) 9
RAF 122
  Bomber Command 187
Red Army (Russia) 15, 32, 69-71, 123, 134, 160
Red Orchestra 176
Reichenau, von 89, 103-104, 124
Reichswehr (Imperial Defence Force) 53-57, 59-61, 63-64, 68, 71, 77, 79-81, 84-85, 87, 90, 93, 102, 141
  confrontation with SA 83-84
  expansion 92, 96, 258
  illicit relationship with Red Army 69
  invasion of Saxony 1923 64
  officers and leaders 77-78, 81, 84-85, 87, 90, 94-95, 101
  requirements 54, 59, 80
  seizes control of government buildings 65
Reichstag 75-76, 89, 98
  fire 84
  Communist members put in concentration camps 171-172
  SPD members arrested 174
Reichwein, Adolf 238
Reinhardt, Hellmuth 148, 151, 156, 190, 192, 216-218, 223, 228
Remer 155, 254
Rhineland
  German reoccupation 94-95, 101, 106, 142, 158
  French occupation 61, 63
Ribbentrop, Joachim von 105
Röhm, Ernst 84-87, 89, 101
  relationship with Hitler 85
Röhricht, Edgar 103-104, 109, 114, 117
Röhricht, Ernst 141
Rommel, Erwin 139, 146, 161, 186, 214, 253
Rote Fahne newspaper 63
Ruhr, French occupation 61, 63, 68, 73
Rundstedt 208
Russian Bolshevik Revolution 41-44, 48, 64, 160
Russian campaign (war against Soviet Union) 66, 152-153, 158-160, 169, 181, 185, 223, 259
  counter-offensive 185, 237

SA (Sturmabteilung 'storm troopers') 76, 79, 83-84, 90
  'wild Concentration Camps' 84, 171
  co-operation with Reichswehr for training 85-86
  execution of leaders (Röhm Putsch) 87-90, 99, 111, 142, 203, 258
  vandalism of Jewish shops 99
Sachsen, Prinz Ernst Heinrich von 87-88
Sack, Dr Karl 102, 105, 116, 165, 213, 227, 230-231
Sauerbruch, Dr Ferdinand 215
Saxon Army 27-28, 30-32
  Royal Saxon Infantry Regiment 106 26, 31
Saxon Assembly of Workers' and Soldiers' Councils 46
Saxon, King of 46-47
Schacht, Dr Hjalmar 115, 179
Scharnhorst, Gerhard 35, 211
Schlabrendorff, Fabian von 185, 187, 189
Schleicher, General 89, 184
Schleicher, Kurt von 77-79, 87, 89